"Deserves a wide readership. [*Scars of War*] presents, for the first time, a thoroughly researched, comprehensive history of the Amerasian issues, thereby filling a significant research gap. For students and scholars alike, it will be an invaluable resource for exploring the politics of paternity and responsibility for the Amerasians of Vietnam. A better understanding of the Amerasian issue can contribute to the development of effective policies for children of foreign soldiers and local women in current and future conflicts and post-conflict regions."

—Lukas Schretter, *Journal of Cold War Studies*

"Rigorously researched, captivatingly written, and compellingly argued, *Scars of War* details the legislative process surrounding migration programs for Vietnamese Amerasians. Thomas offers keen insight into the ways ideas about war, race, gender, and nation intersect in American thought and law."

—Amanda C. Demmer, author of *After Saigon's Fall: Refugees and U.S.-Vietnamese Relations, 1975–2000*

"*Scars of War* offers a new perspective that is important for understanding U.S. policy and also provides a window into the lives of marginalized people in Vietnam. It takes up complex issues of human rights and citizenship at a moment in world history when these problems are particularly visible and troubling."

—Karen Gottschang Turner, author of *Even the Women Must Fight: Memories of War from North Vietnam*

"*Scars of War* makes the important, nuanced assertion that the denial of paternity and parental responsibility has shaped the exercise of American empire in Asia. Many scholars and journalists have explored the history of Amerasians, but not with the thoroughness and singularity of focus that this author deploys."

—Allison Varzally, author of *Children of Reunion: Vietnamese Adoptions and the Politics of Family Migrations*

Scars of War

BORDERLANDS AND TRANSCULTURAL STUDIES

Series Editors:

**Rudy Guevarra
Paul Spickard**

SABRINA THOMAS
FOREWORD BY ROBERT J. MRAZEK

Scars of War

The Politics of Paternity and Responsibility for the Amerasians of Vietnam

University of Nebraska Press | Lincoln

© 2021 by the Board of Regents of the University of Nebraska

Portions of this book were originally published as Sabrina Thomas, "Blood Politics: Reproducing the Children of 'Others' in the 1982 Amerasian Immigration Act," *Journal of American–East Asian Relations* 26 (2019): 51–84; and Sabrina Thomas, "Scholarship during the Coronavirus Pandemic," *Diplomatic History* 45, no. 3 (June 2021): 622–30.

Cover: Audrey Tiernan photograph of Amerasian Le Van Minh in Ho Chi Minh City, from *Newsday*, November 14, 1985. © 1985 *Newsday*. All rights reserved. Used by permission and protected by the copyright laws of the United States. The printing, copying, redistribution, or retransmission of this content without express written permission is prohibited.

All rights reserved

The University of Nebraska Press is part of a land-grant institution with campuses and programs on the past, present, and future homelands of the Pawnee, Ponca, Otoe-Missouria, Omaha, Dakota, Lakota, Kaw, Cheyenne, and Arapaho Peoples, as well as those of the relocated Ho-Chunk, Sac and Fox, and Iowa Peoples.

First Nebraska paperback printing: 2025

Library of Congress Cataloging-in-Publication Data
Names: Thomas, Sabrina, author. | Mrazek, Robert J., writer of foreword.
Title: Scars of war: the politics of paternity and responsibility for the Amerasians of Vietnam / Sabrina Thomas; foreword by Robert J. Mrazek.
Other titles: Politics of paternity and responsibility for the Amerasians of Vietnam
Description: Lincoln: University of Nebraska Press, [2021] | Series: Borderlands and transcultural studies | Includes bibliographical references and index.
Identifiers: LCCN 2021025918
ISBN 9781496200549 (hardback)
ISBN 9781496241030 (paperback)
ISBN 9781496229342 (epub)
ISBN 9781496229359 (pdf)
Subjects: LCSH: Amerasians—Vietnam. | Children of military personnel—Vietnam. | Abandoned children—Vietnam. | Amerasians—United States. | Vietnamese Americans—Legal status, laws, etc.—United States. | Amerasians—Legal status, laws, etc.—United States. | BISAC: HISTORY / United States / 20th Century | SOCIAL SCIENCE / Emigration & Immigration
Classification: LCC DS556.45.A43 T56 2021 | DDC 959.7/00495073—dc23
LC record available at https://lccn.loc.gov/2021025918

Set in Sabon Next LT Pro by Laura Buis.

To my grandma Judy, my grandpa Doug, and my uncle Ricky. Thank you for being here as long as you could. I miss you and hope I am making you proud.

Their very name—Amerasian—tells of their plight. They are not completely American, but not really Asian either. Their Western physical traits, while not enough to make them citizens of the United States, are more than enough reason to their Asian countrymen to ostracize and persecute them.

—SEN. SAMUEL ICHIYE HAYAKAWA, 1982

Contents

Foreword by Robert J. Mrazek   ix
Acknowledgments   xiii
Author's Note   xvii

Introduction   1
1. Setting a Precedent   23
2. Saving Cold War Children   49
3. Becoming Refugees   87
4. Blood Politics   119
5. Window Dressing   153
6. The Amerasian Homecoming Act   177
7. "Like a Home without a Roof"   213
   Conclusion   241

   Notes   247
   Bibliography   321
   Index   341

Foreword

Robert J. Mrazek

When I began my first term as a congressman from the north shore of Long Island in 1983, I never anticipated that in four years I would author the legislation that brought twenty thousand children fathered by Americans during the Vietnam War to the United States.

That story is included in this extraordinary book, *Scars of War,* but it is only one of many. Dr. Sabrina Thomas has compiled a comprehensive and compelling account of the Amerasian experience, how it originated, how it unfolded during the war, and how these Amerasian children were forced to contend with the consequences of the American defeat in that ugly and unnecessary war, in which fifty-eight thousand Americans were killed and at least three million Vietnamese.

Dr. Thomas harnesses a myriad of viewpoints from the Vietnamese and American perspectives, including senior political leaders in the two countries, senators, congressmen, state department officials, aid workers, refugee organizations, and the children and their families. It is a superb achievement, marshaling a wealth of sources for the first time that bring to light the origins of the issue and how it was addressed by both countries over the decades during and after the war. It is a tale of good intentions, missed opportunities, and cynical political manipulation, with Amerasians often pawns in greater schemes. Dr. Thomas deftly chronicles the story without taking sides, letting each of the participant organizations and individuals in the drama express their views and the reasons for their actions.

From the perspective of one who came to the issue late, I found myself cheering on the efforts of so many men and women who dedicated themselves to providing a home in America for those Amerasians who wanted to come. Most prominent among them was my late former colleague, Stewart McKinney, who truly deserves the sobriquet of humanitarian.

Ten years before my own efforts, Stewart led the cause and introduced legislation that provided preferential immigration status to Amerasians because he believed they were just as much American as they were Asian. As Dr. Thomas explains, McKinney emphasized the role of nongovernmental humanitarian organizations like the Pearl S. Buck Foundation in securing "a better future for these sons and daughters of U.S. citizens" by providing Amerasians opportunities to live in America's "more tolerant culture." According to McKinney, Amerasians' American paternity prevented their acceptance into Asian society. As second-class citizens, McKinney continued, "Amerasians faced limited opportunities for education or employment and, therefore, a bleak future."

When I first became aware of the issue in November 1986, the average age of the Amerasians in Vietnam was nearly seventeen. I felt strongly that if they weren't able to come to the United States within a few years, they would reach adulthood and their chances of adapting to a new country would be significantly more difficult.

Looking back, I realize that whatever shortcomings existed in my proposed law resulted from my own mistakes. I drafted the entire piece of legislation, which included a several hundred million dollar appropriation for the transition program in the Philippines, with just my personal staff and the assistance of the House Legislative Counsel. Before its passage in the continuing resolution of 1987, the bill received no public hearings or other serious consideration in the House or Senate. As Dr. Thomas records in her book, the Amerasian Homecoming Act was passed in spite of opposition by the State Department of the Reagan administration, the House Judiciary Committee (the committee responsible for immigration legislation), and the Senate Judiciary committee. However, it was reviewed by the many nongovernmental agencies that would have to play a role in finding landing spots in the United States for thousands of families, and they were enthusiastic.

For better or worse, it changed the lives of twenty thousand Amerasians and their families. In *Scars of War* you will learn of the many complex challenges they faced after leaving Vietnam, particularly Black Amerasians, who faced a much deeper plight both in Vietnam and later in settling in the United States.

A year after passage of the Amerasian Homecoming Act, I began to receive annual reports from the State Department on the practical results of this mass exodus, and I came to wonder if my work to pass the legislation had made a meaningful difference in their lives. The reports highlighted the many abuses that took place as Vietnamese women seeking to leave for the United States used Amerasians as "meal tickets," paying them to pretend that they were their mothers. Other reports indicated that many Amerasians were causing serious problems after their arrival, largely due to their never having gone to school or their having been part of street gangs.

It was only in 2010, when a journalist named David Lamb contacted me to say that he was researching and writing a lengthy piece for *Smithsonian* magazine on the current status of Amerasians, that I learned of the many success stories, the thousands who had completed their education and gone on to have happy and productive lives. I was thrilled to hear his news.

Here, Dr. Thomas presents for the first time a comprehensive account of the entire history of the Amerasian issue, and it is filled with insights on every aspect of the struggle. It is the definitive work for future historians seeking to learn and understand what happened.

Acknowledgments

I began this book in graduate school, intrigued by a photograph of Le Van Minh and numerous other pictures of Amerasians in Vietnam. I wondered how conflict informed the lives of those conceived in war, and how mixtures of race and nationality and questions of paternity shaped their experiences. Like many young scholars, I also worried about doing justice to the subject and to the people whose lives and histories grace the following pages. There are so many who offered and trusted me with their stories and to whom I am grateful. Former congressman Robert Mrazek, the architect of the Amerasian Homecoming Act, was my first official oral history interview. Bob and his lovely wife, Carolyn, welcomed me into their home in upstate New York early in the research process. Bob patiently answered my seemingly endless questions, always with a clear sense of deep reflection that only comes with time, while Carolyn gave me a tour of the town and made sure I was properly fed. Capped off by what became a witty and energetic political debate over dinner with friends, this remains an incredibly memorable experience. Bob's willingness to speak with me, his commitment to having the story about the Amerasian Homecoming Act told, and his optimism about the project convinced me that this was the book I needed to write.

Shortly after meeting Bob and Carolyn, I interviewed Vietnam veterans and activists Bobby Mueller and Greg Kane. Both men were gracious and incredibly honest, and their stories helped fill many of the gaps left vacant by the documents. Only months before his final passing, I had the opportunity to speak with Father Alfred Carroll in the cafeteria of his retirement residence on the Gonzaga University campus. Father Carroll spent a lifetime advocating for Korean

Amerasians, and even at the respectable age of eighty-four his enthusiasm for the Amerasian cause was evident. He was kind and generous and I am so thankful to have met him. I hope his family is able to read this book.

The story of Le Van Minh could not have been told without the contributions of former Huntington High School students Marlo Sandler, Sue (Forte) Gerbavsits, and Tara (Scalia) Quilty, who willingly shared their memories of that powerful photo and their subsequent efforts to bring Le Van Minh to the United States. Not only were our conversations critical to my research, I also found them to be frank and enjoyable. In a different world I imagine we would have all been friends. Thank you for trusting me. I was also lucky enough to do a number of interviews with former Huntington High School staff member Mrs. Gloria Blauvelt. Now in her mid-nineties, Mrs. Blauvelt's emotion for her former students and her impressive sense of humor ensured that both the interview and our postinterview conversations were detailed, informative, and entertaining. The qualities that made Mrs. Blauvelt popular and trusted among her high school students decades ago make her equally engaging now. Thank you.

My research would not have been possible without the helpful hands and hearts of various archivists and librarians. Thank you to those who assisted my project at Gonzaga University and the Jesuit Oregon Province Archives; Auburn University; Howard University; University of Colorado; University of Connecticut; University of California, Irvine; Emory University; and the University of Minnesota. I am appreciative of the wonderful staffs at the presidential libraries of Richard Nixon, Ronald Reagan, and Jimmy Carter, and found the archivists at the National Archives, the Library of Congress, and the Hoover Institution at Stanford University to be incredibly helpful. I would also like to thank the Southern Christian Leadership Conference, the Pearl S. Buck Foundation, and the family of Congressman Stewart McKinney for the use of their records. Finally, I extend my deepest gratitude to former *Newsday* photojournalist Audrey Tiernan for taking the photograph of Le Van Minh that inspired this project.

ACKNOWLEDGMENTS

I was fortunate to spend some time in Huntington, New York, researching for this project courtesy of the financial support of Wabash College and a grant from the Andrew W. Mellon Foundation. I found the Huntington community to be welcoming, supportive, and beautiful. I am especially grateful to archivist Karen Martin and the staff at the Huntington Historical Society and the Huntington Town Clerk's office; Huntington Town Historian Robert Hughes; Brian Hansen of the Huntington Schools Heritage Room, who generously let me dig through piles of yearbook pictures and files; and former Huntington Union Free School District Board of Education member Kathy Barnhart, for her guidance and for sharing her story.

A number of people supported me through this journey. My brilliant colleague Monika Bilka spent numerous hours editing sloppy drafts while listening to my frustrations when the words simply would not form, constantly reminding me that I could, in fact, "do this." I am eternally grateful for our friendship and your patience. My friend and incredibly detail-oriented scholar Joan Miller, who should be teaching college students somewhere, gave the manuscript a thorough and critical read and a final stamp of approval. My dissertation advisor Kyle Longley extended his support and encouraged my work far beyond graduate school. I continue to appreciate his guidance and wisdom. Finally, my aunt Carol Lilly remains the smartest person I know and deserves full credit (and blame) for convincing me to make a career change and begin this journey what seems like a lifetime ago. The completion of this project would not have been possible without her unwavering support and the countless hours she spent listening to my concerns, offering helpful advice, and editing numerous papers, articles, and drafts all while facing her own personal challenges. Thank you.

I am also ever grateful for the unconditional support of my family and friends, especially my mom, Kathy, step-dad, Dusty, sister Stephanie, and partner, Lovell, who, throughout this process, tolerated my stress and anxiety and still loved me. I hope I make all of you proud. I am fortunate to also have the support of my mentor Martha Norkunas, and my grand-aunt Nazi Ingram who, at ninety-two years old, continues to ask me if I need anything and to remind me that I am special. I am also grateful to a number of family friends, including Amy Rundstrom and G. and Bridget Brown, who read the manuscript and offered constructive criticism, and others who just provided a needed (and often bad) joke or a bite to eat. I am grateful and humbled.

Author's Note

The decision to place this particular photograph of Le Van Minh on the book cover was difficult. I did not want to exploit Minh or pose the image as spectacle, and the fact that I was never able to make contact with Minh further complicated the decision. However, after much consultation with colleagues I concluded that the picture is too important to the history to be left out. This photograph is symbolic of the issues of identity, race, and belonging that composed the Amerasian experience in the United States after the Vietnam War. Readers should consider the image and all of its complexities in the context of the history of U.S. intervention in Vietnam and the human consequences of that conflict.

Scars of War

Introduction

Le Thi Ba was barely a teenager when President Lyndon Johnson sent the first U.S. combat troops into South Vietnam on March 8, 1965. Over the next decade, the war fought inside, outside, and over Vietnam disrupted Le Thi Ba's life and the lives of her countrymen and women in violent and irreversible ways. Ultimately, the war killed over three million Vietnamese, disappeared 300,000 others, and obliterated the country on both sides of the divide with five million tons of bombs.[1]

As a young woman coming of age on the outskirts of war-torn Saigon, Le Thi Ba faced a myriad of difficult choices. Like numerous other women in South Vietnam seeking to survive the war and avoid starvation, she likely sought work on or near a U.S. military base collecting American wages in exchange for providing various kinds of services. Perhaps she did domestic work—cooking, cleaning, laundering—for U.S. soldiers or civilians associated with the war effort. Maybe she understood that more intimate labors earned higher wages and joined the thousands of other women who worked in the seedy bars and brothels of Saigon, Bien Hoa, or Da Nang, offering her body and companionship to U.S. soldiers whose souls were shattered by death and defeat. Possibly it was happenstance: a quiet walk to the market, a smile, a wink, and a cheap pursuit by an American man captivated by her beauty and committed to protecting and providing for her at all costs. Or perhaps the intimate encounter between Le Thi Ba and the American soldier was of the more insidious and violent kind, marked by the force and desperation that always accompanies men at war. Regardless of which path she traveled, Le Thi Ba survived the war, and like many other Vietnamese women, along the way she met a U.S. soldier.

While the nature of the relationship between Le Thi Ba and the U.S. soldier is uncertain, what is undeniable is that the encounter created a life. In 1971, two years before President Richard Nixon claimed to have achieved "peace with honor" and withdrew U.S. combat troops from South Vietnam, nineteen-year-old Le Thi Ba gave birth to the first of her four children and the only one fathered by an American serviceman. For the first years of his life, Le Van Minh had a fairly uneventful childhood, raised by his mother and grandmother, Lai Thi Ty, in a poor neighborhood on the outskirts of Saigon. Like the majority of Amerasian children—the progeny of American men and Vietnamese women born as a result of the Vietnam War—Minh grew up without his American father, whose apparent efforts to bring him and his mother to America fell short.[2] However, in 1975, life became more difficult for Minh. Medical records show that at the age of three, Minh acquired poliomyelitis—polio—a debilitating disease that attacked and paralyzed his legs and prevented him from ever walking upright or unaided.[3] That same year, North Vietnam won the war. Amerasians were among its many casualties and bore some of its most tragic scars.

Stories like those of Le Thi Ba, her encounter with the American soldier, and the birth of her Amerasian son were common during the Vietnam War. They are symbolic of a longer and recurring historical pattern of U.S. military intervention abroad, as well as of the ways in which gendered U.S. immigration and citizenship laws support and protect American men, and specifically American servicemen, who create children out of wedlock with foreign women. Le Thi Ba's experience reveals how the tools of survival available in war are also gendered.[4] They are positioned within the broader framework of sexuality and empire that permanently inscribes war upon the lives of women and marks their children as contested sites of war and war memory.[5]

INTRODUCTION

In the decade after the Vietnam War, the battle for war and memory between the United States and Vietnam occurred over the bodies of Amerasian children like Le Van Minh. The majority of the estimated thirty to fifty thousand Amerasians born as a result of the war did not know their American fathers or lacked the necessary documentation to prove their American paternity.[6] In Vietnam's patrilineal society, as in many Asian countries, the stain of illegitimacy dictated the marginalization many Amerasians faced and invited shaming by their families and peers. By making Amerasians easy to identify within a largely homogenous Vietnamese society, race exacerbated illegitimacy, as did their association with the Vietnam War. After the North Vietnamese communists declared victory in Vietnam, mothers of Amerasians feared their half-American children to be threatened by retribution, persecution, or even murder. Seeking to evade such a fate, some mothers destroyed evidence that their Amerasian children existed, including information about their American fathers; others abandoned their Amerasian children entirely to orphanages or to the streets.

While the feared communist retribution failed to materialize, these children with "American faces" became outcasts in their country of birth. Even though they inherited Vietnamese citizenship from their mothers, Vietnam's "dirty little secret," labeled *con lai*, half breed, *my lai*, American child, or *bui doi*, the dust of life, existed as evidence of the mothers' betrayal of their country and served as constant reminders to the Vietnamese of the American "enemy."[7] As a result, many Amerasians sought acceptance and paternal legitimacy. Frequently unable to acquire recognition from their individual fathers, most Amerasians hoped for an acknowledgement of paternity and a gesture of national paternal responsibility through immigration rights to the United States and American citizenship.

In the decade after the Vietnam War, American media outlets brought public attention to the tragic stories of discrimination and abuse facing Amerasians as a result of their "American faces." Photographs of children with typically American features—blond hair, blue eyes, freckles, dark skin, and afros—abandoned in Vietnam, elicited an emotional response from sympathetic Americans, who pressured U.S. lawmakers to bring these "American" children home.[8] Like many Americans during the period, my own introduction to Amerasians decades later came in the form of a particularly powerful photograph of Le Van Minh. In it, Minh is standing on all fours, his legs severely deformed by the polio he contracted years earlier, holding an origami flower made out of aluminum wrappers. A crop of thick brown hair frames his handsome face, and bangs loosely cover his forehead. His piercing brown eyes look directly into the camera. While Minh's physical condition is shocking and induces a number of questions about disability as a social category and an area of historical analysis, for me it was all about his face.[9] Admittedly, I could not reconcile what I perceived to be Minh's "American face" with my own understandings of Vietnam.[10] A subsequent Google Image search resulted in hundreds of pictures of Amerasians whose physiognomy proved equally confusing. Ultimately, this gave rise to a consideration of the complexities that result when war produces children who are both transracial and transnational.

Thus, forty years removed from the morass of the U.S. intervention in Vietnam, I began my examination of how Amerasians came to symbolize the relationship between race, nation, and war. How their bodies represented the ideological divide that defined the Cold War conflict while traversing racial boundaries and national borders. I committed to investigate the weight of words and the power of pictures and specifically sought to understand how the inclusionary rhetoric used by U.S. policymakers to describe Amerasians as "American" in various pieces of legislation was a response to the images of their "American faces" and why that discourse failed to result in American citizenship. I hoped to understand the role of Le Van Minh and how his photograph inspired U.S. lawmakers to pass policies specifically to address the Amerasians in Vietnam. Finally, I sought to make sense of the reverberating effects of the Vietnam War by placing Amerasians at the center of the trauma. As the living reminders of American intervention, abandonment, and defeat in Vietnam, Amerasians remain the war's most visible scar.

INTRODUCTION

Scars of War begins and ends with the legislative process, tracing the U.S. response to the Amerasians in Vietnam over a thirty-year period. It investigates why policymakers and leaders in various humanitarian groups including the African American community deemed a population unfit for the responsibilities of American society, despite the fact that they had American fathers. It argues that while the failure to grant Amerasians U.S. citizenship appeared to be the result of complex U.S. immigration and citizenship laws, their fate was a response to larger geopolitical matters and rooted in deeper issues of race, gender, nation, and war in America.

A diverse array of political and humanitarian actors including journalists and concerned American citizens determined this fate as they responded to the growing numbers of "American-faced" children during the Vietnam War. American humanitarians like Pearl S. Buck and a bipartisan group of U.S. policymakers led by Patsy Mink (D-HI), Stewart McKinney (R-CT), and Robert Mrazek (D-NY) viewed the U.S. response to the Amerasians through the lenses of paternal legitimacy and national identity. Recognizing the inherent challenges in identifying individual fathers and forcing them to claim their children, they advocated for a national paternal responsibility through policies that would recognize Amerasians as American and bring them to the United States.

At the same time, journalists and media outlets brought Amerasians and the hardships they faced in Vietnam because of their American paternity to the attention of the American public. The powerful photographs of blue-eyed, curly-haired children and their tragic stories of discrimination and abuse elicited concern, condemnation, and activism from sympathetic Americans. In 1986 the students at Huntington High School in Long Island, New York, responded specifically to the picture of Le Van Minh with a powerful grassroots campaign that ultimately forced a legislative response from Congress. The international community also reacted to the pictures of Amerasians by calling on the United States to take responsibility for the children it abandoned in Vietnam.

Throughout the twentieth century, images of hungry, injured, and orphaned children of war have proven an incredibly powerful impetus for U.S. lawmakers to pass legislation and Americans to send life-saving assistance and aid. Scholar Laura Briggs writes eloquently about the critical pairing during the Cold War of visual culture and policy initiatives aimed at helping children in distress.[11] In 1937 *Life* magazine's publication of the photograph of the blackened body of a crying Chinese baby sitting alone amidst the rubble of Shanghai, the apparent lone survivor of a Japanese bombing attack, inspired Americans to donate monies for China relief.[12] In 1955 *Jet* magazine's publication of Black teenager Emmett Till's disfigured and swollen body after he was lynched in Money, Mississippi, galvanized the Civil Rights Movement and eventually led to the passing of important Civil Rights legislation.[13] In Vietnam the 1972 *Associated Press* image of nine-year-old Phan Thi Kim Phúc running naked toward the camera, her clothes incinerated by the napalm bomb dropped by U.S. forces on her village, gave credence to the rising antiwar sentiment in America.[14] The iconography of children and war proved as critical for Amerasians. Photographs of Amerasians' "American faces" reminded Americans of U.S. culpability and defeat in the Vietnam War and made it difficult for lawmakers to deny American paternity. In response, they purported to take responsibility by passing legislation that recognized Amerasians as American children but that failed to grant them U.S. citizenship.

The Amerasian Issue

U.S. servicemen have a long and extensive history of fathering and abandoning half-American children abroad. Both historians and scholars of women and gender studies have considered how the gendered framework of militarized intimacies have shaped relationships between military men and foreign women abroad and how the policies that structure them are an extension of U.S. imperialism and colonialism.[15] They have considered the resulting social problems that American paternity and illegitimacy posed for GI babies in the countries of their birth and how their race often complicated notions of national status and identity.[16]

Before Vietnam, U.S. military interventions in Asia produced tens of thousands of Amerasian children. Beginning in 1898, U.S. soldiers fathered an estimated eighteen thousand illegitimate half-American children with Filipina women during America's "splendid little war" and its subsequent war of American imperialism in the Philippines.[17] During the U.S. occupation of Japan, the number of mixed-blood children fathered by U.S. soldiers ranged from official government reports of thirty-five hundred to the two hundred thousand publicized by foreign aid agencies.[18] The tens of thousands of children left homeless or orphaned by the Korean War included an estimated one thousand Amerasians.[19]

In each country, Amerasians' American paternity, illegitimacy, and racial difference marked them for discrimination. Japanese officials worried about the presence of mixed-race children, and specifically Black Amerasians, damaging the racial purity of the Yamato line.[20] Medical doctor and president of Japan's National Public Health Institute, Furuya Yoshio, warned his countrymen that the effects of miscegenation "would leave a scar on Japanese society for many generations."[21] The Japanese were also worried that Amerasians' American paternity marked them as targets for vengeance against the United States and their mothers for having affairs with the American enemy. Eager to rid the country of this potential threat to Japanese society, officials urged the United States, because "the race mix would not pose any problems" in America's "mongrelized" society, to adopt them into American families as U.S. citizens.[22]

The South Korean government was also concerned about its mixed-blood children and the social welfare and publicity problem they posed to the postwar nation-building project. However, President Syngman Rhee also recognized the potential for Amerasian and Korean orphans to accrue "foreign aid from wealthy nations" through international adoption. According to scholar Eleana Kim, adoption became an effective tool of "civil diplomacy," which converted Amerasian and Korean orphans into diplomatic solutions for national security and foreign policy goals.[23]

Although the Amerasian issue in Japan had somehow evaded the scrutiny of the American media, journalists developed an obsession for Korea's mixed-blood orphans.[24] Worried about the damage abandoned half-American children could do to the nation's moral reputation and role as a global "father figure," U.S. leaders encouraged Americans to aid, assist, and adopt Amerasian and Korean orphans.[25] The response was overwhelming, and international adoption agencies that specialized in Amerasian and Korean children and could "move children quickly" stimulated the demand.[26] When the supply of Amerasians could no longer keep up, adoption agencies resorted to the problematic practices of baby hunting and baby buying, contributing to an industry of global sex and child trafficking disguised as child saving.[27]

Press coverage, however, focused on the humanitarian acts of the U.S. servicemen who adopted thousands of mixed race and full-blooded Japanese and Korean children.[28] Adoption enabled servicemen to fulfill their paternalist role in Southeast Asia by becoming figurative fathers to the orphaned children as caregivers and protectors while evading their paternal responsibilities to their actual children.[29] In this way—asserting the power of American paternalism abroad while denying individual American paternity—the United States could continue to project what historian Anne L. Foster describes as its complex and contradictory power over Southeast Asia to "serve both colonial and anti-colonial goals."[30] Adopting Asian and Amerasian war babies became an extension of America's Cold War obsession with stopping communism and spreading democracy. Notable figures, including former first lady Eleanor Roosevelt, humanitarian and author Pearl S. Buck, and then senator John F. Kennedy advocated "saving the Amerasian children," using a Cold War rhetoric in which Americans could help contain communism by adopting Asian children.[31] As Christina Klein writes in *Cold War Orientalism*, by framing the Cold War as "a sentimental project of family formation," adoption allowed ordinary Americans to "identify with the nation as it undertook its world-ordering projects of containing communism and expanding American influence."[32]

In response to the Korean War baby fixation, U.S. lawmakers enacted the 1953 Refugee Relief Act expanding immigration limits allowing more Americans to adopt "eligible orphans." At the same time, U.S. humanitarians began to lobby Congress to grant citizenship to the Amerasian orphans from Korea.[33] According to historian Yukiko

INTRODUCTION

Koshiro, during the congressional debate over the McCarran-Walter Act in 1952, Rosalind Bates, chair of the Southern California Women Lawyers, joined Pastor Sung Tack Whang of the Korea Gospel Church in Los Angeles to request that Congress amend U.S. immigration laws to allow adoptees to inherit the nationality of their adoptive parents. James Finucane, associate secretary of the National Council for the Prevention of War, went further. Finucane insisted the United States establish a commission to examine the records of every American GI baby in the world and grant citizenship to those with evidentiary proof of paternity.[34]

While the requests for citizenship and national paternal responsibility in both proposals were extraordinary, ultimately they went nowhere. U.S. lawmakers avoided any consideration of Amerasians as actual American children and they did not amend or introduce any new laws to address the Amerasians directly. Instead, they continued to view Amerasians in Japan and Korea as a Cold War problem and framed adoption as a Cold War duty, not a parental one. American desires to parent Asian children therefore had insignificant effects on the Amerasian children in Japan and Korea. By 1956 less than four hundred Amerasian and Japanese orphans had immigrated to the United States for adoption.[35] Whereas Americans continued to express high interest in adopting Korean children, by 1962 the supply of mixed race children in Korea had dried up and the Korean government began integrating its remaining Amerasians into Korean society.[36]

Vietnam was different. Unlike the U.S. occupation of Japan—the result of the allied victory in the Second World War—or the Korean War—a multilateral military intervention that ended with an armistice—the United States lost the war in Vietnam. The defeat raised concerns about America's global and moral standing and shook the confidence of Americans who had lost trust in their own institutions and values and who were no longer convinced of their exceptionalism. Historian Christian Appy describes the war as "a kind of awakening," in which Americans learned "hard truths about themselves and their nation on the backs of a people they dehumanized and killed and whose country they wrecked. It was an expensive education."[37]

Although Amerasians in Vietnam shared the issues of paternity, illegitimacy, racial difference, and discrimination with their predecessors in Japan and Korea, they also carried the unique burden of a nation that lost its war and in the process its identity. In addition to being emblematic of American intervention in Vietnam and the Cold War commitment to child saving, these Amerasians represented the nation's military and moral failings—the fifty-eight thousand American lives lost, the nation's abandonment of its South Vietnamese allies, and the immoral behavior of those who survived. For many Americans, the Amerasians represented what historian Linda Kerber describes as "a subterranean tale that haunts the imperial imagination."[38]

Consequently, the United States had a unique response to Amerasians in Vietnam. In the aftermath of the Vietnam War some lawmakers, humanitarians, and adoption workers began to advocate for Amerasians as Americans. They stressed the nation's paternal responsibility to the children it left behind in Vietnam and urged lawmakers to grant them U.S. citizenship. For a decade lawmakers debated the issue through discussions over paternity, responsibility, and identity. Depending on their political agendas at different points, lawmakers disagreed about whether Amerasians were American or Asian, the role of paternity, and the color of Amerasian blood.

Race proved a critical factor. American and Vietnamese leaders, U.S. lawmakers, and humanitarians disagreed on whether Amerasians' race made them American or Asian and which country was therefore ultimately responsible. Skin color compounded the stigma of illegitimacy in Vietnam. It confirmed suspicions of American paternity and marked Amerasians for lives of exclusion and accusations that they were not Vietnamese. In the United States, however, skin color bolstered claims of legitimacy. For those Amerasians whose skin color and physical features aligned with American racial stereotypes of whiteness or blackness, race effectively ascribed them an American identity and made them American. Amerasians whose racial features were less pronounced were assumed to be racially Asian and therefore not American. Black Amerasians proved to be the exception. Although race marked Black Amerasians clearly as the children of Black fathers, members of the African American community rejected assertions that they

INTRODUCTION

were responsible. Rather, leaders pointed to the domestic policies that already disadvantaged them and the racial discrepancy in U.S. refugee and adoption laws that preferred "good" Asian orphans and refugees over Black and brown American orphans and "bad" Haitian and African refugees.[39] The real tragedy, African American civil rights activist Vernon Jordan wrote in 1975, is that "while Americans rush to bring over homeless kids from Saigon, they have yet to evidence any interest in orphans here at home.... It says a lot about American racial feelings that these kids [American orphans] are left without homes while Vietnamese orphans are 'rescued' from their own kin and country."[40]

Questions of Citizenship

Questions of citizenship underscore this work as the ultimate acknowledgment of belonging and national identity. In her 2006 presidential address to the American Historical Association, "The Stateless as the Citizen's Other," historian Linda Kerber placed the Amerasians at the center of questions of citizenship in an increasingly transborder world. Her query of Puccini's opera *Madame Butterfly*, "What passport would the ill-fated child of Madame Butterfly and Captain Pinkerton carry?," illuminated the ways that race, gender, and war have worked in tandem to create citizens and noncitizens, whom Kerber termed the "citizen's other," to reinforce the legitimacy of the state.[41] This research incorporates an analysis of U.S. citizenship law that exposes the gendered ways in which men and women confer citizenship. While children born abroad to American women are automatically citizens, the law ensures that for children born abroad to American men, citizenship is only granted if the father legitimates the child. Thus U.S. citizenship law is inherently gendered along the maternal line. Historically, this policy has proven effective in protecting American men and, in this case, American servicemen, from any responsibility for fathering "foreign" children and excluding those children from any claim to U.S. citizenship.[42] This was the case for the majority of Amerasians in Vietnam, who fell victim to the U.S. system of "natural mothers and legal fathers."[43] Amerasians whose American fathers did not claim them could not secure paternal legitimacy or U.S.

citizenship. Despite the law, however, U.S. policymakers continued to debate whether Amerasians' American paternity did warrant U.S. citizenship and whether their "American faces" were evidence that Amerasians were Americans.

Thus questions of citizenship became the backdrop for the Amerasian experience in America. Humanitarians invoked it as an official marker of paternity and U.S. lawmakers asserted its importance to national identity. Although citizenship never materialized in the legislation, it elicited important discussions not only about whether Amerasians were American or if they could become American but about what it meant, more generally, to be an American.[44] An examination of these conversations demonstrates how race, gender, and war intersected in conceptualizing who can and cannot become a citizen. It further reveals how citizenship remained tied to whiteness and how perceptions of Asians in the United States as "unassimilable foreigners" or "alien citizens" persisted.[45]

During the Reagan administration Congress enacted two pieces of legislation to address the Amerasian issue—the 1982 Amerasian Immigration Act (AIA) and the 1987 Amerasian Homecoming Act (AHA). Although the discourse in support of both bills described Amerasians as children of U.S. citizens, neither actually granted them citizenship. As with their predecessors in the Philippines, Japan, and Korea, because the majority of Amerasians in Vietnam were born out of wedlock, per U.S. law they were not citizens. Yet unlike any previous response, in this case U.S. lawmakers consistently construed Amerasians as American children and amended U.S. immigration law to provide them preferential immigration status as "children of United States Citizens."[46]

After a century of protecting American fathers from the responsibility of paternity and rejecting national paternal responsibility, U.S. lawmakers changed their approach for Amerasians in Vietnam. Yet even as the inclusionary rhetoric appeared to offer Amerasians acceptance and an abstract acknowledgment of American paternity, the legislation did not grant them citizenship. Ultimately the passage of the AIA and the AHA reveals the power of policymakers to perpetuate

INTRODUCTION

a national narrative of inclusivity while enforcing exclusionary practices to protect actual national borders and conceptual racial ones.[47] This book focuses on that space between rhetoric and action and paternity and policy.

Scars of War

Scars of War is the product of a vast body of interdisciplinary works including race, gender, immigration, and critical refugee studies that offer a multilayered analysis of the Amerasian legislation and the Amerasian experience. Beginning in the 1970s, memoirs, letters, reports, and oral histories initiated scholarship on the Amerasian issue. They provided a victim-centered approach that focused on the individual stories of Amerasians and often championed the saving power of adoption and assimilation for Amerasians as part of the Western narrative of Cold War humanitarianism.[48] During the 1980s and 1990s, social scientists contributed numerous studies of the psychological damage to Amerasians caused by abandonment, resettlement, and rejection tied to the AIA and the AHA.[49] Psychologists examined issues of race and identity especially for Black Amerasians who faced rejection because of their race in Vietnam and in the United States.[50] By the 1990s, political scientists and legal scholars were considering how U.S. immigration and citizenship policies shaped the Amerasian experience in deliberate and often exclusionary ways. Importantly, they placed the politics of paternity and the legalities of citizenship at the center of their analysis.[51]

This literature has provided the important and necessary scholarly basis that informs this book. However, a particular debt exists to the scholarship of Kieu-Linh Caroline Valverde and Jana K. Lipman. Valverde first situated the Amerasians firmly within the field of Asian American studies and the Vietnamese diaspora as a new group of Southeast Asian immigrants in her 1992 article, "From Dust to Gold: The Vietnamese Amerasian Experience."[52] By emphasizing their marginalized status "caught between the politics of two nations, between immigrant and refugee status, between two races, cultures, and philosophies, between subhuman and human, and between 'dust' and 'gold,'" Valverde complicated the victim-centered narrative that defined the previous scholarship with geopolitics and race.[53] Valverde's work challenged traditional notions of racial and national borders in important ways. Her examination of the relationship and points of contention between Amerasians and the Vietnamese American community framed the Amerasian issue and the Amerasian population as inherently transnational and rooted in the cross-border militarized encounters responsible for their existence. The debates among policymakers over whether Amerasians were American because of how they looked, or were Vietnamese because of where they were born, conceptualized the U.S. geographic border as a transformative space that could turn Amerasians into Americans. Five years later, in 1997, historian Jana K. Lipman wrote her master's thesis, "Mixed Voices, Mixed Policy," on how the political agendas of the United States and Vietnam dictated the lives of Amerasians in Vietnam.[54] She continued her analysis of policy and people with a deeper consideration of race, paternity, and identity in the AIA and the AHA in her 2011 article, "The Face Is the Roadmap." Lipman joined numerous other scholars of the diplomatic history in rethinking the master narrative of nationalist history, adding new perspectives from below or outside of the country and considering how nontraditional diplomats, including children, create policy.[55] I discovered Lipman's scholarship early in my research and am grateful for the path her work offered for a more extensive analysis of the intersections that complicate and frame the Amerasian experience.

Scars of War follows in the footsteps of Valverde and Lipman. It foregrounds the congressional battles in the debate and recenters the Amerasians within the political history of the Vietnam War. It seeks to understand the influence that the war—infused with colonial ideology, assumptions of racial inferiority, and the shame and guilt of America's sole military defeat—had on the way Americans saw Amerasians, and what that revealed about how Americans saw themselves. Accordingly, it also benefits from more recent works by Allison Varzally (*Children of Reunion*), Rachel Rains Winslow (*The Best Possible Immigrants*), and Kori A. Graves (*A War Born Family*) that situate the

INTRODUCTION

Amerasian issue within the politics of transnational and transracial adoption and migration, family formation, and national reconciliation and the discourses of the Cold War and civil rights.[56] Varzally's analysis specifically challenges the narrative of perpetual Amerasian marginalization by depicting how Amerasians worked to establish a sense of community and create opportunity in the United States. According to Varzally the immigration and resettlement of Amerasians through the AIA and the AHA "expressed the continued, creative efforts of Vietnamese families to reconnect, reestablish, and realize new lives after years of violence, disruption, and loss."[57] Other scholars have begun to expand "the global story of American military imperialism" and the transnational and transracial children born as a result. In their examination of the estimated four thousand GI children born in the South Pacific during the Second World War, Judith A. Bennett and Angela Wanhalla (*Mothers' Darlings of the South Pacific*) discovered that these children, "do not share the same history of systematic and ongoing social exclusion" that defines the experiences of the GI children born in Asia or Germany.[58]

This work began as a policy study, focused on the political process of making legislation and the conflicting political agendas regarding immigrants and refugees during the Cold War. However, the human element requires a socio-cultural approach to expose the voices from below. Accordingly it depends on an array of primary sources. In detailing the legislative process, I relied extensively on U.S. government documents and archives, including a number of presidential libraries and the personal papers, memoirs, and diaries of the various policymakers and political leaders. I searched the records of humanitarian organizations, religious orders, and adoption agencies that focused on Amerasians. I perused the archives of numerous universities with connections to local communities of Amerasians, including Gonzaga University, University of California at Irvine, and the University of Colorado. To understand how the African American community understood Amerasians and Vietnamese refugees, I turned to the archives of the NAACP, the Congressional Black Caucus at Howard University, George Washington University, and Emory University's

Manuscript, Archives, and Rare Book Library. The media archives of CBS, the *New York Times*, *Newsday*, and a number of Long Island newspapers contributed invaluable information about the important role of journalists and news reporters in educating the American public about Amerasians and pressuring U.S. lawmakers to enact policies. Finally, to understand the role of Huntington High School and Le Van Minh, I researched the records of the Huntington Historical Society and the archives of the Huntington Town Clerk and Huntington High School.

Oral history wonderfully complicates this work. The experience of observing and listening to the stories of those so intimately involved in the Amerasian legislation enriches the history in unforeseen ways. In this case the words of Vietnam veterans, humanitarians, lawmakers and former Huntington High School staff and students help guide the narrative.[59] Still, there are a few individuals whose voices are greatly missed. Although their stories underlie each chapter in the manuscript, I was unable to interview Le Van Minh or Audrey Tiernan, whose photograph of Minh led to his immigration and the passage of the Amerasian Homecoming Act. It is my hope that even in their absence I was able to do their stories justice.

In the early stages of my research, I made a deliberate decision to focus on policy and hence on the policymakers and community advocates and activists. After carrying out a few preliminary interviews with individual Amerasians, some of which are included in the book, I decided that I simply could not shoulder the weight of telling their heart-wrenching stories. I remain indebted and in admiration of those who could and whose work my research relies upon for the Amerasian voice.[60] While I understand the cost of this omission, I hope that readers will appreciate my decision to remain as objective as possible and tell only that part of the story that I could manage responsibly.

By examining the legislative process and the networks that garnered support for the Amerasian cause, *Scars of War* contributes both breadth and depth to the existing literature. It also focuses on the tensions between acceptance and recognition and rejection and exclusion that ultimately placed Amerasians in a liminal space: the acknowledged

INTRODUCTION 17

children of Americans nevertheless not recognized as Americans. It thus diverges from existing scholarship by considering the array of actors on all sides of the issue. By detailing the intersection of the top-down narrative of American presidential administrations and U.S. policymakers and the bottom-up experience of local humanitarians, journalists, and community members and Amerasians, *Scars of War* offers a unique perspective that ties the Amerasian plight to the policymaking process.

Organization

The chapters of this book are arranged chronologically. They trace the ways that race, gender, and war have shaped U.S. immigration and citizenship policies for mixed-race persons and people of Asian descent and informed notions of paternity and family that structured the U.S. response to the Amerasians. Each one details how U.S. lawmakers and humanitarians understood Amerasians in Vietnam as Asian foreigners, mixed-race others, or Americans at different points during and after the Vietnam War. They expose the role of media in bringing the plight of Amerasians to public attention through photographs and video images. They examine how U.S. policymakers sought and ultimately failed to reconcile the Amerasians' "American looks" and claims of American paternity with national identity. By recognizing Amerasians rhetorically as Americans without granting them U.S. citizenship, lawmakers failed to fulfill the promises of the policies they passed on their behalf and simply perpetuated their illegitimacy.

The precedent for how U.S. lawmakers perceived Amerasians through the lens of race, gender, and war began centuries before the birth of the first Amerasian in Vietnam. Chapter 1 begins with the initial encounter of photographer Audrey Tiernan and Amerasian Le Van Minh in 1985, to examine the emergence of this precedent in a history of policies and practices that deemed mixed-race populations, racial others, and persons of Asian descent "eternal foreigners." First, it examines the relationship between race, gender, and citizenship and how race mixing and war complicate the issues.[61] It highlights the gendered nature of U.S. citizenship law and how it shaped national membership in deliberately exclusive ways. Second, this chapter roots the precedent for U.S. policymakers' understanding of the Amerasians in Vietnam. It places the practice of denying American paternity and parental responsibility within the "tensions of empire" that framed U.S. interventions in Asia during the nineteenth and twentieth-centuries.[62]

Chapter 2 situates the plight of Amerasians in Vietnam and the humanitarian and political response to them within a Cold War humanitarianism that called upon Americans to save the child victims of communism and the Vietnam War through adoption, assimilation, and integration.[63] It considers how, between 1971 and 1975, the framework of war motivated a group of Amerasian advocates led by humanitarian Pearl S. Buck and Rep. Patsy Mink (D-HI) to describe Amerasians as American children who needed to be "saved" from Vietnam, first through more flexible adoption and citizenship laws and later through mass evacuations like Operation Babylift.[64] It examines how disagreements over the Amerasian hybridity posed their American paternity and Asian maternity at odds and complicated how Americans understood their responsibility towards them.

Chapter 3 continues the analysis of the framework of race, gender, and war by detailing the shifting political and humanitarian discourse in the aftermath of the communist victory in Vietnam. It considers how U.S. leaders sought to redeem the nation from the humiliation and guilt of abandoning American allies and "losing Vietnam" by saving Vietnam War refugees. For U.S. lawmakers and leaders, redemption necessarily transformed Amerasians from adoptable American children to be saved from communism into Asian refugees in need of "rescue and liberation."[65] Efforts to codify that status into law forced U.S. lawmakers once again to confront the merits of American paternity, race, and responsibility.

After a decade of denying paternal responsibility for Amerasians and failing to reconcile their racial hybridity with an American national identity, in 1982 lawmakers changed their minds. Chapter 4 examines the passage of the Amerasian Immigration Act (AIA) and focuses on the congressional debates over whether race or paternity made Amerasians American or Asian and if they were immigrants or refugees. Drawn largely from primary source material, this chapter details the congressional debates about the AIA, which represented an important political shift in the way U.S. lawmakers and leaders understood Amerasians and the nation's responsibility for them. It questions the intent of the various supporters of the AIA and considers why lawmakers and the Reagan administration finally agreed to formally recognize Amerasians as Americans and bring them to the United States but failed to grant them U.S. citizenship. Importantly, it highlights the role of Amerasians in Vietnam, including Le Van Minh, in garnering the support of U.S and Vietnamese leaders for the AIA.

Chapter 5 addresses the outcomes of the AIA, highlighting the weaknesses that limited the legislation's effectiveness specifically for Amerasians in Vietnam. It argues that despite the Reagan administration's public praise of the AIA and its humanitarian effects, the AIA failed to adequately address the problem. Rather, the Reagan administration viewed the issue as a convenient and effective Cold War tool and subjugated any commitment to solving the problems of actual Amerasians to larger concerns over normalizing relations with Vietnam, an obsession with American POWs and MIAs, and growing tensions over Southeast Asian refugees.

Chapter 6 picks up the story of Le Van Minh at the height of bilateral tensions between the United States and Vietnam in 1986. It considers how a powerful picture of Minh and his "American face" motivated students at Huntington High School, policymakers, and a sympathetic American public to bring Minh to the United States for humanitarian reasons. Although those involved appeared to overlook Minh's American paternity and instead focused on his physical deformity, the familiarity of Minh's face proved critical in garnering support for his immigration as an American child and the subsequent passing of the Amerasian Homecoming Act. In detailing the political process to pass the AHA, this chapter reveals the ways in which U.S. policymakers struggled to reconcile the Amerasians' "American face" and paternity with expectations for an American identity and how questions of race and nation more generally remained intimately tied to humanitarianism and the Amerasians.

Chapter 7 examines the implementation of the AHA and its effects on Amerasians in Vietnam. It argues that the AHA brought the Amerasian experience in America full circle. It asserts that while the AHA circumvented the discussions about American blood and evidentiary proof that accompanied the AIA, its reliance on the Amerasians' "American face" to determine eligibility was equally problematic. The AHA forced U.S. authorities to employ a racial rationale that depended on physical signs of whiteness and blackness to determine whether an applicant was American. Notably, as with all previous legislation, the AHA also failed to grant citizenship, maintaining Amerasians' illegitimacy. In this way, the AHA perpetuated the mixed-race otherness and Asian foreignness that had always plagued American attempts to take national responsibility for Amerasians. Importantly, the Amerasians challenge Americans to reckon with the American defeat in the Vietnam War and to examine what the making of American citizenship looks like and what it means to be an American.

Conclusion

The evolution of the Amerasian experience in America is critical to issues of race, nation, and war. Produced from a pattern of U.S. military intervention abroad, the Amerasians are symbolic of the ways in which U.S. laws are inherently gendered to support and protect individual American men from the duties of paternity. The sex-based distinction embedded in U.S. immigration and citizenship law also relieves the United States from national responsibility of caring for fatherless, foreign-born children. However, in the case of Amerasians in Vietnam, the guilt associated with the Vietnam War demanded it. Americans could not ignore the "American faces" of Amerasians produced by the tragedy of the war, but could not fully embrace them either. Thus the inability of U.S. lawmakers to situate Amerasians' "American looks" and paternity in an American identity was consistent with the ways mixed race populations have always confused traditional conceptions of race and nation and with how U.S. laws have excluded them. For a nation uncertain of its identity amid the trauma of losing the Vietnam War, questions of responsibility and citizenship for Amerasians in Vietnam generated important conversations about what it meant to be an American and what it meant to become one.

Fundamentally, this is a war story and Amerasians bear its scars. Beautiful in their mixtures and their complexities, Amerasians carry in them the lessons of Vietnam—conflict, violence, pain, and defeat—and the importance of acceptance, belonging, and identity. They remind us of a past allegiant to fixed borders and boundaries and of a future destined to destabilize them. As such they have often been portrayed as the unintended consequences or the living reminders of a war most wish to forget. Pushed to the margins in much of the existing literature about the war, Amerasians have likewise been marginalized in Vietnam and the United States and denied a national identity. By recentering them as primary actors and agents of conflict and change, this work accords Amerasians their rightful place in the history of the Vietnam War.[66]

| Chapter One

Setting a Precedent

Newsday photographer Audrey Tiernan snapped the picture of fourteen-year-old Le Van Minh in October 1985 while on assignment in Ho Chi Minh City.[1] The daughter of an American serviceman killed in the Vietnam War, Tiernan felt Minh tug at her leg while walking along the river where her father's ship used to dock. "I thought it was a cat or a dog," Tiernan explained. "I looked down and saw that it was a human being. He had a twisted spine, and he was literally scurrying around the streets like a crab. I was so repulsed I couldn't even bring myself to take his picture. But when I looked closer, I said 'Oh, my God, he's an American!'"[2] It took only a moment for Tiernan to recognize the "American" in Minh's face. His sandy brown hair and big brown eyes overpowered the awkward bends and contortions in his limbs and spine, too frail and damaged to hold his body upright. Fascinated by Minh and "the shocking juxtaposition of his sweet, beautiful face and his twisted body," Tiernan focused her camera and took his picture.[3]

In hindsight it appeared fate orchestrated the meeting between Tiernan and Minh. A decade after the war Tiernan's photo of Minh would appear on the pages of the New York newspaper *Newsday*. It would remind Americans of the plight of Amerasians still living in Vietnam and inspire the Amerasian Homecoming Act, a final effort to bring America's children "home." However, the initial interaction between

Tiernan and Minh was much less noble. While her self-described repulsion to Minh was likely a response to his physical deformities and challenges, Tiernan's bewilderment over Minh's condition—animal or human, Vietnamese or American—was consistent with the ways Americans had often perceived mixed-race persons and people of Asian descent as subhuman, racially inferior, potentially dangerous, and perpetually foreign.[4] It illustrates the pervasiveness of an often unspoken and subconscious history of racialized exclusion in America rooted in long-held assumptions of both mixed-race persons as nonwhite racial others and people of Asian descent as non-American foreigners. It is this history that informed Tiernan's understanding of Minh in those first moments and that shaped the confusion about Minh's race and nationality common among those who saw Amerasians, including U.S. policymakers.

Between 1970 and 1995 the Amerasian mixture of race and nation continuously confounded members of Congress, numerous presidential administrations, humanitarians, journalists, and the American public. Unable to reconcile Amerasians' "American faces" with notions of Asian foreignness and the consequences of the Vietnam War, U.S. policymakers took a contradictory approach. At the same time they utilized an inclusionary discourse of family and belonging to recognize Amerasians' American paternity and deem them American children, lawmakers implemented policies that continued to withhold U.S. citizenship.

The precedent for the inconsistent treatment of Amerasians as American children ineligible for birthright U.S. citizenship is firmly situated within the history of race, gender, and war in the United States. It illustrates how these concepts have historically worked in tandem with U.S. immigration and citizenship laws to determine who is and who is not an American and to color the privileges of rights in America white. In this case, denial of citizenship perpetuated the problematic existence of mixed-race persons and people of Asian descent in America to create a population othered twice—by race and nation—from American society. The precedent set centuries before the birth of the first Amerasian assumed them too different and foreign to warrant actual inclusion in the nation through citizenship and ensured they would never be American.

The Benefits of Birth

In America, birthright citizenship is defined by land of birth (*jus soli*) or blood (*jus sanguine*). Citizenship provides both national identity and legal membership in American society and confers access to the constitutional rights, privileges, and protections of the nation.[5] It is a tool of power that simultaneously defines the terms of inclusion and exclusion to shape membership in the nation in specific and deliberate ways and is often structured in terms of ethnic, racial, and gender hierarchies. By distinguishing between those who belong in a nation and those who do not, citizenship provides "the critical juncture in relationships between people when they come to see each other, and are seen by outsiders, as fundamentally, essentially, immutably different from one another."[6] U.S. citizenship—and therefore membership and identity—has historically been colored white and gendered male, thus undermining the inherent inclusivity of a citizenry determined by blood and land. The benefits of birth intentionally privileged white persons over nonwhite persons and men over women. Placed in simple racial terms, to be American meant to be white, and to be nonwhite most often equated to non-American.[7]

For mixed-race persons in America whose bodies blurred the racial lines upon which citizenship relied, the process of ascribing them identities of race for the purpose of recognition and rights began in the seventeenth century. Gender and racial exclusions collectively framed colonial laws to upend the practice of patrilineal descent and relegate the biracial offspring of white slave-owning men and enslaved Black women to the racial category and slave status of their mothers.[8] In colonial Virginia, this law allowed white slave-owning men to expand their slaveholdings simply by reproducing "Black" children. By the end of the century, to be Black was to be enslaved, and therefore "disempowered and dehumanized," even if your father was white.[9] Absent any claim to whiteness, mixed-race persons found themselves othered in colonial society, their liberties limited and their freedom denied through race-based policies that restricted their right to marry, inherit property, and vote.[10]

There were exceptions. Historians have detailed the stories of mulattoes, half-breeds, and quadroons who defied their racial fate in colonial America and married, inherited, or lived as free and white. By the eighteenth and nineteenth centuries, the presence of mixed-race persons, especially those with one white and one Black parent, posed problems in America as skin color proved an unreliable marker of the evidence of the ever-illicit interracial sex.[11] The lighter the skin, the closer to white a mixed-race person appeared and the more difficult it became to deny them rights and membership in the nation.[12] For a country actively working to protect the privileges of whiteness by policing membership, such racial fluidity disrupted the binary that defined race relations in America and thus represented a paramount danger to the purity of the nation.[13]

In an effort, as they saw it, to secure the nation, U.S. leaders enacted laws in which race and gender worked in tandem to other mixed-race persons in America and restrict their access to citizenship. In 1868, the Fourteenth Amendment granted citizenship to African Americans but failed to address the status of mixed-race persons, thus leaving it to interpretation. In their efforts to recodify race and rights and reclaim the racial binary, Southern white leaders othered mixed-race persons into nonwhite racial categories through an assessment of their looks and a measurement of blood.[14] Blood quantum, the "enduring fiction of miscegenation law," attempted to measure the amount of nonwhite blood in mixed-race people to determine their access to "whiteness" and dictate their political, social, and economic status.[15] In cases where ancestry could not determine the amount of blood, or when percentages were not sufficient to legally exclude a mixed-race person from the privileges of whiteness, lawmakers and community members employed the "eyeball test"—the visual measurement of a person's makeup using an assessment of skin and eye color, hair texture, and features, "the shape of the nose, ears, lips, body and skull."[16] For the progeny of one white parent and one racially "other" parent, such practices and policies dismissed any claim they might have made to whiteness and ensured their otherness would be determinative.[17]

During the early twentieth century, eugenicists gave "scientific" credence to ideas of blood quantum and blood contamination as they argued that nonwhite blood infected white blood, causing "mongrolization" and degeneration that would ultimately lead to the extinction of the white race. In 1916 eugenicist Madison Grant wrote *The Passing of the Great Race*, which Adolf Hitler later lauded as "his Bible."[18] In it, Grant conjured the dangers that miscegenation posed to the racial purity and superiority of white Americans and the necessity of relegating mixed-race persons to the racial category of their nonwhite parent. "The cross between white and Indian is Indian, the cross between a white man and a Negro is a Negro; the cross between a white man and a Hindu is a Hindu; the cross between any of the three European races and a Jew is a Jew."[19]

Marriage laws have also been powerful, gendered domestic tools of racial exclusion. Seventeenth-century antimiscegenation laws in the Maryland and Virginia colonies sought to prevent sexual and marital unions between white women and Black men and categorized their mixed-race offspring as Black for the purpose of preserving the binary racial distinctions that structured colonial American society.[20] By dictating who could marry and who received citizenship, marriage laws could prevent interracial unions and preserve the privileges of power for white people, therefore protecting the nation from the presumed racial degradation of miscegenation and the claims of mixed-race persons to property, inheritance, or citizenship.

For children born abroad to American fathers and foreign mothers, domestic marriage laws combined with U.S. immigration law to determine citizenship status.[21] Although U.S. law dictated that blood ties established citizenship for children not born in U.S. territory, the process for children born outside the institution of marriage was, and is, intentionally gendered. For Amerasians in Vietnam, the majority of whom were born out of wedlock, this is the precedent for invalidating their claims of paternity.

In 1864 the federal court case of *Guyer v. Smith* established the precedent in U.S. law of matrilineal descent for children born abroad after the Maryland Court of Appeals determined that mothers bore the primary responsibility for children born outside of marriage. More specifically, according to the court American mothers of children born out of wedlock on foreign soil automatically transmit citizenship to their children but American fathers do not. More simply, despite evidence of their American paternity, children of American fathers were not automatically citizens.[22] In 1952, section 309 of the U.S. Immigration and Nationality Act (INA) reinforced the sex-based distinction established by the *Guyer* case, declaring that a child born abroad out of wedlock "shall have acquired at birth the nationality status of his mother." U.S. citizenship was granted only if the father claimed his child.[23]

In practice, the unequal and gendered application of the law assumed a role of parental responsibility and legal filiation between child and mother and an absence of both between child and father. Consequently, American men faced no legal obligation for the children they produced with foreign women through love, lust, or rape and their children had no legal grounds for U.S. citizenship. In the context of the large U.S. military presence abroad in the nineteenth and twentieth centuries, especially in developing countries with racially distinct populations, the *Guyer* precedent had racially exclusionary implications that would have important consequences for Amerasians of Vietnam.

Race

As mixed-race people in nineteenth century America continued to be racially othered and thus denied the full liberties of their birthright, a growing population of Asian immigrants further challenged the limits of American racial categories and exposed American bigotry toward the Eastern world.[24] Similarly to their mixed-race peers, Asians did not fit into American racial delineations of whiteness or blackness and, as such, challenged the racial rationale upon which the granting of citizenship relied. The geographic and cultural distance that defined Asian foreignness compounded American anxieties over and fascination with the "Oriental difference."[25] Scholar Edward

SETTING A PRECEDENT   29

Said has described the practice of dividing the world into two opposing parts—the developed, civilized, racially superior Occident or West and the lesser developed, uncivilized, racially inferior Orient or East—as *Orientalism*: "a collective notion identifying 'us' Europeans against all 'those' non-Europeans."[26] The juxtaposition of the Orient and the Occident as cultural polarities of geographic distance and racial difference framed American understandings of Asia and Asians as nonwhite, non-American, and foreign. Hence, like their mixed-race peers, the history of Asians in America is a history of othering intended to protect the nation from an "Asian invasion" through the restriction of rights and movement. As part of the effort to prevent people of Asian descent from acquiring membership in the nation or accumulating political power, social and legal exclusions have consistently been framed by questions of whether Asians, regardless of citizenship or generation, could become Americans or if Asian Americans even were Americans.[27]

Beginning with the 1790 Naturalization Law, U.S. citizenship was reserved for "free white persons." With little clarity about what "white" meant at the time, this law made the process of "becoming Caucasian" a crucial part of the politico-cultural saga of European migration and settlement.[28] After the first mass immigration of Chinese laborers entered the country in the nineteenth century to work on the railroads and the mines of the American western frontier, U.S. immigration policies specifically excluded Asians from immigration and citizenship.[29] Race played an important role. Although political leaders and legal authorities agreed that Asian immigrants were not white, they were uncertain as to whether that made them Black. Like mixed-race persons, the inability to easily relegate Asians to either racial category was confusing. Even the U.S. judicial system seemed ambivalent on where to situate them. Facing increasing numbers of Chinese and Japanese immigrants by the mid-nineteenth century, U.S. courts applied the Blumenbach racial taxonomic system to classify the new arrivals as part of the Mongolian or "yellow" race, "a distinct racial group situated somewhere between the '"savage" African and the "civilized" European' and ineligible for citizenship." This intermediary status scared Americans who worried about the threat such a race might pose to the racial order, which depended on the black-white racial binary. It motivated courts to prevent the potential accumulation of Asian political power by restricting immigration rights and denying them citizenship.[30] In the 1880 Oregon circuit court case *In re Camille*, Judge Matthew Deady explained the racial rationale behind Asian exclusion. The Fourteenth and Fifteenth Amendments, Deady asserted, unfairly granted citizenship "to the comparatively savage and strange inhabitants of the 'dark continent,' while withholding it from the intermediate and much-better qualified red and yellow races." Yet such "qualifications" also justified their exclusion: "The negroes of Africa were not likely to emigrate to this country, and therefore the provision [Fourteenth Amendment] concerning them was merely a harmless piece of legislative buncombe, while the Indian and Chinaman were in our midst, and at our doors and only too willing to assume the mantle of American sovereignty, which we ostentatiously offered to the African but denied to them."[31]

In addition to legal exclusions, Asian immigrants in America faced assumptions of racial inferiority that motivated a nativist backlash and racist vitriol from white American and European immigrant workers united in their concerns about the economic threats posed by Asian "coolie" labor.[32] Anxieties were especially high in the western states of California and Oregon, where labor needs in the mines and railroads attracted large numbers of Chinese immigrants and where some worried about the potential problems of naturalized Chinese-American citizens. One Republican senator from Oregon expressed his distaste for such a possibility by pointing out the "practical difficulty" surrounding the Chinese; in contrast with the "fading . . . red man" and the "enslaved . . . Americanized" blacks, "when you open the door to one you open the door to four hundred millions. . . . with this mighty tide of ignorance and pollution that Asia is pouring with accumulating force and volume into the bosom of our country."[33]

Legislative efforts to "protect free white labor" from competition with Chinese "coolie labor" resulted in laws that excluded Asians from property ownership, equal pay, and legal protection. To stifle Asian immigration, certain states levied immigration taxes on "persons who cannot become citizens"—Native Americans, African Americans, and Asians. Massachusetts senator Charles Sumner's valiant yet futile attempt in 1870 to convince Congress to abandon the principle of a racial qualification for citizenship and remove the word "white" from the 1790 law was a direct response to western congressional delegates who staunchly opposed the granting of U.S. citizenship and citizenship rights to Asians.[34]

Americans also worried about the perceived danger of white-Asian miscegenation and the potential threat that such families posed to the racial order and the nation. During the nineteenth century numerous states passed antimiscegenation and restrictive marriage laws aimed at policing Asian sexuality, reproduction, and marriage rights to impede Asians' incorporation into America.[35] Federal legislation reinforced state laws. The 1875 Page Act, 1882 Chinese Exclusion Act, 1892 Geary Act, and the 1907 Gentleman's Agreement barred specific Asians—women and workers—from immigration and citizenship in order to prevent the formation and reproduction of Asian families in America.

As detrimental as they were to the Asian experience in America, these laws still did not temper American anxiety over Asian immigration, settlement, and citizenship, which continued to shape exclusionary immigration and citizenship policies into the twentieth century. The 1917 Asiatic Barred Zone Act denied Asians admission to the United States by classifying them among the diseased, immoral, criminals, "paupers, assorted radicals; and illiterates" and the 1924 Johnson-Reed Act instituted a national-origins quota system that designated Asians as "persons ineligible for U.S. citizenship."[36] Race underpinned these laws. U.S. leaders and the policies they passed failed to distinguish between nationalities and instead grouped Asians into one big "Oriental" category.[37] Unable to claim the characteristics and stereotypes of the white or Black race, Asians in the United States, defined by their difference and distance, became racially othered. Racist designations—the Chinese "coolie," the "yellow peril," the "menacing horde"—were fraught with fears and presumptions of innate inferiority and foreignness.[38]

The U.S. Supreme Court reinforced Asian otherness in the 1922 and 1923 rulings in *Ozawa v. the United States* and *United States v. Bhagat Singh Thind*. In *Ozawa*, the court upheld the exclusion of Asians from immigration and U.S. citizenship because it determined that Asians were not part of the "Caucasian race" and therefore were not "white." In the *Thind* case, the court reframed its ruling from *Ozawa*, insisting that even Asians who were "Caucasian" did not "look white," and so were subject to exclusion from U.S. citizenship.[39] Even the 1952 McCarran-Walter Act, which relaxed existing restrictions on Asian immigration and citizenship, lauded by some as a progressive immigration policy that "removed all racial, gender, and nationality barriers to citizenship," defined the immigration quotas awarded to Asian countries by race rather than nationality. According to the act, any child born to one or more Asian parents, regardless of their place of birth or citizenship, counted against the quota for the specific Asian nation corresponding to their "race"—Japanese, Korean, Vietnamese, etc.—or the general quota for the Asian-Pacific Triangle.[40] Incorporated into the policy was a modern interpretation and application of blood quantum that relegated mixed-race persons to the status of their racially subordinate parent. In his statement vetoing the legislation, President Harry Truman criticized the hypocrisy of the act's discriminatory policies against people from Asia and its inherently racist implications: "The countries of Asia are told in one breath that they shall have quotas for their nationals, and in the next, that the nationals of other countries, if their ancestry is as much as 50 percent Asian, shall be charged to these quotas. It is only with respect to persons of oriental ancestry that this invidious discrimination applies.... These provisions are without justification."[41]

Yet Truman's words fell on deaf ears. It was not until 1965 that the Hart-Cellar Immigration Act, described as the "most dramatic rethinking of immigration policy in the last half-century," finally replaced the national-origins quota system with preference based on family relationships and reunification as well as labor needs.[42] The result was a massive and unintended influx of Asian immigrants to America that rekindled the nineteenth-century racialized fears of a "yellow peril" and an invading "yellow horde" that would take American jobs.[43] Even after the "model minority" epithet reracialized Asians in the United States into the example of successful assimilation, juxtaposing them against the alleged failings of African Americans, notions of Asian foreign otherness persisted. Although the new stereotype allowed white Americans to countenance Asian Americans as citizens, nevertheless because "whiteness was not an option" as it has been for Southern and Eastern European immigrants, they remained racially othered—unassimilable and permanently foreign.[44]

Decades before Audrey Tiernan met Le Van Minh, Amerasians had suffered from the repercussions of these long-standing racialized and exclusionary policies and practices, used to distance both mixed-race persons and people of Asian descent from whiteness and thus restrict their access to immigration and citizenship.[45] The sex-based distinction had particularly devastating consequences. During the twentieth century, this additional form of discrimination accompanied U.S. military forces into Asia, effectively eliminating potential claims of American paternity or nationality for most Amerasian children born abroad.

The Imperial Precedent

Anxieties over the darkening of America and the persistent equation of race and nation—white and American—accompanied U.S. imperial expansion at the end of the nineteenth century. The acquisition of new lands in the Caribbean and the Pacific inhabited by darker-skinned, foreign populations coincided with increasing domestic concerns over the race and rights of African Americans and nonwhite immigrants from Europe and Asia.[46] The subsequent debates over citizenship and status for those living in America's newly acquired territories demonstrate the extent to which the racial binary and an ideology of white superiority informed the U.S. imperial project to construct colonial categories of white citizens and nonwhite subjects.[47] The conflation of race and nation to divide citizens from subjects along racial lines proved increasingly problematic to the nation's notions of Empire. After the annexation of Puerto Rico in 1898, American fears of miscegenation and racial degeneration led members of the U.S. Supreme Court to express their concerns about granting Puerto Ricans U.S. citizenship. Justice Edward White worried that "if the Constitution automatically granted citizenship to Puerto Ricans, then American citizenship might be dismantled and the people of the United States enslaved . . . the language of physical degradation suggests a moral and racial tainting thereby rendering the body of the American citizens incapable of citizenship."[48] White inferred that the power of race to corrupt the nation through citizenship justified denying U.S. citizenship to Puerto Ricans.

Tensions between race and nation also emerged in the Pacific, where American investors, missionaries, and reporters continued to define Asians as the ultimate nonwhite foreigners and thus "antithetical to the prevailing ideas of what it meant to be an American."[49] In Hawaii, American imperialists plotting to acquire more land applied their anti-Asian sentiment to exploit existing tensions between native Hawaiians, deemed "whitish" and assimilable, and the Asian immigrants who lived and labored on the islands and whom they perceived in racial terms as unassimilable, undesirable, and diseased.[50] Hence, when the 1900 Hawaii Organic Act established the territory of Hawaii and conferred U.S. citizenship on all Hawaiians, it excluded Hawaii's Asian population. The denial of citizenship to 60 percent of Hawaiian residents was a continuation of the exclusionary U.S. immigration and citizenship laws already applied to Asians. It also reflected the racial rationale of U.S. leaders who believed that, like Puerto Ricans, Asians would contaminate the nation.[51]

While Americans feared the detrimental effects of granting U.S. citizenship to people from Asia, American men continued sleeping with Asian women and fathering half-American and half-Asian children. Whereas racism framed U.S. policies and practices that excluded Asians, gender ensured the rejection of Amerasians. By the turn of the century, the sex-based distinction in U.S. law had sufficiently protected numerous American men from paternal responsibility and the

SETTING A PRECEDENT   35

nation from culpability for the half-American children they fathered abroad. However, the law proved simultaneously more powerful and problematic in Asia, where Amerasians faced the double exclusion of mixed-race otherness and Asian foreignness.

The American response to the estimated eighteen thousand American-fathered mestizos born as a result of U.S. intervention in the Philippines in 1898 set the precedent for how U.S. leaders would ultimately address Amerasians in Vietnam.[52] The half-American, half-Filipino mestizos introduced new concerns into domestic conversations in America about race mixing and citizenship as U.S. authorities struggled to understand hybridity within the colonizing confines of war and empire.[53] More than three years of imperial conquest structured American perceptions of mixed-race Filipinos as "nonwhite" racial others.[54] Viewed through this prism, America's war in the Philippines was a race war fought between the civilized white and the uncivilized nonwhite. Instead of interpreting the Filipino resistance through the lens of America's own revolutionary history, Americans viewed it as a clear violation of the natural racial order. They believed that such blatant disobedience justified U.S. intervention on the islands and a strategy of extreme brutality and "exterminism."[55]

The common belief that Filipinos—the people, the culture, and their environment—had the power to decivilize white people and turn them into savages heightened existing racial anxieties. "The tropics," Army Lieutenant Conrad Stanton Babcock wrote in his journal circa 1902, "do funny things to Caucasians at times."[56] But Babcock and others also believed that white Americans held an equally intoxicating power to civilize worthy Filipinos and to recivilize Americans who had "gone wild" in the Philippines. In fact, while addressing one U.S. soldier whose "mental balance had slipped," Babcock employed measured modern American discipline to bring him back to civilization. After a hefty dose of his stern command to "Drop that gun!" Babcock explains, "His wildness left him in a flash . . . he dropped his rifle instantly."[57] The "savagery" of the war and the ferocity of the fighting in the Philippines became a template for future American wars in Asia, as did the practice of American men sleeping with

Asian women and fathering and abandoning their mixed-race Amerasian children.[58]

The power to civilize, decivilize, and recivilize complicated American notions of paternity and responsibility for the mestizo children. Fears of miscegenation and racial degeneration combined with anti-foreign sentiment to shape the American response to what U.S. leaders viewed to be a mestizo problem.[59] Although U.S. authorities continued the practice of racializing those mestizos raised by their Filipina mothers, they took a very different approach to mestizo orphans. The assumption was that children raised by Filipina mothers in the Philippines could not escape the decivilizing effects of their native environment and their mothers' love. But a civilizing opportunity did exist for those absent any maternal influence and specifically for those mestizos with white American blood. Hence, by inverting the rules of blood quantum to account for the amount of white blood running through their veins, orphaned mestizo children fathered by white American men could become white and, potentially, American.[60] In response to the realization that there were numerous "white American" children orphaned in the Philippines, white American expatriates began to assert a sort of transnational paternity in which they supported, protected, and educated their "white" children while also urging U.S. officials to recognize the nation's paternal responsibility for the orphans and grant them citizenship.

Such recognition of race and responsibility fully displayed American racism. White American expatriates did not extend support or provide services to the orphaned mestizo children of African Americans, for whom the traditional rules of blood quantum remained. Unlike the "white blood" that liberated their mestizo peers from darkness and decay, the "black blood" of those fathered by African American men, allegedly evidenced by their dark skin and "comically oversized lips," excluded them from whiteness and hence consideration for U.S. citizenship.[61] Ultimately, neither the white nor Black mestizos actually received blanket U.S. citizenship. Unconvinced that American paternity, regardless of the father's race, conferred the racial or cultural characteristics of whiteness, U.S. authorities continued to classify the mestizos as non-American.⁶² The inconsistency with which Americans created, racialized, and excluded the American mestizos was a notable precursor to Amerasians in Vietnam almost a century later, but with one important exception. After the Vietnam War whiteness and Blackness marked Amerasians as potential Americans, while more ambiguous or Asian racial characteristics excluded others as "others."⁶³

Wars

Anti-Asian sentiment in America continued throughout the twentieth century. The racialized colonial and Orientalist ideology perpetuated the notion of Asians as inferior and uncivilized, manifesting itself in domestic concerns over immigration and economic competition and international fears of foreign conflict. During the Second World War, U.S. leaders and soldiers carried their racialized understandings of Asia and Asians into the war with Japan. The Japanese proved a formidable military foe. American misperceptions of the Japanese, framed in a "four-hundred year intellectual development of European concepts of the colored other," continued to warrant the brutality of American soldiers against people they viewed as "savages, children, madmen, and beasts."⁶⁴

U.S. leaders, simultaneously impressed and concerned by Japan's military prowess, once again depicted the war in racial terms. Whereas a benevolent paternalism dictated the discourse of war in the Philippines, America's war against Japan was a battle for the preservation of Anglo-Saxon civilization and the white race. Accordingly, American racism and anti-Asian sentiment were on full display. Leaders depicted the Japanese as aggressive but inferior imitators of the white race who claimed to be the sole champions of civilization in Asia.⁶⁵ Famed U.S. War correspondent Ernie Pyle described the Japanese as "subhuman and repulsive," and American soldiers, he claimed, viewed the Japanese "the way some people feel about cockroaches or mice."⁶⁶ During the postwar occupation of Japan, U.S. leaders reconfigured their racism into an "enlightened paternalism," acknowledging Japan's capacity for democracy, but only with America's help. Secretary of State John Foster Dulles expressed the concerns of many Americans that because of their race, the Japanese, like all other Asians, were untrustworthy. "The Oriental mind," Dulles explained, "was always more devious than the Occidental mind."[67]

At the onset of the Cold War, the Orientalized and racialized discourse of Asian inferiority that shaped Dulles's anxiety continued to accompany the new global outlook, in which U.S. leaders were now committed to a world divided along ideological lines rather than racial ones and to preventing the spread of communism. The "loss" of China to communism in 1949 bolstered both the anticommunist and racial fears that the fight against communism was also a fight to protect white and Western superiority. Concerns about the Chinese "Yellow Peril" and the Russian "Red Peril" and presumptions that Russians were really Asiatic and therefore the true evil in the East motivated further U.S. intervention in Asia.[68]

In Korea, U.S. fighting and occupation forces placed forty thousand troops below the 38th parallel in defense of democracy. As in the Philippines and Japan, racialized colonial notions of Asian inferiority persisted. U.S. media reports continued to dehumanize the North Koreans to the status of livestock and bugs. The North Koreans, the *Los Angeles Times* reported, were like "droves of cattle," and U.S. victory in battle "was like scraping ants off with a stick."[69] In August 1950 the *Los Angeles Times* revealed that U.S. soldiers had revived the word "g——" to describe the North Korean communists. First used to degrade Filipinos during the Spanish-American War in 1898, it was fraught with historical, racial, and colonial connotations.[70] Later, during the Vietnam War, the term, which intentionally failed to distinguish between enemies and allies, was the most common racial epithet used to dehumanize Asians.[71] In boot camp, American soldiers trained to "kill, kill, kill the g——" and to think, "If it's dead and Vietnamese, it's VC" learned to view all Vietnamese as inferior. Such a dehumanizing discourse of war in Asia returned to the United States with soldiers, perpetuating beliefs of Asian inferiority and shaping the way Americans tended to view all Asians.[72]

Like their counterparts in Europe and their predecessors in the Philippines, U.S. soldiers stationed in Asia after the Second World

SETTING A PRECEDENT 39

War also fathered children with Asian women. But as a result of the sex-based distinction in U.S. law and the specific exclusion of Asians from immigration and citizenship during much of the period, Amerasians were excluded from citizenship. When Japanese radio announced the birth of the first Amerasian child born as a result of the U.S. occupation in 1946, the Japanese were as worried about the presence of mixed-race children in Japan as U.S. officials were about having to take responsibility for them.[73] While the Japanese tended to approve of Amerasians fathered by white Americans, they despised those fathered by African Americans. In 1953, the president of Japan's National Public Health Institute stated publicly his concern that Black Amerasians, considered genetic and social degenerates, would pass on their non-Japanese features to their descendants and pose a great threat to Japanese society.[74] Such anti-Black prejudice existed across Asia where Black Amerasians suffered harsher discrimination, abuse, and marginalization because of their race.[75]

While U.S. officials denied responsibility for Amerasians in Japan they had less success ignoring the "American" children in Europe. Specifically, the "brown babies," offspring of African American men and European women, perpetuated American fears of miscegenation and confusion over mixed-race populations. Although African American soldiers composed only 10 percent of U.S. military forces in Europe during the Second World War and fathered less than 2 percent of out-of-wedlock children, obsessions over the interracial relationships between Black soldiers and white European women and racist beliefs about the carnal dangers of Black male sexuality led many Americans and Europeans to believe that African Americans fathered the majority of war babies.[76] As a result, authorities labeled the children a "Black" problem and relegated responsibility for their care and upbringing to the African American community, whose "Negro GI" men left their children behind.[77]

In contrast to the American mestizos in the Philippines and Amerasians in Japan, the "Blackness" of the brown babies excused white European mothers from their maternal obligations and masked the reproductive responsibility of white American soldiers who fathered children in Europe. In what was now a common practice regarding the mixed-race offspring of American men, U.S. leaders recognized the brown babies as the children of African American men but declined to grant them U.S. citizenship.[78]

Thirty years later, Americans concerned about Amerasians in Vietnam ignored the nation's previous approach to the mixed-race, American-fathered children born in Europe and Asia. Rather, advocates lauded the French model of national responsibility toward its mixed-race, French-fathered métis children. Like the American mestizos in the Philippines, the métis challenged French colonial policies that sought to sustain a clear distinction between the "civilized" French citizen colonizers and their uncivilized, native colonial subjects.[79] Similarly, because the majority of métis were born out of wedlock, per French law they did not automatically inherit French citizenship unless their father claimed them. The result was a growing population of fatherless "orphans" that French authorities worried would grow up to resent France and become enemies of the empire. Consequently, French colonial administrators viewed the métis as subversive threats to French national identity and the colonial project. To allay these perceived dangers, French colonial authorities uprooted those orphaned métis deemed worthy of inclusion into the French empire from the degrading influences of their indigenous environments and families and placed them in French-run institutions where they became "civilized" French citizens.[80] The transformation of the métis from subjects into citizens relied on beliefs about the powerful "civilizing effects" of "French blood" and the insertion of race into the 1928 French nationality law.[81]

Hence, by the time French forces faced defeat at Dien Bien Phu to end the First Indochina War in 1954, race and blood rendered the métis valuable members of the French empire. Empire therefore motivated the relocation of twenty-five thousand Eurasian children to France after the war, and justified French financial support and French citizenship.[82] Amerasian supporters and American humanitarians, hoping the nation would finally take paternal responsibility, cited the French approach as a model, conveniently dismissing the imperial motives and

SETTING A PRECEDENT   41

racism behind French actions. American advocates insisted that the United States must also transport its Amerasian children from Vietnam and welcome them to the United States as American children.[83]

Gender

Gendered assumptions were central to the pattern that led U.S. military personnel to produce, abandon, and reject children abroad. In addition to the sex-based distinction in U.S. immigration and citizenship law and long-held assumptions of Asian racial inferiority and deviance, Americans also imposed gendered notions of femininity and sexuality and geographic concepts of conquest on Asian women. Asian women faced the double burden of a racialized and gendered "Orientalization" that stereotyped them as compliant, demure, and exotic.[84] The history of U.S. militarism in Asia is also a history of U.S. military prostitution and the objectification of Asian women. When U.S. Commodore Matthew Perry opened Japan's doors to foreign trade in 1854, he introduced American men to the Japanese geisha and the Asian prostitute, who shaped conceptions of Asian women as simultaneously seductive and sinister. Nineteenth-century encounters between American men and Asian women in the ports of Japan coincided with an influx of Chinese immigrant women to the United States, who were often associated with prostitution and were viewed by Americans with distrust, especially in the American West. The Chinese prostitute reinforced the image of the sinister Oriental seductress and resulted in the 1875 Page Act barring the importation of Chinese women for immoral purposes.[85] In accord with the expectations about colonized women of color during American imperialism and Asian immigration, U.S. soldiers in Japan, South Korea, and Vietnam believed in their own racial and cultural superiority and anticipated Asian women as being readily sexually available. In response to such racialized and gendered interpretations of imperial power and play by American servicemen, a massive prostitution industry oriented to the military emerged that commodified the sexual domination of Asian women by American men.[86]

During the Second World War, the siren voices of the mythical

"Tokyo Rose" further exoticized the image of the "Orientalized Asian" by allowing U.S. soldiers to simultaneously "transfer their racial fantasies and hostilities."[87] The emergence of military-endorsed prostitution during the postwar U.S. occupation of Japan gave American servicemen the opportunity to act out their visceral fantasies on the bodies of Asian women. Hence the Japanese geisha, followed by the Korean comfort woman and later the Vietnamese bar girl, facilitated the emergence of lucrative sex and service industries in Asia. Some military leaders believed prostitution an unnecessary evil that interfered with soldier effectiveness, while others saw it as a necessary component of normalizing the lives of soldiers in very abnormal conditions.[88] Whatever the opinions of individual leaders, however, the presence of U.S.-regulated brothels contributed to the perception that the majority of Asian women were prostitutes. While obviously untrue, this belief set the precedent for soldier behavior toward women in Asia, including Vietnam.[89]

Ironically, the stereotype of Asian women as submissive, docile, and sexually subservient to the needs of men also contributed to the increasing numbers of American soldiers marrying Japanese women after the Second World War. The Asian war bride, transformed from paramour to paragon of virtue through a "domesticated Orientalism," became a common occurrence on U.S. military bases in Japan and South Korea.[90] To quell the trend, U.S. military policy reinforced U.S. immigration and citizenship laws to police soldier marriages and prevent Asian women from immigrating to the United States. War Department directives required military approval of all U.S. soldier marriages. However, while authorities expressed concerns about overseas soldier marriages generally, the "miscegenous unions" proved "the most distressing."[91] U.S. military leaders actively discouraged soldier marriages with Asian women on the grounds that U.S. law excluded Asian nationals as "aliens ineligible for citizenship."[92] Different perceptions of German and Japanese women as potential wives—the latter presumed inferior and sexually immoral—translated to an unequal application of military fraternization and marriage policy and the reliance on prostitution in Asia.[93] It is not surprising, therefore, that the majority of the 114,000 wives admitted to the United States under the 1945 War Brides Act were white, European, and English speaking. In addition, the 1947 Alien Brides Act that allowed Asian wives to immigrate to the United States as "'alien spouses' otherwise considered 'inadmissible because of race'" included numerous provisions that made immigration impossible for most couples.[94]

A decade later American perceptions of Asian women extended into Vietnam, as did the efforts of U.S. leaders to restrict and regulate sexual and conjugal relations. The emergence of South Vietnam's "entertainment" industry, fully equipped with massage parlors and brothels, coincided with the increasing numbers of U.S. servicemen in the country between 1965 and 1973.[95] During the Vietnam War, thousands of Vietnamese women flocked to U.S. military bases for employment as laundresses, maids, and cooks. Others came as "mama-sans," "hooch-girls," and prostitutes to work in the brothels that sprouted up on army bases with names inviting play and frivolity—Sin City, Disneyland, and Boom Boom Parlors. Many were built under the directive of military leaders—division commanders, two-star generals, and colonels—to whom Washington had given "considerable discretion" in regulating prostitution.[96]

Americans tended to view Vietnamese women through the same anti-Asian lens that shaped a history of exclusionary and racist policies and practices. U.S. military leaders emphasized the dangers posed by Vietnamese women, whom they viewed as racially inferior and potential communist subversives. They were the seductive and sinister Vietnamese prostitutes whose exotic Asian beauty and feminine docility had been corrupted by communism, and who would seduce an American serviceman into her bedroom before viciously cutting his throat.[97]

Consequently, the obstacles for U.S. servicemen committed to marrying their Vietnamese girlfriends despite assumptions of racial inferiority and allegiance to communism were deliberately overwhelming. In addition to the extensive security and background checks required for potential Vietnamese spouses, military officials used paperwork, red tape, and the high cost of immigration as obstacles to prevent soldier marriages.[98] Emmanuel J. Holloman, a U.S. Army interpreter stationed in Vietnam from 1966 to 1971, believed that racism motivated commanders to make the marriage process so challenging. According to Holloman, "A few blacks, but mostly whites, felt that the Vietnamese weren't equal to us. So they made it real difficult to marry one."[99] Others, including some Asian American soldiers, echoed Holloman's claim. After requesting permission to marry his Vietnamese girlfriend, the military superior of one Asian American soldier stated, "Man you don't want to marry one of these 'g——s' over there. They're not civilized, and if you take her back home with you, people won't be able to handle her cause she's not civilized and you wouldn't be able to trust her once you get back to the States." The commander added, "once you get back, you'll see all those blonds and stuff, and you'll look at your wife and she'll be this old farmer chick—this g———and you'll want to get rid of her. You'll be embarrassed when you get back because she's Vietnamese."[100]

While discouraging soldiers from marrying Vietnamese women, U.S. authorities continued to encourage servicemen to engage in sexual relationships with them in order to boost soldier morale, provide comfort, and reinforce the masculinity necessary to keep soldiers fighting like men.[101] Although such intimate encounters were often strictly relationships of convenience for the soldier, some evolved into consensual, long-standing, and loving relationships. Others took the violent and racialized form of the war itself. The belief that the Vietnamese were racially inferior and inhuman paired with the anticommunist sentiment that defined U.S. intervention in Vietnam to justify the sexual assault of Vietnamese women. As journalist Susan Brownmiller famously wrote, "When men are men, slugging it out among themselves, conquering new land, subjugating new people, driving toward victory, *unquestionably* there shall be some raping."[102] When asked about the rape of Vietnamese women during the war, marine Sergeant Scott Camil responded, "It wasn't like they were humans.... They were a g—— or a Commie and it was okay."[103]

Although the Amerasian children produced during the Vietnam War posed challenges for U.S. authorities, little had changed since the nation faced similar questions of paternity and responsibility for the American mestizos in the Philippines. The military still supported soldier sex in Asia while protecting U.S. soldiers against paternal responsibility for their children. Some military leaders viewed the responsibility of paternity as counterproductive to the maintenance of a well-oiled fighting machine by depriving combat "of some of its appeal."[104] They feared that forcing American men to take responsibility for their offspring would only encourage foreign women to seduce American men and have their babies in order to get a free ride to the United States.[105] Subjecting soldiers to paternity suits, child support payments, and the responsibilities of fathering could undermine the war effort as it would "miss the existential and deeply gendered point of mayhem."[106] Hence, military leaders relied on the sex-based distinction in U.S. immigration and citizenship law and the *Guyer* precedent of matrilineal descent to defend soldier-fathers from paternity claims and ensure that the U.S. military had no legal responsibility to care or provide for the out-of-wedlock children of American servicemen.

Even for those soldiers with legal unions and legitimate children, military policies and practices sought to inhibit the legal formation of transnational/racial families. It took U.S. serviceman Michael Schado two years of red tape to secure a marriage certificate from the American Embassy to marry his Vietnamese fiancée in 1970. It was another fifteen years before Schado could acquire an exit visa for his legitimated Amerasian child.[107] U.S. Ambassador to Vietnam Graham Martin harbored a specific belief that regardless of relationship status, legal union, or paternity, the Vietnamese were not and could not become Americans. As the United States frantically withdrew from Vietnam in April 1975, Martin made the evacuation of American citizens his primary concern, excluding common-law Vietnamese wives and their children as illegitimate dependents of U.S. servicemen.[108]

Regardless of the specific scenario—prostitution, marriage, rape—U.S. leaders made conscious and deliberate calculations about the sexual needs of male soldiers and "how Vietnamese women could best meet those needs." In each case, the decision-making process exposed the faulty rationale behind the sex-based distinction in U.S. law when applied to military presence abroad.[109]

Discourse and Diplomacy

By the time the United States began to engage in Vietnam, U.S. leaders were well versed in the racialized and gendered colonial discourse of Asian inferiority that had shaped previous U.S. actions in Asia.[110] Likewise, the nation still grappled with the place of mixed-race people in America. Informed by the Orientalist and racialist discourse that shaped American perceptions of Vietnam prior to U.S. intervention, U.S. leaders extended their colonial ideology into Vietnam in a deliberate effort to assert American superiority and power.[111] Diplomatic historians have written extensively about the ways that U.S. leaders incorporated race and racial assumptions into U.S. foreign policy decisions and how the apparent global solidarity of nonwhite populations concerned U.S. leaders ideologically committed to self-determination but practically anxious about losing newly decolonized nations to communism.[112]

Thus despite their anticolonial rhetoric, U.S. leaders approached Vietnam with clearly misguided colonial assumptions about the intellectual, physical, and racial characteristics and capabilities of the Vietnamese.[113] The Truman administration's decision to support French recolonization of Vietnam reverted to the racialized colonial arguments of racial inferiority, intellectual capacity, and fitness for self-government. U.S. leaders perceived the Vietnamese to be intellectually incapable of government—"attractive and even loveable," but "essentially childish."[114] American ignorance was not solely race-based, as America had very little prior interest in Vietnam and therefore few reference points or personal knowledge about the capabilities of the Vietnamese people. In fact, by the end of the French Indochina War the majority of American intelligence about the country came from French colonial authorities. Consequently, French colonial discourse combined with America's own racialized colonial experiences guided how U.S. leaders viewed the Vietnamese people, their ability for self-government, and their capabilities for war.[115]

Despite, or likely because of, the misguided racialized and gendered presumptions of U.S. leaders about the colonial character of the Vietnamese and the paranoid efforts of four U.S. presidents, America did eventually "lose" Vietnam. The defeat shattered the nation's confidence in its military superiority and exposed the reprehensible actions of American soldiers in war, damaging America's global humanitarian and moral credibility. In the process of losing the war, some posit that America lost its identity, veiled by a collective amnesia regarding the war and its consequences. As we will see, Amerasians became a crucial part of the new war narrative of American victimization, noble soldiers, and a humanitarian victory.

Conclusion

The Amerasian story is well situated within a history of race, gender, and war in the United States. Long before a young Massachusetts senator named John F. Kennedy stressed that Vietnam was "our offspring, we cannot abandon it, we cannot ignore its needs," U.S. soldiers stationed abroad had already produced, abandoned, and ignored numerous populations of mixed-race children in Europe and Asia.[116] Although some American men did willingly and lovingly legitimate and parent their half-American sons and daughters, in most instances, and specifically in cases of clear racial difference, they shirked their paternal responsibility. U.S. leaders, worried that fatherhood and foreign families would limit the resolve of U.S. soldiers and undermine the effectiveness of America's fighting forces, encouraged such behavior. U.S. laws also protected soldiers from parental responsibility in the interest of national security. The sex-based distinction in U.S. law made it legal to deny the children fathered by U.S. soldiers abroad paternal legitimacy. Additionally, while the militarized conditions that created Amerasian children in Vietnam mirrored those in other countries, America's military defeat there compounded issues of citizenship and illegitimacy. The dynamics of the Vietnam War, combined with a history of exclusionary policies and practices toward mixed-race persons and people of Asian descent in America, shifted the discourse regarding citizenship and responsibility. Ultimately leaders, laws, and war helped cast the majority of Amerasians in Vietnam as a population ineligible for U.S. citizenship.[117]

The process of othering mixed-race persons and people of Asian descent remains a persistent problem in America. The complexities of race and belonging for mixed-race persons reveals the ways in which citizenship is tied to whiteness and how the perception of Asians in the United States as "unassimilable foreigners" or "alien citizens" shaped U.S. immigration and citizenship laws, which in turn reinforced and perpetuated those same conceptions. The contradictory approach of policymakers who knew Amerasians were the offspring of American men but failed to grant them citizenship is evidence of how citizenship is wielded in an effort to protect and promote the privileges of power.[118] In this case, such privileges are inherently gendered as well, embedded in the license of American men to produce a population of others without the responsibility to parent or protect them. As America went to war in Vietnam, however, the future of abandoned, half-American children and the implications for U.S. foreign policy during the Cold War worried humanitarians, who pressed Congress to reconsider the nation's paternal responsibility.

| Chapter Two

Saving Cold War Children

Born in Hillsboro, West Virginia, in 1892 to Presbyterian missionaries, humanitarian and author Pearl S. Buck spent most of her formative years in Zhenjiang, China. There the blond-haired, blue-eyed American girl quickly learned the meaning and dangers of mixing race, faith, and foreignness with war. China left an indelible mark on Buck, who embraced the nation and its culture so much that she mastered the Chinese language before her native English tongue and preferred the Chinese translation of her name, Sai Zhenzhu, to its American original. She also studied the Confucian way. "If America was for dreaming about," Buck later explained of her early life, "the world in which I lived was Asia."[1]

Even after returning to the United States in 1910 at the formidable age of eighteen, determined to reassimilate into her home country and culture, Buck's feelings of alienation forced her to constantly negotiate the cultural, racial, and national divides that placed her nationality and her lived reality at odds. According to one family member, Buck "never felt like she belonged," and "didn't feel like she was an American. . . . It handicapped her terribly."[2] As a writer, Buck viewed herself as a human conduit to a cross-cultural global community that united the East and the West and sought to reconcile her internal struggles with nationality and belonging through her novels.[3]

In her 1930 novel *East Wind West Wind*, Buck first coined the term "Amerasian" to describe the half-American, half-Asian children that began to surface in China, "a new group of human beings, a group that Asians do not know how to deal with, illegitimate as well as mixed in race."[4] Unlike many of her American contemporaries during the period who viewed racial mixing as a national threat, Buck insisted it was necessary and positive. Miscegenation, she believed, produced a racially hybrid and superior population innately disposed to cross-cultural collaboration.[5] Mixed-blood children, she claimed, were "smarter and better looking than full-bloods of either parent's race. Most certainly they are tougher."[6] Buck viewed Amerasians specifically through the lens of her own transnational experience, as the perfect hybrid blend of race and nation inherently able to traverse the international and racial divides. Buck saw herself as a bridge between the East and the West, and Amerasians as key to a more inclusive and globalized world.[7]

Buck's own experience living on the margins of race and nation as a white American girl in China during periods of conflict made her sympathetic to the Amerasian condition and the dual exclusion they faced—denied both an American identity by their Asian maternity and an Asian identity by their American paternity.[8] Hence Buck committed to providing Amerasians a place to belong by encouraging American families to recognize their parental responsibilities to Amerasians and adopt them.[9] "There is nothing more important, for our nation right now," Buck claimed, "than for our government and people to respond to these helpless babies and say, 'we recognize our responsibilities.'"[10]

In 1949 Buck established Welcome House, a permanent foster home for mixed race children that eventually evolved into the Pearl S. Buck Foundation (PSBF), an international adoption, assistance, and support agency specializing in seeking placement for the tens of thousands "otherwise unadoptable" Amerasians born from the Second World War.[11] During the Vietnam War, the PSBF joined other international adoption agencies and humanitarian organizations including the Holt Adoption Agency, International Social Services, and Save the Children in addressing the needs of Vietnamese and Amerasian children affected by the war.¹² In 1967, the first year of international adoptions between the United States and South Vietnam, the PSBF successfully placed thirteen South Vietnamese children in American homes.¹³ That same year Buck implemented Father's Anonymous, a program designed to collect child support contributions to assist the Amerasian children in Japan, South Korea, and Vietnam. Concerned Americans could donate monies anonymously for the care, education, and welfare of Amerasians. In its short duration the program yielded only 151 responses, the majority from the wives and mothers of U.S. military personnel and one from a future inductee whose family offered to "pay now and sin later."¹⁴

Even amidst her efforts to convince Americans to adopt Amerasian children, Buck understood that in terms of actually solving the Amerasian problem, adoption had its limits. As long as U.S. troops continued to father Amerasians abroad and the U.S. government failed to accept responsibility for them, adoption "could never be more than a 'selective medication,' and certainly not a 'universal remedy.'"¹⁵ Buck did not believe that removing all Amerasians from Vietnam was the answer either, especially for those Amerasians who wanted to stay with their Vietnamese mothers and relatives and who would face tremendous emotional and psychological problems if forced to leave.¹⁶ Although adoption and assistance might offer some relief to certain Amerasians, Buck understood that the United States had to address the fundamental issues of paternal illegitimacy and national identity. Even though Amerasians did have Vietnamese citizenship, absent their American father they became an inferior and marginalized population in Vietnam. "Every child of an American cannot set up his own family registry in the Asian country in which he is born, nor am I sure that this would solve the problem if he could. . . . The boys," Buck explained "would still have no family backing and a girl with only her own family registry is still a prostitute."¹⁷

The answer, Buck insisted, was for the United States to assert its national paternal responsibility for Amerasians by recognizing them as American children and legitimating them through U.S. citizenship. Formalizing kinship ties with Amerasians would erase questions of paternal responsibility, make adoption and immigration easier, and provide Amerasians a national identity, self-worth, and opportunity.[18] During the Vietnam War, Buck attempted to make this case political. She employed an inclusionary discourse that downplayed Amerasians' racial hybridity, and instead emphasized their blood ties to the United States through their American paternity, to urge U.S. policymakers to take responsibility. "Do we, their fathers' people, not owe them something?" Buck asked.[19]

Between 1971 and 1975 a bipartisan group of U.S. policymakers and humanitarians responded to Buck's charge. Believing the nation to hold a specific paternal responsibility for the "American" children abandoned in Vietnam, they advocated for more liberal adoption and citizenship laws, to bring Amerasians home to the land of their fathers. To garner political support for more flexible legislation, proponents used a discourse of race, nation, and family to ascribe American racial categories to Amerasians and grant them U.S. citizenship. Classifying Amerasians as white or Black American children would help convince Americans of their duty to save them from Vietnam. Opponents, however, including African American leaders, viewed such efforts to racialize Amerasians into Americans as disingenuous and emphasized the "other" side of the Amerasian mixture. They insisted that race did not make Amerasians American but rather confirmed that they were Asian and were therefore neither American children nor an American responsibility. The spirited political debates about Amerasians' race, their paternity, and questions of American responsibility for them presented a paradox for policymakers, who proved unable to reconcile Amerasian hybridity with U.S. law.

Forming Families and Foreign Policy

The PSBF's commitment to the adoption of mixed-race children was part of a global humanitarian concern that emerged out of the tremendous numbers of people displaced, persecuted, and orphaned during the Second World War. Historian Michael Barnett argues that after World War II the world got serious about saving lives.[20] As Americans embraced humanitarianism as part of their nation's exceptional global responsibility to rescue and provide refuge for the world's persecuted and oppressed, humanitarian organizations sent their resources across national borders to aid and assist those unable to help themselves.[21] To reinforce the nation's moral duty, assuage concerns about aiding the "wrong kind" of people, and justify the sending of food and aid to former enemies, U.S. leaders focused specifically on "saving" children. On December 22, 1945, President Harry Truman declared his hope that the majority of displaced persons and refugees allowed entrance into the United States "will be orphaned children."[22] Indeed, over the next two decades numerous U.S. immigration and adoption policies and programs welcomed displaced children and orphans from Europe and Asia into the United States, including a growing population of half-American offspring of American servicemen.[23]

During the Cold War, the battle for global ideological domination wed humanitarianism and family to U.S. foreign policy.[24] Leaders politicized aid for saving children as the key to promoting the benefits of democracy abroad, pairing images of suffering (often nonwhite and foreign) children with the nation's Cold War duty to rescue them.[25] Notions of happy American childhoods and nuclear, white, Western families juxtaposed with harsh images of parentless and abandoned "children fleeing from Communism," convinced many Americans to embrace transborder child-saving acts of sponsorship and adoption as a moral responsibility and a civic duty.[26] Adoption specifically provided white Christian families the opportunity to save young bodies and souls by converting foreign children into god-loving, democratic American citizens.[27] As objects of rescue and redemption in need of parental protection and care, the Cold War's most vulnerable victims became the ultimate symbols of communism's incompetence by representing communism's failure to protect its children and America's exceptional ability to parent them.[28]

The emergence of transnational adoption agencies that specialized in Asian and Amerasian children, like the PSBF and the Holt Adoption Agency, further tied American families to U.S.-Asia relations. They stressed that American families could facilitate positive geopolitical relations between the United States and Asia, prevent further losses of Asian nations to communism, and alleviate the threat of anti-Americanism abroad by adopting Amerasians and instilling in them pro-American and prodemocracy sentiment. Such "patriotic pronatalism" linked citizenship and national security with parenthood and family and encouraged Americans to help contain communism by adopting Asian children.[29] "Hybrid Asian and American families created through adoption," Buck wrote in a 1952 article in the *Saturday Review*, "could eventually facilitate better political relations between the U.S. and Asia."[30]

Middlebrow intellectuals and Hollywood's celebrity elite found the adoption of exotic Asian and Amerasian children and the formation of multiracial and multicultural families especially appealing. They embraced the opportunity to contribute to racial progress and viewed transracial and transnational adoption as politically just, and suddenly these adoptions were in vogue.[31] Songwriter Oscar Hammerstein III, *The King and I* star Yul Brenner, and Pulitzer Prize–winning author James Michener all adopted (and Michener later returned) Amerasian children from Welcome House.[32] In 1972 actress Elizabeth Taylor and her husband Richard Burton also expressed their interest in adopting an Amerasian. "Though this may be a romantic whim," Burton wrote to Pearl Buck, "We would like . . . an 'Amer-Asian' for we feel that the terrible dichotomy between East and West could be resolved in small in our own household."[33]

But as Cold War tensions continued to send American troops abroad to combat communism, the emphasis on adopting foreign babies shifted to concerns about the growing numbers of hybrid "American" babies born abroad and what might happen should the United States continue to abandon and ignore them. During the Vietnam War, fears that orphaned and stateless half-American children might become purveyors of anti-Americanism were spread to encourage Americans to adopt.[34] In August 1967, Oregon Republican congressman John R. Dellenback warned the Oregon state legislature that Amerasians "were a special kind of orphan," stateless and "without country," and hence "condemned to anger and bitterness."[35] That same year, a *New York Times* story about a sixteen-year-old Japanese Amerasian who raped and strangled three women seemed to prove Dellenback's point. According to the report, psychologists recognized the crime as the "youngster's violent revenge" for the social slights, discrimination, and abuse he suffered in Japan because of his American paternity and illegitimacy. At his indictment, the Japanese national press service *Kyodo* explained, "The scars of war remain in the form of mixed-blood children, alienated from society."[36] Pearl Buck agreed, and in 1971 she explained to the *Washington Post* that while Amerasian adoption remained a moral responsibility and civic duty, in the midst of the Vietnam War it had also become critical for national security. "These children who have no country are going to be a menace. They're angry. They're very angry. And our men have been abroad so long that some children are now 20 years old. I'm afraid there's a danger the Amerasians will go over to the Communists."[37]

As adoption agencies during the Vietnam War tapped into American fears and patriotism, humanitarian organizations appealed to the parental instincts of Americans concerned about the fate of abandoned "American" children in Vietnam in promotional materials for child sponsorship, assistance, and aid. Pamphlets for the Save the Children agency depicted images of crying Vietnamese and Amerasian orphans in cages with the heart-wrenching captions: "At Least 500,000 Vietnam War Orphans," "80% of Babies & Toddlers are Dying," "150,000 are Sons & Daughters of US Servicemen."[38] Some materials also politicized their humanitarianism by asserting the nation's paternal responsibility to save Amerasians in Vietnam and demanding the U.S. grant them citizenship: "Support legislation to confirm these children's U.S. citizenship and bring them home for permanent foster care in the U.S."[39]

Individual advocates, including Buck, also began pressing for American citizenship, recalling France's response to its Eurasian offspring during the First Indochina War. By granting the métis French citizenship, they argued, France correctly rescued its children from the obscurity of a marginalized and stateless existence and ensured they had a homeland.[40] France had apparently set the proper precedent for dealing with mixed-race children in Vietnam.[41] Commending France for its example of national paternal responsibility, advocates wondered, "Why haven't we recognized our children?"[42] By 1971, the efforts of adoption agencies and humanitarians to save Amerasians from Vietnam for the purposes of family, national security, and responsibility finally caught the attention of U.S. policymakers, who saw Amerasians as another humiliation from what seemed to be an endless war in Southeast Asia.

Nixon's Resistance, 1971–1973

In the final year of Richard Nixon's first term as president, what appeared to be a growing and embarrassing humanitarian problem for the United States amid a failing war effort in Vietnam spurred an international response and created demands that the U.S. government do something about its orphaned children. In July 1971, international childcare agencies met with U.S. government officials, including Rep. Patsy Takemoto Mink (D-HI), Sen. Edward "Ted" Kennedy (D-MA), and representatives from the U.S. Army and Air Force, to discuss the Amerasian issue. According to the *Washington Post* those in attendance concluded that Amerasians were an American problem and that "the U.S. has a responsibility for American-fathered children and all children victimized by the Vietnam War."[43] Yet Nixon's attention remained firmly focused on the growing domestic and political discontent with the Vietnam War. Consumed with his own paranoia and declining popularity amid an ill-fated decision to expand the war into Cambodia, Nixon had little interest in the Amerasians. Central to Nixon's aversion to even acknowledging the issue was his belief that the abandoned children of U.S. soldiers would simply add another black mark to America's questionable war record and invite meddlesome scrutiny of the behavior of U.S. soldiers in Vietnam.[44]

During Nixon's presidency media coverage of the war sometimes exposed the bad behavior of U.S. soldiers, causing irreparable damage to the reputation of the military at home and abroad. The American public learned the details of Charlie Company's March 16, 1968, massacre of 504 Vietnamese civilians in the hamlet of My Lai in January 1972 when Seymour Hersh, a reporter for the *New Yorker*, published his exposé on the My Lai cover-up. Hersh's interviews with U.S.

soldiers who described similar events in which American GIs slaughtered Vietnamese of all ages shocked many Americans, who were already losing trust in the war effort and in U.S. leaders. Army Private Terry Reid admitted to Hersh, "Sometimes I thought it was just my platoon, my company, that was committing atrocious acts. . . . But what we were doing was being done all over." Such stories further incited antiwar activists, who repeatedly condemned such atrocities and the immorality of U.S. soldiers.[45] Americans who once believed that morality, virtue, and freedom guided the nation's military were now, reportedly, hurling accusations of "baby killer" at returning soldiers to shame them for their part in Vietnam.[46]

The acknowledgment that U.S. troops were making babies with Vietnamese women and then abandoning them seemed yet another troubling example of U.S. soldier immorality. American mothers, according to Don Luce, the head of International Voluntary Service in Vietnam, "would be upset to know their sons were sleeping with Vietnamese girls."[47] Since there was no actual proof of paternity in the majority of the Amerasian cases, it was simply easier for the administration to deny than to acknowledge them. As Pearl Buck explained, for many Americans "the very idea of American servicemen fathering babies overseas is unthinkable, therefore the children do not exist."[48]

Hence, the Department of Defense (DOD) avoided implicating its soldiers and instead wrote policies insisting it did not condone the "irresponsible and immoral behavior" of American servicemen. In its efforts to circumvent even the possibility of such disorderly behavior, the DOD claimed that it gave priority to "character guidance and other programs to provide servicemen an opportunity to channel their off-duty activities into wholesome pursuits."[49] To address the issue of loneliness that arose from family separation and placement in a foreign environment, the DOD pointed to the variety of virtuous activities, entertainment options, and strict rules that prevent such unsavory acts.[50] As in previous wars, one Korean War veteran explained, the general belief was that "our men don't do that (make babies), they play volleyball for relaxation."[51]

Instead of recognizing Amerasians as the children of American fathers and therefore an American concern, the DOD denied all responsibility. Officials asserted that emotion and compassion had inflated the magnitude of the problem. In 1971, responding to international condemnation surrounding embarrassing reports that U.S. soldiers fathered and abandoned tens of thousands of half-American children, Alexander Haig, a member of the president's national security team, countered that only fifty-four hundred "illegitimate children of racially mixed parentage" existed in Vietnam and that the majority were not abandoned but lived with their mothers or other relatives. Furthermore, Haig claimed that the approximately four hundred Amerasian orphans living in Vietnam were Vietnamese, not American, and must be treated the same as all of Vietnam's child war victims and raised within the "framework of the Vietnamese society." U.S. efforts, according to the DOD, "should continue to focus on strengthening services for all families and children in Vietnam."[52]

By denying any responsibility for Amerasians and failing to criticize the actions of its soldiers abroad, the DOD maintained that "the care and welfare of these unfortunate children . . . had never been and is not now considered an area of Government responsibility nor an appropriate mission for the Department of Defense to assume."[53] According to *Washington Post* reporter Tom Tiede, the United States did not even officially recognize the existence of Amerasians. White House aides wrote it off as a State Department matter, he claimed. "And the State Department, through an official of the Agency of International Development says: 'We have no program for the children, and none is contemplated.'"[54]

This was not entirely true. Although the Nixon administration did not have any clear plan to acknowledge or address the Amerasians, increasing media attention and political pressure did force White House staff to ponder a solution. On April 28, 1971, H. R. Haldeman, Nixon's chief of staff, expressed his growing concern about Amerasians to Nixon's special counsel on foreign affairs and communications, John Scali: "I'm sure that you've noticed the newest press attack with regard to the 'thousands' of illegitimate children in Vietnam. . . . This is the sort of thing that I hope you will be pointing out to us in the months ahead. Is there anything we should be doing with regard to this problem so that it is not blown up into a significant issue?"⁵⁵

Dismayed that neither the DOD nor the State Department had any plans to care for or assist Amerasians, Scali sought a solution to the problem.⁵⁶ His efforts, however, could not outpace the political criticism from some members of Congress. Iowa Democratic senator Harold Hughes inflamed public and political sentiment on the issue when he told the United Press International that the United States had an obligation to the thousands of, as UPI put it, "unwanted, unloved, and often uncared for Vietnamese children fathered by US soldiers," but that the Pentagon, "refuses even to acknowledge the existence of the children fathered by our soldiers." Absent any recognition of the nation's paternal responsibilities, there was no plan, Hughes explained, "to take care of the children when US troops are withdrawn."⁵⁷

Stuck between a resistant Nixon administration and the growing ire of a disgruntled Congress and disillusioned public, Scali reverted to U.S. precedent and advocated for reviving the programs established after the Korean War to address the Amerasians in South Korea—private relief assistance through orphanages, international adoption programs, and financial aid. The "Korea model," according to Scali, presented an excellent compromise. It allowed the United States to take responsible humanitarian action toward Amerasians in Vietnam without having to address soldier behavior or admit culpability.⁵⁸ However, some humanitarian organizations strongly disagreed that the Korea model should be replicated in Vietnam. In 1965, Paul Cherney, the general director of International Social Services, a nongovernmental organization focused on protecting children worldwide, concurred with the government of South Vietnam and argued that the Korea model's focus on orphanages and adoption created more problems than it solved. The primary objective, Cherney asserted, must be the restoration of children and orphans to their families, not their adoption into new ones. Building orphanages, he insinuated, simply encouraged parents to abandon their children in the belief that they would have better care and education, while doing nothing to address the actual problems of discrimination, illegitimacy, and abandonment. As one child welfare worker wrote, "let us not make the same mistakes we made in Korea."[59]

Nixon administration officials ignored such concerns and approved the Korea model. They believed that the optics of saving children would benefit the administration and improve military morale while at the same time allowing the United States to avoid taking responsibility. Photographs of U.S. troops building orphanages and stories of American families embracing their adopted Vietnamese and Amerasian children could counter criticisms of troop immorality and child abandonment.[60]

Despite its promise however, Scali knew it would be difficult to make the Korea model work in Vietnam. In his report to Haldeman, Scali admitted that while the Korea model appeared a palliative remedy, the bilateral cooperation and collaboration that enabled success in South Korea was absent in South Vietnam. Donald L. Ranard, the director of Korean affairs at the State Department, agreed. In his report on the Korean Amerasians, Ranard lauded South Korea's willingness to give the United States "permission to operate mixed-blood orphanages and cooperation in emigration of mixed-blood children." According to Ranard, the key to success in Korea was the "willingness of the Government and the Koreans themselves to perpetuate the eminently satisfactory relationship between American and Korean nationals." Only with the same set of favorable circumstances could the United States achieve similar outcomes in Vietnam.[61]

However, that was not the case, as South Vietnam was increasingly distrustful of its American ally, whose own people and soldiers seemed to be losing faith in Nixon and the war. In June 1971, U.S. Marine colonel Robert D. Heinl described the deterioration of the U.S. military in the *Armed Forces Journal*: "individual units avoiding or having refused combat, murdering their officers and noncommissioned officers, drug-ridden, and dispirited where not near-mutinous."[62] Furthermore, South Vietnam's president Nguyen Van Thieu increasingly understood Nixon's policy of Vietnamization as code for the slow American abandonment of South Vietnam and the war rather than a winning war strategy. Their suspicions made the South Vietnamese very wary of U.S. intentions regarding Amerasians specifically and resistant to sending any of their children to the United States. Many feared that Americans would abuse or exploit Vietnamese and Amerasian children for political gain. Communist radio stations broadcast reports that America planned to sell the children "to plantation owners and capitalists as child slaves."[63] Ultimately, South Vietnamese officials opposed the mass adoption or evacuation of Vietnamese children they believed should be raised and cared for in Vietnam.[64]

The claim by South Vietnam that Amerasians were Vietnamese children sparked discussions among humanitarian organizations and political advocates about the extent of U.S. responsibility, kinship, and national identity. Seeing an opportunity to relinquish assertions that the United States had a national paternal responsibility for Amerasians, the Nixon administration quickly embraced South Vietnam's position, explaining to the *New York Times* that U.S. officials did not consider the Amerasians an American issue because they were not American citizens.[65] In July 1971 William H. Sullivan, deputy assistant secretary for East Asian and Pacific affairs, expressed the administration's support for the integration of Amerasians into Vietnamese society without any distinction from full-blooded Vietnamese children. According to Sullivan, the United States agreed with South Vietnam that Amerasians were Vietnamese children and wished to "avoid any American action, such as special legislation or special treatment for racially-mixed children."[66] Some humanitarian organizations, including International Social Services and Church World Service, reinforced the administration's position. Contracted by the U.S. government to aid and assist the child victims of the Vietnam War, both organizations believed that despite their apparent American paternity, for the purpose of family, Amerasians—the majority of whom, they noted, were raised by their mothers or Vietnamese relatives—were Vietnamese and should be treated as such. Furthermore, they argued that, per U.S. law, Amerasians "are not Americans," and are therefore ineligible for U.S. citizenship.[67] Categorizing Amerasians as Vietnamese rather than American children strengthened the Nixon administration's resolve to ignore international pressure for the United States to take responsibility and to strictly adhere to U.S. nationality law. Absent paternal legitimacy, Amerasians were not American citizens and therefore not America's responsibility.

Legislation

Seeking to force the Nixon administration to take national paternal responsibility for the Amerasians, congressional representatives Patsy Mink and Donald M. Fraser (D-MN) publicly criticized the U.S. government's long history of ignoring the Amerasian problem. Rather than lauding the French or pointing to the Korea model as an option for success, they reminded Americans that the thousands of Amerasians in Japan and Korea who preceded those in Vietnam also grew up ostracized in a society that swept them under the rug. "The U.S. Government," Fraser exclaimed, "had a hand on the broom."[68] In May 1971 Mink and Fraser cosponsored HR 8462, the first major bill to address the Amerasians of Vietnam. The bill proposed to issue special immigrant visas for Amerasian orphans in Vietnam and remove "existing immigration barriers" to their "adoption or care by families in the United States."[69] Mink appealed to the moral goodness of American exceptionalism, humanitarianism, and family, proclaiming that America "must not abandon this moral responsibility" and must care for and protect these poor, innocent children and provide them a home. She described Amerasians as "the most defenseless victims" of the war and insisted on America's responsibility by asserting that they "must grow up and live in a world we have created by our presence in Vietnam."[70]

Mink certainly had an empathetic constituency in her home state of Hawaii, where a complex history of immigration, race, and race mixture resonated with residents. After watching an NBC report on Amerasians in 1971, one constituent wrote Mink, explaining, "My husband and I were particularly struck by this newsreel because, coming from Hawaii, we look upon *hapa haole* [mixed-race] children as being especially precious."[71] Even with such an emotional appeal, the bill found little support among House leadership. House chairman Peter Rodino (D-NJ) rejected the opportunity for the United States to fix its track record on the issue. Rodino denied numerous requests for a hearing on the bill, stating, "Present law covers the situation."[72] The bill died in the Judiciary Committee.

Less than a year later, in April 1972, a bipartisan group of senators who all served in the Second World War, Republican Mark Hatfield (OR) and Democrats Harrison Williams (NJ) and Harold Hughes (IA), presented SB 2497 to the Foreign Relations Committee. The bill proposed to establish the Vietnam Children's Care Agency. It authorized the president to collaborate with the government of South Vietnam to provide welfare assistance and adoption for all child victims of the war, but specifically for the growing Amerasian population. Concerns in the Democratically controlled Congress that investing more money in South Vietnam even for humanitarian purposes might prolong U.S. involvement in the war stalled the bill. It, too, never made it out of committee.[73]

The withdrawal of U.S. troops from South Vietnam during the spring of 1973, however, offered new hope for legislative efforts to aid and assist Amerasians. As Americans celebrated the homecoming of soldiers and prisoners of war, they began to grapple with the nation's culpability and the human toll of the war, including millions of Southeast Asian refugees, displaced persons, and child victims.[74] The failure of the U.S. military to achieve peace or victory in Vietnam exposed America as fallible, and shattered the faith that it was a force for good in the world. Additionally, the war birthed a new skepticism toward U.S. leaders, their claims, and the ethics of their motives. In 1971, 58 percent of Americans believed the war to be both immoral and a mistake, and by 1973 only a third of Americans trusted the government.[75] The painful downfall of the Nixon presidency resulting from the Watergate scandal and the revelations of the extent of Nixon's crimes further disillusioned Americans. Saving Amerasians salved the conscience of those looking for some sliver of redemption or hope that the nation was still exceptional.

In June 1973, two months after the last major group of U.S. forces left Vietnam, NBC released its one-hour prime time special, *The Sins of the Fathers*.[76] The program exposed American viewers, already inundated by disturbing media reports and images of the war's child victims, to the specific challenges now facing Amerasians in Vietnam. The title was a damning acknowledgment of American paternal responsibility for the now twice-forsaken Amerasians. Reporter Robert Northshield began the broadcast by explaining how American fathers produced and then abandoned half-American children, whom he described as "left behind—but doomed to live." After initially implicating U.S. soldiers, Northshield shifted the blame for Amerasians' plight as poor and marginalized orphans to Vietnamese racism and intolerance. Relieving viewers of any personal guilt, Northshield pandered to notions of American benevolence and exceptionalism. According to Northshield, the departure of America's "gentle warriors" from Vietnam left Amerasians facing a "generosity gap," not a paternity gap. When Americans left Vietnam, Northshield stated, "they took with them much of the compassion and caring these children [Amerasians] ever knew." American soldiers "cared but they had to leave."[77] Absentee fathers were not the problem, the report implied; rather Amerasians suffered from a deficiency in American humanity.

The program meshed the visual power of film with assertions of national paternal responsibility and the exceptionalism of American benevolence to mobilize good-hearted Americans to rescue a population no longer protected by U.S. soldiers. The *New York Times* described how images of crying, distraught, and abandoned "American faced" children in the program, "the astonishingly beautiful to the horribly maimed," triggered the empathy of American audiences, who now imagined themselves as the children's parental savior.[78] Their "American faces" reminded viewers that Amerasians were not just children damaged by the war but "American" children. They were the living memories of the fallen soldiers Americans hoped to remember, born from a war most wanted to forget.

The immediate response was emotional and intense. Concerned viewers wrote their congressional representatives and local adoption agencies in support of aiding and saving Amerasians from Vietnam. For the Nixon administration, the program compounded the rising pressure to solve the "people problems" created by the war and injected new energy into policymakers and humanitarian organizations intent on forcing U.S. action. Once again political efforts ensued to make it easier for American families to adopt Amerasians and grant them U.S. citizenship. Rep. Patsy Mink led the charge.

Mink was no stranger to struggle. The first Nisei woman to graduate from the University of Chicago law school and the first Asian American woman to serve in Congress, Mink carried the scars of discrimination, marginalization, and exclusion. By 1973 and in her ninth of what would be a twenty-four-year congressional career, Mink had proven an ardent supporter of the antiwar movement and liberal causes. She held a tireless commitment to improving the lives of immigrants, racial minorities, women, and children through policy. The "plight of orphans in Vietnam fathered by U.S. servicemen" was of particular concern to her. Mink surmised that her home state of Hawaii was uniquely qualified to parent and protect all the Vietnam War orphans and, specifically, Amerasians, whose mixtures "could easily blend into the State's polyglot society."[79] She strongly believed that race and illegitimacy marked the Amerasians for exclusion from Vietnamese society. According to Mink, "a child who is racially mixed and is orphaned and is to grow up in overcrowded institutions will be faced with virtually insurmountable odds."[80] She also insisted that the United States must assert its national paternal responsibility through immigration and adoption to parent and protect Amerasians who, she believed, were U.S. citizens. Mink argued that since Amerasians have "one parent who is an American and one parent who is Vietnamese," they should be able to enter the country "as if they were citizens of the United States."[81]

In March 1973 Mink requested congressional support for HR 3159, legislation "for the relief of certain orphans in Vietnam" through an expedited adoption process and special immigrant visas. In promoting the bill, Mink revived her previous arguments for the failed HR 8462 and again argued that Congress must remove every potential barrier to American families adopting Amerasian orphans and bringing them to the United States.[82] This time, however, Mink referenced *The Sins of the Fathers* and the images of half-American children in the program to stress the importance of family ties and remind policymakers of the "plight of the orphans." She also alluded to Northshield's description of America's "generosity gap" and the exceptional and moral obligation of the nation to rescue its child victims of war. Finally, Mink pointed to the urgency of time in saving "Vietnam's dying orphans" from the dire situation left by the U.S. withdrawal and the long and cumbersome adoption process.[83]

Mink's concerns were well founded. Although South Vietnam's Ministry of Social Welfare reopened adoption and assistance services, including ones geared specifically toward Amerasians, time proved the most daunting challenge.[84] A 1973 congressional study found that the mortality rate was the most urgent problem facing Vietnamese orphans, while the Pearl S. Buck Foundation reported that the majority of Vietnamese infants released for adoption died before the paperwork was complete. Most of them, the study found, perished in "squalid, poorly equipped, understaffed, and overcrowded" orphanages.[85] U.S. news outlets blamed the deaths on the South Vietnam government. In May 1973 *Newsweek* criticized the Republic of Vietnam for dedicating a measly 1 percent of the national budget to the care and welfare of "its crippled, diseased, or orphaned children." The twenty-five thousand mixed-blood babies, the article claimed, suffered the most.[86] South Vietnam's minister for veteran affairs, General Pham Van Dong, defended his country's limited financial commitment to its orphans by blaming the war and, less explicitly, the United States. The country's poor economic situation was, Dong claimed, a result of the war, and orphaned children "are spenders at a time when we need productive returns on our investment."[87]

Even while defending its treatment of orphans, South Vietnam officials vehemently denied claims that Amerasians faced harsher treatment or discrimination and continued to insist publicly that they were cared for and accepted into Vietnamese society. Intent on discovering the truth about the orphanages and Amerasians, Mink traveled to South Vietnam in August 1973 and quickly discovered the fallacy of Dong's claims and the burden that illegitimacy placed on Amerasian orphans. "More than half of the sickest, most neglected, close-to-death children in the reception centers I visited were inter-racial babies," Mink reported. Following her discussions with Vietnamese government and social welfare officials and as a result of what she saw, Mink concluded that neither Black- nor white-fathered Amerasians "would be accepted into Vietnamese society." Upon her return, Mink insisted that the Nixon administration address Amerasians separately from other Vietnamese orphans, and immediately amended her bill to grant adopted Amerasians U.S. citizenship.

Citizenship was a critical part of Mink's bill since Amerasians approved for adoption immediately lost their Vietnamese citizenship. Under U.S. law, these same children remained ineligible for U.S. citizenship for a two-year period in which they were essentially stateless. Recognizing the potentially dangerous implications of statelessness for a population already facing other forms of exclusion, Mink argued that granting immediate U.S. citizenship was crucial in order to eliminate any issues of identity or nationality and any potential residency or status problems.[88] According to Mink, not only would citizenship motivate American families to adopt Amerasians "as a personal way to help alleviate war-caused suffering," but their paternity demanded it.[89] In her appeal for public support, Mink reminded Americans that Amerasians were American children and that Americans must save them before addressing the other "people problems" from the war. She argued, "If we are unwilling to even help our own, how can we even think of help for all orphans?"[90] South Vietnamese officials agreed. In 1973, two years after insisting that Amerasians were Vietnamese children and thus a Vietnamese responsibility, South Vietnam changed its mind. The United States, they argued, "should grant immediate citizenship so that the child is not left in some kind of legal limbo."[91]

Even with South Vietnam's revised stance, the Nixon administration remained unmoved in its opposition to Mink's bill. The Department of State and Department of Health, Education, and Welfare specifically questioned the intent and practicality of implementing such policies. Both departments pointed to the potential problems associated with mass adoption and immigration, reminding Congress of the poor optics associated with "Americanizing" the adoption process.

Amerasians, they continued to insist, were Vietnamese children and a Vietnamese problem. Furthermore, they argued that the Vietnamese people would not appreciate another U.S. "attempt to solve Vietnamese problems" by imposing American programs and solutions; nor would they welcome Americans favoring one group of Vietnamese children over others. Deeming Amerasians a "special" population would only prove detrimental for them in Vietnam, where race and illegitimacy already marked them as different.[92]

There were other concerns as well. Opponents remained unconvinced that Americans had actually fathered all Amerasians and expressed deep concerns about evidentiary proof of paternity. "We will have to offer some means of identifying them," one concerned congressional colleague wrote Mink. While skin color, features, and hair made it easier to identify "some of the black Vietnamese-American children," there was no clear way to identify others.[93] The Nixon administration agreed. "Paternity would present many legal problems," including finding the father and legitimating those children whose fathers did not claim them.[94] Mink had prepared for such complications and made preliminary efforts to investigate all possible evidentiary sources, including genetic and biological testing. She even researched current existing scientific methods for measuring blood. Heather Sigworth, the Director of the Children's Legal Status Project, expressed her surprise to Mink that the physical anthropologists and hematologist she consulted on the issue "knew of no way that Caucasian-Vietnamese or Negroid-Vietnamese mixed genetic heritage could be established with measurable reliability."[95] The hematologist, Sigworth explained, "was quite sure that blood-typing would be of no assistance," while the anthropologist knew of no tests that could measure the amounts of different kinds of blood.[96] Although well intentioned, Mink's reversion to "blood quantum" was highly problematic, as it resurrected the outdated and racist assumption that people have different kinds of blood and that blood determines nationality.

Still, Mink knew that absent any evidentiary proof of paternity, authorities were limited to supporting documentation—mother's affidavit, the testimonies of neighbors and orphanage workers, and the child's appearance. However, the Nixon administration deemed the reliance on such prima facie evidence insufficient and continued to support only legislation that assisted all Vietnamese orphans "without ethnic distinction" or any need to establish paternity. Ignoring South Vietnam's recent shift on the issues of adoption and citizenship, the Nixon administration supported the Republic of Vietnam's initial stance that "children born in Viet-Nam of Vietnamese mothers are Vietnamese citizens regardless of their paternity or legitimacy."[97] Once again, Mink's bill died in committee.

Mink, however, had hit a nerve. Political pressure for adoption and citizenship for Amerasians intensified, as did the media coverage and humanitarian calls to save Amerasians. In May 1973 the U.S. Agency for International Development (USAID) requested that the government modify immigration and nationality law to grant Amerasians in Vietnam U.S. citizenship both as a national recognition of paternal responsibility and to ease and expedite the adoption process.[98] In June a group of Mink's congressional colleagues, Republicans Howard Robison (NY) and William Steiger (WI) (both World War II veterans) and John Anderson (IL), proved Amerasian immigration was a bipartisan concern when they presented a second bill, HR 8381. The bill proposed to confer U.S. citizenship on Amerasians for the purpose of adoption. According to Steiger, "by bestowing U.S. citizenship on these children, we will clearly indicate to the South Vietnamese that we are willing to accept our responsibilities and that we want to provide them [Amerasians] all the care, rights, and privileges that we grant all American citizens."[99] Despite the persistent and bipartisan effort, the House Judiciary Committee, chaired by decorated World War II veteran Peter Rodino, declared that citizenship for Amerasians "was out of the question" and refused to pass the bill out of committee.[100]

Still, the growing bipartisan awareness by policymakers worried about the postwar consequences for the people of Vietnam continued even after U.S. troops withdrew. One of the most outspoken advocates of American humanitarian aid for Vietnam refugees and war victims, Sen. Ted Kennedy, urged the Nixon administration to remember that even after the war, America's primary responsibility in

Indochina would be "to the people who live there."[101] In 1973, Kennedy proposed three amendments to the Foreign Assistance Authorization Act authorizing $5 million to assist and adopt the South Vietnamese children disadvantaged by the war. In his effort to gain political support, Kennedy reminded Congress that both Saigon and Washington had long neglected the Vietnam War refugees, orphans, those crippled and maimed by the war, and the Amerasian children, whom he deemed "a special concern."[102] Kennedy believed the United States must shoulder the humanitarian burden it helped create in Southeast Asia and he criticized the administration's failures. Specifically, Kennedy condemned the State Department for undermining the "legitimate efforts" of some American officials to meet the humanitarian needs of children.[103] It was time for Americans, he said, "to pause and open our eyes to the plight of the children in Indochina." In order to heal "the wounds of war," the United States must address the issues facing Amerasians.[104] Although the Senate Foreign Relations Committee issued a report recommending further consideration of Kennedy's bill, no additional action ever occurred.

Black Amerasians

Tensions over race, identity, and responsibility undergirded the political debates and public discussion over adopting and assisting Amerasians. American and Vietnamese officials clashed over whether Amerasians were American or Vietnamese and who was ultimately responsible for their condition and subsequent care. Vietnamese authorities simultaneously resisted America's child-saving methods, insisting the country that created the war could not claim to rescue its victims, and demanded the United States assert its responsibility to aid and assist all of Vietnam's children affected by the war. Disagreements over rescue and responsibility also framed much of the discord among adoption advocates and organizations, including the PSBF. Agencies disagreed over the consequences of American paternity and whether adoption or aid was the better solution.

Just as American advocates and humanitarians emphasized that Amerasians' "American looks" marked them as targets for racial injustice in Vietnam, many Vietnamese agreed that race and blood made Amerasians a problem. In a reversal of America's own historical understanding of blood quantum and racial contamination, it was widely accepted in Vietnam that Amerasians' "American blood" caused a moral degeneracy that turned them into cultural misfits incapable of adhering to the norms of Vietnamese society. In her psychological study of the psychosocial and adaptational issues facing Amerasians in Vietnam, Joyce Anis discovered that many Amerasians internalized the stigma attached by Vietnamese family members and peers of being wild, criminal, homeless, and bad. According to one Amerasian, "a lot of older people think that Amerasian kids are hard to raise because they have a mixture of blood . . . they pretty much categorize us as bad kids."[105]

Although Amerasians often described the prejudice they faced in Vietnam as a result of their American features and "American blood," race proved an even bigger factor. American social service and adoption experts agreed that the estimated fifteen thousand Black Amerasians living in Vietnam faced a dire situation.[106] As in the United States, Vietnam had a deeply rooted history of racial and class hierarchy that characterized whiteness as good, beautiful, and evidence of wealth, and blackness as bad, ugly, and a marker of peasantry and poverty.[107] French colonialism and the more recent engagement with France's African colonial troops during the First Indochina War further aligned notions of race and beauty with European standards. Hence the white skin and European features of the white-fathered Eurasian were more desirable than the darker skin tones and African physical characteristics of the Black métis.[108]

The Vietnam War compounded existing anti-Black racism by introducing American racial tensions and stereotypes of African Americans as poor, uneducated, and criminal to Vietnam. In his interviews with Amerasians from Vietnam, child psychiatrist and Vietnam Veteran Robert McKelvey discovered that because whiteness equated to physical attractiveness in Vietnamese society and blackness did not, Black Amerasians faced intense discrimination and "more than their share of difficulties."[109] As with the Eurasians, race privileged white

Amerasians, who were often valued for their beauty, while disadvantaging Black Amerasians, considered physically unattractive.[110] Additionally, while many non-Black Amerasians grew into their American features—nose shape, hair color, height—and were often able to obscure them through childhood, Black Amerasians could not escape their skin.

This was particularly problematic for orphans. According to Thich Nhat Thien, head of a Buddhist social-welfare center in Saigon, "the black children are a big problem . . . but white children are very easy to care for because Vietnamese women are happy to have them."[111] The willingness of Vietnamese mothers to parent their white Amerasian children further revealed the insidious ways that race penetrated Vietnamese society. Dark skin—undeniable evidence of a Vietnamese mother's sexual immorality and her sexual relationship with a Black man—brought shame to the Vietnamese family, ruined her reputation, and marked her as a prostitute.[112] Hoping to hide or discard their shame, mothers abandoned their Black Amerasian children at hospitals, orphanages, or to the streets at a ratio of seven-to-three over white Amerasians. In 1971 Black Amerasians composed an estimated 10 percent of all Amerasians in Vietnam but accounted for 52 percent of those in orphanages.[113] According to Sister Françoise, head of the Caritas Orphanage in Saigon, the Vietnamese viewed such abandonment as "good for the family but sad for the child."[114]

Black Amerasians raised by their mothers or extended family members often experienced childhoods hidden away, shunned and ridiculed by parents, neighbors, and classmates. School appeared to be a particularly challenging environment as Vietnamese peers teased Amerasian classmates about race, paternity, illegitimacy, and the negative assumptions now associated with their mothers. On average, Black Amerasians were more likely to have been in fights than white Amerasians, and 33 percent of Black Amerasians had no schooling in Vietnam compared to only 13 percent of white.[115] The Vietnamese grandfather of Black Amerasian Thong described the relentless abuse his grandson faced from classmates, who passed his house after school shouting, "The black American! The black American!" Thong's grandfather "wished his daughter had fallen in love with a white soldier instead of a black one" because "there would be no trouble sending a white Amerasian child to the local school."[116] Twenty-six-year-old Black Amerasian Luong Hung and two others describe their own feelings of race in Vietnam:

> I feel ashamed that my mother was with a black man, and now I have to carry that.

> When I go to store and they saw me come, some the people [sic] they throwing things at me . . . they say I am black, or something.

> I don't know how they would treat someone who has lighter skin, but for me having dark skin, they did not like. Those who have dark skin they think are ugly—we don't look good with dark skin.[117]

By 1971 U.S. officials stationed in Vietnam largely accepted that race was a problem for Amerasians and the U.S. Embassy noted that the "black child may have a more difficult time growing up in Vietnam than other children."[118] Recognizing that race compounded the stigmas of illegitimacy and foreign paternity for Black Amerasians and ensured them a difficult existence in Vietnam, social welfare and humanitarian organizations like International Social Services (ISS) argued that, unlike the general Amerasian population, which must be treated the same as all Vietnamese children, saving Black Amerasians required their immigration to the United States.

In February 1972 Gloria Emerson's article, "Part Vietnamese, Part Black and Orphan," appeared in the *New York Times* and brought the problematic existence of the Black Amerasians in Vietnam to the attention of the American public. Appealing to the racial sensibilities of a post–Civil Rights America and emphasizing the power of family, Emerson suggested that "any child who grows up without a family, which is the focus of Vietnamese life, and is also black, confronts obstacles that a Westerner cannot easily imagine."[119] Assumptions of a shared transnational racial kinship between Black Amerasians and African Americans prompted some to place responsibility for Black Amerasians on the African American community. According to Wells

Klein, the general director of the ISS, absent a Black community in Vietnam and lacking any other references to this part of their identity, Black Amerasians will "grow up and live in relative social isolation." Bringing them to the United States was the only answer.[120]

Vietnamese officials also viewed Black Amerasians as an undesirable population and admitted that racial difference stigmatized them as racially inferior foreigners and prevented them from assimilating into Vietnamese society.[121] The family members of many Black Amerasians supported such claims. Vo Thi Nen, the grandmother and caretaker of a Black Amerasian grandson, explained that her grandchild was "too different from the other children in our community. I think he would be better off in the United States."[122] Considering America's racial history in which whiteness often defined what it meant to be an American, there is irony in the assumption that a transnational racial kinship linked Black Amerasians to African Americans and made them American. African Americans, advocates insisted, must take responsibility for "their" Black children.

Some African American community leaders agreed that because the Black Amerasians were racially Black, African Americans had a responsibility to parent and protect them. In 1971 Juanita Williams, wife of civil rights leader Hosea Williams of the Southern Christian Leadership Conference (SCLC), visited South Vietnam to address troubling reports of racial discrimination, drug abuse, and drug addiction among African American soldiers.[123] While Hosea Williams visited basecamps, military prisons, and firebases, the wives of American diplomats and bureaucrats stationed in Vietnam gave Juanita a tour of local orphanages. Initially uninterested because she "thought it was just another one of those orphanage type things," Juanita soon became concerned by the numerous mixed-race children she saw there.[124] In a 1972 interview, Williams described her concerns that Black Amerasian children faced racism and discrimination in Vietnam: "There were so many mixed black babies in these orphanages and then we really got concerned... the Vietnamese people are very prejudiced.... and when a baby was born black, they wouldn't want these babies... they would ostracize these babies."[125]

As the first lady of one of America's strongest civil rights organizations, Williams believed that she had the power to help these "black babies," and committed SCLC to building an orphanage in Vietnam specifically for Black Amerasians and to finding African American families to adopt them.[126] Despite her efforts, very little support emerged from the Black community. The Black press largely ignored the issue, except for Era Bell Thompson's 1972 article in *Ebony Magazine*, "The Plight of Black Babies in South Vietnam."[127] Thompson detailed the racial discrimination facing the children, while insinuating that the real problem was that Vietnamese women were taking advantage of Black men by getting pregnant for the purpose of military money and immigration rights.[128] The lack of coverage in the Black press reflected a general lack of interest among African Americans, who were more concerned with the disproportionate number of Black men dying in Vietnam, economic inequality, and protecting the civil rights gains of the previous decades.[129] Many African Americans also resented the assertions by humanitarian leaders like ISS's Klein that they were responsible for Black Amerasians when other groups of Americans were not accountable for their abandoned children. Specifically, African Americans rejected the accusation that America's badly behaving soldiers were Black, and the accompanying insinuations of Black male promiscuity, rape, and child abandonment. By December 1972, lacking the support of the Black community and coverage by the Black press, SCLC officially terminated the program, having failed to adopt out even a single Black Amerasian child.[130]

Disparities within the adoption system framed African American neglect of the Amerasian cause. Constant reporting in mainstream newspapers like the *New York Times* and the *Washington Post* about the challenges facing Vietnamese orphans and the need for American families to adopt fueled a perception within the Black community that the U.S. government cared more about foreign children than it did about Black and brown American kids.[131] Social service workers also worried that increasing interest among American families in adopting foreign children might subvert resources for the forty thousand "hard to place" Black, Native, Puerto Rican, and handicapped

American children currently in the foster care system.[132] Black social workers were particularly outspoken about the dangers of interracial adoption for Black children. In 1972 the National Association of Black Social Workers (NABSW) released a formal statement opposing interracial adoption on the grounds that preserving Black identity and culture were best accomplished when a Black child is raised within a Black family.[133]

Even while the African American community generally resisted presumptions of racial kinship and responsibility for Black Amerasians, many Black adoption and social welfare agencies expressed discomfort with white American families adopting Black Amerasians.[134] Espousing the same assumptions of transnational racial kinship that their white counterparts used to demand racial responsibility by the Black community, Black adoption and social workers argued that this "discrete group of American-fathered black children" was racially Black, and therefore must be placed with Black families. The Child Welfare League of America supported the position that despite their Asian mothers and the good intentions of white adoptive families, Black Amerasians "are labeled 'Black' as soon as they land in the United States." Thus "only a Black family can teach such children how to cope with the complexities involved in Black-White relationships in the United States," foster Black consciousness and pride, and promote a feeling of group identity.[135]

To promote intraracial adoption the NABSW and Black adoption agencies established adoption assistance programs to recruit and assist Black families to adopt Black children and provide aid to Black Amerasians in Vietnam. In response to the demands of Black agencies, on October 3, 1973, USAID and the Department of Health, Education, and Welfare formed the Interagency Vietnamese Adoption Committee (IVAC), a sixteen-member consortium of adoption agencies including Holt International, Church World Service, Afro-American Family and Community Services, and the Black Child Development Institute, dedicated to the care and placement of Black Amerasian orphans with African American families.[136] A belief in transnational racial kinship guided the IVAC's focus on family, home, and racial identity as it aimed to provide the Black Amerasian "with loving parents (or parent) who can give him the ethnic identity which is more related to his own."[137]

Apart from the efforts of Black adoption and social service agencies, Black political leaders in Washington DC and the newly founded Congressional Black Caucus (CBC) mirrored the general sentiment within the Black community on the Amerasian issue. Formed in 1971, the CBC sought to hold the Nixon administration accountable to the needs of America's minority communities, including investigating racism in the U.S. military, increasing aid to Africa, addressing America's economic inequality, and ending the war in Vietnam. Its National Black Political Agenda, released in March 1972, focused on addressing the needs of Blacks in America and Africa, supporting Black troops, and denouncing "Black participation in wars which suppress revolutionary struggles in the Third World."[138] Members of the CBC did in fact believe they held a global racial responsibility to their transnational racial kin, but defined that kinship in diasporic terms. While African ancestry and Atlantic migration linked African Americans to Black South Africans fighting apartheid and Black Haitians fleeing persecution, Black Amerasians had no such claim. They were children of the Pacific, not the Atlantic, and therefore excluded from the diaspora and the CBC's agenda.

Ending the war in Vietnam was of particular concern for the CBC, whose members viewed the war as unnecessarily and disproportionately taking both the lives of black men and the resources they believed could help African Americans. In May 1972 a frustrated Rep. John Conyers Jr. (D-MI) condemned the continuation of the war and situated it in racial and economic terms: "There has been no Vietnamization program for the American poor who have not been given the training and assistance to fight their own battles. They have been left as they were—deprived, powerless, and trapped. It is not necessary to go to Asia to see the victims of Vietnam. One need only walk through the streets of any slum or ghetto in any city of the land."[139] Members were also committed to racial equality and justice for Black soldiers and veterans as they returned from war. In response to the

Nixon administration's failure to address racism in the U.S. military, CBC Chairman Charles C. Diggs Jr. declared that the CBC would oppose additional funding for soldiers "in countries where the human dignity of black soldiers has been violated."[140] Seeking to avoid any negative publicity regarding Black servicemen, CBC members also rejected assertions that African Americans were racially responsible for Black Amerasians. They too viewed accusations of paternity and child abandonment as condescending and hypocritical and questioned why white communities were not asked to shoulder the same burden. The CBC remained silent on the issue.

Ultimately, attempts to foster a transnational racial kinship between Black Amerasians and African Americans to alleviate the Amerasians' specific racialized suffering failed to spur the African American community to action. Despite assumptions that race made Black Amerasians African Americans, Black community and political leaders recognized the inequity of demanding African American paternal responsibility at the same time that white soldier-fathers escaped any similar expectations. As the war in Vietnam finally came to an end, race continued to complicate how Americans understood Amerasians and guided how policymakers legislated for them. In the final moments and immediate aftermath of the war, they rushed to rescue the now twice-abandoned "American" children from Vietnam, only to reracialize and thus renationalize them later as Vietnamese, erasing their American faces and absorbing them into the larger population of refugees fleeing Vietnam.

Operation Babylift

Patsy Mink watched as the paranoia, drama, and downfall of the Nixon administration in 1974 consumed the attention of the American public and drained the life out of her legislative efforts to adopt and grant Amerasians citizenship. As the North Vietnamese forces advanced quickly on South Vietnam in early 1975, first attacking the central highlands, then turning north to Pleiku, Hue, and Da Nang before heading south to Saigon, another legislative opportunity emerged. Tired of the war, Americans stood silent as their allies fell, resigned to the realities of South Vietnam's defeat and America's failure. Hoping to salvage some semblance of victory from the war, U.S. policymakers turned their attention from adopting Vietnamese children to rescuing the U.S. citizens in Vietnam and approved $300 million to evacuate Americans for humanitarian purposes.[141]

At the same time, numerous reports from humanitarian organizations generated concern about the fate of Vietnam's orphaned children and specifically Amerasians, believed to be a primary target for communist vengeance.[142] Reports that Amerasians faced murder, sterilization, and even slavery because of their American paternity sounded the alarm of a government-executed Amerasian bloodbath. In South Vietnam locals gossiped that if the Communists found Amerasians, they would slit open their bellies, pull out the livers, and eat them.[143] In the city of Ban Me Thout rumors surfaced that the Vietcong killed younger Amerasians and enslaved older ones.[144]

To elude such a fate many mothers and family members of Amerasians rid themselves of "evidence" that they had collaborated with the American enemy by discarding their Amerasian children. The PSBF reported that in the days preceding the Communist victory, Vietnamese mothers, consumed with fear about the future, began "throwing their kids over the walls of orphanages" in the hopes that the United States would save them.[145] Historian Trin Yarborough writes, the day that Saigon fell a "dozen of abandoned children, some as young as two years old, with half-Vietnamese, half-American faces . . . had been pushed frantically into the streets or left at orphanages by terrified Vietnamese mothers or their family members convinced the Communists would murder anyone ever connected to the American enemy."[146] By abandoning their children and destroying any evidence, including birth certificates, photographs, and paperwork showing that their Amerasian child or its American father had ever existed, mothers effectively erased any documented proof of American paternity and claim to legitimacy.[147]

Sensing the urgency of the situation, political advocates quickly revived legislation to expedite the adoption process to bring the Amerasians to the United States and award them citizenship. On March

18, 1975, Rep. Paul Tsongas (D-MA) introduced HR 5187, "a bill to confer U.S. citizenship on certain Vietnamese children and to provide for the adoption of such children by American families." Citizenship was necessary, according to Tsongas, to speed up the adoption process but, more importantly, because "the United States bears a special responsibility to these children."[148] Granting Amerasians citizenship would ensure their evacuation from Vietnam along with all other U.S. citizens.

While Tsongas's bill lingered in the Judiciary Committee, photographs and graphic stories of abandoned and terrified Vietnamese and Amerasian orphans filled the pages of humanitarian promotional materials and U.S. newspapers. The images of Amerasians and their "American faces" specifically garnered public support for U.S. rescue efforts, and Pres. Gerald Ford knew he had to respond. Ford had already proven himself sympathetic to the Amerasian cause. In 1973, while serving as Nixon's vice president, he praised the way France handled its Eurasians as the "most humane and generous" approach.[149] As president, Ford also understood the moral, humanitarian, and political opportunity that saving orphaned children from Vietnam presented for the country to "salvage something from the horror of the war."[150] Rescuing half-American children from the clutches of communism might bring redemption to a nation haunted by the ghosts of its fifty-eight thousand fallen soldiers and its abandonment of its South Vietnam ally. Ford also understood that he could no longer continue to maintain the position of his predecessor that Amerasians were Vietnamese children and a Vietnamese problem. Images of child war victims were bad enough, but the faces of Amerasians simply could not be ignored.

On April 3, Ford announced Operation Babylift—an emergency evacuation of two thousand Vietnamese and Amerasian orphans for adoption by American families.[151] While the Babylift appeared to be a victory for Amerasian advocates and political proponents like Mink and Tsongas, the celebration proved short-lived. Images of the tragic crash of one of the Babylift military rescue planes, which killed seventy-eight Vietnamese and Amerasian orphans as it left Saigon, quickly consumed horrified Americans, some of them anxious families awaiting their adopted Babylift children. Sheila Weidenfeld, the press secretary for First Lady Betty Ford, described the crash as "the ultimate disaster in a country of endless disasters—a cruel attack on the most innocent victims of war, and when they were so close to safety and comfort and familial love."[152]

Although saddened by the crash, the Ford administration took advantage of the tragedy and the Babylift generally, which curiously airlifted children away from their homeland at the end of the war, to gain public support for the evacuation efforts in Vietnam.[153] In the days before the Babylift began, U.S. Ambassador Graham Martin assured Dr. Phan Quang Dan, South Vietnam's deputy prime minister for social welfare, that the "evacuation of thousands of war victims will help to sway American public opinion in South Vietnam's favor. When the children arrive in the United States, the press, television, and radio will give ample publicity to the matter and the impact will be enormous."[154] Years after the war, former CIA officer Frank Snepp recounted how the Ford administration had "hoped that the spectacle of hundreds of Vietnamese babies being taken under the American wing would generate sympathy for the South Vietnamese cause around the world" and pressure Congress to send aid to the flailing Thieu regime in its final days.[155]

Although the desired support for South Vietnam failed to materialize from the Babylift, the sentiment surrounding it and the plane crash did spur the Amerasian advocates in Congress to, once again, act. On April 7 Republican senator Bob Packwood (OR) introduced SB 1368, a sister bill to Tsongas's HR 5187, the legislative culmination of the previous failed policy efforts of Mink, Steiger, and Robison.[156] Unlike their predecessors, these bills took clear and full national paternal responsibility for the Amerasians, formally recognizing that "thousands of children were fathered in Vietnam by United States citizens" during the war and that America had a "special responsibility" to care for and adopt these "citizens of the United States."[157] In promoting the bill to his Senate colleagues, Packwood called upon their parental instincts and the nation's obligation to protect Amerasians. "We have a responsibility," Packwood explained, "to do what we can for the Amerasian children. They are young and defenseless and most would not be there were it not for the lengthy American presence in South Vietnam."[158] Despite the apparent opportunity presented by the Communist victory for swift action, both bills met the fate of their predecessors and never advanced out of the Judiciary Committee.

Hence, while the Babylift elicited strong emotions from U.S. policymakers and inspired Americans to adopt the orphans, including First Lady Betty Ford, who professed that the "photographs of crying orphans in Vietnam made her 'want to adopt them,'" it failed to obtain the foreign policy outcome President Ford desired. In South Vietnam, the evacuation of Vietnamese babies appeared to be yet another example of American exploitation in which U.S. interests superseded any concerns for the Vietnamese people. While watching one of the Babylift planes depart for the United States, one Vietnamese army officer expressed his disgust with his former ally, "It is nice to see you Americans taking home souvenirs of our country as you leave—china elephants and orphans."[159] U.S. policymakers like Sen. Edward Kennedy also questioned the rationale of the U.S. approach.[160] Although the Babylift may have given Americans short-term relief from the war, Kennedy argued, it was unfeasible "to think about all Americans adopting 850,000 orphans or half orphans." Rather than bringing all of Vietnam's war orphans to the United States, he continued, America must aid the orphans in Vietnam.[161] Although Kennedy's words largely fell on deaf ears, his stance reflected an important shift among policymakers regarding humanitarian aid and refugees that would have important implications for Amerasians.

The African American Response

As Operation Babylift galvanized many Americans to adopt Vietnamese and Amerasian orphans, African Americans remained largely unmoved. In 1975 *Ebony* magazine reported that the federal government's role in Operation Babylift upset African Americans concerned that such efforts and the allocation of resources to save foreign Vietnamese children only served to exacerbate the "browning of child welfare" in America.[162] In the months after the war, increasing interest in foreign adoptions combined with declining numbers of white American babies available for adoption created a "white baby famine" that appeared detrimental to the crisis levels of Black, brown, and mixed-race American orphans already awaiting families.[163] Furthermore, the preference of white families to adopt any foreign child regardless of age or special needs over Black and brown domestic children continued to prove problematic. One week after Operation Babylift, Ursula Gallagher of the U.S. Department of Health, Education, and Welfare questioned why American families that traditionally wanted to adopt healthy white infants were now willing to take "older, handicapped Vietnamese children" instead.[164] Vernon E. Jordan Jr., president of the National Urban League voiced his disgust with both the infatuation with foreign adoption and the Babylift, which he claimed was a myth "sold as an example of American generosity and concern for homeless waifs who might suffer untold harm if the North Vietnamese take over the South." According to Jordan, "the real tragedy here is that while Americans rush to bring over homeless kids from Saigon, they have yet to evidence any interest in orphans here at home."[165]

Doubts about America's obsession with foreign adoptees appeared justified after the predicted "blood bath" of Amerasians never occurred, and when reports emerged that some of the "rescued" Babylift orphans were in fact, not orphans at all.[166] However, as Americans grappled to assimilate the nation's humiliating military defeat, the humanitarian efforts to save Vietnamese and Amerasian children from communism became part of a bigger and deliberate effort to redefine the American experience in Vietnam. Unable to glorify American military heroism or triumph after the war, the focus on saving orphaned children from the dangerous clutches of an "uncaring" Vietnamese communist government enabled U.S. leaders to begin to reconstitute the nation's military defeat in Vietnam as a humanitarian victory.[167]

Yet Congress remained resistant to passing specific Amerasian legislation that members believed may expose the country to further criticism and embarrassment. Ignoring the bipartisan opportunity presented by Mink, Tsongas, Steiger, and Robison to take national paternal responsibility for the children fathered by U.S. soldiers, most U.S. policymakers prioritized their political futures and continued to conflate the conditions specific to Amerasians with all of Vietnam's child war victims. According to psychologist Robert McKelvey, U.S. politicians were unwilling to act on behalf of Amerasians as a result of North Vietnam's victory in the war. They feared that bringing Amerasians to the United States might appear "to be aiding and abetting the enemy" and could result in political repercussions.[168] As a result, congressional leaders showed little appetite for any formal recognition of American paternity, citizenship, or identity for Amerasians and thus failed to pass any legislation on their behalf.

Legislative impotence on this issue spoke volumes about the limits of American humanitarianism: the humanitarian impulse lost to the priority of protecting U.S. soldiers from paternal obligations and U.S. borders from unnecessary infiltration. An acknowledgement of paternity would surely have brought additional calls for U.S. citizenship, forcing policymakers to consider making an exception to nationality law and making Amerasians immediately eligible for immigration to the United States as the "sons and daughters of U.S. citizens." Although citizenship could resolve many of the issues Amerasians faced, it would require the U.S. government to address the discrimination, poor living conditions, and alleged persecution of Amerasians still in Vietnam and to act abroad on their behalf. Having little desire to open up those doors, U.S. policymakers followed the precedent set in previous wars and adhered to U.S. nationality law, formally acknowledging neither U.S. paternity nor citizenship. Ironically, ignoring their American paternity and deeming the Amerasians Vietnamese children allowed the United States to burnish its reputation for disinterested humanitarianism.

Conclusion

Between 1971 and 1975 Rep. Patsy Mink and her colleagues, along with a number of humanitarian organizations and Amerasian advocates, used an inclusionary discourse to pressure the United States to accept its national paternal responsibility by bringing the Amerasians to America and awarding them U.S. citizenship. Their efforts forced U.S. leaders to consider the nation's humanitarian and paternal responsibility to "save" the Amerasians in Vietnam. But unable to come to terms with Amerasians' racial and national mixture, policymakers, humanitarians, and leaders of the African American community simply ignored it. They continued to conflate race and nation to deem Amerasians fully American or Vietnamese at different points in the war. The failure to acknowledge the complexities of hybridity placed the Amerasians' American paternity and their Asian maternity in conflict.

Over the next decade, paternal deniability became increasingly difficult. As U.S. leaders sought to heal the wounds of the war and revive American exceptionalism through moral and humanitarian acts targeting the enormous number of Southeast Asian refugees pouring out of Vietnam, Amerasians faded to the background. By the time U.S. media outlets began to report again on Amerasians, the "American-faced" children were older and their physical "American" features more clearly formed. Many could now describe the exclusion they faced from Vietnamese society and assert their own agency in their desire to "come home." From 1975 to 1980 U.S. policymakers would walk an increasingly fine line along which they acknowledged the nation's paternal responsibility for Amerasians as American children while denying them U.S. citizenship.

| Chapter Three

Becoming Refugees

Elected to Congress in 1970, Rep. Stewart McKinney (R-CT) quickly established himself as a champion of social justice and social welfare programs. The wealthiest member of Congress at the time, the Ivy League graduate, Air Force veteran, and self-proclaimed "liberal Republican" won reelection eight times in his overwhelmingly Democratic fourth district. During his political career he quickly earned a reputation as a humanitarian and an advocate for society's forgotten and invisible populations.[1] On entering office, McKinney acted out of a sense of moral obligation to help both the child victims and refugees of the Vietnam War through adoption and humanitarian aid. In 1973 McKinney wrote one troubled constituent, "I share your deep concern over the tragedy of the orphaned and abandoned children left in the wake of the Vietnam War." In 1975 he told another that "to ignore our [United States'] moral obligation to the refugees would further discredit us."[2]

Like many of his congressional colleagues, including Patsy Mink, McKinney expressed specific concerns about Amerasians, whose paternity he believed made them Americans and America's responsibility. Pointing to the social ostracism that they "will undoubtedly face" in Vietnam because of their illegitimacy and racial mixture, McKinney called for changes to U.S. immigration law to allow "the offspring of our servicemen" to come to the United States.[3]

America's eventual defeat in Vietnam muted McKinney's calls to save the Amerasian children. As Saigon fell In April 1975, U.S. officials hastily prepared to evacuate Americans and one hundred and thirty thousand "at risk" Vietnamese and Cambodians. Not surprisingly, a sense of guilt and concern emerged across the country for "the plight of 'those we left behind.'"[4] The powerful images and sounds of frightened, injured, and desperate people fleeing their homes and the sad stories of displacement and anguish of those the United States had once vowed to protect jarred Americans and further disrupted the convictions of some that the nation was an exceptional and moral force for good in the world.[5] As Americans wondered and worried about what the U.S. military defeat and the abandonment of allies meant for the nation's future, a need to do something, including saving fleeing refugees, took hold. One *New York Times* editorial insisted "the U.S. could not shed its moral responsibility for thousands of Vietnamese who had trusted the U.S. in the past."[6] Hoping to redeem the soul of the country by rescuing refugees, U.S. leaders sought to distance the nation from its role in the war, bury the sentiment of American wrongdoing, and in the words of U.S. Secretary of State and National Security Advisor Henry Kissinger, "put Vietnam behind us."[7]

Redemption, however, required revising the war narrative so that it absolved the nation of its immorality and inhumanity in Vietnam and reminded Americans of their history of heroism and humanitarianism. Stewart McKinney agreed, but stressed the necessity to take responsibility for the consequences of the war. "We must now work," McKinney wrote to one worried Connecticut voter, "to recapture our old image of ourselves as we bind our national wounds and rebuild that war-devastated country."[8]

The new narrative was a powerful yet ahistorical account of America "winning" in Vietnam through selfless and moral acts of assistance and aid to the victims of communism. In "the gendered language of paternalism," America now claimed victory in Vietnam through the "rescue and liberation" of refugees.[9] By reframing U.S. intervention as an act of moral and benevolent guidance and recasting U.S. soldiers as kindhearted "gentle warriors" sent to save the Vietnamese people, not kill them, leaders hoped to rebuild the trust of the American people and reclaim the nation's exceptionalism.[10] Furthermore, focusing the nation's efforts on saving the refugees, rather than its role in making them, would place the country on the "right side" of history.[11]

For McKinney, taking responsibility for Amerasians was a critical piece in rebuilding the nation's image. He rejected the concerns of his colleagues that Amerasians were bitter reminders of American immorality and failure in the war and who were thus eager to ignore their American paternity and group them within the larger population of Southeast Asian refugees. Rather, McKinney believed that "saving" Amerasians from Vietnam—recognizing their American paternity and bringing them "home" to the United States—was clear and powerful evidence that the nation was good, moral, and humane. But the refugee exodus created a humanitarian crisis in Southeast Asia that undermined attempts to recognize Amerasians as a special population of American children deserving of adoption, immigration, and citizenship. Reports of the suffering now facing all Southeast Asian refugees made Amerasians' American paternity and the subsequent abandonment and discrimination that once rallied a bipartisan group of U.S. policymakers and humanitarians to their cause less notable. As Southeast Asian refugees to be saved rather than American children to be claimed, Amerasians were not, as previous Amerasian advocates had tried to suggest, one of us, but a mere subset of them. As such, Amerasians did not need an act of national paternal responsibility; however, they did still need American heroes to rescue them. Grouped among the persecuted victims of communism, Amerasians reinforced both the new narrative of America's humanitarian victory in Vietnam and the Cold War conflict that again posited a democratic America against a communist Vietnam. Thus as the more general refugee challenge pushed questions of paternity, immigration, and citizenship aside, U.S. policymakers integrated Amerasians into broader discussions about U.S. responsibility to aid, admit, and resettle Southeast Asian refugees.

Between 1975 and 1980, the United States faced the global and domestic repercussions of the nation's military loss and subsequent refugee exodus from Southeast Asia. While U.S. leaders sought to secure a humanitarian victory in Vietnam through the rescue of Southeast Asian refugees, some policymakers, including McKinney, continued to advocate for saving Amerasians specifically and rejected efforts to absolve the nation of paternal accountability by integrating them into the larger refugee issue. Tensions between those who believed Amerasians to be American and those who saw them as Asian refugees triggered questions over the merits of American paternity, race, and responsibility that translated into an uneven application of U.S. immigration and citizenship laws for Amerasians.

Rescuing Refugees

On May 1, 1975, one month after welcoming the first group of Operation Babylift evacuees at San Francisco International Airport, President Ford terminated the U.S. rescue operation in South Vietnam. Despite Ford's insistence that America had a moral obligation to save its former allies, U.S. forces left behind millions of "high risk" Vietnamese supporters, collaborators, and government officials along with tens of thousands of Amerasians.[12] In his final efforts to evacuate the remaining American personnel and as many "deserving" South Vietnamese as possible, U.S. Ambassador Graham Martin worried that the trepidation of many Americans fathers over deserting their Vietnamese dependents and Amerasian children might hinder his mission.[13] On April 29, a frustrated Martin asked U.S. National Security Advisor Brent Scowcroft, "Perhaps you can tell me how to make some of these Americans abandon their half-Vietnamese children, or how the President would look if he ordered this?"[14]

Graham was right to be concerned. The American public would likely not have responded kindly to images of American men abandoning their children in Vietnam at the same time that the nation was forsaking its ally. Yet Graham's question of how to balance the urgent need to get U.S. citizens and certain Vietnamese out of Vietnam with the optics of separating American men from their Amerasian children revealed a larger conflict between national interests and humanitarian concerns that shifted how U.S. policymakers understood

Amerasians in the postwar era.[15] Martin's reference to Amerasians as "half-Vietnamese children" is also notable, considering that previous debates among policymakers and humanitarians tended to emphasize their American side. While issues of paternity, race, and responsibility largely shaped discussions during the war over whether Amerasians were American or Vietnamese, after the war national status became the crucial determinant.

The Ford administration perceived the refugee crisis that followed the evacuation in both humanitarian and political terms.[16] Ford believed that the United States had a moral imperative and an ideological obligation to rescue and resettle the Southeast Asian refugees before they fell victim to communism. However, he also understood that these refugees were valuable assets in America's continuing Cold War conflict. Their flight from communism validated decades of Cold War rhetoric about the dangers of communism and the greatness of democracy. On April 3 Ford proclaimed, "I believe that the will of the South Vietnamese people to fight for their freedom is best evidenced by the fact that they are fleeing from the North Vietnamese . . . they want freedom."[17]

Furthermore, the exodus reinforced the postwar humanitarian victory narrative that U.S. leaders were now trying to tell. By placing the refugee plight in Cold War terms and insisting that all those fleeing be designated only as refugees, the United States could recast the war as a humanitarian victory. The designation of "refugee" was particularly important for two reasons. First, it affirmed that those leaving Southeast Asia did so in fear of reprisal from communist regimes. Second, it helped garner the necessary response from the international community and the United Nations High Commissioner on Refugees (UN-HCR) to share the burden of addressing this "great human tragedy."[18] Hence, the eventual admission and resettlement of 130,000 Southeast Asian refugees through the Indochina Refugee Migration and Refugee Assistance Act in the months after the war was, in many ways, a selective and "calculated kindness" by the administration.[19] Furthermore, by linking the refugee crisis to the Communist victory in the war, and stressing the urgency of rescue, the Ford administration contributed to a new postwar narrative that affirmed the benevolent and necessary nature of U.S. intervention in Vietnam. Saving the refugees could therefore further U.S. foreign policy objectives, as the postwar narrative required a villainous Vietnam and a victimized America, an America committed to standing strong against the evils of communism and rescuing its remaining victims.[20]

To further distract their constituents from concerns that refugees would exacerbate an already stressed economy, U.S. policymakers framed the Vietnamese refugees within the growing push to protect human rights. Although the nation's humanitarian history of "rescue and liberation" was a familiar trope, human rights activism was a newer manifestation of American benevolence.[21] Emerging from the transnational nature of the 1960s rights revolutions that linked domestic inequalities with global injustice, human rights activists believed U.S. foreign policy stood at odds with American values. Specifically, they condemned America's disregard for human rights violations in the name of Cold War allegiances as undermining any claim the nation had to moral superiority.[22]

Hence, activists sought to align U.S. foreign policy with America's stated democratic values. In 1973 Rep. Donald Fraser (D-MN) led a "congressional revolution" on human rights, introducing a wave of legislation that made human rights a formal priority in foreign policy. Fraser believed the United States had a global duty to protect the universal rights of all people and that "consideration for human rights in foreign policy, is both morally imperative and practically necessary."[23] After the Vietnam War, human rights became a way to mitigate the legacy of the war, shifting attention and blame from America's own immoralities and inhumanities to the evils abroad. By situating American efforts to save the Southeast Asian refugees within the global movement to eradicate human rights abuses and evildoers, the nation could reclaim the moral high ground it lost in the Vietnam War and "redefine America to Americans."[24]

"Good Refugees"

Still, even after expressing overwhelming support for Operation Babylift and the evacuation of U.S. allies from South Vietnam, the American people appeared uncertain of what to do about the refugees. While support for rescuing them was strong, the majority of Americans had no interest in bringing them to the United States. In May 1975, a Gallup poll revealed that 54 percent of Americans opposed admitting Vietnamese refugees to the United States.[25] Congress was equally resistant as members worried about integrating refugees from Southeast Asia into a society bitter over the war and increasingly strained by a struggling economy. Sen. Joseph Biden (D-DE) accused the Ford administration of inadequately informing Congress of the number of refugees coming to America. Senate Minority Whip Robert Byrd (D-WV) insisted the administration screen the "undesirables"—"barmaids, prostitutes, and criminals"—out of the resettlement process. According to Byrd, "there is no political support for it in the country."[26]

Despite such resistance, Ford continued to push Congress to support the resettlement of Vietnamese refugees. He insisted, "The vast majority of Americans today want these people to have another opportunity to escape the probability of death." To galvanize support for finishing the job of resettling the rescued refugees now filling U.S. reception centers, the Ford administration reminded Americans of their moral responsibility to these "good refugees," 60 percent of whom were children and who, Ford claimed, "ought to be given an opportunity." As the victims of communism, Ford argued, the Vietnamese refugees were no different than the seven hundred thousand Hungarian and Cuban refugees already resettled in the United States, refugees he described as being "good citizens."[27]

Even as the president appealed to America's moral responsibility to save the refugees, Cold War politics and U.S. foreign policy drove his concern.[28] The "good refugee" indebted to the good American savior was a critical part of the rescue and liberation narrative and necessary to a U.S. humanitarian victory in Vietnam.[29] U.S. leaders reminded Americans that unlike the Third World refugees from Cuba and Haiti, the Vietnamese refugees arrived in family units, with education, skills, and English language competency, along with an expectation to repay the American "gift of freedom" with hard work and gratitude.[30]

Once again, African American leaders had concerns. They were particularly critical of the attention being given to the Vietnamese refugees and their characterization as "good refugees." The post–World War II *reracialization* of Asians in America from the unassimilable, unskilled, undesirable, and racially inferior "bad" immigrants into the upwardly mobile and politically nonthreatening "model minority" came at the expense of African Americans.[31] Part of what historian Ellen Wu describes as "the post-Exclusion inclusion" of Asian Americans in American society juxtaposed the social and economic success of the model minority Asian against the poverty and struggle of African Americans, to depict the heights to which minority populations could rise with hard work and strong cultural values.[32] While Americans viewed certain racial minorities, immigrants, and refugees as competition for jobs and housing and pariahs subsisting on America's social welfare system, they lauded the "model minority" as evidence that while race did not hinder achievement, it was an indicator of it.[33] Hence, when syndicated newspaper columnist Joseph Alsop pointed to the "staggering achievements" of model minority Asian Americans and the alleged failures of bad minority African Americans in the *Washington Post*, he attributed the difference to race.[34] Despite the alleged racial inadequacies of African Americans, however, a disproportionate number of Black men served, sacrificed, and died in Vietnam, a war that diverted attention and money away from the Civil Rights movement and the fight for racial equality.[35] Yet when African American veterans returned home battered and bruised from battle, they still suffered under the presumption that they were bad minorities and that people of Asian descent were good.

The racial differentiation embedded in the minority myths exacerbated longstanding tensions between Black and Asian communities in America over resources and rights. Hence, African American leaders pushed back against the Ford administration's efforts to secure funding for the resettlement of Southeast Asian refugees, pointing explicitly to its disparate effects on the Black community and to the nation's racially uneven approach to refugee policy. On May 8, 1975, the Congressional Black Caucus expressed empathy with the refugee plight while citing concerns about spending more money on Vietnamese refugees instead of on American citizens struggling to survive the economic crisis. Congressman Ronald V. Dellums (D-CA), an advocate for peace and disarmament during the war and a member of the House Armed Services Committee, went further: "We lost the war in Vietnam, and now we bring thousands of its victims to a nation which has deserted its war on poverty, permits rapid expansion of its unemployment ranks, does little to correct inequitable distribution of power and wealth, and taxes unevenly and regressively its citizens."[36]

Black leaders were especially worried that the resettlement of Vietnamese refugees would unfairly burden African American communities and further distract attention from critical civil rights legislation. According to the CBC, refugees needed housing at a time when thirteen million Americans were housing deprived, including one-third of Black families. They also required education in a period in which eight to ten million Americans were unemployed and the unemployment rate for Black youth sat an incredible 40 percent, double that of all American youth. At the same time the Ford administration seeks to aid and assist Vietnamese refugees, the CBC explained, it has failed to pass housing and employment legislation for Americans.[37]

In the last days of the final evacuation of Saigon, African American columnist and political conservative William Walker implored Black Americans to consider the effects of adding two hundred thousand refugees to the millions of Americans already unemployed and poorly housed. "History tells us that every time this nation opens its gates to hordes from any foreign country, they get preferential treatment over us. So, no matter how the pot melts, we always remain on the bottom.... Are the obligations to Negroes less sacred and conscionable than the implied if not questionable obligation to the Vietnamese?"[38] Despite the assurances of House leader Tip O'Neill (D-MA) that Southeast Asian refugees were not a threat to Black employment because "there are so many jobs that are available," the CBC announced that without the Ford administration's commitment to expand social aid to America's "'domestic refugees,' including minorities, the poor, and others made jobless by the recession," its members would not support the refugee relief bill. On May 9, 1975, both Black members of the House Judiciary Committee—John Conyers (D-MI) and Barbara Jordan (D-TX)—voted against the bill.[39]

For many CBC members, the uneven approach of the United States to racially different refugee populations reinforced the disparate ways that race shaped how U.S. leaders understood human rights and dictated U.S. refugee policy. In September 1975, the attempted suicide of William Isidore, a Haitian refugee being held in a U.S. detention center in Florida, brought national attention to a newer, less numerous, and darker-skinned refugee population. After fleeing the violent persecution of Haitian leader "Papa Doc" Duvalier and seeking asylum in the United States, Immigration and Naturalization Services (INS) officials detained Isidore along with eighty other Haitians and held them in a Florida jail for over two months. Even though Duvalier had an abysmal record on human rights, U.S. leaders dismissed concerns because Duvalier was anticommunist and a friend.[40] According to U.S. officials, Duvalier's regime was authoritarian, not totalitarian, and therefore, unlike their Southeast Asian counterparts, Isidore and the other Haitians had no fear of persecution.[41] Rather, it was economic opportunity that drove the Haitians to U.S. shores, and thus they were not refugees in the true sense of the word but "economic migrants" and therefore not eligible for asylum.

At the same time INS officials denied the asylum claims of over fifteen hundred Haitian refugees, the United States accepted seventeen thousand Vietnamese and two hundred thousand Cuban refugees into the country.[42] For many, evidence of racial bias was apparent. While the guilt of war coupled with the model minority myth and assumptions about the "good refugee" helped disrupt a history of racialized and exclusionary immigration policies against Asians and justify the resettlement of Vietnamese refugees, the "bad minority" label attached to dark-skinned populations only hurt the efforts of those fleeing Haiti. In condemning the seemingly biased approach to refugee policy by U.S. officials, Father Antoine Adrian and Dr. Paul Lehmann, Chairman of the American Committee for Protection of Foreign Born, explained, "The racial overtones of the treatment accorded black Haitian refugees stands in tragic contrast to the generous

United States government provisions for Cuban refugees who are, except for a few, white and skilled."⁴³

Adoption proved another area of discontent for CBC members, who noted that despite wartime efforts to force African Americans to take responsibility for "their" Black Amerasian children, after the war agencies discriminated against African American families wanting to adopt. Two weeks after Operation Babylift commenced, three Black social service agencies—Afro-American Family and Community Services, the Black Child Development Institute, and Homes for Black Children—accused Babylift organizers of deliberately ignoring eligible Black families interested in adopting Black Amerasians. In fact, only five of the over three hundred Black Amerasians evacuated through the Babylift were referred to the forty Black families awaiting children.⁴⁴ Alfred B. Herbert Jr. of the Black Child Development Institute condemned the situation as another example of an unevenly applied policy. The placement of part-black Vietnamese children with white families, Herbert asserted, was a "gross neglect of resources within the black community."⁴⁵ The Interagency Vietnam Adoption Committee also criticized adoption agencies for bypassing Black families, many of whom had been waiting for two years to adopt an American child, and for failing to grasp the importance of race for Black Amerasians. According to IVAC executive secretary Evelyn Eggleston, adoption by Black families was the best chance for Black Amerasians. She claimed they had a right to come to the United States because their fathers were American, and they needed the necessary tools to survive racism in America and achieve a healthy ethnic identity. "The children appear more like American Blacks than Orientals," Eggleston explained, and "our history of acceptance of the mixed child better prepares us to deal with a child who will be classified as Black once in this country."⁴⁶

Still, IVAC's complaints and the concerns of African American leaders over discriminatory priorities had little effect. U.S. refugee policy remained racially uneven and concerns about interracial adoption persisted, while discussions about Black Amerasians largely disappeared from the debate. After ending its program in Vietnam, IVAC refocused its efforts on adopting African American children, who composed over 60 percent of those awaiting adoption in America into Black families.[47] As Americans turned their attention to the upcoming 1976 presidential election, Black leaders found their concerns further neglected as another group of Americans needing rescue from Vietnam took center stage.

POW/MIA

In the months after the war, Americans turned their attention from rescuing Southeast Asian refugees from communism to saving Americans believed held captive in Vietnam or still missing from the war. What would become an American obsession with prisoners of war and an uncompromising demand for a full accounting of those still missing in action in Vietnam subverted the futile and short-lived attempt by the United States and the Democratic Republic of Vietnam (DRV) to normalize relations. Early on, DRV officials recognized the value of the American POW/MIA issue for future diplomatic talks. As they captured Saigon in April 1975, Communist leaders prepared to offer the United States an accounting of American MIAs and even returned three sets of American remains in exchange for the over three billion dollars of reconstruction aid promised by President Nixon.[48] However, after Premier Pham Van Dong described U.S. aid as compensation for the U.S. "criminal war of aggression" in Vietnam, there was little chance for normalization.[49] Still smarting from the embarrassment of defeat in the war, U.S. leaders had no interest in further humiliation afterwards. Henry Kissinger proved particularly petty in his punitive postwar approach. Rather than conceding to Vietnam's demands or negotiating over American POW/MIAs, the State Department "issued a stiff denunciation" of Dong's statement and imposed harsh sanctions on Vietnam that included a damaging trade embargo accompanied by international isolation. Absent a full accounting of American MIAs, the Ford administration declared, there would be no diplomacy.[50]

Hanoi made efforts to meet U.S. demands. In November 1975, believing they could quell tensions further disrupting an already weak

Vietnamese economy, officials repatriated the remains of twenty-three Americans and released the "last prisoners of war"—the "Ban Me Thout Twelve"—a group of mostly American civilians captured in the final offensive.[51] Rather than compelling U.S. cooperation, however, these acts validated the claims of U.S. leaders and the increasingly powerful National League of Families of American Prisoners and Missing in Southeast Asia that Vietnam continued to imprison and torture American soldiers and hide the remains of the missing.[52] Ironically, and despite the attention given the issue by U.S. leaders, the Vietnam War produced a lower number of American MIAs than any previous U.S. war, about 4 percent.[53] However, the POW/MIA issue proved politically potent for U.S. policymakers and an American public eager to embrace its own victimization and to again see Vietnam as its enemy.

The 1976 presidential election further elevated the issue on the political stage. The same year the Socialist Republic of Vietnam finally reunified that nation under the Communist flag, California governor and Republican challenger Ronald Reagan criticized President Ford for being weak on Vietnam and the MIA issue in particular. Reagan demanded a full accounting of American MIAs in Southeast Asia and promised that, unlike his predecessor, he would obtain that accounting in the first week of his presidency.[54] To combat Reagan's stinging critique, Ford also embraced the demand for a full accounting, ending any hope for negotiations with Vietnam. By the time Ford lost his reelection bid to Georgia peanut farmer Jimmy Carter, the POW/MIA issue was paramount in the political calculations of policymakers eager to turn their attention from rescuing refugees to saving Americans from Vietnam.

Victims of War

By 1977 what historian Edwin Martini describes as "the American War on Vietnam" took its toll. For two years the United States had punished Vietnam for its war victory through harsh economic sanctions and political isolation that crippled the nation's economy and sent many Vietnamese searching for safety and stability in neighboring countries.[55] Severe weather, food shortages, and border disagreements with China and Cambodia compounded the effects and created more refugees. Concerned by the exodus now straining their resources and borders, U.S. allies in Asia turned to newly elected president Jimmy Carter to resolve the situation. As a presidential candidate Carter was optimistic that he could heal the nation of its "Vietnam War scars" through humanitarianism, normalization, and an appeal to human rights.[56] But as president he found that the MIA/POW issue hindered his efforts. Despite the fact that a *New York Times*/CBS poll showed that 66 percent of Americans supported sending humanitarian aid to Vietnam, U.S. policymakers, insistent that Vietnam must provide a full accounting of American MIAs before any further negotiations over aid or normalization, were simply unwilling to help.[57]

Ironically, it was America's obsession with saving its captive and missing soldiers from Vietnam that reintroduced the Amerasian issue to the American public. Journalists, eager to break stories on American POW/MIAs, found "American-faced" children wandering the streets of Ho Chi Minh City instead. By 1978 the growing flight of refugees from Vietnam by land and by boat brought more media attention and international coverage to the issue.[58] That same year "Rosie," a Vietnamese woman and mother of an Amerasian child, garnered the interest of the American public when she began proposing to foreign journalists that the U.S. government follow in the tradition of the French government and begin airlifting its children home.[59] Once again, the gripping pictures and stories of Amerasians complicated the redemption of a nation now vying for the memory of the war and staking claims to its own victimization. Once viewed as a population that Americans could save from communism, first as potential American children available for adoption and assimilation and then as persecuted refugees, by 1977 the existence of Amerasians impeded the healing process. Their "American faces" having visibly matured by now into more "American" features, Amerasians no longer reminded Americans of Vietnam's cruelty but rather of America's immorality.

Beginning in 1977 films like *The Deer Hunter* and *Apocalypse Now* joined novels, memoirs, and television shows in bringing Vietnam "home" into American cultural memory. By focusing on the American experience in Vietnam and replacing Vietnamese victims of the war—children burned by napalm and villagers executed at My Lai—with traumatized American soldiers, fractured communities, and sinister Vietnamese figures, popular culture relieved Americans of their collective guilt for the war and reiterated that they were the war's ultimate victims.[60]

At the same time, popular television shows also publicized the plight of Amerasians to a mass American audience. On December 31, 1979, the popular television show M*A*S*H aired the episode, "Yes-sir, That's Our Baby," in which the staff of the fictional 4077th find an abandoned Amerasian baby. Although the show was based on the Korean War and thus the mother was Korean and the baby half-Korean, the premise of the episode clearly referred to more recent events in Vietnam. The show immediately evoked notions of transnational kinship between the American servicemen and the baby. Unlike the abandoning mother, whom the doctors describe in the racialized terms of the "sneaky Asian" as "too cagey, slipping in and out without nobody seeing her," the child is immediately pronounced a "good baby," "strong, beautiful," and able to bring out the maternal instincts of "Auntie" Margaret.[61]

The episode had two clear messages. First, by recounting the numerous, often unfounded reports of the persecution and murder of Amerasians after the Vietnam War, the show emphasized that because of their mixed race, Amerasians faced lives of misery and discrimination in their homelands, where Amerasian boys were "emasculated" and girls "slaughtered." Second, in a rare and powerful rebuke of the cumulative failure of culpability, the episode depicted that neither the mother of the Amerasian, the local community, nor the U.S. military wanted to take responsibility for the baby.[62]

The show also exposed the hypocrisy of American inaction with regard to the issue. In a heated interaction in which a U.S. military official declared that the child was "not an army matter" and that the army was not responsible for "what happens when a soldier gets lonely," an angry Hawkeye responded, "Not an army matter? You jackass! Where do you think that child came from? You've got people in

American soldier suits running around out there making babies and then making tracks. Don't you think it's about time it became an army matter?"[63] Later in the episode, as a South Korean government official explained to Hawkeye and Colonel Sherman Potter that while France, Great Britain, and the Netherlands had taken responsibility for their military babies, offering them support and citizenship, "the United States, where all men are created equal refuses to do this."[64]

In the end the 4,077th did what U.S. troops had always done with their out of wedlock children born abroad, it reabandoned the baby to a local monastery, concerned about its future but unable or unwilling to be responsible. The Pearl S. Buck Foundation acted as a consultant on the episode and some of the criticism of U.S. military inaction seemed to derive directly from PSBF promotional materials. Although the episode was uncharacteristically grim for the popular television show, it brought public attention to Amerasians by broadcasting the issue into the living rooms of American viewers.

The Filiation of *Fiallo v. Bell*

Ultimately, neither Rosie's pleas nor the *M*A*S*H* episode spurred the massive airlifts for which many had hoped. Instead, amidst rising alarm over a renewed public interest in America's war babies, the Department of Defense released its most current policy regarding GI babies, directive 1344.3. The policy simply restated the official U.S. policy in place since the Second World War: in cases of paternity claims against American and allied personnel, "no individual in the military service will be required or requested to admit paternity."[65] The DOD considered complaints by foreign mothers against a member of the military for child support to be unfounded unless legitimated by the judgment of a court of record in the United States.[66] The policy had proven an effective barrier against paternity claims by foreign women, protecting American servicemen from any responsibility for fathering "foreign" children and excluding those children from any claim to U.S. citizenship.[67]

In 1977 the U.S. Supreme Court reaffirmed the DOD's policy when it issued the *Fiallo v. Bell* ruling.[68] The decision upheld the 1952

Immigration and Naturalization Act and the sex-based distinction embedded in U.S. immigration law for jus sanguinis citizenship claims.[69] According to the 1952 law, unwed American mothers automatically transmitted birthright U.S. citizenship and therefore immigration preferences to children born abroad with foreign fathers while unwed fathers did not.[70] In *Fiallo v. Bell*, three unmarried American fathers and their children challenged the sex-based distinction in U.S., law arguing that it violated both equal protection and due process by excluding unwed fathers from the definition of *parent* and their children born outside of marriage from the definition of *child*.

In its ruling upholding the sex-based distinction, the Court pointed to the intention of U.S. immigration law. According to the Court, the law clearly reflected the specific concern of the U.S. Congress to protect the relationship between the child and its natural mother.[71] A similar consideration of the relationship between child and father was more difficult, the majority argued, because of the perceived absence of family ties and the "lurking problems" of proving paternity.[72] Consequently, the law reflected "an intentional choice not to provide preferential immigration status by virtue of the relationship between an illegitimate child and its natural father."[73] Citing Congress's plenary power to regulate immigration, the Court argued that the sex-based distinction was rational and no different than any other requirements for citizenship such as age or residency.

Because the opinion of the Court was that Congress had the power to prefer unwed mothers over unwed fathers and that the sex-based distinction was a political question, not a judicial one, each of the three claims in *Fiallo* was denied.[74] Cleophus Warner, a naturalized U.S. citizen, had petitioned for his son Serge, born out of wedlock to a foreign mother in the French West Indies. The other two families included Trevor and Earl Wilson, permanent resident aliens of the United States who petitioned the court to have their father Arthur, a citizen of Jamaica, immigrate. Finally, Ramon Martin Fiallo Jr., a U.S. citizen by birth and the out-of-wedlock son of Ramon Fiallo-Sone, a citizen of the Dominican Republic, had petitioned for immigration preference for his father as the parent of a U.S. citizen. Each of the claims failed on the basis of proving paternity.[75]

In addition to tragically affecting the plaintiffs, the ruling in *Fiallo v. Bell* created problems for Amerasians in Vietnam. By upholding the sex-based distinction in immigration law implicit in the U.S. citizenship ruling, the court ensured that the majority of the sons and daughters of American men living in Vietnam after the war had no claim to American paternity, U.S. citizenship, or preferential immigration status. More importantly, when placed in the context of the large U.S. military presence abroad, the ruling continued to protect American servicemen from parental accountability following liaisons with foreign women.[76]

The Orderly Departure Program

The historical idealization of America as a nation of immigrants and a beacon of hope has largely shaped the nation's refugee policy committed to saving the world's displaced, persecuted, or threatened.[77] The repeal of the national origins quota system by the 1965 Immigration and Naturalization Act was still rather new to Americans in the period after the war in Vietnam, as were the increasing numbers of Asian and Latin American immigrants and refugees. For policymakers and a public still recovering from the nation's military failure in Vietnam, the refugees from Southeast Asia were especially troubling. In the six months after the Communists took South Vietnam in April 1975, 125,000 Vietnamese refugees entered the United States. By 1979 America welcomed fourteen thousand Southeast Asian refugees each month.[78] The "land people" and "boat people" from Southeast Asia composed the "largest nonwhite, non-Western, non–English speaking group of people ever to enter the country at one time."[79]

While educated, English-speaking, skilled, urban, middle-class families composed most of the initial postwar wave of Vietnamese refugees resettled across the United States, the second wave brought a very different demographic and elicited a different response from Americans.[80] One year after *Fiallo v. Bell*, Vietnam "began hemorrhaging boat people as its inhabitants risked the dangers and violence of the seas."[81] The massive outflow of refugees turned international humanitarian attention both to the dire situation in Vietnam and also to the difficulties facing first-asylum countries in Southeast Asia expected to absorb the large refugee populations.[82]

The United States responded by increasing its number of Indochina refugee admissions from twenty-five to fifty-three thousand per year and extending the Indochinese Refugee Assistance Act. However, many Americans resisted the expansion of refugee quotas. Not only did this refugee wave include increasing numbers of ethnic Chinese, Cambodians, and Laotians, it was also largely filled by poor, uneducated, unskilled, single men, women, and children. Unlike the first group, the new refugees required government assistance upon their arrival, making them competitors for housing, jobs, and welfare with lower- and working-class Americans.[83] As one worried American saw it, "All money and jobs must be for Americans while we still have a country. The Vietnamese must go elsewhere."[84]

Yet some policymakers saw the refugee crisis as an opportunity to resurrect American exceptionalism through humanitarian and moral acts and redeem the nation's failures in Vietnam. Supporters of U.S. refugee policy stressed the symbolism of achieving some success in Vietnam, even if it was humanitarian rather than military. In 1979 Congressman Henry A. Waxman (D-CA) referenced an article in the *Los Angeles Times* explaining that the humanitarian efforts of the United States on behalf of the Vietnamese refugees was an opportunity for all Americans, particularly the young, to regain the pride that existed prior to the Vietnam War. According to Waxman, "the saving of Vietnamese and Cambodian lives can help reverse some of the terrible consequences of that war."[85]

In the Senate, Strom Thurmond (R-SC) reminded his congressional colleagues of America's history of humanitarian greatness by declaring that, as the "flow of refugees from Southeast Asia has become a torrent of suffering, death, and human disaster," America "has been at the forefront" of the global response and that "this was and is proper."[86] Sen. Samuel Ichiye Hayakawa (R-CA) made the American response personal: "We ourselves are boat people. Every American owes something to those fragile wooden vessels."[87] Vice President Walter Mondale also called upon congressional leaders to follow in America's tradition of global humanitarian leadership, eliciting the tragic memories of the world's failure in 1938 to save the ill-fated Jews of Germany and Austria from Adolf Hitler's wrath. The world, he exclaimed, did not listen, but America would remember now and lead in Indochina, fulfilling its role as the "Mother of Exiles," welcoming the Indochinese refugees, whose talents and energies would enrich the nation.[88]

While Thurmond, Hayakawa, and Mondale conjured up America's image of global humanitarianism and its immigration narrative, opponents once again questioned the role of race in refugee policy. They argued that because the newcomers included legal and illegal immigrants and refugees from Asia, Latin America, and the Caribbean who were racially, culturally, and linguistically different from most Americans, they exposed the vulnerability of and posed a national threat to America's borders.[89] Likewise, African American leaders continued to condemn the racial undertones of U.S. policies committed to aiding the "boat people" of Southeast Asia while simultaneously discriminating against the "black boat people" fleeing Haiti.[90] The resettlement process that placed Southeast Asian refugees in predominately Black and low-income communities during a depressed U.S. economy further exacerbated the existing racial tensions. In Charlotte, North Carolina, Black residents expressed their frustrations with the 350 Southeast Asian refugees living in their neighborhoods. Black residents, including a number of Vietnam veterans, accused the refugees of taking jobs, housing, educational resources, and governmental assistance from American community members in need. Charlotte resident Ronnie Durham spoke for many African Americans when he noted that Black people were consistently denied the social services and assistance so generously given to the Southeast Asian refugees. Durham exclaimed: "You got white people come out and pick them up and give them things and take them here and take them there.... that bothers you. You don't see them doing it for black people.... Our people are struggling and these people come over and everything's so easy for them. I don't think it's right."[91]

Other residents expressed sympathy for the refugees and agreed that the United States had a responsibility to help, but argued that assistance should not come at the expense of Black Americans and that the refugees should be placed in white communities where there was less economic stress and more opportunity. Reverend James Frieson, president of the Baptist Ministers Conference, suggested a more insidious racial agenda at work. Frieson argued, "We feel, if America has a secret to make these people self-sufficient, perhaps that ought to be turned around to help black people." He continued, "if black folks can't pass the education competency tests, how can they teach these refugees to speak English and get jobs and function in three or four months? If they got some kind of secret, let's help everybody."[92]

Washington Post journalist William Raspberry also questioned America's motives. Raspberry criticized America's commitment to causes outside its borders at the same time American citizens faced tremendous domestic and economic challenges. America's humanitarian agenda in Southeast Asia, Raspberry posited, was the direct result of guilt from the Vietnam War that should be directed toward alleviating economic inequality at home.[93] Rep. Clarence D. Long (D-MD), chairman of the House Subcommittee on Foreign Operations and Related Agencies, shared Raspberry's sentiment. "I think Americans are getting awfully tired of the cost of this Vietnam War," exclaimed Long, "It is the most expensive war we ever lost."[94] The resulting tension did little to make the newcomers feel welcome in their new homeland. After surviving her journey from Saigon by boat, twenty-four-year-old Khanh Dung complained, "We can't get along too well with our neighbors. We don't talk to them and they don't talk to us. I think they don't like us."[95]

American opposition to refugee resettlement was not confined to African American communities or even to those Americans struggling under the effects of a strained economy. Americans with personal connections to the Vietnam War also found it difficult to dissociate these new immigrants and refugees from the enemy. Many still associated Asians with the "g——," the Vietcong, and an alien and foreign threat.[96] Jack Fortner, an official with the Immigration and Naturalization

Services, falsely claimed as fact that "many young, male, Vietnamese refugees are former Vietcong."[97] Unlike their "model minority" counterparts, the perceived foreignness of the second wave of Southeast Asian refugees, their association with the Vietnam War, and their immediate dependence on American social welfare services awakened colonialist stereotypes of Asia, Asians, and Asian Americans as foreign and dangerous. This time, Americans feared the dreaded "yellow peril" threatened to destroy America by economically sucking the nation dry.[98]

In California, Senator Hayakawa sought to counter the fears of residents who believed that the refugees were going to drain the state of its resources. In a state where over 30 percent of refugees were resettled by 1979, Hayakawa framed the refugee debate in racialized and Cold War terms.[99] Hayakawa, the Canadian-born son of Japanese immigrants and a naturalized U.S. citizen, called for expanded immigration laws to meet the needs of Southeast Asian refugees, reminding Americans that Asians were "good," ambitious immigrants who did not abuse welfare. Asians, Hayakawa explained, "are readily accepted by most communities as they have made a good record for themselves. . . . They are hard-working and self-sufficient." Furthermore, providing them assistance was the "charitable and humane" way to attain a moral victory from the Vietnam War and to expose Vietnam's communist government as "the totalitarian, racist tyranny that it is."[100] Hayakawa proved to be an interesting and controversial figure whose policy positions often appeared at odds with his own background. Although a vocal proponent of liberal refugee and immigration policies, Hayakawa also advocated for total assimilation and demanded that newcomers "forego the national, ethnic, and cultural identities of their homelands and *become* American."[101] Still, Hayakawa believed the United States had a moral and democratic obligation to rescue and resettle Southeast Asian refugees and he showed specific concern for children. He was adamant that the federal government provide the necessary resources to aid, assist, and educate the refugees, including teaching them job skills and the English language to ensure they did not become financial burdens and could fully assimilate into America.[102]

While Hayakawa focused on meeting the needs of all Southeast Asian refugees, his congressional colleague in the House, Stewart McKinney, turned his attention solely to the Amerasians. Worried that the refugee problem distracted from the needs of the American children still languishing in Vietnam, on April 4, 1979, McKinney introduced HR 3439, the United States–Asian Immigration Act. Built on the foundation of previous legislation that sought to provide Amerasians immigration and citizenship rights, McKinney's bill proposed to give paternal legitimacy to Amerasians and allow them to immigrate to the United States as the "sons and daughters of U.S. citizens."[103] He believed that grouping Amerasians with all other refugees only worsened their plight and ensured that very few Amerasians would even have the chance to immigrate to America. As he saw it, the U.S. immigration system deliberately denied Amerasians' claims to American paternity and excluded them from immigrating to the United States under the category reserved for family reunification, thus forcing them to apply through the nonpreference category.[104] Amerasians who qualified for permanent immigrant visas did so not in preference class (1), unmarried sons and daughters of United States citizens, or preference class (4), married sons and daughters of U.S. citizens, but under the lowest preference class (8), other qualified immigrants.[105] According to McKinney, the othering of Amerasians in U.S. immigration policy was an inadequate solution to the increasingly dire Amerasian situation. Because the nonpreference category attracted a number of applications that exceed the total quota limit, "the children of American citizens have little or no chance of entering the United States."[106]

McKinney therefore sought to challenge the intent of U.S. immigration law. Believing Amerasians to be just as much American as they were Asian, his bill proposed to amend the admissions provisions of the Immigration and Nationality Act to provide Amerasians preferential treatment. In promoting the bill, McKinney appealed to American humanitarianism, the inclusionary character of American democratic ideology, and American paternal responsibility. He emphasized the importance of nongovernmental humanitarian organizations like the

PSBF in securing "a better future for these sons and daughters of U.S. citizens" by providing Amerasians opportunities to live in the "more tolerant culture" of the United States.[107] According to McKinney, Amerasians' American paternity prevented their assimilation into Asian society, as most of their countrymen considered them to "exist outside the mainstream of that society."[108] As second-class citizens, McKinney continued, Amerasians faced limited opportunities for education or employment and, therefore, a bleak future.

In the post–civil rights era, American policymakers were all too familiar with the challenges that second-class citizenship posed to an American ideology that espoused equality. Perhaps this was McKinney's justification for concluding this reference with a call for American humanitarian and paternal responsibility for these children of American citizens. It is because of the U.S. presence in Asia, McKinney asserted, that Amerasians exist, and due to U.S. immigration law that categorizes them as "other" applicants, that they continue to live in dire circumstances.[109]

In his passionate support for the bill, McKinney invoked the notion of family unification and reunification. After all, McKinney reasoned, as the children of American men, Amerasians were American citizens. However, U.S. law only granted American citizenship to the legitimate children of U.S. fathers born abroad and that required a recognized marital union or documented acknowledgment of paternity.[110] Since most Amerasians did not know their American fathers outside of, perhaps, a first name, photograph, or place of birth, obtaining an acknowledgment of paternity proved almost impossible. While accounting methods for Amerasians were largely unreliable, in 1979 the PSBF reported that in Vietnam alone, an estimated ten thousand Amerasians existed with no way to identify or locate their American father.[111] In many instances, the American father did not even know that he had fathered a child or denied such allegations.[112]

To address the weaknesses of U.S. law and Department of Defense directive 1344.3, which released U.S. servicemen from any paternal responsibility, McKinney's bill adopted the French approach and placed the United States in the role of national surrogate father.

The problem, McKinney argued, was not the Amerasian whose father already had or wanted to legitimate his child. Rather, this bill addressed the needs of the rest of the Amerasians, who in most cases never knew their American fathers or had no way to find them. Regardless of the specific circumstances, current U.S. policy ensured that biological American fathers had no formal responsibility to children they did not claim. McKinney hoped his bill would alleviate the harms that resulted.

Much like the Nixon administration, the Carter administration had little interest in Amerasians apart from the larger refugee issue. In fact, by the time McKinney proposed his Amerasian legislation to Congress, the administration was struggling to balance the domestic opposition to refugee resettlement with its Cold War commitment to humanitarianism and human rights. In May 1978, Vice President Mondale described the refugee situation as the world's "most pressing and tragic human rights problems" and declared, "I believe there is no more profound test of our government's commitment to human rights than the way we deal with these people."[113] Six months later, over 375,000 refugees from Vietnam populated the refugee camps in neighboring Southeast Asian countries and tens of thousands more refuge-seekers were arriving on the shores of Malaysia, Indonesia, the Philippines, and Hong Kong.[114] Frustrated with the overwhelming numbers of refugees seeking settlement, leaders in first-asylum countries wondered why Vietnam's Communist army could defeat the United States but proved unable to stop a "mere fleet of refugee boats" from departing its shores.[115] The United States was also concerned. The tens of thousands of boat-people fatalities and Vietnam's reported persecution and expulsion of its ethnic Chinese minorities troubled the Carter administration and caused Secretary of State Cyrus Vance to condemn the Vietnamese government as a human rights abuser.[116]

In order to address the refugee outflow and to stop the thousands of drowning deaths at sea, the United Nations High Commissioner for Refugees (UNHCR) established a memorandum of understanding with the government of Vietnam in 1979 by creating the Orderly Departure Program (ODP). The ODP hoped to provide a safe, orderly, predictable, and legal means for people to leave Vietnam.[117] The agreement, which Sen. Ted Kennedy praised as the proper humanitarian response to the "urgent plight of the 'boat people' floundering throughout Southeast Asia," allowed immigrants and refugees from Vietnam, including Amerasians, to depart for family reunification and humanitarian reasons.[118] Qualifying Vietnamese citizens were designated either as immigrants or as one of three categories of refugees: (1) family members of United States citizens, (2) former employees of the U.S. government, or (3) other persons closely associated or identified with the U.S. presence in Vietnam before 1975.[119] The issue of family reunification was critical for UNHCR, which considered reunification to be one if its basic functions. Seeking to rectify its humanitarian image, the United States also prioritized reunification, specifically targeting those left behind during the war: friends, allies, and Amerasians.[120]

Ironically, however, neither the UNHCR nor the Carter administration actually valued reuniting Amerasians with their American fathers. While the ODP identified Amerasians in Vietnam as the children of American fathers, it failed to include them in category (1) of the program, family members of U.S. citizens. Rather, Amerasians qualified for the ODP only in category (3), "other persons" associated or identified with the U.S. presence in Vietnam. Including Amerasians in category (3) did enable those Amerasians who could not prove their paternity to leave Vietnam. However, few in this category were able to immigrate, due to the limited spaces available and the preference for those listed under categories (1) and (2). And the distinction between refugee and relative in the ODP reinforced the notion that Amerasians were not one of "us"—American children or even relatives of U.S. citizens—they were instead, one of "them"—"other" Asian refugees.

For U.S. policymakers who felt a sense of responsibility or guilt to act on behalf of Amerasians but who were still unable to accept them as American children, the ODP provided the perfect compromise. Its inclusionary language recognized Amerasians' American paternity and their persecution by the Vietnamese Communist regime while excluding them from the privileges of that paternity by continuing to classify them as "others." The contradictory approach of inclusionary discourse and exclusionary policy in the ODP reflects the complicated relationship that U.S. policymakers would maintain with the Amerasians of Vietnam over the next decade and that would dictate all future Amerasian immigration policies. The transnational and transracial makeup of Amerasians continued to confuse U.S. policymakers conflicted about who was responsible for Amerasians and where they actually belonged. U.S. leaders unable to reconcile the Amerasian mixture of race and nation committed to a contradictory approach that acknowledged Amerasians as the children of American fathers but did not recognize them as real American citizens.

These contradictions were also apparent in the political discussions over McKinney's United States–Asian Immigration Act. By October 1979 the U.S. Department of Health, Education, and Welfare, the Department of State, and the Department of Justice reviewed and opposed McKinney's bill. The State and Justice departments were particularly critical in their comments, denying that the immigration of Amerasians to the United States as the children of U.S. citizens qualified for the status of family unification.[121] Such opposition exposed a disconnect among some U.S. leaders who, on one hand, agreed with the assumed American paternity of Amerasians and acknowledged the discrimination and abuse Amerasians faced in Vietnam as a result of it, but insisted that this in itself did not make them American children. U.S. immigration and nationality law supported the apparent contradiction. Opposing policymakers simply pointed to both the sex-based distinction in the law that defined Amerasians as illegitimate and the critical inability of Amerasians to provide evidentiary proof of American paternity. They disregarded any visible evidence of biological filiation with American fathers and maintained that no legal distinction between Amerasians and other Vietnamese children in postwar Vietnam existed—Amerasians were Asian children, not American—and therefore had no claim to U.S. citizenship.

Unwilling or perhaps unable to acknowledge how such rationale for excluding Amerasians perpetuated a history of racialized exclusion against mixed-race persons and people of Asian descent, the Carter administration based the majority of its criticism of McKinney's bill on two specific issues—the determination of American paternity and the potential economic burden on American taxpayers. In each case, McKinney struck back. Regarding paternity, the bill proposed the creation of a review board to determine paternity claims using nontraditional documentation, including government documents, photographs, letters, and/or proof of past financial support from the assumed American father. To address fears that Amerasians would become economic burdens, the bill required an American financial sponsor for each Amerasian applicant. This stipulation, McKinney claimed, would prevent Amerasians from becoming public charges.[122] But the Carter administration remained steadfast in its rejection of the bill. Rather than viewing it as an opportunity to address the half-American children born in Asia or to give credence to McKinney's insistence of U.S. responsibility, the administration dismissed the bill as a measure that would unnecessarily increase the workload for INS officials and place an economic burden on American taxpayers.[123] It maintained that the ODP was the best solution to address all Southeast Asian refugees.

The administration's position incited McKinney's ire and he accused the administration of using bureaucratic rather than humanitarian eyes in its blatant rejection of the bill.[124] It was a clear contradiction of America's fundamental inclusionary core, which underlay the nation's narrative of open shores and shelter for the plight of the less fortunate. Overlooking such an important piece of the American fabric was especially problematic in this case, according to McKinney, because the Amerasian situation was "a problem caused by the citizens of our Nation."[125]

The PSBF also criticized the administration for its inaction on the Amerasians. Between 1979 and 1981, executive director John Shade sent numerous requests to President Carter inviting him to visit the Buck House in Perkasie, Pennsylvania, and to live up to his reputation as a humanitarian and a Christian by becoming the first president to publicly acknowledge the Amerasian issue.[126] Citing a busy schedule, Carter did not accept Shade's invitations. Shade also requested that the DOD show the *M*A*S*H* episode to all new U.S. military arrivals to Asian posts, informing American soldiers of the potential consequences of their actions. This request, too, never materialized. By October 1980, HR 3439 was dead.[127]

The 1980 Refugee Act

Although the Carter administration fell short on the Amerasian issue, they resurrected U.S. world leadership on refugee resettlement. On March 17, 1980, in response to the overwhelming numbers of refugees coming to the United States and a year of political squabbling over admissions numbers, quotas, and money, Congress passed the 1980 Refugee Act. As the first piece of U.S. legislation to address refugees as distinct from other immigrants, this act formally recognized that while immigrants left their homes willingly, refugees did not.[128] Thirty-nine years after the United Nations defined refugees as anyone "unable or unwilling to return to their country of origin owing to a well-founded fear of being persecuted," not just those fleeing communist regimes, the United States aligned itself with international law and formalized the refugee admissions process. The 1980 Refugee Act increased annual refugee admissions to fifty thousand, empowered the president to exceed that limit in emergencies, included claims for asylum, and established the Office of Refugee Resettlement in the Department of Health and Human Services.[129] However, the act had little effect on Amerasians, whose claims of persecution as a result of paternity and illegitimacy failed to elicit any special consideration. They continued to be grouped among all other Southeast Asian refugees.

Becoming American

As former California governor Ronald Reagan celebrated his victory in the 1980 presidential election, increasing media coverage about the half-American children in Vietnam inspired policymakers to take a closer look. In his *New York Times* article "The Plight of the Children Abandoned in Vietnam," journalist Bill Kurtis reminded the American public that when America left Vietnam in 1975, it also left thousands of American children behind. These "living reminders of the war" now wandered the streets of Saigon, homeless, parentless, and hopeless.[130] After half a decade of insisting Amerasians were just another population of Southeast Asian refugees, Kurtis's work conjured up notions of kinship and family. One American wrote President Reagan in response to Kurtis's article imploring the president to bring these American children home: "We have a tremendous obligation in conscience to these particular children, who are of our race and blood." Another American challenged Reagan's inaction: "This is a moral issue and your help is needed. Where do you stand?"[131]

The emotion and sympathy evoked by the article proved complicated in an era defined by increasing social and economic conservatism and anticommunist nationalism. The six to eight million immigrants and 166,000 refugees living in the United States by 1980 strained the U.S. economy at a time when there were seven million unemployed Americans and an unemployment rate hovering at 7.1 percent.[132] For many Americans the nation's immigration problem appeared to be out of control, and demands for a more restrictive immigration policy clashed with the nation's Cold War humanitarian ideal—to save the world's poor and persecuted from communist countries.

The challenge for the newly elected president was to honor the American tradition of providing a beacon of hope to the world's oppressed, hopeless, and poor while meeting the demands of the conservative political environment and his own Republican Party.[133] The arrival one year earlier of 125,000 Cuban refugees fleeing communism and thousands of Haitians fleeing persecution further complicated Reagan's charge. By the time he took office, what to do with the tens of thousands of unsettled Cuban *marielitos* and Haitian refugees confined to U.S. prisons and military bases forced Reagan to reconsider the porousness of U.S. borders, the expanded refugee admissions from the 1980 Refugee Act, and the "changing face" of legal immigration.[134] President Reagan addressed this challenge in his 1981 statement on U.S. Immigration and Refugee Policy by evoking the "myth of universalism" that portrayed the nation as inclusive and tolerant of outsiders: "We shall continue America's tradition as a land that welcomes peoples from other countries. . . . At the same time, we must ensure adequate legal authority . . . to enable us, when sudden influxes of foreigners occur, to decide to whom we grant the status of refugee or asylee."[135]

Conclusion

As the nation entered a new era with new presidential leadership, small yet significant steps of progress emerged in support for specific Amerasian legislation. Although McKinney's HR 3439 failed to pass in Congress, the discussions it elicited over paternity, race, and responsibility kept the Amerasians alive in the minds of U.S. policymakers and humanitarians. While previous presidential administrations had failed to accept them as an American responsibility, the Reagan administration would do just that, emphasizing the nation's efforts to take paternal responsibility for its children by finally passing the 1982 Amerasian Immigration Act. Nevertheless, the Amerasian mixture continued to confound U.S. lawmakers, resulting in a contradictory policy. Even as they agreed to formally recognize Amerasians' American paternity, they disagreed about what that meant and whether Amerasians were in fact, American.

Chapter Four

Blood Politics

As the newly elected president Ronald Reagan entered the White House in January 1981, Rep. Stewart McKinney brought the plight of Amerasians once again to the House floor with the Amerasian Immigration Act (AIA).[1] Similar to its predecessor legislation, which had floundered several years before, the AIA amended U.S. immigration law to provide the tens of thousands of Amerasians in Southeast Asia preferential immigration status, classifying them as the "children of United States Citizens."[2] In order to qualify for the AIA, Amerasians had to show proof of American paternity, obtain an American sponsor with guaranteed legal custody and financial responsibility for five years, and separate from their Vietnamese family members, including their mothers, who had to relinquish their parental rights.[3]

In his speech, McKinney urged House members to reconsider including half-American children among the larger group of Southeast Asian refugees. He again implored Congress to take responsibility for its abandoned children in Vietnam and grant them citizenship, and reminded members of the actions of other Western countries regarding their mixed-race war babies. As had many before him, McKinney pointed to the French, British, and Dutch, who had granted "no-fault" citizenship to their Eurasian children while criticizing the United States for ignoring its "bastard sons and daughters."[4] By virtue of parentage, McKinney reasoned, Amerasians who were being persecuted in Vietnam because of their American paternity should have the right to immigrate and claim U.S. citizenship. "There is no argument," McKinney explained "including all the ones expounded upon by the administration, for this Nation to deny what has always been its policy, that a child born of an American parent is an American child—either parent, father, or mother."[5]

It was this understanding of the issue coupled with a hopeful interpretation of U.S. citizenship law that motivated McKinney to frame the AIA as an inclusionary policy that recognized Amerasians' American paternity and welcomed them "home." However, while the AIA offered a pathway to naturalized citizenship through immigration, its failure to grant Amerasians birthright U.S. citizenship reflected the continued inability or unwillingness of U.S. policymakers to reconcile the Amerasian mixture of race and nation with the sex-based distinction in U.S. citizenship law. During the political process to pass the AIA the same political and humanitarian actors who previously advocated for changes to U.S. adoption, citizenship, and immigration laws, including McKinney and the PSBF, expanded their base to incorporate a diverse array of advocates, including church leaders, members of the media, and Vietnam veterans. Together, they took a more aggressive approach in advocating that Amerasians were American children. While continuing to condemn the sex-based distinction in U.S. immigration law, they intensified their discourse regarding paternity and race to ascribe an American identity to Amerasians. Proponents specifically emphasized the race-making power of American paternity to convince Americans that Amerasians were "our children" in Vietnam.[6]

During the congressional debates over the AIA, disagreements about paternity, race, and national responsibility for Amerasians put members of Congress and the Reagan administration at odds. Those who supported the AIA advocated for the recognition of Amerasians as American children, American citizens, and an American responsibility. Their position reflected a historical appreciation for how the U.S. presence in Asia had induced Asian immigration to the United States and a sense that citizenship is the true mark of belonging. Advocates demanded that the U.S. government take responsibility for the consequences of a war it had initiated. They also criticized the gendered nature of U.S. citizenship law, targeting the sex-based distinction that denied Amerasians citizenship.

In contrast, those in opposition to the AIA insisted that although Amerasians were a tragic humanitarian consequence of the war, without an identified American father to legitimate them they were not American children and had no claim to U.S. citizenship. Their objections were also rooted in a longer history in the United States of excluding Asians from immigration and citizenship and sought to distance the nation from any culpability.[7] To justify their position, opponents pointed to U.S. law, which they noted only granted citizenship to persons born abroad whose U.S. citizen fathers claimed them. Of course, this was the very point of the AIA. By defining Amerasians as persons "fathered by U.S. citizens," the bill effectively asserted a claim of American paternity, legitimacy, and responsibility for them. At the same time the AIA reinforced the position of its critics by creating a specific immigration category for Amerasians, thus implying that Amerasians were "aliens, not citizens."[8]

Concerns about citizenship and responsibility loomed large for Rep. McKinney and Amerasian supporters and advocates like Fathers Alfred Keane and Alfred Carroll, both of whom worked with Amerasians in South Korea. In his 1980 testimony before Congress, Father Keane, a Maryknoll missionary who served as head of the St. Vincent's Home for Amerasian Children in South Korea, depicted the injustices experienced by Amerasians in that country.[9] Without Korean or American citizenship, Amerasians, he claimed, were stateless. As the children of U.S. citizens, Father Keane explained, U.S. law should grant Amerasians U.S. citizenship, which would facilitate an American identity.[10]

Thus the political process to pass the AIA into law put questions of paternity, legitimacy, and responsibility on full display. As lawmakers considered whether Amerasians were American children or Asian foreigners, they framed the debate within a discourse of blood politics.[11]

Immigrants and Refugees

President Reagan entered the White House with a clear conservative domestic and Cold War foreign policy agenda. After blaming his predecessors for "weakening" America, he committed his administration to rebuilding the nation's trust in its leaders, restoring America's military dominance, defeating communism, and healing the country after the Vietnam War.[12] Reagan believed the U.S. defeat in Vietnam had crippled the nation and he made the restoration of American pride and patriotism a central focus of his presidential administration. His aggressive anticommunist, anti-Soviet foreign policy resulted in the largest peacetime increase in defense spending in history and a renewed focus on, and respect for, American military veterans.

Diverging from his predecessor's humanitarian narrative that based the nation's greatness on its ability to save Southeast Asian refugees from communism, Reagan focused his attention on reviving American exceptionalism through the redemption of U.S. soldiers and the U.S. military. In 1981 he became the first U.S. president to mention Vietnam in his inaugural address, situating the war effort within a longer tradition of heroic military endeavors and wrapping "all American wars, and all the American soldiers who had died in those wars, in a single flag of patriotism and sacrifice."[13] Rather than ignoring what was still a painful memory, Reagan commended Vietnam veterans for their service and offered public praise for men and women he described as honorable heroes and a war he identified as a "noble cause."[14] Americans responded fervently to the new nationalism and absorbed Reagan's message through his words, commercial products, and popular culture. Seeing an opportunity for profit, corporate executives placed a price tag on ideas and symbols that had once inspired mass protest and dissent.[15] Chrysler incorporated patriotic images of American flags and cowboys and an appropriately titled theme song, "The Pride is Back," into its advertising. Hollywood also contributed full-screen patriotic imagery and military messaging with films like *Rambo: First Blood* (1982), *Missing in Action* (1984), and *Top Gun* (1986), each depicting the heroism and strength of U.S. soldiers involved in the Vietnam conflict.[16] Reagan wanted more Americans to feel pride in their service members and their country so he used rhetoric and policies to perpetuate the notion of a strong nation with superior military capabilities and noble soldiers.

However, racism and nativism also infiltrated this "rebirth of America and Americanism," which historian Christian Appy describes as "relentlessly upbeat" and optimistic.[17] At the same time eager Americans embraced the new nationalism and commenced what was now a Cold War conflict with Vietnam, concerns about illegal immigration from developing countries compounded the difficulty of facing the nation's humanitarian responsibility toward Southeast Asian refugees. The growing overall presence of Black and brown newcomers who were seen as taking American jobs, abusing welfare, and committing crimes led many Americans to believe the nation had lost control of its borders. As a result, some citizens demanded a more restrictive immigration policy and a more selective method that would save only certain kinds of refugees from communism. Writing about these issues during the 1980s, political scientist Elizabeth Hull noted, "Americans are beset with anxieties, for which aliens now, as in the past, provide convenient scapegoats."[18]

The growing anti-immigration sentiment proved especially problematic for refugees from Southeast Asia. By 1980 immigration restrictionists pointed to the waning public enthusiasm for those still fleeing the region and the heavy financial burdens that resettlement services imposed on taxpaying Americans and local governments.[19] Some, including Rep. Frank J. Sensenbrenner (R-WI), wondered if the aid could be sustained. "At a time when our unemployment rate is going up, when we are spending about $1 billion per year for refugee resettlement costs, the people of the United States are warm, they are hospitable, but there is also a limit to how much we can afford at a time of rampant inflation and deficit budgets."[20] Others, like Joseph Sureck, the INS district director in Hong Kong, argued that five years after the war those coming to America were no longer refugees fleeing a "well-founded fear" of persecution as defined by the 1980 Refugee Act, but rather "economic migrants" motivated by opportunity.[21]

Restrictionists like Sureck advocated replacing the nation's open-door policy with a "screen door" meant to police entrance into the country.[22]

At the same time, immigration proponents were making their case. In 1981 the Select Commission on Immigration and Refugee Policy (SCIRP) released its report on current U.S immigration law and practice, with recommendations for reform.[23] The commission reflected the broad range of societal interests of its diverse membership, which included lawmakers, business executives, labor leaders, and representatives from different ethnic groups. Although the report, *U.S. Immigration Policy and the National Interest*, found illegal immigration to be a serious problem, it concluded that legal immigration, including refugee resettlement, was economically and socially beneficial to the country. SCIRP suggested that, in spite of popular assumptions, migrants and refugees from Asia, Latin America, and the Caribbean were particularly valuable, as they assimilated easily, worked hard, and contributed to society. Legally admitting these groups on the basis of family reunification, job skills, and refugee status was, therefore, in the national interest. Still, the American people seemed unmoved by the findings. SCIRP chair and president of Notre Dame University Father Theodore Hesburgh acknowledged the failure of the report to change public opinion. "As a general rule," Hesburgh observed, "the American public . . . has been negative toward the admission of immigrants and refugees to the United States. . . . It is the most human thing in the world to fear strangers."[24]

However, the intent of the commission had always been political and it did manage to motivate Congress toward immigration reform by addressing both the benefits of legal immigration and also the consequences of illegal immigration. Decoupling legal and illegal streams of migration allowed President Reagan to align his political stance with his personal views shaped by his time in California, where migrant labor drove much of the economy and informed a free-market conservatism that leaned toward open borders to meet the labor needs of big business. Reagan believed that immigrants benefited the nation and also understood that reducing the number of Indochinese refugees undermined his Cold War commitment to save those escaping communism and his vilification of communist Vietnam.[25] A number of administration hard-liners, including Secretary of State Alexander Haig and UN Ambassador Jeanne Kirkpatrick, agreed that a generous refugee admissions policy strengthened the nation's anti-communist and anti-Vietnam stance.[26]

Regardless of the Reagan administration's or SCIRP's position on immigrants and refugees, many Americans tended to embrace an understanding of America's open-door policy that stressed the importance of assimilation and becoming American*ized*. Unless immigrants "want to learn to be Americans," twenty-one-year-old Cindy Lane declared to the *Wall Street Journal*, "they shouldn't be here."[27] Lane's sentiment was common during the period, as questions of assimilation and integration suffused the debates over immigrants and refugees. It also reflected the nation's efforts to grapple with what it meant to be an American and what it meant to become one. These questions now pervaded the congressional debates over the AIA and the nation's paternal responsibility for Amerasians.

The Debate

On November 17, 1981, members of the House of Representatives Subcommittee on Immigration, Refugees, and International Law began discussing two bills that addressed the immigration rights of illegitimate children fathered by U.S. citizens abroad: HR 3405, introduced by Rep. Barney Frank (D-MA), and the AIA. Frank's bill challenged the sex-based distinction in existing U.S. immigration law by seeking to require illegitimate children born to foreign mothers abroad "to acquire or transmit certain immigration benefits by reason of its relationship with its natural father."[28] The AIA also challenged the sex-based distinction in U.S. law by providing those Amerasians without paternal legitimation admission to America as "children of United States Citizens."[29]

Among those in attendance were two of the AIA's most ardent supporters, Pat Schroeder (D-CO), the first female congressional representative from Colorado, and the outspoken Frank. Elected to Congress in 1980 after an eight-year stint in the Massachusetts legislature, Frank, a

New Jersey native and Harvard Law graduate, was a constant champion of civil rights. In 1987, he would become the first openly gay member of Congress. Frank strongly criticized the sex-based distinction in U.S. citizenship law in which American mothers, but not fathers, automatically transmitted citizenship to their children. In practice, the unequal and gendered application of the law assumes a role of parental responsibility and legal filiation between child and mother and an absence of both between child and father. Frank believed this to be a grave injustice. The law, he argued, ensured that American men, and in the case of Amerasians, U.S. servicemen, faced no legal obligation for the children they fathered with foreign girlfriends or lovers, and their children had no legal grounds for citizenship. The parental relationships, Frank argued, should receive equal treatment; therefore the citizenship of its natural father should give any child the right to all immigration benefits.[30]

Schroeder also took issue with the sex-based distinction and the practice of paternal irresponsibility within the U.S. military. Raised in a military family, she won election to the House of Representatives in 1972 as an anti–Vietnam War, pro–women's rights candidate. One of only fourteen women in the House, Schroeder was quickly versed in challenging male-dominated institutions like Congress and the U.S. military. She once told a congressional colleague who questioned her ability to mother and govern that "I have a brain and a uterus and I use both." As the first woman on the Armed Services Committee, Schroeder was active on military issues and dedicated her efforts to improving and protecting the lives of military spouses and families. She viewed the policies on Amerasians as the perfect example of an irresponsible U.S. military that too often sacrificed the rights of women and families in war.[31]

Supporters of both bills joined Frank and Schroeder in criticizing the sex-based distinction in U.S. law, condemning how the law contributed to military paternal irresponsibility. However, those in opposition had their own concerns about tarnishing the redeemed reputations of America's "noble warriors," while needlessly implicating individual U.S. soldiers, who had most likely moved on with their lives, as fathers.[32] Although there was no official political stance from any specific U.S. veterans organization, large numbers of individual Vietnam veterans feared passage of the bill and its legal implications for fatherhood and child support. According to Greg Kane of the Vietnam Veterans of America, many veterans were petrified that "some Amerasian kid" would knock on their door when they had their "family all around them."[33] Proponents disregarded such concerns, insisting that the AIA had no power to identify individual fathers or reunite them with their Amerasian children.

More concerning for political opponents, however, was the fear that such legislation would open a back door to fraud and more illegal immigration. Government agencies, including the Immigration and Naturalization Service, spoke out against the AIA expressing concerns with changing U.S. laws. In response to Father Keane's specific request for U.S. citizenship for Amerasians, Leonel J. Castillo, a former INS commissioner, explained that three basic principles structured current immigration law—family unification, labor needs, and political asylum. Since the U.S. government did not recognize Amerasians as American children, Amerasians, according to Castillo, "did not fit into any of these principles."[34]

In its opposition to the AIA and in defense of its position that Amerasians were not American children or a U.S. responsibility, the Reagan administration, as had the Carter administration, pointed to evidentiary problems inherent in verifying paternity for Amerasians who lacked the documentation to prove paternity by blood.[35] Disregarding the reasons for the lack of evidence of paternity and dismissing suggestions of U.S. culpability because of its role in the war, the administration argued that requirement of proof of paternity was rational and "based on a valid governmental interest in limiting fraudulent alien entry into the United States on the basis of questionable blood relationships."[36] Thus Frank's bill concerned policymakers who worried that it encouraged "unacceptable" foreigners to sneak into the country illegally by exploiting American men as fake fathers or persuading unrelated American male citizens to claim paternity. The State and Justice departments also opposed the AIA. They pointed to the possibility of fraud inherent in the bill, the lack of probative evidence, and the reality that there was no "natural father asserting paternity."[37] The administration feared that because no father existed, or at least there was no evidence to prove that one did, there was no way in the AIA to legitimize any claim to paternity or prove an Amerasian was American.

The administration's resistance to claiming Amerasians as American children is notable considering that their plight aligned nicely with Reagan's "selective embrace of refugees" fleeing communism and his conservative ideas of family.[38] But while Amerasians were exactly the kind of refugees that fit into the administration's anti-Communist foreign policy agenda, Reagan's commitment to redeeming the actions of the U.S. military and the reputations of American soldiers of the Vietnam War made their family statuses more challenging.[39] While Reagan espoused strong families as the key to American success, to many Americans Amerasians stood as a continuing reminder of the country's failure in Vietnam: evidence of the immorality of U.S. soldiers, the nation's abandonment of its allies, and the Communist victory. Hence, while the Reagan administration could have supported the reunification of Amerasian children with their fathers by encouraging American men to take their paternal roles seriously, it was more concerned with protecting their privacy and reputations.[40]

Both Frank and Schroeder quickly criticized the administration's hypocrisy toward family and responsibility and its assertion that the AIA opened a back door to illegal immigration. Not only did both members of Congress believe Amerasians to be American children, the AIA included them in the previously established immigrant and refugee admissions numbers under the United Nations' Orderly Departure Program, ensuring that they were not an additional burden on the U.S. immigration system. Furthermore, Schroeder condemned the irresponsibility of the administration, which she claimed endorsed the proliferation of military babies.[41] Still, the administration remained adamant in its position that without scientific evidence there could be no proof that the fathers of Amerasians were in fact American. Therefore, it argued, both bills simply encouraged illegal immigration.[42]

The insistence that only scientific evidence could prove paternity and determine nationality seemed odd to many AIA supporters, especially in light of the physical and undeniable proof visible on the very bodies of the population in question. Disregarding the reality that not all Amerasians had clearly defined "American" looks, proponents continued to assert that by merely examining the features of Amerasians anyone could easily read their paternity and thus their claim to citizenship. In fact, it was what Amerasians looked like that initially captured the sympathy of American humanitarians and policymakers. In addition to the numerous photographs that appeared in reputable media sources, including the *New York Times*, the Reagan administration's acknowledgment of the large U.S. military presence in Vietnam during the war and its own recognition that Amerasians faced discrimination due to their American paternity seemed to undermine its argument.[43]

Clearly troubled by the administration's position, Schroeder reminded Congress that no such problem of proof existed in Asia, where the ability to identify Amerasians as American had resulted in their subjection to tremendous discrimination.[44] Testimony from John Shade, Father Keane, and former State Department and Americans for International Aid employees affirmed Schroeder's claim. "There is no problem in identifying the Amerasians; for example their hair, eyes, color of skin, facial features and other characteristics are evident," retired State Department employee Henry Sandri explained.[45] Frank and Schroeder believed it to be nonsensical for the Reagan administration to acknowledge that the discrimination Amerasians suffered in their birth countries was a direct result of their American looks while simultaneously denying their American paternity.

Frank aggressively challenged the requirement of scientific evidence, asserting that the heart of the problem for the Reagan administration was one of race, racism, and race mixture. Its real concern, according to Frank, was not that the children fathered by European or Australian men would sneak into the country illegally, but that the children of Asian mothers would.[46] In other words, Frank surmised that the Reagan administration, while agreeing that the physical characteristics of Amerasians made them American, simultaneously deemed them Asian and therefore non-American.[47]

Yet race and race-mixture were also problematic for Frank and Schroeder. While both criticized the Reagan administration for its apparent racialization of Amerasians as Asian because of how they looked, they employed the same racial rationale to deem them American. In each case, the administration and Congress conflated race and nation. This was troubling because both sides depended upon subjective, preconceived, and racialized notions of what an American and what a non-American actually looked like. In this case, the American looked Black or white and the non-American looked Asian. Almost a decade earlier Dr. James R. Dumpson, dean of the School of Social Service at Fordham University and a member of the Edward Kennedy Study Mission to South Vietnam, discussed the rationale behind assumptions of race and nationality for Amerasians. Considering the composition of the U.S. military forces in Vietnam during the war, Dumpson argued it was logical to assume that white or Black Americans fathered the majority of Amerasians.[48] However, Dumpson also pointed to the limitations of American racial categories, explaining, "I think we are so accustomed in our country to say white and black, that we forget that we have other ethnic groups too. I am sure some of those children [Amerasians] were fathered by Puerto Ricans or Asian Americans. When we say black, we mean nonwhite."[49]

Despite the reality of the heterogeneity of the U.S. population and the issues with grouping all nonwhite persons as Black and conflating race and nationality, legislators focused their discussion of Americanness on those Amerasians they deemed to be Black or white. They excluded Amerasians with Latin American or Asian American fathers and those whose looks they found more difficult to identify.[50] Consequently, the arguments of both Frank and Schroeder and the Reagan administration shared a racial rationale rooted in the longer history of racial relegation, exclusion, and othering of mixed-race persons in America. Each side simultaneously used race as evidence of filiation and difference.

As Representative Frank pressured legislators to produce a solution for the evidentiary problem, the Reagan administration, wanting to deny Frank's accusations of racism, introduced the blood test. Known today as the DNA test, it was in its infancy in 1981. Nevertheless, the administration claimed that by examining the antigens in the blood, it could determine whether an individual was American.[51] Such a blood test, it argued, would be useful in scientifically determining the individual father, and in cases where there was no father available to test, the blood of the child could determine in which part of the world the child originated.[52] According to Cornelius Scully, the director of the Office of Legislation, Regulations and Advisory Assistance in the Bureau of Consular Affairs, the test could tell if "an individual who now lives in Seoul was fathered by an American rather than by a Frenchman or rather than by a Moroccan, or rather than by somebody else."[53] The test, the administration posited, was so specific that it "may be able to differentiate between a Kentuckian and a New Jersyite."[54] Documents later submitted by the Center for Disease and Control (CDC) quickly disproved the administration's claims that a blood test could determine whether or not someone was American.[55] However, the nature of the assertion, the impending debate surrounding it, and the shocking failure of Frank or Schroeder to question the validity of such a blood test reeked of an outdated and troubling racial ideology. The underlying assumption that people have different kinds of blood and the assertion that blood can determine nationality was extraordinarily misguided. Such claims, reminiscent of the controversial notion of blood quantum, revived the arguments of early twentieth-century eugenicists who warned against miscegenation as leading to racial degeneration.[56] Fundamentally, these discussions reveal how thoroughly a racialized ideology continued to shape the ways U.S. leaders understood and structured national identity.[57]

The Priest and the Missionary

As lawmakers debated the racial relevance of Amerasians and their claims of paternity, a number of humanitarian actors pressured legislators to accept a national paternal responsibility for the "American" children abandoned in Vietnam. From his office at Gonzaga University in Spokane, Washington, Father Alfred Carroll, the head of the Korean Amerasian Program, initiated a massive congressional letter writing campaign in effort to gain political support for the AIA.[58] Including a passionate plea to President Reagan, Carroll appealed to notions of nation and family. "I beg of you" Carroll implored, "to support this legislation which will allow these youngsters the rights of their paternal heritage. These youngsters who ... have the virtues to become good Americans." Carroll also wrote Rep. Walter Fauntroy (D-DC) a founding member and chairman of the Congressional Black Caucus. To Fauntroy, Father Carroll conveyed a message of transnational racial kinship, explaining the necessity of his support and that of the CBC for Amerasians, who he claimed in "many cases were black children."[59]

In 2013, some thirty-four years later, the life and light in Father Carroll's big brown eyes remained vibrant as he discussed the beloved program he developed in 1975.[60] Carroll's wide, mischievous smile deceived the lines of age and wisdom that danced across his face and the frail body that frustrated him with the unavoidable limitations of its eighty-four-year-old frame. "Inspired by God" while watching Saigon fall to the Communists in April 1975, Father Carroll initiated the Vietnamese Program to provide Vietnamese refugees filling the resettlement camps in Washington state with scholarships to Gonzaga University.[61]

In 1979 Father Carroll turned his attention and mission to Amerasians in South Korea after psychology professor and counselor Joseph Moisan asked for his assistance in obtaining a scholarship for an Amerasian student his family planned to host. According to Carroll, Moisan explained that coming to America and attending school was the only way this young Amerasian man "could be in contact with his father's heritage, learn English, [and] gain a superior education."[62] Father Carroll agreed to pray about Moisan's request and the "misery of Amerasians, the moral responsibility of Americans, and the need to cooperate with the goodness of Mr. Moisan."[63]

By 1980 Father Carroll had become a champion of the Amerasian cause. Partnering with Father Alfred Keane, he labored to bring other Korean Amerasian "sons and daughters" of American citizens "home."[64]

Keane, by then the director of Amerasian affairs for Americans for International Aid, was a leading figure in the push for transnational adoption, believing it to be the best solution, especially for younger Amerasians. Although he had lived in Asia since 1958, Father Keane's first introduction to Amerasians did not occur until Christmas Eve, 1970, when he noticed a group of children described by his parishioners as the "outcasts," warming themselves at a stove near the back of his chapel. Moved by the problems facing the children because of their "American faces," Father Keane took up the cause of South Korea's large Amerasian population.[65] In 1979 he lobbied relentlessly for McKinney's HR 3439, calling on over twenty-five congressmen to support the bill. Like Father Carroll, a fundamental belief in family, nation, and faith drove Keane's activism for Amerasians, who both priests believed were American children and American citizens who should have the "right to come home."[66] In fact, according to Father Carroll, the initial efforts of both men focused on pressuring policymakers to grant Amerasians U.S. citizenship. It made sense, he explained, that the children of American citizen fathers would be American citizens. However, the growing economic and social concerns over foreigners coming to America during the Reagan era ensured that citizenship was unlikely. Congress, Carroll explained, "wouldn't have anything to do with it."[67]

Five years after the Vietnam War, members of Congress continued to hear the discontent and, sometimes, racism in opposition to Vietnamese immigrants and refugees. Illustrative of this sentiment were the comments of one concerned couple from Greenwich, Connecticut, who wrote to their congressman Stewart McKinney that the Vietnamese immigrants were not "of the same caliber of the immigrants of the early 1900's [sic] who sought freedom and had pride in themselves to work and provide for themselves. They sought no financial aid—quite a comparison to what these immigrants are *demanding today.*"[68] More hostile complaints cited the tax burden and unemployment that accompanied refugees and pointed to their connection to the war. One angry American described his position to the *New York Times*: "These people didn't have the guts to fight for their own country. They are lazy, corrupt and cowardly . . . and they breed like flies . . . we have too many Orientals now. We are losing our national character."[69] Father Carroll received numerous letters expressing similar sentiments compounded by economic angst and vitriol toward Amerasians specifically. "Haven't you heard of unemployment in this country?" asked one anonymous writer. "Who is going to support these bastards?" Another threatened, "We are going to send every Asian brat right back where they came from, and you with them . . . we're going to rid the country of foreign trash."[70]

Despite such resentment, Father Carroll and Father Keane continued to advocate U.S. citizenship for Amerasians. They understood that the patrilineal culture of many Asian countries, including South Korea and Vietnam, necessitated paternal legitimacy, and that "in Asia, the children belong to their father."[71] For those Amerasians abandoned by or unknown to their individual American father, the curse of illegitimacy meant the absence of identity through name, nationality, ancestry, and family, all of which directly determined access to education, marriage, and jobs.[72] In daily life, illegitimacy made them victims of abuse, harassment, and exclusion; in Korea they were marked as the *ai-ee-no-koo*, "person who belongs to no one," and in Vietnam as "half breed" or the "dust of life."[73] In Vietnam the association of Amerasians with the war further complicated their existence. Although Amerasians did have Vietnamese citizenship, Vietnam officials considered them the "children of the enemy" and insisted the United States take its children home.[74]

Fathers Keane and Carroll agreed. They believed that U.S. leaders could alleviate the consequences of illegitimacy for Amerasians by taking national paternal responsibility and granting them U.S. citizenship.[75] "All we really need," Keane explained, was for the "American government to admit the truth. These are children of U.S. citizens, their own flesh and blood. But if we get the government to say that, what it means is that these children will have a category . . . by which they would be able to immigrate to the United States."[76] In fact, Father Keane spent much of 1980 and 1981 on Capitol Hill unsuccessfully lobbying lawmakers to grant Amerasians citizenship. After having his efforts rejected by lawmakers uninterested in even discussing it, however, Keane accepted that they were fighting a losing battle.[77] Frustrated with the failure of U.S. leaders to accept a collective paternal responsibility and cognizant of the challenges facing a push for citizenship, both men focused their efforts on the more attainable goal of passing the AIA. At every chance, however, Keane and Carroll emphasized Amerasians' Americanness and reminded policymakers that Amerasians "are children of U.S. citizens."[78] Their hope was to convince legislators who viewed them as Asian children or foreign immigrants that they were in fact American.

The Flight Attendant and the Humanitarian

In the mid 1980s Christian motivational speaker Zig Ziglar described Jodie Darragh as a typical middle-class mother and homemaker: smart, pretty, compassionate, and energetic.[79] As a stewardess for Eastern Airlines during the 1970s, Darragh witnessed the miserable conditions of the Amerasian children in Vietnam while volunteering to chaperone Vietnamese and Amerasian orphans to the United States for adoption. As with Fathers Carroll and Keane, faith inspired Darragh to act on behalf of the children and she believed that rescuing them from the dire conditions in Vietnam was "God's work."[80] In 1974 Darragh expressed her own desire to adopt a Vietnamese girl whose mother had abandoned her to the An Lac orphanage in Saigon and whose Vietnamese father refused to relinquish his child. "The father loves his little girl," explained Darragh, "still I wish we could buy her little dresses."[81] In 1975 she and her husband Richard "Dick" Darragh, a ticket office manager for Eastern Airlines, founded Americans for International Aid, an international volunteer agency based in Marietta, Georgia. Through this organization volunteer flight attendants used their free travel passes to fly "mercy missions" to escort children from developing countries like Vietnam to adoption agencies, relief missions, hospitals, and American families awaiting the chance to adopt.[82] During Operation Babylift, Darragh played a critical and controversial role in the mass evacuation of Vietnamese and Amerasian orphans, many of whom lawsuits would later reveal were not orphans at all.[83]

Still, Darragh believed that her actions were righteous as she and Dick continued to dedicate their lives to "serving, and saving, children."[84]

Arguably, Darragh's most important role was uniting the efforts of political and nonpolitical advocates on the Amerasian issue. In 1973 Darragh first brought the Amerasians to the attention of future senator and eventual cosponsor of the AIA Jeremiah Denton. Shortly after, Darragh met Father Keane, whom she appointed as the director of Amerasian affairs for Americans for International Aid in 1978. In 1979 she allied her organization with the PSBF to support McKinney's United States–Asian Immigration Act, and in 1981 and 1982 Darragh lobbied on behalf of the AIA and supported granting citizenship to Amerasians. Amerasians, she insisted, "are humans who deserve all the rights U.S. citizenship can afford them."[85] During the Reagan administration, Darragh proved a reliable Amerasian proponent and a fierce ally of Representative McKinney. She testified before Congress in support of the AIA and all of its subsequent proposed revisions and proved an effective and sympathetic spokesperson able to keep the issue in the public eye.[86]

From the PSBF headquarters in Perkasie, Pennsylvania, executive director John Shade described the failure to grant Amerasians U.S. citizenship as a "human rights violation" perpetrated by an irresponsible U.S. military.[87] During his tenure at the foundation, Shade contributed an aggressive humanitarian voice in support of the AIA. He characterized America's previous failures to take responsibility for Amerasians through more reasonable adoption policies and the granting of U.S. citizenship to be a bipartisan legislative failure of epic proportions. In 1981 Shade publicly criticized the nation's problematic history of producing mixed-race GI babies in Asia beginning with the Filipino mestizos in 1898. Like many Amerasian supporters, he often compared the Americans unfavorably to the French in their handling of the issue. Shade was also unapologetically critical of what he termed "U.S. military birth control"—the nonfraternization policies that overlooked brothels and the military practice of discouraging servicemen from marrying Asian women and quickly removing or returning home those soldiers who desired to do so. "America," Shade argued, "cannot continue fathering thousands upon thousands of mixed-race children each year and abandoning them when they see life."[88] It was not, however, just the military that drew Shade's wrath; it was the way the military policies and practices worked in tandem with the sex-based distinction in U.S. citizenship law. Together, Shade argued, the laws allowed U.S. officials to ignore the half-American offspring fathered by U.S. servicemen, whom he described as "the flesh of our flesh and the blood of our blood."[89]

For Shade, the Amerasian issue incorporated three major concerns—fatherlessness, race, and age. In accord with Fathers Keane and Carroll, Shade contended that the absence of the father was the key to Amerasians' plight since children without fathers in Asian societies do not legally exist. Race compounded fatherlessness and illegitimacy as it often made Amerasians easy to identify, visibly disrupting the largely homogenous Asian societies in which they lived. Amerasians, Shade explained, "represent disorder in an otherwise ordered world."[90] In Vietnam, Shade claimed, "an uncomfortable memory of war" further complicated the Amerasian existence. The Socialist Republic of Vietnam does not recognize the children of its former enemy as citizens, Shade claimed, and thus Amerasians exist as "non-persons," lacking even the basic provisions of life.[91]

Although Shade believed that Amerasians were half-Americans and "half-Americans are Americans," he also noted that the rapidly maturing population of Amerasians in Vietnam required urgent action.[92] At the same time that Amerasians grew into their "American" features, making their paternity undeniable, age transformed Amerasians from innocent children into troublesome teenagers. Sympathetic Americans committed to saving helpless children from Vietnam ironically had little interest in rescuing young adults. The older they became, the less adoptable Amerasians were and the more difficult it would be for Americans to accept the notion that these children deserved citizenship. As the *New York Times* reported in July 1982, "time is running out for America to claim its children. They will always, indelibly, be American. They will not long remain children."[93] Furthermore, Amerasians who had already reached adolescence could now recognize their own racial differences and the resulting discrimination and social exclusion. The consequences of illegitimacy, Shade argued, already gripped many Amerasians as they "understand their origins and know that acceptance and integration within their Asian home countries will be slow and hard coming."[94] In her study of Vietnamese Amerasians, psychologist Joyce Anis found that most Amerasians became aware of their mixed identities between six and fourteen years of age. Many recognized their phenotypic differences of skin color, facial features, and hair along with the absence of their biological fathers through the harsh words and hard punches of family members and classmates.[95] One Amerasian girl became aware that her eye shape, hair color, and skin tone were different from her classmates only after they began to tease her: "Maybe 7 or 8 years old they started calling me half breed, you know, and then I realized oh I have a Vietnamese mother and American soldier father. And my face was different, you know, my nose was higher because over there most people have a flatter nose, their eyes are smaller and I have bigger eyes."[96]

Understanding the harm caused by Amerasians' awareness of their Americanness, Shade remained adamant that U.S. policymakers grant them citizenship. He believed it illogical that they even be in the same discussions with immigrants and refugees considering they were the children of American fathers. Because Amerasians are American, Shade exclaimed in 1981, they "'have more right to be citizens of this country than Cubans and Haitians.'"[97] In his testimony before Congress regarding the proposed AIA in November 1981, Shade continued to assert that Amerasians were American citizens. By recognizing them as children of American fathers and on that basis expediting their departure to the United States, the AIA, Shade claimed, was "in line with the traditional formal U.S. Government position that basic human rights are obligations owed by all governments to its citizens."[98] As with Fathers Carroll and Keane before him, Shade too found his demands for citizenship largely ignored by U.S. policymakers unwilling or unable to fully embrace Amerasians as Americans. Still, Shade's vocal dedication to the Amerasians on behalf of the PSBF would prove central to the passage of the AIA.

The Politicians

Rep. Stewart McKinney first met the Darraghs and Father Keane in 1978. They shared a personal sense of responsibility for a population they understood to exist only as the result of U.S. foreign policy and war. In his 1982 testimony before the Senate Judiciary Committee in support of the AIA, McKinney expressed his frustration with the direction of the debates, "I have a difficult time after all these years even using the word 'immigration' in the same sentence with these [Amerasian] children. In essence, these are not immigrants. These are American children."[99] McKinney's Republican colleague in the Senate, Jeremiah Denton (R-AL), a Vietnam veteran and former prisoner of war, cosponsored the AIA with McKinney. A native of Mobile, Alabama, Denton attended the U.S. Naval Academy and earned a graduate degree from George Washington University in 1964 before deploying to Vietnam. In July 1965, after only one month of flying combat missions in the Vietnam War, enemy forces shot down Denton's plane and captured him. Over the next seven years Denton's North Vietnamese captors starved, tortured, and beat him. On May 17, 1966, Denton managed a small retribution after blinking the word T-O-R-T-U-R-E in Morse code during a North Vietnamese propaganda interview to a horrified American television audience. When asked about American war atrocities in that same interview, a defiant Denton replied, "I don't know what is happening in Vietnam because the only news sources I have are North Vietnamese. But whatever the position of my government is, I believe in it, I support it, and I will support it as long as I live."[100]

After almost a decade as a POW, Denton finally found himself on a flight home in 1973 as part of Operation Homecoming.[101] Serendipitously, airline stewardess Jodie Darragh accompanied him.[102] Perhaps in the midst of friendly conversation Darragh described to Denton her experiences transporting Vietnam War orphans to America and she spoke specifically of Amerasians. Although Denton was primarily concerned at that time with his own reintegration into American society, over the next decade Darragh and Americans for International Aid kept him informed about the Amerasians.[103]

After his election to the U.S. Senate in 1981, the devout Catholic, right-wing conservative, and father of seven became the first Republican from Alabama elected to the U.S. Senate since Reconstruction. Denton gained a reputation in Washington for his passionate commitment to restoring morality to the nation with a specific focus on children, teenage chastity, adoption, and the preservation of the nuclear family. The pro-life proponent committed much of his agenda to preserving and protecting the lives of children. He was a strong advocate for the Head Start programs and for promoting adoption as an alternative to abortion among teenage mothers. In 1981 Ronald Reagan signed Denton's Adolescent Family Life Act into law, encouraging voluntary and confidential adoption options for pregnant teenagers. That same year Denton held hearings as the chair of the Subcommittee on Aging, Family, and Human Services on incentivizing American families to adopt infants and special needs children, including racial minorities.[104]

As senator, Denton also remembered the Amerasians. He spoke again to his old acquaintance Darragh, who introduced him to Father Keane, whose faith-based work and focus on family she knew would spark Denton's interest.[105] As a war veteran, Denton knew that the problem of illegitimately fathered children overseas was real. It was an issue of morality, family, and faith. Like McKinney, Denton vehemently believed in the nation's moral responsibility and paternal obligation to Amerasians. For these reasons he agreed to partner with his House colleague to cosponsor the AIA. Amerasians, Denton explained, "must not be abandoned by this Nation as they were abandoned by their fathers."[106] It was time, Denton strongly believed, for America to "bring these children home."[107]

Although Denton's commitment to Amerasians reflected a political career dedicated to "caring about the born," his biggest contribution to the AIA was his support for the Reagan administration's insistence on amending the language of the bill regarding the fathers. Seven months removed from the fiery exchanges in the House over "looks" and "blood" and having had its evidentiary argument for blood tests debunked, the Reagan administration refocused its resistance to the

AIA on protecting veterans and the nation's reputation from the implications of paternity. Specifically, the administration opposed the House version of the bill because it identified the presumed father as an active member of the U.S. military. Denton suggested a more general definition that would affect a broader population of Amerasians—replacing the military requirement for paternity with the less specific "U.S. citizen."[108]

The esteemed member of the Veteran's Affairs Committee clearly spoke for many of his military brethren concerned with protecting the individual identities of American servicemen and the image of the U.S. military and Vietnam veterans in particular as he reminded the Senate that the fathers of many Amerasians were nonmilitary and nongovernmental personnel.[109] Denton's claims certainly aligned with the beliefs of the administration, whose main concern, according to U.S. ambassador and assistant secretary for consular affairs Diego Asencio, was the requirement that the father was a "member of the U.S. Armed Forces at the time of conception."[110] Despite McKinney's attempt to clarify that the AIA did not make any effort to "identify the actual father" but only to establish that the child had a U.S. citizen father, the administration remained adamant that civilian U.S. citizens fathered "substantial numbers of these children." In order for the administration to support the bill, they argued that the language must change.[111]

No longer concerned apparently with fraud and immigration, the administration carefully centered its position on the bill around protecting the image of U.S. servicemen abroad and, in turn, maintaining a policy of irresponsibility.[112] When asked by Sen. Alan Simpson (R-WY) if the administration might consider a long-term solution to the Amerasian problem given the continued presence of U.S. troops in Asia, Ambassador Asencio replied with laughter, "I just can't imagine what that could be," before continuing with the very vague, "I think we would have to take the effects of stationing troops abroad as a given, and adjust accordingly."[113] Simpson did not push for further explanation.

Still, Denton's sponsorship of the AIA placed the conservative politician in an unlikely alliance with a progressive media then generating

American sympathy for Amerasians through television documentaries, photographs, and stories. Even famed *Washington Post* political columnist Mary McGrory, who previously blasted the Reagan administration for its "shameful treatment" of Amerasians, commended Denton for his commitment to the issue.[114] Even so, Denton fell short of supporting citizenship for Amerasians and used the term *citizenship* much more cautiously than his political counterpart in the House. Without specifically claiming that Amerasians deserved citizenship and thereby fully recognizing them as American children, Denton did advocate for their right to immigrate and live in the country of their fathers where he believed they would have a better life. The AIA, Denton claimed, would "give the Amerasian children the same immigration preference enjoyed by other children of American citizens" and provide "these children of Americans the benefit of their birthright."[115]

The Veterans and the *Bui Doi*

In December 1981 a "special edition" of *Newsweek* magazine brought the challenges facing Vietnam veterans years removed from the war to the attention of Americans. The article, soon to become a book, profiled the men of Charlie Company and the enormous struggles they experienced readjusting to American society after fighting a losing war.[116] The article exposed the prevalence of alcoholism, addiction, and suicide among Vietnam veterans and offered a tragic picture of the enormous and long-lasting physical and psychological effects on those who served and who returned home to an unsympathetic public that did not honor them for their sacrifices.[117]

In 1978 Vietnam veteran Bobby Muller, an intelligent, charismatic, and tough-talking New Yorker, founded the Vietnam Veterans of America (VVA), an organization dedicated to assisting Vietnam veterans and addressing the larger meaning of the Vietnam experience.[118] Muller enlisted in the Marines in 1967 to avoid the draft and, in his own words, to "prove his manhood."[119] Eight months into his deployment, Muller took a bullet to the chest that severed his spine, leaving him paralyzed from the chest down. He spent a year recovering at Kingsbridge VA hospital in the Bronx, New York, where the horrendous conditions in the dilapidated and overcrowded facility motivated Muller to advocate for Vietnam veterans.[120] Under his leadership, the VVA sought to improve veterans' benefits in education, counseling, health care, and addressing the effects of Agent Orange. Muller also made it his mission to help veterans overcome the trauma of the war.

Although a number of other veterans' groups also emerged to address the unique challenges faced by Vietnam veterans, the VVA soon became the largest and most politically powerful.[121] In 1981 the VVA had the necessary political leverage to help veterans become reconciled to their experiences by returning to Vietnam.[122] Despite the absence of diplomatic relations between the two countries, Muller believed that American and Vietnamese war veterans could find resolution on shared issues, including Agent Orange and soldiers still missing in action. The purpose, Muller explained, was "to relate to the Vietnamese as people instead of relating to them as . . . g——s."[123]

In December of that year, Muller and three other combat vets flew to Hanoi on the first of many trips of reconciliation. *New York Times* reporter Bernie Weinraub accompanied the group. Weinraub wrote a series of articles about the trip and on December 27, 1981, his fifth report, "Tears as the Past Is Remembered," described the "swarms of begging half-American children" that surrounded the veterans every time they left their hotel in Ho Chi Minh City.[124] It also included numerous photographs of "American-faced" children with the VVA veterans complete with captions that emphasized Amerasians' "Americanness" and their desire to be American. One caption explained how the children touched the arms of the veterans, "besieged them with photographs and letters, struggled to speak English and gazed at the four with awe."[125] Weinraub framed the children as another tragedy of the war, and his story caught the attention of *Times* publisher Arthur Sulzberger, whose interest in the Amerasians led to a series of editorials. The publicity about Amerasians by such a reputable media source increased public awareness and desire to help the half-American kids on the streets of Vietnam.[126]

The timing could not have been better. Weinraub's article appeared a month after the initial House hearings on the AIA. While those hearings revealed greater congressional support for the bill than McKinney's 1979 legislation, the AIA seemed destined for failure as well because of the Reagan administration's arguments regarding proof of paternity, fraud, and blood tests. Unlike previous stories about Amerasians that focused on their victimization by the Vietnamese Communists, Weinraub's reports skillfully linked Amerasians directly to American veterans and the United States, implying to readers that Amerasians were American children. Just like the twenty-five hundred U.S. servicemen missing from the war, Weinraub insinuated Amerasians too, were Americans and the nation had a responsibility to bring them home. At the same time, Weinraub shifted the blame for Amerasians and their dire existence from the Vietnamese Communists to an irresponsible U.S. government. It was not, the *Times* reported in July 1982, that Vietnam will not let Amerasians out, but that "America won't let them in."[127]

The VVA took its second trip of reconciliation in May 1982. The agenda for this trip included discussions with Vietnamese officials concerning Amerasians, MIAs, and the effects of Agent Orange. CBS news reporter Mike Wallace joined the trip. Upon arriving in Ho Chi Minh City, young Amerasian street kids surrounded Wallace and the VVA members, asking them if they were their fathers. Among the group was one freckle-faced, hazel-eyed ten-year-old named Le Van Minh whose clear "American face" and severe physical deformities captured Wallace's attention. Likely because of his physical challenges, his "American" features, and his age, Minh's Amerasian peers often deliberately placed him in front of Western tourists and journalists. The more attention and sympathy they could garner from foreigners, the more money they could make. Although Minh's physical challenges were the result of polio, those who saw Minh often wrongly assumed him to be the victim of Agent Orange poisoning, which made him an even more tragic figure. Most people could not stop staring at him.

Since the end of the Vietnam War the accounts of media outlets, humanitarian organizations, and visitors contributed to the popular, but often false, narrative that all Amerasians in Vietnam were abandoned, orphaned street children whose "American faces" marked them for discrimination and marginalization.[128] In reality, while reports did validate their marginalized status in Vietnamese society, the majority of Amerasians in Vietnam were not homeless or orphans. A 1994 study found that 75 percent of Amerasians surveyed identified their mother or grandmother as their primary caretaker, and 8 percent lived with adoptive parents.[129] However, repeated reports of half-American children asking Western visitors "Are you my daddy?" strengthened assumptions that Amerasians were orphaned and homeless.

Recognizing the domestic and geopolitical power of pity, U.S. and Vietnamese officials reinforced the portrayal of Amerasians as homeless and suffering war orphans but shifted the narrative in terms of who was to blame.[130] Vietnam officials condemned the United States for abandoning its children and promoted the Amerasians as just another example of the hypocrisy of an American democracy that failed to fulfill its international and humanitarian obligations. Vietnamese leaders insinuated that just as the United States had *Americanized* the war before deserting its South Vietnamese allies, U.S. soldiers had *Americanized* and then abandoned their Amerasian children.[131]

Seeking to move the conversation away from the sexual improprieties of their soldiers abroad, members of Congress and the Reagan administration presented the Amerasians as the persecuted orphan victims of the evil Vietnamese Communists. By framing Amerasians as a population the United States could save from communism rather than one it irresponsibly reproduced, American leaders could enhance the nation's global humanitarian reputation and condemn communism and Vietnam.[132] The ability of Americans to personalize the Amerasians and recognize them as both abandoned and American children proved critical to the U.S. postwar narrative. Only by imagining Amerasians as forsaken and ascribing them an American identity could the United States properly "save" them from communism. As historian Laura Briggs writes, "an infant alone is a disturbing picture" that calls us to "pick the child up and comfort it if its parents cannot be found."[133]

For their part, Amerasians begging on the streets of Saigon were also well versed in the power of story, and they invested fully in the American narrative. Survival on the streets required a certain kind of savvy, and Amerasians quickly discovered that the combination of their "American" looks with their individual stories of abandonment and abuse proved particularly effective at provoking an emotional response from Westerners that equated to food, goods, and money. By exploiting the lingering tensions of war and guilt and employing the power of their paternity, some Amerasians perfected the art of an emotional diplomacy critical to their survival. Those Amerasians with clear "Western" features—blue eyes, blond hair, dark skin, afros, freckles—were better equipped to acquire more goods from onlookers.[134] Americans in particular soothed their guilt through giving, in hopes that these tiny contributions might atone for their sins and offer Amerasians some relief.

With "the personality and the physical situation to really be a tear jerker for folks," Le Van Minh proved a gifted diplomat.[135] VVA leader Greg Kane met Minh on numerous trips to Ho Chi Minh City and observed him telling different versions of his personal story to sympathetic Americans. After watching Minh and a younger Amerasian change their stories for Mike Wallace who appeared taken by the tales, Kane warned Wallace, "you know, this kid has eight different stories, which story is he telling you?"[136] Although the story that Minh told was generally true, the details around his homelessness and his abandonment seemed to shift depending on the audience. When Minh begged for money to feed his mother, stepfather, and brothers, he understood that he could provoke a more lucrative response from Westerners by making himself an orphan who was first abandoned by his American father and then rejected by his Vietnamese mother.[137] At times, Minh would falsely claim that his mother had died. However, Kane admits that regardless of the stories they told, Amerasians were "out on the street for one reason or another and Amerasian kids did not get treated well."[138] Such story-shifts by Minh and other Amerasians were central to their survival, an assertion of agency critical for a population with very little power.

With his 1982 *60 Minutes* documentary "Honor Thy Children,"

Wallace managed to capture the plight of Amerasians in Vietnam along with an Emmy nomination. His report highlighted the tragedy of Amerasians' abandonment and marginalization in Vietnam and incited American sympathy and support for Amerasians at a critical point for the AIA. Like Weinraub, however, Wallace did not blame American fathers for deserting their children or Vietnam's Communist government for persecuting them. Rather, he suggested that the real culprit was the U.S. government. The Reagan administration, he implied, prevented American veterans who wanted to father their children from retrieving them from Vietnam. Perhaps taking a cue from Reagan's own revisionism that blamed inept U.S. civilian leadership rather than an ineffective military for losing Vietnam, Wallace insinuated that the U.S government, not the American people, continued to act inhumanely in Vietnam.[139]

To prove the point that the Amerasian problem was one of policy rather than persons, Wallace presented evidence throughout the report that Amerasians were, in fact, Americans and not Vietnamese. He also profiled the frustrated efforts of two U.S. servicemen whose attempts to retrieve their Amerasian children had been ignored by U.S. officials, who insisted their children were not Americans. One boy, he explained, claiming to be an American said "he felt like an American . . . because he had an American father." Vietnam veteran Roger Bott appeared visibly frustrated with the U.S. government's unwillingness to assist in bringing his Amerasian son home. Bott also emphasized his child's Americanness, explaining to Wallace, "It seems the older he gets . . . the more American he looks."[140]

Other veterans shared Bott's resentment and likewise blamed the Reagan administration for deliberately keeping their children in Vietnam. A few months prior to Wallace's report, veteran Gary Tanous of Washington State sent a handwritten plea to President Reagan to intervene in bringing his Amerasian daughter, Jeanna Mare Tanous, to America.[141] According to Tanous, Hanoi refused to grant his daughter an exit visa to leave Vietnam despite the fact that Tanous had legitimated her through marriage, making her a U.S. citizen. Jeanna even possessed a U.S. passport.[142] Months later, having never received a response from the president, an exasperated Tanous blamed Reagan for his daughter's situation and condemned the administration's refusal to recognize her as an American. "I have received absolutely no cooperation from American authorities. They don't want anything to do with a Vietnamese and they keep reminding me that Jean Marie is half Vietnamese."[143]

Wallace also interviewed John Shade, who continued to attack the irresponsibility of U.S. leaders and implied that their failure to act on behalf of Amerasians was criminal. According to Shade, regarding "the children we fathered in wedlock and out of wedlock in Asia, we have had a silent policy of child abandonment, because that's what it is, it is child abuse."[144] Some Vietnamese mothers agreed. Between 1980 and 1982, numerous women wrote to U.S. officials asking for permission for their Amerasian children to emigrate to the United States. One mother implored all Americans to remember their offspring in Vietnam: "We hope you don't forgetting We [sic] children orphans right now living VN."[145] During his report, Wallace described the numerous Vietnamese mothers who gave letters and photographs to Western journalists and tourists asking them to help their Amerasian children leave Vietnam. When asked why she would allow her children to go to the United States without her, one mother explained that in America, they would have education, protection, and care.[146] Such pleas exposed Vietnam's indifference toward Amerasians and reminded Americans that Amerasians in Vietnam were citizens without a state.[147]

In the closing moments of his show, amid an array of photographs of "American-faced" Amerasian children, Wallace summed up the futile situation facing Amerasians in Vietnam for his audience. "Only a handful of Amerasian children," Wallace explained, "perhaps a dozen, have been able to immigrate to the United States from Vietnam." He reminded viewers that Vietnam was willing to release all Amerasians to the United States and that the AIA was currently under consideration in Congress.[148]

"Honor Thy Children" aired on September 19, 1982, in the midst of the final congressional debates over the AIA. For many American viewers the report was a powerful visual reminder of America's war in Vietnam and of the nation's responsibility to the Amerasian children. Surprisingly, Wallace did not profile Minh and his cameraman failed to capture even his image. Still, Wallace reminded American viewers that they had a responsibility to save Amerasians in Vietnam, which they could do by pressuring their congresspersons to pass the Amerasian Immigration Act. One week later, Sen. Denton referenced Wallace's report in Congress. He reminded the members of both the House and Senate of the public attention the television program brought to the issue and its emphasis on passing the AIA in the current congressional session. According to Denton, "With each day that we delay, the Amerasian children who are our responsibility because they are half American, are further away from escaping the discrimination that is caused by their mixed heritage."[149]

Amerasian advocates including Fathers Keane and Carroll and John Shade also increased their pressure on Congress to pass the AIA. They knew for the legislation to be successful Congress had to disassociate Amerasians from Asia and accept them as American children. Accordingly, while lobbying congressional representatives, Father Keane deliberately stopped using the term "Amerasian" and instead referred to the children as the "abandoned Americans left in Asia."[150] This was a critical semantic shift that further served to ascribe Amerasians an American identity. Congressmen McKinney and Denton followed in Keane's footsteps. In the June 1982 Senate hearings on the AIA, Senator Denton urged his colleagues to recognize Amerasians as Americans, explaining that "the word 'Amerasian,' of course, derives its first two syllables from 'America.'"[151]

Their efforts appeared to pay off. On September 28, 1982, the AIA unanimously passed the Senate, and Denton quickly urged House members to consider the *60 Minutes* report and to pass the AIA without delay.[152] On October 1, 1982, the House did pass the AIA, but not before amending the Senate version of the bill to protect Amerasians from exploitation once in the United States.[153] The amendments, according to Sen. Ronald Mazzoli (R-KY), preserved "the spirit of the bill" in recognizing Amerasians' American paternity and offering immigration rights while eliminating potential problems.[154] The House version included safeguards to ensure the legitimacy of the sponsorship process and required the involvement of the state child welfare agencies and public and private agencies familiar with international adoption and placement. It also directed the attorney general to file regular reports regarding the bill and its effects on family separation and dislocation.[155]

Members of the House lauded the passage of the AIA as a bipartisan victory and commended the efforts of McKinney, whom Rep. Hamilton Fish Jr. (R-NY) labeled "the conscience of the Congress," for bringing the Amerasians to the forefront of public attention.[156] McKinney credited "citizen supporters" for developing a "national lobbying network that would make many politicians jealous."[157] As did previous policies, and limited by the sex-based distinction in U.S. immigration and citizenship law, the AIA contributed a new framework for how policymakers would approach contested identities of race and nation, navigating between the national narrative of inclusivity and the perennial concern for the security of U.S. borders. After years of refusing to formally recognize Amerasians' American paternity and insisting that they were just like all other Vietnamese refugees, U.S. policymakers now eagerly embraced Amerasians as "our children" and the "forgotten sons and daughters of U.S. citizens."[158] But while they used an inclusionary discourse to describe Amerasians as Americans, they declined to include citizenship in the bill, and thus excluded them from the rights and privileges accorded to Americans. Furthermore, even after Congress passed the AIA, the Reagan administration continued to insist that without evidentiary proof of their "American blood," Amerasians were not really American. Nonetheless, the AIA served as formal recognition by the U.S. government of Amerasians' American paternity and provided a pathway for some Amerasians to immigrate to America.

Conclusion

The process of passing the AIA exposed how the racial and national ambiguities in the Amerasian mixture vexed American understandings of identity and belonging. By the time the AIA became law, a general consensus about Amerasians existed among U.S. policymakers, humanitarians, and the American public. Amerasians were the children of American fathers conceived as a result of the U.S. presence in the Vietnam War. Their American paternity subjected them to abuse, discrimination, and exclusion in Vietnam. The majority of them did not know their fathers and were therefore illegitimate. They were largely poor, uneducated, and undernourished, and they were getting older. They were one of the most tragic scars of the American conflict in Vietnam.

Over the next three years, Amerasians in Vietnam would continue to fall victim to diplomatic tensions between the United States and Vietnam, hindering efforts at reconciliation. Both countries continued to politicize Amerasians to their own ends. Vietnam pointed to the failure of the AIA to allow the mothers or relatives of Amerasian children to immigrate with them to the United States and condemned the absence of U.S. citizenship in the bill. The United States continued to condemn Vietnam's discrimination against Amerasians as evidence of the evils of communism.[159] Each government blamed the other for the program's inefficiency and both ignored the effect on the Amerasian children, victims of the entire process.[160]

| Chapter Five

Window Dressing

President Reagan signed the Amerasian Immigration Act into law on October 22, 1982, describing it as a reflection of American humanitarianism and a commitment to family reunification.[1] Representative McKinney and Senator Denton joined Reagan at the signing ceremony along with Father Alfred Keane's sister Judy and her two daughters, two Korean Amerasians sent by Father Carroll named Eddie Choi and Jini Choi (unrelated), Jodie and Dick Darragh, and John Shade. President Reagan deemed the AIA a "good and humane law."[2] He declared it to be a "major step" in the national effort to meet its moral responsibility to children who, "through no fault of their own," have "frequently lived in the most wretched of circumstances and often have been ostracized in the lands of their birth."[3] The AIA, he claimed, would reunite "these children with those who will love and care for them" and it "recognized the rightful claim of Amerasian children to American citizenship."[4]

Three days after signing the AIA, President Reagan sent congratulatory letters to all of the major political actors involved in passing the bill. He personally thanked Father Keane for bringing the "thousands of children born in Asia to United States citizen fathers to the attention of the American public and government."[5] He also specifically commended Senator Denton and Representative McKinney for their efforts on behalf of the Amerasian children, whom he described as "forgotten by our laws, but not by our people." The AIA, Reagan reiterated, was "the first step toward welcoming these children home."[6]

Reagan's warm words of belonging and acceptance, however, proved misleading. The AIA did not welcome Amerasians "home" nor did it reunite them with their American fathers or families. Although the AIA did formally recognize Amerasians as "children of United States citizens" and gave them immigration preference to the United States, a number of limitations—financial requirements, family separation, the absence of diplomatic relations with Vietnam—greatly restricted the AIA's effect. Furthermore, citizenship was not part of the bill. At the same time Congress criticized Vietnam for denying Amerasians the "dignity and rights of true citizenship" and for its treatment of Amerasians as others, its own members refused to even discuss the issue of citizenship in debating the bill. Such an omission ensured that absent the legitimation of their individual American fathers, Amerasians were not legally American citizens.[7]

Between 1982 and 1986 the AIA failed to adequately address the Amerasian problem in Vietnam, proving more semantic than substantive. Viewing the Amerasians as convenient and effective political tools in its continuing Cold War conflict with Vietnam, the Reagan administration subjugated the interests of Amerasians to other issues. Specifically it focused on the normalization of diplomatic relations between the United States and Vietnam and the domestic debates over immigration generally.

Legal Limitations

Amerasian advocates had applauded the signing of the AIA into law as a positive step by the Reagan administration toward recognition of national paternal responsibility. However, in addition to the exclusion of citizenship, they criticized limitations in the legislation that deterred or disqualified Amerasians from applying. First, although the AIA designated qualifying Amerasians as immigrants, only those who had guaranteed financial support from an American family or private charitable agency could benefit. Since most Amerasians neither knew an American family or agency willing to sponsor them nor had access to the resources required to make such connections, this requirement effectively presented an insurmountable barrier to emigration.

Second, the AIA only allowed for Amerasians themselves to relocate to the United States. It did not include their biological mother or other family members, thus rendering it a policy of family separation. Critics argued that this omission contradicted the fundamental tenets of an inclusive, humanitarian, and family-focused immigration policy. It unnecessarily divided families and separated children from their birth mothers. In 1982, the majority of Amerasians in Vietnam were still children who would not or could not abandon their Vietnamese families to immigrate. For Amerasian children to benefit from the legislation, they had to leave their mothers, who were forced to relinquish their parental rights, and move to a foreign country where they did not speak the language or understand the culture. For those Amerasians younger than eighteen who did immigrate to the United States but who did not have the benefit of adoption, the U.S. foster care system became their new home.[8]

Prior to its passage Vietnamese officials had voiced concerns over the proposed requirement of family separation, viewing it as evidence that U.S. policymakers were not really committed to cooperation on the Amerasian issue. They emphasized that their willingness to assist in expediting the departure process for Amerasians depended upon America's ability to keep families together.[9] Donald Colin, the head of the U.S. Refugee Program responsible for the departure of Amerasians, summed up Vietnam's position, saying Hanoi would not allow Amerasian children to leave alone, and "they don't intend to cooperate if the mothers are split from their children."[10]

Some mothers of Amerasians felt equally strongly and demanded that they, too, should be included in the bill. Many of the mothers CBS reporter Mike Wallace interviewed in the spring of 1982 were terrified of the prospect of sending their children to the United States alone. When Wallace asked these mothers if they would let their Amerasian children go to America without them, one mother replied, "No . . . the mother and the children go together." Another mother gave a more emotional response, explaining, while on the verge of tears, "He's my only son."[11]

Once the AIA became law, many mothers feared being left behind. One group of seven Vietnamese mothers wrote U.S. officials explaining that because of their Amerasian children, they too were victims of discrimination and abuse. They asked the U.S. government to "save us out of the present miserable living" in Vietnam.[12] Nevertheless, the Vietnamese government's request and the mothers' pleas had little effect. Instead, U.S. officials questioned the motives of Vietnam's leaders in seeking to include women in the AIA who were condemned as prostitutes and traitors in Vietnam. Such a response further hindered collaboration between the two governments, ensuring that the AIA simply "cannot be made to work in Vietnam."[13]

Notably, the exclusion of mothers and family members from the AIA also reflected, ironically, the Reagan administration's commitment to "family values" and to winning the Cold War by remasculinizing the nation.[14] During his 1980 presidential campaign, Reagan, once divorced and often described as having a "frosty" relationship with his kids, embraced the family-values agenda of conservative evangelical voters.[15] In the post–Civil Rights era, white evangelicals held the previous decades of progress toward racial and gender equality responsible for degrading the country by destroying the family and specifically upending the role of the father. The answer to the nation's ills and immorality, according to evangelist and leader of the Moral Majority Jerry Falwell, was the restoration of the white, nuclear, patriarchal American family complete with a "breadwinning father, stay-at-home mother, and well-tended children."[16] Fathers, Falwell believed, should be strong and powerful providers and leaders. Weak men, he preached, "have weak homes, and children from these homes will probably grow up to be weaker parents leading to even weaker homes."[17] For many Americans the man who cast himself in the image of an American hero in the Oval Office and projected individual and national images of manliness embodied the qualities, values, and characteristics of the traditional American father.[18] Hence, many white, evangelical voters viewed Reagan's midwestern masculinity (credited to his Illinois roots), optimism, and staunch anticommunism as a paternal "symbol of strength in troubled times."[19]

The exclusion of the mothers from the AIA reinforced the patriarchal notions of family that informed the family-values agenda and also upheld the sex-based distinction in U.S. immigration and citizenship laws. Literally removing the mothers from the lives of their children figuratively recentered American men in their traditional and patriarchal role as fathers and emphasized the moral and paternal goodness of their efforts to save their children from Vietnam. According to UNHCR officer Frank Poli, paternal preference was evident in the power given the father by U.S. law to legitimate Amerasians and substantiate citizenship. By ignoring the fact that Amerasian children "might want to bring their mom," and forcing mothers to surrender their parental rights and release their children to U.S. authorities, the AIA legally severed the mother-child bond.[20]

Considering the failure of Congress and the Department of Defense to address the habit of U.S. troops fathering and abandoning half-American children abroad, a policy of family separation seemed especially problematic.[21] Even Representative McKinney, the AIA's co-sponsor, noted that one of its major flaws was that it failed to address the continued fathering of children by American servicemen in Asia and that it did not apply to children born after the passage of the act.[22] In light of the administration's failure to address what he believed to be the fundamental problem regarding Amerasians, the Pearl S. Buck Foundation's John Shade explained, "We must expect that such births will occur, as nothing material has changed in Asia, considering the deployment of nearly 200,000 U.S. troops in seven Asian locales. Such is not conjecture; it is certainty."[23]

Critics were equally concerned that the absence of diplomatic relations prevented the AIA's implementation in Vietnam. Contrary to the administration's public praise of the AIA and the assurances that it would bring Amerasians in Vietnam "home," the administration clearly understood the difficulty of implementing the AIA in Vietnam. One week before the final Senate vote on the bill the president addressed the issue in his daily press briefing. Included in his briefing memo regarding the legislation was the statement that the AIA "does not automatically benefit the Amerasians in Vietnam."[24] The State Department also communicated to Congress that although the AIA would work in some countries, given the lack of diplomatic or consular relations it could not be implemented in Vietnam.[25] Importantly, critics noted that even as Vietnam expressed an interest in compromising over the AIA, the Reagan administration refused. The administration appeared to value maintaining a sense of conflict with Vietnam on the Amerasian issue over finding a resolution. As Michael Nebeker, Thailand director of the PSBF explained, "Congress wrote the bill as if it were saying 'Let's make a nice gesture toward the Amerasians—but don't really let the bastards in.'"[26] Over the course of its short lifetime, the limitations of the AIA severely inhibited it from facilitating any mass immigration of Amerasians to the United States and had almost no effect in Vietnam. Indeed, after three years of implementation only 165 Amerasians immigrated to the United States under the AIA, 156 from South Korea and only four from Vietnam.[27]

Amerasian advocates also voiced their consternation over the exclusion of citizenship.[28] One month after the bill became law, John Shade wrote to President Reagan, commending the AIA as a "milestone" and "positive movement."[29] However, he also asserted that the denial of birthright citizenship to Amerasians was one of the AIA's most serious flaws. According to Shade the exclusion of citizenship was inconsistent with legislation that defined Amerasians as the "children of U.S. citizens."[30] The contradiction he posited was problematic and likely arose from the administration's politicization of the AIA as a "humanitarian remedy" and part of the administration's Cold War agenda rather than an actual solution to the Amerasian situation.[31]

Other advocates noted that the AIA did provide those Amerasian children adopted by American families or sponsored by U.S. citizens an easier path to naturalization. However it ignored the majority of Amerasians, who did not qualify for sponsorship or were too old for adoption and too young for their mothers to send them to America alone.[32] In addition, advocates deemed the requirement that an Amerasian child abandon its Vietnamese family in order to obtain U.S.

citizenship "not afforded by birthright, but by a naturalization process," to be "unfair, unethical and morally wrong."[33] Absent birthright U.S. citizenship the AIA failed, according to Shade, to remedy the lives of most Amerasians.[34] The AIA did nothing, Shade declared, to assist in these cases.[35] Despite recognizing Amerasians' American paternity, the AIA still deemed Amerasians not American enough to be citizens.[36] Under the AIA Amerasians who desired to become American citizens joined other foreign immigrants and refugees in the naturalization process, earning their citizenship through residency and passing the citizenship test. Despite their American paternity Amerasians remained foreigners.

The Human Problems

Ronald Reagan was largely unconcerned by the criticisms of the AIA and had little interest in addressing the legislation's flaws. He assumed office in 1981 riding a rising tide of American conservatism driven by a weak U.S. economy and a shifting political landscape due to demographic changes.[37] For the first time since 1954, conservatives controlled the U.S. Senate, and defenders of the Vietnam War, including Sen. Jeremiah Denton—the cosponsor of the AIA—replaced its critics in Congress. Like Reagan, Denton was promilitary and believed in showing national strength through tough talk and action. He blamed an inept U.S. government for the defeat in Vietnam and insisted that America could have won the war had it "fought to win." According to his wife, Jane, Denton believed "you don't get peace by losing respect all over the world."[38]

Key members of the Reagan administration also believed in governing through strength. During his confirmation hearing to become secretary of state, General Alexander Haig told the Senate Committee on Foreign Relations that it was time "to shed the sackcloth and ashes" the country had been wearing since the Vietnam War.[39] Secretary of Defense Casper Weinberger defended the rebuilding of the nation's military forces as necessary to meet the "immediate and dangerous threat posed by the Soviet Union" and help "erase some bad memories of the Vietnam War."[40]

Reagan personally contributed to the escalation of the Cold War through an aggressive anticommunist rhetoric that reminded Americans that they were good and that communists were bad.[41] He believed reviving rather than resolving the Cold War conflict with Vietnam to be critical to restoring American strength and pride and destroying the "Vietnam syndrome" that still plagued the country.[42] Reagan committed his administration to what would become known as the Reagan Doctrine, a muscular anticommunist and anti-Soviet foreign policy also intended to punish Vietnam.[43] As living evidence of the dangers communism posed to Americans, or at least children who looked like Americans, Amerasians were an important political and Cold War diplomatic tool in America's pursuit of a "war by other means" with Vietnam.[44]

While Reagan invested fully in the Reagan Doctrine, which depended on cutting taxes for the wealthy and increasing defense spending, he struggled to convince the American people of his human side.[45] In fact, throughout his presidency the former New Deal Democrat showed limited interest in the social issues that most directly affected the lives of the American people. During his first term in office, Reagan's advisors continuously voiced their concerns about the president's humanitarian image, or lack thereof, and they believed the AIA could offer the president a "win" with the American people. In 1982 Reagan's trusted advisor Lyn Nofziger sent a memo to White House staffers explaining the importance of the AIA in convincing the American public that Reagan worried about human issues, especially the plight of children and families. "One of the President's problems," Nofziger explained, "is that the public thinks he doesn't care about people."[46] By supporting the AIA, President Reagan could show the American public that in fact, he "cares a little bit about people."[47]

The "Great Communicator" had come honestly by his reputation of not caring about people. By combining his family values agenda with an aversion to big government, Reagan made it his mission to dismantle the social welfare apparatus that he attributed to Lyndon Johnson's Great Society and that he deemed the primary cause of the country's economic struggles.[48] The massive tax cuts and increased defense spending that defined Reagan's first term created an economic prosperity that affected only a select few. It failed to "trickle down" to the majority of Americans. Reaganomics proved disastrous for those who depended on social welfare programs like Aid to Families with Dependent Children.[49]

By the end of his first term, Reagan's domestic policies had alienated specific segments of the population and resulted in the tripling of America's debt, stagnant wages, and a growing and massive wealth disparity. It also succeeded in creating the perception of a nation divided into "tax payers and tax takers."[50] To mobilize popular support against government assistance, the administration vilified the "takers" as being poor women and racial minorities—the "welfare queen"—convincing many voters that his human concern had a price tag and a color.[51]

Democrats were quick to voice their opposition. They accused Reagan of being insensitive to human problems and particularly tone deaf on issues of racial equality, justice, and fairness. They pointed to his long history of opposing civil rights and condemned his cuts to domestic and social welfare programs, including food stamps. The Reagan Revolution, Democrats argued, was largely an attack on America's poor families, women, children, and racial minorities. In stark contrast to the majority of white Americans, these groups saw Reagan as "distant, cold and dangerously insensitive."[52]

Thus, for an administration in need of showing a more compassionate side, saving Amerasians from Vietnam by supporting the AIA appeared a wise political calculation. Nofziger knew the images of abandoned "American-faced" children in Vietnam and their stories of abuse and discrimination would have a powerful impact on the American public. Americans saw the victimization of "American-faced" children as more evidence of the evils of communism and an extension of the American experience in the Vietnam War. By supporting the AIA and "saving" Amerasians from Vietnam and from communism, Reagan could remind Americans that U.S. intervention in Vietnam remained benevolent, heroic, and necessary. Furthermore, it would show that Reagan cared about Amerasians.[53] Indeed the beauty of the legislation for the Reagan administration was in the limitations and contradictions. Officials could laud the AIA as a humanitarian success and take credit for saving "American children" from Vietnam and communism without any actual cost to the country.[54]

Normalizing a Diplomacy of the Dead

At the same time the Reagan administration claimed to be taking responsibility for Amerasians through the AIA, Vietnamese officials were increasingly agitated about the Amerasians. They viewed the "American-faced" population to be a sore spot that brought unwanted negative attention to Vietnam and caused problems within Vietnamese society. As their participation on the AIA and the ODP previously revealed, they also believed they could use the Amerasians as leverage for normalizing relations with the United States, perceived to be necessary in order to revitalize Vietnam's economy and secure its international standing.[55]

While Vietnamese leaders appeared able to suppress their animosity for their former enemy for the perceived good of the country, American leaders proved less gracious.[56] The Reagan administration had little desire to normalize relations. Reagan's anticommunist stance encouraged the continuation of the Cold War conflict with Vietnam. However, U.S. leaders could not deny diplomatic relations with Vietnam outright. In an effort to toe the line, U.S. officials appeared willing to reopen talks but insisted that a number of issues must be resolved first—Vietnam's occupation of Cambodia, a full accounting of American MIAs, and the release of reeducation camp prisoners and Amerasians.[57] In order to prove its willingness to meet U.S. demands, Vietnam attempted to cooperate on each issue. Rather than rewarding Vietnam for its efforts, the Reagan administration moved the bar in an effort to "bleed Vietnam white."[58] Thus while the Reagan administration appeared to favor normalization, it prevented actual progress toward it by blaming Vietnam for failing to do its part.[59]

This was the same approach the administration employed with the AIA. It praised the legislation for addressing the needs of Amerasians while refusing to consider the limitations that prevented the majority of them from benefiting and blaming Vietnam for the policy's failure in that country. The tactic proved incredibly effective. By praising the AIA, the administration convinced many Americans the legislation had solved the issue, causing public interest and media coverage of Amerasians to wane. At the same time the Reagan administration focused attention on the other Americans left behind in Vietnam. U.S. demands for a full accounting of the twenty-five hundred American MIAs overshadowed continuing concerns about U.S. responsibility for Amerasians.

Upon entering office, President Reagan understood that to resurrect American exceptionalism, the country needed to absolve itself of the guilt associated with the Vietnam War. Americans had to rid themselves of the anxiety that they had abandoned their brethren—the living and the dead—in a losing war effort.[60] Reagan's emphasis on Vietnam veterans and dead or missing soldiers was an important part of his Cold War anticommunist agenda and the effort to refashion public memory of the war as a noble cause worthy of America's attention.[61] He lauded Vietnam veterans as heroes and condemned Vietnam for withholding the names and remains of American POWs and MIAs.[62]

Under Reagan, American veterans of the Vietnam War had their service and sacrifice commemorated in parades, ceremonies, and memorials that helped diminish the sense of betrayal and rejection many felt from their own countrymen when they returned home from the war.[63] On Veterans Day in 1984, a crowd of a hundred thousand attended the formal dedication of the Vietnam Veterans Memorial in Washington DC. Reagan presented the shiny, V-shaped, black granite wall as a place of reconciliation and proof that America finally had begun to heal from the war.[64]

On April 30, 1985, Reagan commemorated the ten-year anniversary of the end of the Vietnam War by telling Congress that any possibility of normalizing relations with Vietnam depended on Vietnam's willingness to provide a full accounting of American MIAs.[65] Reagan emphasized his "personal dedication to this great national effort" and detailed the actions of the U.S. government "in our national goal of returning any servicemen who may still be held captive in Southeast Asia; the fullest possible accounting of those still missing; and the repatriation of all recoverable remains of those who died serving our Nation."[66]

One month later, on Memorial Day, Reagan reiterated the U.S. position. He reminded a hopeful crowd that the war in Southeast Asia "still haunts" the families of the missing and that without a full accounting, it would never end. "Today," Reagan said, "a united people call upon Hanoi with one voice: Heal the sorest wound of this conflict. Return our sons to America. End the grief of those who are innocent and undeserving of any retribution."[67] He also reminded Americans that a decade removed from the war, Vietnam was still communist, evil, and America's enemy. Even as his staunchest allies testified that there were no more American POWs remaining in Vietnam, Reagan continued to promote unsubstantiated claims and "evidence" that Americans were alive in that "d—n Communist sink hole."[68]

The Amerasian and MIA issues shared some common threads—the Vietnam War, abandonment, victimization—and the Reagan administration used them both in negotiations for normalization. However, the administration did not view them equally. While supporting the AIA and claiming to bring American children home had improved Reagan's humanitarian reputation and contributed to the narrative of American benevolence in Vietnam, it failed to keep the attention of the American public. Rather, Americans were obsessed with the stories of Americans held captive a decade after the war by an uncooperative Vietnamese government and the heroic American efforts to save them.[69] Blockbuster movies including *Rambo, First Blood*, part 1 (1982) and Part 2 (1985), and *Missing in Action* (1984) depicted heroic American veterans of the war saving surviving POWs from the torture and captivity of the barbarous Vietcong. Such a historical "inversion of victimization," in which Americans were the victims and the Vietnamese the victimizers, indoctrinated Americans to Reagan's Cold War view of Vietnam as America's perpetual enemy.[70]

The Reagan administration lent validity to the mythmaking, expanding the POW/MIA section of the Defense Intelligence Agency, devoting more resources, deploying a special team to Southeast Asia to solicit information on potential POW/MIAs from refugees, and coordinating efforts with the National League of Families of American Prisoners and Missing in Southeast Asia (NLF).[71]

For many Americans the effects of the MIA issue were deeply personal. During the 1980s retired Special Forces colonel James "Bo" Gritz organized private and futile raids into Laos to rescue POWs who he believed had been "abandoned by their government to cruel Asian communist slavery."[72] Arguably obsessed with the MIA/POW issue and his own power to "keep the forces of darkness at bay," wealthy businessman Ross Perot began funding secret and unsuccessful forays into the jungles of Vietnam to find and free POWs. The efforts of both men were extreme, earning them impressive reputations among the political MIA advocates known as the "Rambo set." However they also contributed to an aggressive public awareness campaign waged by the Reagan administration in coordination with the NLF to increase media coverage and raise "domestic consciousness of this issue to the highest level since the end of the war."[73]

For most Americans the escapades of the Rambo set failed to resonate, but the testimonies of Vietnam veterans and surviving POWs did. While campaigning in support of the AIA in 1982, former POW Sen. Jeremiah Denton described his own experience at the POW/MIA Recognition Day: "Let the Southeast Asian communists understand that the American people do hold them responsible for past and continuing atrocities and aggressions. We cannot appeal to the morality of those who have no morality. We cannot rely on the goodwill of those who have no goodwill. We cannot depend on the civilized impulses of those who behave as barbarians.... They respond only to the determination and, if necessary, the force to hold them responsible for their actions ... we will get the accounting of our MIA."[74]

Three years later, in 1985, in testimony before the Subcommittee on Asian and Pacific Affairs, former director of the Defense Intelligence Agency Lt. Gen. Eugene F. Tighe Jr. called attention to the nation's moral obligations deriving from the war. Tighe referred not to America's duty to save Amerasians from Vietnam but to the twenty-five hundred

American MIAs and those reportedly still languishing in Vietnamese prisons. He described America's commitment to this cause as "a great tribute to the human concern of the greatest nation on earth."[75]

Considering the nature of war in general and the Vietnam War in particular, with its heavy artillery, bombings, and plane crashes that literally obliterated human remains, such a demand seemed rather idealistic and largely unattainable. In no previous wars had the United States imposed such requirements. In comparison to the seventy-eight thousand missing and eighty-five hundred unidentified Americans after the Second World War and the eight thousand still missing from the Korean conflict, the twenty-five hundred American MIAs from Vietnam represented markedly few casualties.[76] As with the Amerasians, Reagan's insistence on a full accounting was less about resolution than about extending the ideological Cold War battle with Vietnam. He saw the POW/MIA issue as central to transforming the memory of the war from an American tragedy to a noble cause, with America's missing soldiers as honorable victims of a war from which they needed rescue.

In the same way that Vietnam denied American accusations that it treated Amerasians badly and prevented them from leaving the country to come to the United States, Vietnamese officials challenged the Reagan administration's assertions that they secretly held living American soldiers captive and deliberately hid the remains of the missing. In fact Vietnam surrendered its own postwar problems, including hundreds of thousands of Vietnamese MIAs for whom it lacked the resources to find or identify, and continuously expressed its devotion to resolving the American MIA/POW issue for the sake of normalization.[77]

The irony of America's obsession with its missing dead soldiers over its living children was not completely lost. One distraught U.S. citizen wrote the PSBF asking "why . . . representatives can go to Vietnam to negotiate for dead MIA's [sic] but cannot or will not or do not negotiate for live children?"[78] Despite the recognition by administration experts that the majority of "live sightings" were false or pertained to Americans or Europeans who were not prisoners of war, the administration recognized the political value of keeping the issue alive and persisted in its commitment to get a full accounting of the missing and the dead.[79]

At the same time, the administration continued to insist that Vietnam was hiding the requested information on MIA/POWs in order to prolong the conflict. In 1985 the assistant deputy director of the DIA responsible for investigating the claims of American MIA/POW sightings in Vietnam admitted that there had been only two firsthand live sightings reported since 1980. He disclosed, "We have not been able to prove that Americans are still being held captive in that part of the world."[80] The false reports, the administration asserted, were part of Vietnam's mission of misinformation to divert efforts away from investigating real live sightings.[81]

During Reagan's second term, however, a chorus of criticism grew that the administration had used the missing for political gain. Journalist James Rosenthal published "The Myth of the Last POW," a scathing article in the *New Republic* magazine exposing the administration's politicization of American MIAs.[82] Rosenthal argued that America's obsession with the MIA/POW in Vietnam was not about the missing soldiers but rather the fact that the United States had lost the war. The MIAs, Rosenthal explained, "have become a matter of American honor, and their return a symbolic restoration of that honor."[83] The cruel truth, Rosenthal contended, was that the Reagan administration, like the Nixon administration, was exploiting the issue for political gain.[84]

Even Anne Mills Griffiths, the sister of an MIA and the director of the National League of Families, was increasingly frustrated by the aggrandizement of the issue by activists like Ross Perot. Griffiths too, criticized the administration, telling Rosenthal that the MIA/POW issue had been used to justify the administration's foreign policy positions and as a scapegoat for its failed policies.[85] The families of the missing, Griffiths exclaimed, "have had their hopes raised by politicians, publishers, filmmakers, and lawyers in pursuit of self-promotion and profits." While she maintained that the effort to account for and recover the remains of Americans killed in Vietnam must continue, such efforts were far removed from "sustaining the cruel delusion that there may be Americans alive in Vietnam."[86]

The politicization of the MIA/POWs had a critical effect on Vietnam's Amerasians. The Reagan administration pointed to both Amerasians and the missing American soldiers as evidence of the injustice and cruelty of a communist Vietnam. By prioritizing the MIA/POWs over Amerasians in negotiations over normalization, the administration tied the opportunity for Amerasians to continue to come to the United States to the impossible task of a full accounting of MIAs. Thus as a result of America's obsession with recovering the bones of its dead soldiers, "the living American prisoners in Asia languished in bureaucratic limbo."[87]

Fixing the Flaws

However, most Americans remained unaware that Amerasians were still in need. After passing the AIA, Reagan officials consistently misrepresented the real effects of the policy it so publically praised, especially in regards to Amerasians in Vietnam. Specifically, it failed to distinguish it from the Orderly Departure Program (ODP) utilized by all Indochinese refugees. Although a subset of the ODP, the AIA was specific to Amerasians, enabling those who could meet its strict requirements to come to the United States as immigrants rather than refugees. The difference was important. As immigrants, the United States recognized Amerasians' American paternity and offered a path to permanent residency and naturalization, whereas refugees had no such benefits. But since the limitations set by the AIA excluded the majority of Amerasians, most could only emigrate in category 3 of the ODP as "other" refugees.[88]

Too often, administration officials and media outlets incorrectly credited the AIA for the successful immigration of Amerasians from Vietnam who had actually benefitted from the ODP. For example, in April 1984 the *New York Times* reported that since the AIA there has been a significant increase of Amerasian children coming to the United States from Vietnam.[89] The emigration of the nine Amerasian orphans depicted in the story, however, was no different than the twenty-four American citizen Amerasians who had immigrated to the United States before the AIA was law. Both groups arrived through the ODP.[90]

By 1984 evidence that both the AIA and the ODP had failed to produce significant results for Amerasians in Vietnam led to questions about the Reagan administration's commitment to resolving the Amerasian issue. There is a gap, freelance writer Joseph Cerquone wrote about the AIA, between what has been said and what has been done.[91] Frustrated political advocates and humanitarians demanded the administration "open the doors which should never have been shut" to Amerasians, who U.S. law clearly states "are American citizens."[92] Public condemnation of the AIA's false advertising ranged from accusations of American racism to charges of inhumanity. Many sympathized with the words of one concerned citizen who expressed her displeasure to Reagan in 1983, writing: "I am usually proud to be an American, but when I realize that the racism and close-mindedness of overpaid bureaucrats is what is keeping hungry Amerasian children from warm loving homes, I am ashamed to say I am a citizen of the same country."[93]

Rep. Stewart McKinney had pined over the various limitations and flaws of legislation he once hoped would bring positive change to the lives of Amerasians.[94] Having now accumulated data on the AIA's ineffectiveness, McKinney and other AIA supporters identified three main problems that needed to be addressed: the sponsorship requirement, the slow processing of applicants, and the barriers to implementation in Vietnam. On July 12, 1984, McKinney wrote to House subcommittee chairman Romano Mazzoli (D-KY) to request a review of the AIA, which, he explained, "seems to be experiencing difficulty. . . . I would like to know why. . . . and I am wondering if it might be a good idea to review the program to see how and if it is working."[95]

While Mazzoli may have approved such a review, his attention at the time was elsewhere. A divided U.S. Congress sparred with administration officials over how to balance Reagan's Cold War refugee priorities for those fleeing communism with growing domestic anxieties over the changing demographics of newcomers and general concerns about illegal immigration.[96] As Congress moved toward a more restrictive approach, the Reagan administration remained committed to preserving the allocations specifically for Indochinese refugees. It was "America's moral duty" to "support the forces of freedom in Communist totalitarian states," Sec. of State George Shultz explained.[97] Hoping to strike a balance through legislation, Mazzoli and his Senate colleague Alan Simpson committed to passing comprehensive bipartisan immigration reform.

Simpson was an advocate for more restrictive immigration laws and a reduction in refugee admissions. The U.S. Army veteran who served in occupied Germany after the Second World War and chaired the Veteran's Affairs Committee held conservative views of limited government and immigration. He was a major antagonist to open-door immigration policies and was specifically critical of family unification as a category of immigration.[98] However, Simpson had also supported the AIA and, like McKinney, he was increasingly critical of its ineffectiveness. He was agitated that "after going through the anguish of passing an Amerasian legislation" in 1982, most Amerasians emigrated through the ODP.[99] Simpson found it troubling that Amerasians refused the AIA because they did not want to leave their mothers but were accepted into the ODP with numerous family members who he believed did not qualify as refugees.[100] Indeed, according to James Purcell, director of the Bureau for Refugee Programs, thirty-five hundred Amerasians and fifty-one hundred of their relatives had immigrated to America through the ODP between 1982 and 1986.[101] Purcell, however, gave a compelling response on behalf of Amerasians to Simpson's criticisms of the ODP. The AIA requirement of family separation for a population he described as "exactly the persecuted people the 1980 Refugee Act was supposed to help" was unconscionable. Unless Congress changed the AIA, there was no other choice, he explained, than for Amerasians to flee that country through the ODP.[102]

Stewart McKinney recognized that shifting views of immigration and refugee admissions now informed how some lawmakers understood the Amerasians and the AIA. As a result, he likely expected a fight when he made his first request for a formal review. Moreover, the Reagan administration's reluctance to even acknowledge the AIA's weaknesses, particularly for Amerasians in Vietnam, heightened his concern. Rather than listening to the criticism or attempting to fix the problems, the administration insisted that the ODP was a sufficient solution to that country's specific Amerasian problem.[103] U.S. officials even denied Vietnam's request to discuss the problems that hindered the ODP and restricted the AIA, leaving hundreds of Amerasians in limbo on the streets of Saigon: "We don't really see any necessity for talks. The orderly departure program is the only program set up to take Vietnamese refugees, and it is working."[104]

But the ODP was not working for Amerasians. On September 11, 1984, to quiet the critics and reassure the country that the administration was doing everything possible to bring Amerasians in Vietnam "home," Sec. of State George Shultz reaffirmed the administration's commitment to the issue. He declared Amerasians a "special humanitarian concern" and introduced a new subprogram to the ODP that would allow Amerasians in Vietnam who did not qualify for the AIA to immigrate with their family members to America as refugees.[105] The administration also introduced two "special initiatives" to resolve what it deemed the most critical humanitarian issues in Vietnam. The first was to resettle in the United States all political prisoners still interned in reeducation camps in Vietnam, and the other to fulfill Shultz's promise to admit all of the remaining Vietnamese Amerasians and their family members by 1987.[106] Shultz explained that "because of their undisputed ties to our country," over the next three years the United States would increase the annual allotment in the ODP to five thousand Amerasians in order to "accept all Asian-American children and their qualifying family members presently in Vietnam."[107]

Hoping that a resolution on Amerasians could still improve relations and lead to normalization with the United States, Vietnamese authorities again agreed to cooperate on Shultz's proposal, providing the Reagan administration a political victory that quashed the concerns of critics. They also took the expanded allotment seriously and immediately doubled the number of Amerasians approved to leave Vietnam through the ODP from twenty-two hundred in 1984 to four thousand in 1985. Shultz used the increase as evidence of the initiative's success, but once again, rather than praising Vietnam for cooperating, the administration blamed the country for failing to locate all remaining eligible Amerasians and thus falling short of the allotment.[108]

The criticism, however, was disingenuous. While Vietnam approved more Amerasians to leave the country under the ODP, less than 50 percent of those actually immigrated to the United States. In 1984, of the twenty-two hundred Amerasians approved to leave Vietnam only 937 successfully immigrated. In 1985—the year Amerasian departures peaked—of the four thousand approved only 1,498 arrived in America.[109] The numbers revealed that Vietnam was not to blame for the failure to meet the announced goals. Vietnamese officials clearly did approve Amerasians for immigration. Rather the onus lay with the United States, whose officials did not accept qualified Amerasians at equal rates.[110] Furthermore, Schultz's promise to expand the ODP allotment for Amerasians in Vietnam never materialized. Amerasian applicants continued to be counted as part of the general allotment for the entire ODP refugee program, eighty-five hundred per year.[111] The expectation that the Vietnamese could locate all of the remaining Amerasians for the program was also misguided. The task of disseminating information throughout the country and locating Amerasians residing in rural areas within the three-year time frame proved impossible.[112]

Vietnamese leaders justifiably took offense at U.S. accusations of obstruction and incompetence. They charged the United States of deliberately slowing the flow of ODP admissions to restrict Amerasian arrivals, thus avoiding actual responsibility for its abandoned children. By December 1985 the growing backlog of over twenty-two thousand ODP applicants approved by Vietnam to leave but still awaiting acceptance by the United States validated Vietnamese claims. It also exposed Amerasians as pawns in a Cold War game from which both countries sought to capitalize. Thus in January 1986, Vietnamese leaders blamed the United States for a backlog of sixty thousand ODP cases. As punishment, Vietnam suspended the ODP and ordered all Westerners to leave the country. The only path for Amerasians to leave Vietnam had disappeared.

Observing the missteps of the Reagan administration with regard to the AIA, Stewart McKinney determined he had to do more. On April 16, 1985, McKinney took advantage of the emotion and media coverage surrounding the ten-year anniversary of the end of the war. One year after he first wrote House subcommittee chairman Mazzoli, McKinney tried again: "Because of the ten year Vietnam anniversary, there has been a renewed interest in the Amerasian children in Vietnam and what is being done to bring them to the United States. In light of this, I would appreciate being able to have the enclosed remarks and questions read to the State Department official that will be attending your hearing on the Reauthorization of the Refugee Act. . . . Your continued interest in this issue and assistance in clarifying the concerns recently raised with regard to the Orderly Departure Program is appreciated."[113]

As he awaited a decision on his request for oversight hearings on the AIA, McKinney contacted a number of humanitarians and refugee assistance agencies, including the PSBF, Jodie Darragh, and Father Alfred Carroll for feedback on the program. The results offered some conflicting reviews, but largely revealed a shared desire that the AIA be amended.[114] There was general agreement that the requirement of a guaranteed financial sponsor in the United States deterred Amerasians who did not know how to locate a sponsor and imposed an excessive and "unreasonable" financial risk on the sponsor.[115] From Vietnam, where he worked to help Amerasians leave, Greg Kane of the Vietnam Veterans of America argued that sponsorship was an unnecessary and unfair burden and should be eliminated. The United States, Kane asserted, needed to treat Amerasians like either normal refugees or immigrants, rather than assigning them a special category. Neither refugees nor immigrants required sponsorship to come to America; only Amerasians did.[116]

Further troubled by the slow processing time associated with the AIA, its political advocates confronted State Department spokesman Frank Sieverts. Quick to deny any wrongdoing, Sieverts deflected questions about the numerical limits of the AIA and instead pointed to the fifty thousand refugees, including many Amerasians, who arrived in America from Asia each year. He blamed the small number of Amerasians immigrating through the AIA on family size and suggested applicants use the ODP instead. According to Sieverts, "the Refugee Act of 1980, as opposed to the Amerasian Immigration Act, is more 'flexible' and encompasses McKinney's bill.... It also allows families to come to the U.S."[117] The number of Amerasians leaving under the AIA was small, according to Sieverts, because Amerasians from Vietnam do not leave the country alone and thus very few apply or qualify.[118]

Like McKinney, Vietnamese officials were also ready for change. Since 1982 they had publicly declared their willingness to cooperate on numerous proposals to expedite the departure of Amerasians from Vietnam. By 1985, after facing much discrimination and marginalization as children, many Amerasians had matured into troublesome teenagers who were no longer just a public relations problem for Vietnam but a domestic societal concern. In October, Vietnam's foreign minister Nguyen Co Thach urged a delegation of American war veterans to take Amerasians with them when they left: "These are your children. I would welcome anyone to come and take them away."[119]

However, the Reagan administration had no incentive for any mass exodus of Amerasians out of Vietnam. The Amerasian issue had proven a convincing and critical Cold War tool. Amerasians, the missing American soldiers, and political prisoners were all evidence of the injustice and cruelty of a communist Vietnam. Vietnam countered by pointing to America's refusal to discuss the issue formally or to make any special provisions for Amerasians specifically beyond the ineffective AIA. The issue proved an opportunity for Vietnam to expose America's hypocrisy. Critical of the Reagan administration's insistence on a full accounting for MIAs, Vietnamese officials accused the United States of being more concerned with its dead soldiers than its living children.[120]

During the three years after the passage of the AIA, American actions on behalf of Amerasians fell far short of the promises and inclusionary rhetoric that accompanied the passage of the bill. Despite their words of concern for the abandoned "children of America" and claims of the nation's responsibility for them, there was very little progress toward an actual solution.[121] Even McKinney's efforts to simply review the program proved futile, forcing him to propose formal amendments in 1987 to rectify the AIA's limitations. Wider-ranging concerns about immigrants and refugees, and the Cold War conflict with Vietnam, overshadowed efforts to actually improve the prospects for Amerasians in Vietnam. Furthermore, the Reagan administration found the "American-faced" children in Vietnam to be convenient and effective political tools. By acknowledging them as American children, condemning the discrimination they faced in Vietnam, and supporting legislation that appeared to "save" them from communism, Reagan could simultaneously show the American people his own humanity and chastise the nation's Cold War enemy for its lack of compassion.

Conclusion

By 1985 Amerasians in Vietnam were aging out of childhood. The youngest were almost teenagers. Having grown out of the cute button noses, fair skin, and baby hair of their youth and into their "American" features, freckles, and hair textures, many Amerasians were now accustomed to their marginalized status in Vietnam. The stories of rescue, hope, and opportunity once used to promote the AIA and the photographs of handsome Amerasian boys and pretty Amerasian girls excited to come to the United States to find their fathers had largely disappeared. American newspaper editors understood that pictures of dirty teenagers or stories about abandoned young adults did not garner the sympathy of readers or sell newspapers. Besides, the passage of the AIA effectively alleviated concerns about them that Americans had previously held. Most believed the AIA was working, based on media reports and stories of Amerasians now living with their new American families. Portrayals of the AIA's success were so convincing that after its first year of implementation, veterans' organizations no longer listed the Amerasians among the major points for resolution with Vietnam.[122]

Still, the AIA had failed to provide a pathway to immigration for Amerasians in Vietnam and by 1986 the ODP and AIA together accounted for only an estimated 12 percent of the thirty thousand Amerasians believed still living in Vietnam.[123] Efforts by Stewart McKinney,

Father Carroll, the Darraghs, and the PSBF to improve the AIA failed to create real change, and by 1986 the American public had moved on from the issue.[124] It would do a double-take, though, in response to a photograph of an Amerasian teenager named Le Van Minh, whose "American face" and severely deformed legs would finally force U.S. lawmakers to make things right for Amerasians in Vietnam.

| Chapter Six

The Amerasian Homecoming Act

Son Tran arrived in Huntington, New York, in July 1974. The seventeen-year-old was one of fifteen Vietnamese students to earn a one-year scholarship from American Field Service (AFS) to attend school in the United States, and the only recipient at Huntington High School (HHS). While Son completed his senior year at HHS and looked forward to returning home to Saigon, his family half a world away struggled to survive the collapse of South Vietnam in the final days of the war. In April 1975, Son's father wrote him explaining that Son could not safely return to Saigon and that his family planned to "get out of Vietnam."¹ The fearful concern expressed by Son Tran's father for his family's escape and his son's safety confirmed the dangers many Huntington residents associated with North Vietnam and communism. Worried about the future of their "seventh son," Son's American family, the Flemings, asked the Huntington community to help Son stay in the United States. In an overwhelming response, Huntington residents joined with the HHS students and staff to save Son from the consequences of the war and provide him safety, acceptance, and opportunity in America. The *Long Island Press* reported that, "Son Tran may be the latest youth who can't go home again—but no one in Huntington seems to mind. In fact, everyone is working overtime to keep the young South Vietnamese exchange student in town."² In

June 1975 guidance counselor Lois Stamberg and the HHS chapter of AFS initiated the Son Tran fundraiser, to aid "the homeless student" in his efforts to stay in the country. It seemed that the entire community had committed to keeping Son Tran safe in America.

As in many small towns and tight-knit communities across the United States, the Vietnam War left lasting scars on Huntington.[3] Nestled amid the big, beautiful trees of the Long Island countryside forty miles northeast of New York City, Huntington was an ethnic, racial, and economic melting pot. Despite its heterogeneity, Huntington was segregated into two neighborhoods literally divided by the tracks of the Long Island Railroad: the white and affluent Huntington Village and the working class Huntington Station, home to the town's ethnic, immigrant, and racial minority populations.[4]

During the 1960s, Huntington's attempts to combat the growing effects of urban blight and decay with urban renewal upended the lives of many Huntington Station residents and added to the existing tensions over racial and economic inequality, integration, civil rights, and the Vietnam War.[5] The war divided neighbors, disrupted families, and inserted political tension into once amicable social gatherings. Local families sacrificed forty-three sons to the conflict, including two whose remains were never found—Air Force lieutenant Jonathon Bednareck and Navy carrier pilot, Lieutenant William N. Meese. Such loss and sacrifice weighed heavily on Huntington residents, who shared the burden of the war with other small communities across the country. "The deaths of others took something out of all of us," a local reporter wrote. "The same with the wounded and of those who served in a far-off foreign land."[6] Unlike other small towns, however, where a "blood sacrifice" in Vietnam was the grim consequence of economic frustration, Huntington offered affluence, education, and hope to its Vietnam generation.[7]

In August 1969, the Huntington August Peace Project convened over one hundred local townspersons to protest a war they declared to be a mistake. Although the United States had good intentions in Vietnam, explained one Vietnam veteran who attended the protest, "we are destroying a country, we promised to free."[8] Still, even those

Huntington residents who condemned the war remained steadfast in their support for the service and sacrifice of U.S. soldiers and committed to helping those most affected by the war. In 1967 a group of local women concerned that domestic tensions over the war ultimately harmed those serving in Vietnam founded the Huntington Women in Support of Our Men in Vietnam, an apolitical group intended "to support the morale of Huntington men in Vietnam."[9] In 1971 the group erected the nation's first living memorial to the war, a grove of forty-three Japanese Kwanzan cherry trees planted on the town's village green to commemorate the forty-three Huntington men who died in Vietnam.[10] Members chose the Kwanzan trees specifically as symbolic of the soldiers' sacrifice "because the blossoms fall while they're in their full beauty, not after they have faded . . . just like warriors."[11] Two years later, Huntington joined the rest of the nation in celebrating the homecoming of American prisoners of war and the return of Capt. David E. Baker, who spent seven months as a POW after being shot down over Cambodia.[12] On April 5, 1973, the local paper, the *Long Islander*, extolled the virtue of town residents who, regardless of their views on the war, "never forgot the men who served."[13]

Huntington residents and their Long Island neighbors showed similar concerns for American allies and victims of the war in Southeast Asia. A number of local families, including the Flemings, offered shelter and opportunity to those, like Son Tran, whose lives the war upended. Here the discourse of service and sacrifice often used to describe Huntington's support for the war and its soldiers was replaced by a narrative of "rescue and liberation," buttressed by a deep conviction of America's exceptional benevolence.[14] The 1967 arrival and successful schooling of a thirteen-year-old Montagnard, Hakin Lienghot, and his subsequent graduation from Stony Brook High School in 1972 sparked *Newsday* to describe Lienghot's experiences as tapping into a "vein of American idealism," a story "of one child who was eventually made homeless by war, and of a Long Island community that welcomed him."[15] In August 1975 the *Bethpage Tribune* called on local families to sponsor Vietnamese refugees, emphasizing that the most important quality a sponsor must have "is a kind and generous heart" and "a moral commitment to offer food, clothing, and shelter to the refugees."[16] In 1979 *Newsday* reported on Camille and Stan Noren of nearby Bethpage, who fostered refugee siblings Tuyen, Thap, and Quan Voung, who had fled Vietnam by boat before landing in a Staten Island orphanage. The Noren's selfless act exemplified the good will of many.[17]

The efforts of the HHS students and staff and the Huntington community to save Son Tran from Vietnam were consistent with a local culture of selfless service, sacrifice, and humanitarianism, as well as a deep connection to the Vietnam War. The next generation of Huntington youth, although born one step removed from the war, shared similar humanitarian impulses. They came of age with the rhetoric, idealism, and hope that characterized Ronald Reagan's exceptional America in which the Vietnam War was noble and U.S. soldiers were heroes.[18] Hence, by the time members of the HHS student government began their grassroots campaign to bring Amerasian Le Van Minh to the United States from Vietnam for humanitarian reasons in the fall of 1986, students were well versed in their nation's exceptionalism and in their community's humanitarian acts of saving. The efforts of HHS students to save Le Van Minh inspired a disparate group of concerned Americans, humanitarians, and journalists to encourage politicians to pass the Amerasian Homecoming Act to allow all Amerasians in Vietnam to immigrate to the United States. A decade removed from the Vietnam War and years after the Amerasian Immigration Act failed to produce any tangible results, the HHS student's persistence in bringing one Amerasian child to America infused new life into the Amerasian issue. Their efforts forced Americans to once again remember the children they abandoned in Vietnam.

The Photograph

One might imagine the tenor of hope and expectation swirling around the halls of Huntington High School in August 1986. A new school year had begun and, unbeknown to the members of the HHS student government, they were about to embark on something bigger than college entrance exams and applications. By the end of the school

THE AMERASIAN HOMECOMING ACT 181

year HHS would garner the political spotlight on the national and international stage.

In November 1985 sixty-three-year-old Gloria Blauvelt, a public relations worker for the Huntington School District, came across Audrey Tiernan's photograph in *Newsday* of Le Van Minh, the fair-skinned Vietnamese boy with severe leg deformities and a twisted spine crawling on his hands, begging for money, on the streets of Ho Chi Minh City.[19] Like many other *Newsday* readers, the powerful picture struck her hard. "It stopped me in my tracks," Blauvelt recalled decades later.[20] Perhaps idealistic in her own thinking, Blauvelt knew she had to do something to help the "crippled boy" in the photo, who she believed had to come to America.[21] With the support of HHS principal Jim Salvatore, Blauvelt showed the photo and the accompanying article to the HHS student government and challenged them to do something. Upon seeing it, student body president David Zach, and committee members Marlo Sandler, Sue Forte, and Tara Scalia (the only junior in the group) gasped out loud. The picture, Zach explained, disturbed them, an "image of a contemporary crawling like a crab in ragged clothes."[22] Years later, Marlo Sandler still remembered the photo, "the severity and the deformity around his hips and his skinny upper legs . . . he looked like an animal. His face was sort of this perfect-like, beautiful, childlike innocent face, but his body was so contorted and animal-like."[23]

Motivated by the photo, the student council accepted Blauvelt's challenge and focused on bringing Minh to the United States and getting him the medical care they assumed could save his life.[24] However, the task proved more formidable than any of the students could have imagined. The absence of diplomatic relations between the United States and Vietnam, and Vietnam's suspension of the ODP eight months earlier, had eliminated the only means for people from Vietnam to immigrate to the United States. Without diplomatic intervention, there was no legal way for Minh to come to the United States for medical care.

Not to be deterred, the students persisted in their cause with encouragement from Blauvelt and Tiernan. During the fall semester, they initiated a petition to bring Minh to America for medical treatment. In true grassroots campaign fashion, the students hit the pavement around Huntington, collecting signatures from residents at HHS football games, back-to-school nights, and other school-sanctioned events. They spent hours at the Walt Whitman Mall armed with clipboards and pens, talking to community members and asking them to "Help Bring Le Van Minh to the United States." Everywhere the students went they took Tiernan's photograph of Minh. They showed it to their neighbors and others in the community and spoke to them of the responsibilities that resulted from war. Marlo Sandler remembers the picture was a conversation starter that triggered lots of emotions. "Many people who saw the picture and saw what we were doing said, 'Oh I saw that, I saw that in *Newsday*'; it had left a mark with many people."[25] Tara Scalia remembers the emotional reaction of one man at the Walt Whitman Mall who asked to sign the petition. "He was crying," Scalia remembered, and he "carried a copy of the *Newsday* picture in his hand." After signing the petition, Scalia heard the man mutter to himself as he walked away, "My conscience was bothering me."[26]

While the four members of the HHS student government led the petition signing enterprise, Sue Forte remembered a complete community effort including students, families, teachers, and neighbors.[27] One Staten Island family even offered to adopt Minh, while a businessman proposed to fly him to America.[28] For the HHS staff, like social studies teacher Wayne Lackman who the students remember fondly as offering much support and guidance, the opportunity for students to experience a living lesson in civics, social studies, culture, and diplomacy seemed too good to be true. *Newsday* quoted a Spanish teacher, Yvonne Brady, speaking to her ninth-grade class: "We're talking about a boy in Vietnam—reaching out to another culture. . . . To bridge the gap that exists between countries is to be able to understand."[29] Still, not everyone in Huntington supported the students. Some made comments like "We don't need any more dogs and cats in the United States," and "'Why don't you help one of our own?'"[30] According to Blauvelt, a number of local Vietnam veterans also firmly opposed the campaign. She noted, "They were polite but did not want anything to do with it, and I didn't blame them."[31]

The students also lobbied for support outside of Huntington, sending petitions and Tiernan's photo of Minh to school districts across the nation. *Newsday* detailed the students' daily efforts, and major news networks like CBS provided national television coverage. By November the students had successfully collected twenty-seven thousand signatures from twenty-seven states and three foreign countries in support of Minh's emigration.[32] With petitions in hand, the students took the next step, contacting their congressman and HHS alumnus, Robert Mrazek (D-NY).

A Humanitarian Case

From the moment she encouraged the HHS students to bring Le Van Minh to the United States, Gloria Blauvelt was determined to protect the kids and the project from becoming a "political football." She recognized that the response to Minh's photo "was a humane reaction that just hit everybody right in the heart" and believed the HHS campaign to be strictly humanitarian.[33] As the students embraced the hard work of their campaign, Blauvelt quietly and strategically established a network of humanitarian support to help navigate the politics and bureaucracy of U.S. immigration law and refugee resettlement. She also contacted various medical professionals seeking treatment for Minh's legs. "The only reason we could get him here" Blauvelt explained, "was to make it humanitarian and to use humanitarian resources." Additionally, Blauvelt sought to keep the students, to whom she credits all the success, in the spotlight. "The kids were superb, they never showed any self-importance."[34]

Blauvelt proved a savvy and strategic media manager. As a former high school sports reporter for the *Long Islander* and then a public relations specialist for HHS, Blauvelt kept media attention on the students, Minh, and the medical urgency of Minh's condition.[35] Hence, local media sources focused the story on Minh's medical condition and framed the students' efforts within a discourse of humanitarianism. Anna-Simms Phillips, the associate producer for WCBS-TV, was admittedly attracted to the human interest side of the story and described the students as "courageous" and determined to save the "throw-away" children left behind in Vietnam.[36] Just as *Newsday* consistently described Minh as the "crippled" or "handicapped" Amerasian, the students insisted that they wanted to improve the quality of his life by providing him the medical care necessary so that he could walk.[37] Marlo Sandler remembers wondering if Minh "would ever be able to stand upright or walk . . . going back to the first image of his posture on all fours, how long can he live like that?"[38] Representative Mrazek, too, contends that Minh's medical condition was the sole motivation in pushing for his immigration. There was a chance, Mrazek explains, "with our fine medicine here in the United States to conceivably do something that could help the boy that could not be accomplished in Vietnam. This was an exceptional case."[39]

However, Minh's case was not really that exceptional. American journalists and humanitarian organizations had been reporting on the sad condition of Amerasians in Vietnam for a decade. Bernie Weinraub's stories in the *New York Times* and Mike Wallace's *60 Minutes* report on CBS had reinforced the accounts from delegations of Vietnam veterans returning to Vietnam confirming the large population of homeless, orphaned, and abandoned Amerasians, and further propelled more media coverage. In July 1983 the discovery of over 250 Amerasians sleeping on the sidewalk had prompted the American Council of Voluntary Agencies, the U.S. Catholic Conference, and the Pearl S. Buck Foundation to propose the construction of an Amerasian processing center in Ho Chi Minh City. While Vietnam supported the proposal and asked for U.S. assistance in building such a center, the Reagan administration had rejected it.[40]

Minh was likely among those taking up residence on Ho Chi Minh City's sidewalks; however, *Newsday* avoided making the connection or grouping him among the tens of thousands of other Amerasians living in Vietnam. Even those journalists who reported on Minh's family history and his fluctuating story about his mother failed to tie his tales of abandonment, abuse, and family separation to the broader Amerasian narrative. Initially Minh stated he was an orphan as the result of the deaths of his mother and stepfather, then later he described the abandonment and abuse his (now alive) mother inflicted upon him, before finally revealing the "tearful parting" with his mother in Hanoi. While it remained unclear which of Minh's stories was true, each telling revealed a common thread within the experience of Amerasians, who reported suffering, abandonment, and physical abuse from family members and peers because of their American paternity. The emotional trauma from separating from their mothers was also common for those Amerasians who left home to shed their illegitimacy or those who emigrated without their mothers, as required by the AIA.[41]

Yet rather than situate Minh within the larger Amerasian context, reporters continued to frame his story as unique. They failed to question how Minh was an "orphan" if in fact he had a mother or challenge the moral or legal rationale of taking Minh from his mother without her consent. Also missing was any discussion about the existence or responsibility of Minh's American father. Instead, reporters made very few references to Minh's American paternity while emphasizing the humanitarian necessity of his medical condition. Journalists seemed to imply that the efforts on Minh's behalf were not because he was an American boy or that he represented tens of thousands of other Amerasian kids just like him. Minh was a single boy facing enormous medical challenges that just a little American humanitarianism could fix.

Nevertheless, Minh's American paternity appeared undeniable in Tiernan's photograph. Viewed in color, the picture clearly showed Minh's light brown hair and eyes. In black and white the photograph darkens the color of both. However, media reports made an appeal to racial kinship when describing Minh, assigning him stereotypically American features while omitting reference to his American paternity.[42] More specifically, *Newsday* reporters consistently described Minh as having *blue* eyes. In November 1985, Jeff Sommer introduced Minh to *Newsday* readers as having "light-brown hair, pale skin and hazel eyes" that identify him "immediately as an Amerasian."[43] One year later, in November 1986, reporter Paul Marinaccio described Minh with "straight black hair, blue eyes and freckles," and a few weeks later, "A street beggar with blue eyes and freckles who crawls on all fours."[44] In March 1987, reporter Irene Virag, in reference to the difficulties facing Minh explained that the absence of diplomatic relations between the United States and Vietnam "makes it impossible to bring a single blue-eyed child to the land of his fathers."[45] One month later, Virag described Minh specifically as "the blue-eyed boy who lives half a world away." It was not until Virag met Minh in May 1987 that her description became more realistic, "hazel eyes and severely cropped hair."[46]

There is no question that just as policymakers utilized a discourse of inclusion to employ an assumption of filiation between America and her Amerasian "sons and daughters" to pass the AIA in 1982, similar methods assisted Minh's immigration five years later. Likely, those reporters who had not seen Minh in person or who failed to examine the photograph in color simply projected their own ideas of what Minh looked like into their stories, inserting their personal assumptions that Minh's American father, presumed white, would necessarily have passed the trait of blue eyes on to his son. They possibly knew that such a description of his physical characteristics would garner the sympathy of *Newsday* readers, who would recognize Minh as American, ultimately selling more papers. Or perhaps when reporters looked at Minh, they simply saw what they wanted to see: a fair-skinned, half-American boy with blue eyes.[47]

The use of a racialized discourse of inclusion personalized Minh's medical condition for many readers. Blue eyes may have made Minh more plausibly American and thereby worthy of humanitarian assistance. Certainly, Minh's eyes made an impact on the HHS students. Thirty years later, Tara Scalia and Marlo Sandler remembered Minh's "big beautiful eyes" and how they looked "totally American." In hindsight, Sandler wondered whether perceptions of Minh's blue eyes and his American looks somehow spoke to the group of white teenagers. "I really wish I could go back in time," Sandler reflected, "and determine where that factored in."[48]

The very clear connotation in blue eyes of whiteness carries bigger questions about Minh's case. Would the reaction from *Newsday* readers, the HHS students, or the Long Island community have been the same had Minh's face not been so familiar? Would the HHS students have perceived Minh as their contemporary had he been full Vietnamese and "crippled" rather than Amerasian? How might they have responded had Minh been a Black Amerasian? Such questions went unanswered as the students gathered signatures to support bringing Minh to America for humanitarian reasons at the same time that Americans grew tired of saving Vietnamese refugees they believed were no longer a humanitarian concern.

The Congressman and the Amerasian Boy

Elected to Congress in 1982 only a few weeks after the AIA became law, Rep. Robert Mrazek admittedly had little knowledge of Amerasians. Before entering politics, the Huntington High School alumnus and Cornell graduate served in the U.S. Navy from 1967 to 1969. After leaving the Navy, Mrazek joined the staff of U.S. senator Vance Hartke (D-IN). By 1986, Mrazek had served a four-year stint as a member of the House Appropriations Committee and the Foreign Operations Subcommittee, which oversaw foreign aid and immigration and naturalization services. Nonetheless, Mrazek was unfamiliar with the Amerasian issue when he picked up his copy of *Newsday* and saw Tiernan's photograph of Minh. It was, Mrazek exclaimed, "one of those very arresting photographs which I remembered, of this strikingly handsome little boy."[49]

It was not until a visit from the students of HHS, however, that Mrazek was forever connected to Minh and the Amerasian issue. In November 1986 Zach, Forte, Sandler, and Scalia presented Mrazek with the twenty-seven thousand signatures they had collected in support of bringing Minh to the United States for medical treatment. Aware that Vietnam had suspended the ODP months earlier and of the contentious relationship between the two countries, Mrazek had doubts about the prospect for success.[50] Regardless, the hopeful idealism of the HHS students touched him: "you have these teenagers looking at you with open-wide doe-eyes thinking, you know, you're the Congressman, you can pull it off. I felt I had to at least follow through to see if there might be something I can do."[51]

Amid the diplomatic stalemate between the two countries over what U.S. leaders viewed as Vietnam's refusal to release Americans being held as political prisoners or to provide a full accounting of American MIAs, Mrazek understood that room for cooperation on Amerasians did exist.[52] In the fall of 1986 U.S. officials were actively seeking to restore the ODP on American terms in order to bring political prisoners and Amerasians to the United States. Richard Childress, a senior National Security Council official, and John C. Monjo, State Department officer in the Bureau of East Asia and the Pacific, held a secret meeting with the Vietnamese Minister of Foreign Affairs, Vo Dung Giang, to specifically discuss a bilateral agreement to allow Amerasians to immigrate. In light of the tensions over the stalemated ODP, which had not processed an Amerasian applicant for almost six months, Childress and Monjo proposed a new program that would operate independently of the ODP and free from the oversight of the UNHCR, allowing American officials to interview and approve Amerasian applicants.[53]

Mrazek recognized the desire of the U.S. State Department to revamp the ODP program on its own terms. Viewing the opportunity for diplomacy over Minh's fate as having potential for progress on the other shared humanitarian issues, Mrazek went to work. Within a few weeks of meeting with the HHS students, Mrazek met with Nguyen Dang Quang, the first secretary of the Vietnamese mission to the United Nations, to discuss the possibility of diplomatic cooperation on Minh's case. They agreed that it would generate positive publicity and possibly benefit both countries politically. The HHS students also contacted Quang, writing him a letter they hoped would endear him to their cause. They pointed to the benefits of Minh's immigration for Vietnam and the shared humanity and "mutual compassion" that tied both countries to Minh, whom they described as a "symbol of the tragedy of war."[54] "We are aware" they wrote, "that your nation's medical resources may be burdened as a result of the past conflict. Therefore we would like to assist in a small way by bringing Le to the United States for medical treatment."[55]

Shortly thereafter, Mrazek and the HHS students, along with Gloria

Blauvelt and the photographer Audrey Tiernan, who was covering the event for *Newsday*, visited Quang's New York office.[56] The students knew immediately that the meeting was a very big deal. "I remember we were so nervous," recalls Sandler, "and we had to miss school that day and we all put on our professional-looking clothing. I just remember that we felt so out of our league, and like such little kids." Tara Scalia agreed: "We were so excited when we got that invitation and we thought the Vietnamese would see that we were trying to do a good deed. I'm not sure we realized everything else going on at the time . . . communism and so many other barriers."[57] Still, by all accounts the meeting was respectful and positive. Quang listened intently to the students' plan for Minh and he ultimately endorsed bringing Minh to America, announcing that Vietnam would make an exception to the suspended ODP and grant him an exit visa. The students were ecstatic, with David Zach exclaiming, "Mr. Quang has put the ball in our field. It is now up to us to contact our government and hopefully get it to be as responsive as the Vietnamese have been."[58]

For Vietnam, such a humanitarian gesture meant positive publicity at a time of high diplomatic tensions with the United States. The Reagan administration was consistently accusing Vietnam of humanitarian violations against Amerasians, political prisoners, and American MIA/POWs. It also meant a possible breakthrough in getting Amerasians out of Vietnam. The three thousand Amerasians included in the ODP backlog were now mostly teenagers and young adults.[59] Largely unemployed, uneducated, and homeless, these Amerasians gathered in Ho Chi Minh City, where they engaged in petty crimes, became a public nuisance, and proved a problem for Vietnamese officials.[60] Amerasians who begged Western visitors for food and money also brought negative publicity to the country. Some reports suggested that the Vietnamese government institutionalized many homeless Amerasians in orphanages or labor camps.[61] Thus Quang could not overlook the opportunity that approving Minh's emigration offered. He professed Vietnam's willingness to cooperate on the Minh case while pointing to the bigger Amerasian problem in Vietnam and urging the U.S. government to expedite the relocation of all other Amerasian youth to the United States.[62]

For the students, the meeting with Quang appeared to be a turning point. Suddenly they felt like something could actually happen and that Congressman Mrazek was now fully engaged in their cause. The media attention and the students' celebrity increased as reporters from major news networks began appearing in Huntington, tracking the students down at the mall and at school. Marlo Sandler remembers a reporter who came to her house to do a "weird, fluffy human interest story" about her as a teenager "who is trying to make a difference in the world."[63]

Media coverage of Amerasians intensified as reporters once again focused their pens and cameras on the dire existence of the abandoned Amerasians still living in Vietnam. The resulting stories and powerful video footage of Minh being carried around Ho Chi Minh City on the back of his best friend Ti educated the HHS students about the broader Amerasian issue. According to Sandler, the video haunted the students, who now realized the larger scope of the Amerasian problem. They also began to feel guilty "that we weren't also bringing Ti over or trying to help . . . it was a reminder to us that we were only doing what we can to bring this one child, but there are so many."[64]

As they grew in understanding of their humanitarian cause and the scope of the Amerasian issue, the students began to worry about the politics. It was on this topic that Gloria Blauvelt's dogged determination proved most fierce. The woman who first introduced the students to Minh and who had thus far guided, protected, and encouraged their grassroots efforts to bring him to the United States had no intention of letting political agendas subvert their cause. At the age of ninety-six, Blauvelt still emanates passion and love for her HHS students as she recounts the events surrounding Minh. Despite the challenges of time, she retains a sharp wit. She is direct, warm, and funny, with an indomitable spirit, and her memories of these specific students are as clear as if the entire affair was yesterday. "This was all about the students," Blauvelt explained, "it was about Minh and being humanitarian, I never wanted it to be political."[65]

The U.S. State Department also appeared to want to prevent Minh from becoming political, initially proving much less willing than Vietnam to cooperate with its communist foe. In response to Vietnam's concessions to expedite Minh's emigration, the State Department rejected the Vietnamese condition that Minh forego the required ODP interview and medical examination. Frank Sieverts, the spokesman for the Bureau for Refugee Programs, insisted that Minh proceed through the normal ODP process, which included both the interview and exam to confirm his identification and assess his medical condition.[66] However, with no diplomatic relations or a functioning ODP, Vietnam refused to let American interviewers and medical teams into the country to conduct such exams. So Sieverts suggested a compromise. Instead of granting Minh an individual exception, the U.S. government, he explained, could simply place Minh's name among the three thousand other Amerasians awaiting departure under the ODP.[67]

Considering the condition of the ODP, Sievert's suggestion seemed a meaningless solution that failed to meet the request for expediting Minh's departure for medical "urgency." Even for those Amerasians in Vietnam already approved for immigration, the backlog meant that often their departure date exceeded the one-year expiration on their ODP medical exams, placing them in a static category, "Persons Approved but Not Medically Clear," in a suspended program.[68] As the suspension continued this category grew, resulting in ever fewer Amerasians leaving Vietnam. In 1985, 1,498 Amerasians left Vietnam under the ODP. In 1986, after the suspension of the program, only 512 (who had been approved before the suspension) departed.[69]

Thus, despite its claims of humanitarian concern for all Amerasians, five years after finally supporting the AIA there was very little U.S. government interest in cooperating with Vietnam over Minh. Even Mrazek's attempts on Capitol Hill to obtain support for Minh's case hit resistance from the State Department. After a personal plea to Secretary of State Shultz to grant Minh an immigration exception for humanitarian reasons, Mrazek received a "perfunctory letter" from the State Department expressing that "they wish they could but they were not going to cooperate" on this issue.[70]

By January 1987, as the second semester of classes began, the HHS students started to realize the broader implications of their efforts to bring Minh to the United States. Specifically, they understood the opportunity his case presented to both countries to finally reestablish diplomatic relations and perhaps reconcile some of the emotional effects of the war. Over the next few months, the students embraced the opportunity to participate directly in the American political process—meeting with Vietnamese officials, collaborating with their congressman, and lobbying Congress. Lutheran Immigration and Refugee Services (LIRS) in Manhattan advised the students on the political strategy that would garner the best results. As one of the agencies contracted with the U.S. government for refugee resettlement and concerned with the current status of the ODP and Amerasians, LIRS employees encouraged the students' efforts, hoping they could help revitalize the program. LIRS associate director Marta Brenden believed Minh's case brought a human element to the diplomatic stalemate: "You are raising a real life situation for all these people to think about while they negotiate."[71]

Ironically, LIRS already knew about Minh and had attempted to facilitate his immigration a year earlier. The students offered new hope and LIRS employees advised them to be strategic in pushing a small and select group of Congress members to support expediting Minh's case.[72] As part of their new political approach, the students traveled with Blauvelt and Tiernan to Washington DC, where they hand delivered their petitions to Representative Mrazek's office. Along the way, the students had an emotional visit to the Vietnam Veterans Memorial, where Tiernan sketched her father's name. "Despite the bitter cold," Marlo Sandler explained, "we just could not leave that memorial. Its impact on all of us was devastating."[73]

At the same time the students were perfecting their political strategy, Mrazek and Quang solidified their own political footprint on the case. When reports that officials from both countries had reached an agreement to allow Amerasians to immigrate to the United States proved premature, both men extended their efforts to reach a successful bilateral solution on Minh.[74] Mrazek framed his approach within the

THE AMERASIAN HOMECOMING ACT   193

Reagan-era language of reconciliation. According to Mrazek, "Helping Le could demonstrate the mutual concern of our people over the cost of war."[75]

By March 1987 the persistence of the HHS students in New York combined with Mrazek's political influence in Washington DC finally began to sway individual members of Congress. In the preceding months, Marzek spent hundreds of hours talking to individual members of Congress about Minh. He used every possible opportunity to make his case, from the House floor to the gym. His efforts paid off as Mrazek managed to gain the support of the majority of the House to bring Minh to America for medical treatment. Although the House made a bipartisan effort on Minh's behalf, Mrazek most credited Tiernan's powerful photograph for garnering support. The picture, Mrazek admits, moved members of Congress to varying levels of emotion. Even those who initially resisted Mrazek's personal pleas proved sympathetic to Minh's story and the discrimination he faced after seeing the photo. For many policymakers, Minh simply "looked" American and his face was "a bitter and painful reminder of the war."[76] Now more confident in his congressional standing on the issue, Mrazek sent a letter to Secretary Shultz that included the signatures of 306 of the 435 House members who supported a humanitarian exemption for Minh that would allow him to come to America without the required interview or medical exam.[77]

In response to growing congressional support, the State Department finally agreed to expedite the immigration process for Minh. By April the Vietnamese government located Minh, who they said expressed his desire to leave Vietnam, and granted his exit visa. Minh, who spoke very little English at the time, later revealed that he had not given his consent and did not want to leave Vietnam for America.[78] He claimed Vietnamese security guards accosted him in front of the Caravelle Hotel in Ho Chi Minh City.[79] But by then it was too late for Minh to change his fate. In May, Mrazek and Tiernan flew to Vietnam to meet Minh and bring him "home." No longer simply a high school humanitarian project, Minh had been transformed into a politically symbolic gesture between two countries. Minh, Mrazek exclaimed, could be the "first step to removing some of the roadblocks" to normalizing relations.[80]

Becoming American

In lobbying Congress to bring Minh to the United States, Mrazek and the HHS students and their supporters emphasized the humanitarian urgency of his case because of his need for medical care. However, once the State Department agreed to cooperate with Vietnam to bring Minh to America, those involved began to stress Minh's American paternity through a discourse of kinship and family. Before the school made a public announcement, a proud Gloria Blauvelt told the members of the HHS student government that Minh was "coming home." "It felt like we had just won the Super Bowl," Sandler remembered "we were crying and jumping up and down."[81] After the initial excitement, Sue Forte remembers the entire school committed to planning and preparing for Minh's arrival.[82]

To celebrate the students' successful efforts, Huntington High School declared April 27 "Le Van Minh Day." At the event Robert Mrazek spoke to the students in front of television cameras and reminded them of their humanitarian success: "Very soon you will have a chance to meet a young man whose life you've saved . . . you should be proud. Your high school is responsible for bringing Le out of a life of misery to a new life in America."[83] Local folksinger Patricia Shih performed an original song about Amerasians left behind in Vietnam. Her lyrics aroused notions of national paternity, "Papa, you're in my heart. Do you want to keep our lives apart?"[84] Amerasian teenager Anh Dung Nguyen also spoke to the HHS students of his experience in Vietnam and America. *Newsday* reporter Irene Virag poignantly explained that although Anh never met his American father, a soldier who left Saigon when Anh was an infant, Anh still held on to the dream of finding him and kept a framed photograph of him by his bed.[85] Anh's own testimonial was even more gripping as he expressed the common hope of many Amerasians—that coming to America and becoming American would fill the hole left by their absent fathers. Coming to America, Minh will feel "reborn,"

Anh told the HHS students. "Half my blood is American" and "I am one of the lucky ones."[86]

One month later, Mrazek arrived in Vietnam and Virag provided a detailed narrative of Minh's trip "home to the land of his unknown father."[87] Virag's reports described the budding relationship between the congressman and the Amerasian teenager in a framework of paternal responsibility. Mrazek also described his interaction with Minh in familial terms. "I feel like a prospective father," Mrazek stated the day before leaving for Vietnam: "I have the same sense of expectation and concern for the unknown as when I was awaiting the birth of my first child."[88]

The bond between Mrazek and Minh developed quickly. Photos captured the tall congressman carrying Minh like a child, cradling the "small, crippled boy" whose thin arms wrapped tightly around Mrazek's neck.[89] Virag related the sentimental moments between man and child to *Newsday* readers as those special moments that fathers share with their sons: Mrazek putting drops of medicine in Minh's eye before dabbing it with a tissue, sharing pictures of his children and wife, and playing black jack with Minh in his hospital room. Minh, for his part, told of his life on the streets, of hunger, danger, and survival, and of his best friend Ti.[90]

Only the emotional reunion between Minh and Tiernan, whose photograph had initiated the efforts for Minh, could compete with Mrazek's moments. If Mrazek stood in the shoes of a loving American father, Tiernan embraced the role of the caring mother as she "stroked Minh's withered legs," "tousled his hair," and comforted him with a small brown teddy bear.[91] By all accounts Tiernan was a "lifeline" for the HHS students throughout the entire process, as she had a special relationship with Minh, for whom she desperately wanted a better life. "She was so emotionally invested in him," remembers Marlo Sandler, "not the bigger thing, but just this boy. . . . there was something very personal for her about her feelings for Minh."[92]

The compassion and care shown to Minh by both Tiernan and Mrazek helped keep Minh at ease during the initial phase of his emigration from Vietnam. While in the isolation ward for refugees in a

Bangkok hospital, recovering from a contagious eye infection that delayed his departure, Minh's Americanization continued with an introduction to American medical care and culture. A video captured the excitement of Minh's first physical therapy sessions, in which his American nurses celebrated his first few steps. Moments later, the camera zoomed in on Minh making an origami flower he gave to his nurse, who exclaimed, "He's got beautiful eyes!"[93] According to *Newsday* reports, Minh perused pictures of the White House and the Statue of Liberty, ate M&Ms, and listened to Simon and Garfunkel, Jimi Hendrix, and the Cars on his new cassette player. These were, Virag wrote, "symbolic ways" in which Minh moved "a little closer to America."[94]

In America the students at HHS also moved closer to Minh. They anxiously awaited his arrival and tried to imagine how Minh felt, knowing he was coming to a new, foreign culture. For the HHS teenagers, pictures of Minh wearing American sneakers, listening to music, and playing cards transformed the "crippled" boy living on the other side of the world in Tiernan's first photograph into a real person rather than a street kid and beggar.

Teachers at HHS took the opportunity to situate Minh's case and the school's efforts into a larger context of diplomacy, determination, and human compassion. The students who had worked relentlessly to bring Minh to America now began to wonder more about him. They imagined the life he was leaving, thought about "his mother who had ordered him into the streets when he was 10" (Minh later recanted this story and explained he had spoken out in anger), and were hopeful for the life he would have.[95] The focus of the HHS community also shifted from the humanitarian urgency of Minh's twisted spine to the familiarity of his "American face." Sixteen-year-old Dina Boccio pointed to the picture of Minh that had made him famous, a photo in which one cannot deny nor turn away from Minh's physical condition. But Boccio was no longer looking at the awkwardly bent legs that initiated the humanitarian calls to save him. Perhaps finally free to voice what many were thinking when they saw Minh's picture, Boccio exclaimed, "Look at that face, how could you not do anything? We had to do something."[96] They also wondered about his paternity, curious about the American father, the man "of whom he knows nothing." According to Sandler, the question of Minh's American father lingered for the group "as something that we hoped eventually we, or someone else in this process could help with."[97] But none of the kids, or adults, seemed to know how.

By the time Mrazek carried Minh off the airplane into a crowd of television and newspaper reporters and HHS students at New York's John F. Kennedy Airport on June 4, 1987, the congressman and the Amerasian teenager had formed an indelible bond. "I didn't go to Vietnam to find a son," Mrazek told Virag, "and yet I've fallen in love with this boy."[98] Minh, too, seemed comfortable with the congressman, calling him "Daddy" and clinging to him as they stepped off the plane, where media questions and camera flashes instantly engulfed them. The HHS students were also there. Crying, laughing, and hugging each other, they welcomed Minh to America with posters and huge banners, "Welcome Home Le" and "We Love You." They also presented him with a number of gifts: an HHS school jacket to represent his acceptance into the HHS "family," a copy of the book *A Day in the Life of America*, and a small American flag. HHS senior Alison Mixer cried upon seeing Minh, exclaiming, "When you look at his smile and the sparkle in his eyes . . . you can see he's so beautiful."[99] Marlo Sandler summed up the feelings of many HHS students, "This entire year we thought of Le as a project . . . now we realize he's a human being. . . . It's amazing. . . . We're changing a person's life."[100]

At the press conference Mrazek commended the students for their persistence and hard work in bringing Minh to America. He reminded the students that they had "truly changed the life of this young man" and that "Minh begins a new life in the U.S. today." Secretary Quang also attended, taking the opportunity to remind Americans that Minh was one of many Amerasians in Vietnam. Amerasians in Vietnam, Quang explained, "are the children of the United States."[101] Quang also stressed his hope that Minh's case could result in improved relations between the two countries.

Newsday captured the emotion of the moment. A photograph from the press conference depicts the beaming smiles of the students, the pride emanating from Gloria Blauvelt, the apprehension of Minh hidden under his white and purple baseball cap, and on everyone's face, a bit of fatigue. Yet the photo also revealed something else. Rep. Mrazek stood center stage holding Minh for the cameras and talking to reporters while the HHS students surrounded him on either side. Marlo Sandler, Tara Scalia, and Sue Forte held each other's hands. They looked up at the towering congressman and the teenager they worked so hard to bring to the United States, unable to touch or talk to him. The picture was prophetic. Despite Blauvelt's best efforts, Minh's arrival signified a new phase for the HHS students, who felt their role diminished by the limelight. Having accomplished Minh's rescue, politicians, political agendas, and photo ops took priority and literally pushed the students aside. "The reporters and cameras kept piling in and telling us to get out of the way," a frustrated David Zach exclaimed.[102] Tara Scalia also recollected having very little contact with Minh when he arrived at the airport, managing only a quick hello to the young man she remembers seeing a little frightened and overwhelmed, before he was whisked away. Marlo Sandler felt the whole affair was really political and recalled the students left the airport with a "bad taste in our mouths."[103] As Gloria Blauvelt celebrated the students' success and the fact that Minh was "safe in America," all the students agreed that their relationship with Minh after he arrived was much less personal than they had envisioned.[104]

Lessons Learned

Fame, fanfare, confusion, and fear filled Minh's first few weeks in America as the coverage of his "becoming American" kept him in the media spotlight. *Newsday* detailed the happenings of "Minh's First Day Home" as he watched cartoons, played with crabs, and swam in Centerport Harbor.[105] The media cameras also followed the four HHS student council members the following week when they met with Minh for the first time. *Newsday* described the emotion and pride the students felt as they touched Minh's arm, "jiggled his foot," and "tossled [*sic*] the boy's close cropped hair" to "convince themselves that he wasn't an illusion." In the front-page photo, the huge smiles of the students and Minh seem to confirm that "this was the beginning" of a wonderful relationship between the students and Minh.

Marlo Sandler, however, remembers the experience a bit differently. "I remember there was a little bit of awkwardness around just physically touching him—like would it hurt? Would he not want us to touch him? What would be the right way to interact with him physically? I think we were also inclined to want to just hug him but we didn't know if that was appropriate."[106] Shortly thereafter, at the HHS graduation, Minh made his first public appearance. During the ceremony Gloria Blauvelt and Audrey Tiernan received honorary diplomas and a standing ovation. Minh "shied away from" the camera flashes and stares and "kept his head down."[107] Sandler remembers feeling uncomfortable at the graduation as "it felt like he [Minh] was just being trotted out for accolades. It didn't feel good. It felt like everybody was staring at him, like he was a zoo animal or something. It was like he was being used."[108]

The fanfare chased the HHS students too. As a result of their efforts, Huntington High School was one of six finalists selected for the 1986–87 *Newsday* Long Island High School of the Year for Community Service. Shortly after Minh arrived, David Zach told reporter Gail Ellen Daly of the numerous phone calls he received following a television appearance, including from a magician who "asked me to become his helper and travel all over the country with the act."[109] Gloria Blauvelt also remembers being approached by film studios to discuss the possibility of making a movie about Minh's life. East Bay Studios contacted Marlo Sandler for permission to cast her likeness on screen. They even copyrighted a movie script about Minh's rescue titled "My Father's Not Home," calling it "a universal story" that would expose "the plight of ALL Amerasian children."[110]

As the HHS students discovered the consequences of the national spotlight, Minh too found his transition to America to be far from idyllic. Like many Amerasians, Minh struggled with issues of loss, assimilation, and identity. Psychologists attributed these issues to abandonment by both the Amerasians' American fathers and their biological mothers. According to psychologists Robert McKelvey and John Webb, paternal abandonment of Amerasians often resulted in poverty, ostracism, and shame, ensuring a disadvantaged life of diminished educational and vocational opportunities in the countries of their birth. For many in Vietnam, including those living on the streets, the additional rejection by their Vietnamese mothers from fear, despair, or disgrace had long-term psychological consequences like depression and anxiety. In fact, studies found that Amerasians from Vietnam generally suffered from more psychological issues and higher levels of distress than other Vietnamese immigrants, due primarily to parental separation, rejection, and to entering the United States alone as unaccompanied minors with little formal education. Black Amerasians also had the additional issue of race to contend with.[111]

Further compounding the feelings of loss were the humiliation and rejection that often accompanied a failed search for their fathers once in America. Dartmouth psychologist Kirk Felsman explained that as Amerasians matured, many began questioning their own identity, marriage, and family, and finding their own fathers became consuming.[112] In 1985 a survey by the U.S. Catholic Conference Migration and Refugee Services found that the need for Amerasian children to connect with their American fathers was emotional and "deeply ingrained," and had been for many the primary motivation for migrating.[113] Despite the assistance of private organizations like the American Council for Nationalities Service in New York City and private individuals like Father Carroll, who continued to help Amerasians immigrate and naturalize, no official mechanism to help Amerasians with their search existed.

Moreover, American policies worked to protect the identity of the fathers at the expense of their children. Thus according to the U.S. Catholic Conference survey, by 1985 only 2 percent of Amerasians had reunited with their fathers upon arrival to the United States.[114] The potential demands for child support and fears that a half-Vietnamese child could disrupt the lives of American men took precedence over the desires of Amerasian children to find their fathers.[115] According to Vietnam veteran Greg Kane, a lot of veterans feared having to face the bad choices they made in Vietnam and a vocal minority condemned efforts to connect Amerasians with their American fathers, telling U.S. officials, "you have no right to bring these kids here." According to Kane, the last thing "a guy who is struggling to deal with the war itself" needs is "some memory coming to haunt him."[116] In his efforts to locate potential fathers for the purpose of establishing evidentiary proof of paternity, Father Carroll continued to interact with many American men who he claims agreed to acknowledge paternity only if it could be kept secret from their American wives and children.[117]

Failed father searches had major implications for issues of paternal abandonment and mental health for the Amerasian children. For them, the inability to fulfill the fantasy of family reunification contributed to feelings of isolation that had defined their lives as *bui doi* in Vietnam and now defined them as outcasts in America.[118] The absence of citizenship added to their alienation. Only through the legitimation of the father and the resulting birthright citizenship could Amerasians fully grasp and be embraced by their Americanness.

Thus by 1985 the inclusionary, yet contradictory, language of the existing Amerasian legislation—the AIA and the ODP—complicated the issue of belonging and citizenship. On the one hand Amerasians were the children of American fathers but on the other they were noncitizen refugees.[119] To help alleviate the confusion in its own work, Lutheran Immigration and Refugee Services reminded employees that although American policy legally defined Amerasians as the children of U.S. citizen fathers, and in many cases the children "looked like" American children, without paternal legitimacy, birthright citizenship was not automatic. Additionally, the State Department did not accept documents they deemed potentially inaccurate from Vietnam, including birth certificates, for the purpose of establishing citizenship.[120]

LIRS also expressed concerns about the dangers of assimilation for Amerasians. Due to their "American looks," LIRS officials explained, many Americans too quickly forced Amerasians into American cultural and racial categories. They assumed that blond hair, afros, or freckles equated to an easy adaptation into American culture. There was an ethnocentric assumption by many Americans that Amerasians would most benefit by becoming American as fast as possible, ignoring the potential harm that could result. According to LIRS officials, imposing American culture and heritage to protect Amerasians while denying them their Vietnamese heritage was troublesome. Such a practice, LIRS warned, left the Amerasian "doubly rejected." Assimilating into a new culture was just as difficult "for those who 'look American' as for those who do not" and Amerasians, "are as much Vietnamese as any other Vietnamese nationals that we serve."[121]

Minh experienced all of these challenges. During his initial interview with U.S. immigration officials in Thailand, he expressed remorse over leaving his friends in Vietnam and refused to speak with the interviewer about his life, pushing away and turning his back.[122] His Vietnamese interpreter, Xuan Bell, voiced concerns over Minh's behavior and what she perceived as a swift transition to America. Bell observed, "Whatever family has him will have a hard time. He's never lived in a family before."[123]

Still, Mrazek hoped that Minh could adjust reasonably well. To help ease Minh's transition, Mrazek and his family housed Minh for a few weeks before moving him to his permanent foster home in Centerport, New York, with Eugene and Nancy Kinney. It was during the move to the Kinneys' that Minh received the upsetting news that even in the United States there was no medical solution for his legs. Minh would have to use crutches to walk for the rest of his life.[124] The students, too, were affected. Tara Scalia recalled, "I think we were all sad because that was the reason we brought him here to fix him. When you're sixteen you think you can fix everything."[125]

The next few months were a whirlwind of emotion for Minh and the Kinneys. It was not long before the warnings of LIRS employees, Xuan Bell, and others came true regarding the potential harm caused by fast-tracking Minh's assimilation. Minh had a difficult time adjusting to his new life. Although he "looked American," Minh did not speak English or understand American culture. His supposed rescue from Vietnam had removed him from the only life and family he had ever known into an unfamiliar American society where he must have felt abandoned. The community of friends and supporters that welcomed him at JFK airport dissipated quickly after his arrival, and students at HHS turned their attention to summer vacations and college. Sue Forte remembers that after Minh arrived, "it was sort of like, now he's here and he's doing his thing and he's getting his attention. We were going to college. . . . It was not my focus after that."[126] By August, Forte, David Zach, and Marlo Sandler departed for college and Congressman Mrazek, the man Minh called "Daddy," returned to Washington.

Even as Mrazek's office reported that "Minh is adjusting well to his new life and has developed a fondness for pizza," the expectation of a quick assimilation created tension between Minh and his adoptive family.[127] "There were a lot of complications behind the scenes that I did not see right away," Mrazek later admitted.[128] Even with the Kinneys' patience and love, the cultural differences proved challenging. Assumed small things like the timing of dinner or going to school overwhelmed Minh, who was "used to eating at midnight after begging in front of the Rex hotel," and who "did not want to go to school; he could not read or write and he rebelled against it."[129] Likely yearning for some semblance of home and missing his family in Vietnam, Minh told Mrazek "I miss my mother, I want my mother to come." In August, Minh filed the paperwork to begin the long and tedious process to bring his mother and half-siblings to the United States through the ODP.[130]

By November, *Newsday* reported the "Americanization of Le Van Minh is a slow process." The article examined the cultural and language barriers Minh still faced, his affinity for sleeping on the floor, eating at odd times as he did on the street, and the longing for his mother.[131] The Kinneys blamed their challenges with Minh on the quick transition and his "lack of orientation." While pointing to his medical condition to justify the expedited departure, Mrazek, too, admitted that more time to prepare for his arrival in America would have made a difference. "I think taking him from this street environment and bringing him to America has resulted in an accelerated transformation from boy to man."[132] Shortly after, Minh left the Kinneys' for a new foster home. Minh's foster mother, Nancy Kinney, explained that during the time Minh stayed with them, "We had a lot of trouble raising him. He was very resistant to school and had no desire to get up in the morning. He wanted dinner at midnight because that's when he'd eaten on the streets in Vietnam."[133]

By February 1988, Minh lived in Oakdale, New York, his third foster home since coming to America. He was the twelfth Vietnamese or Amerasian foster son for Mary and Edwin Holter, whose home provided Minh some familiarity and normalcy. Minh lived with other boys who spoke Vietnamese, understood his culture, and looked like him. One year later, Minh moved again, this time to live with his newly emigrated mother and half siblings in Utica, New York, before finally relocating to San Jose, California, where his family settled among the growing Vietnamese community.[134] Although Minh's assimilation was not the success story first anticipated, his journey became the impetus for new legislation that would affect the lives of tens of thousands of Amerasians still living in Vietnam.

Are You My Daddy?

Robert Mrazek had hoped that the bilateral cooperation needed to bring Minh to the United States could bridge the diplomatic divide with Vietnam enough to restart the stalled ODP. Prior to his arrival in Vietnam to retrieve Minh, Mrazek had scheduled a meeting with Vietnamese officials to investigate such possibilities. Once there, however, Mrazek knew another discussion was also necessary. As he walked around Ho Chi Minh City, Mrazek noticed the dozens of Amerasian kids who followed him. These were children, Mrazek remembers, who "stood out so starkly from what is a racially pure society, particularly the black Amerasians and those with Caucasian eyes. They were surrounding me and talking about taking them to the land of their fathers."[135]

Mrazek's experience with Amerasians in Vietnam reinforced similar reports from numerous foreign visitors to Ho Chi Minh City since the war ended. Fortunately, Mrazek was in a position to do something. After speaking with some of the children through an interpreter and discovering that they could not attend school or obtain employment and suffered discrimination because they were half-American, Mrazek realized that Minh was just the first step.¹³⁶ According to Mrazek, he knew that he had to provide a way for those Amerasians who wanted to come to the United States.¹³⁷ Although Amerasians could apply to immigrate to America through the ODP, Mrazek believed he had to address their situation independent of it. The Reagan administration continued to fall short in its efforts to renegotiate the ODP with Vietnam, due to tensions over the MIA/POW issue, Vietnam's occupation of Cambodia, and the ODP backlog. However, Mrazek hoped that since Amerasians were the children of American fathers, Americans would overcome the "compassion fatigue" that now defined many of the lingering issues from the Vietnam War and be more sympathetic to their cause.¹³⁸

Mrazek found Vietnamese officials, including Foreign Minister Nguyen Co Thach, favorable to his proposal to address Amerasians separately from the ODP, treating them as immigrants, not refugees. The classification of Amerasians as immigrants was critical for Vietnamese officials, who continued to insist that Amerasians did not qualify as refugees since they received the same treatment as all other Vietnamese citizens. It was, Mrazek claimed, "a sore point" for the Vietnamese, who watched their former agreement with American officials in October of the previous year implode after the Reagan administration refused to bend on the issue. For Mrazek it was a step forward and he felt confident that he could get something done in Congress to this effect.¹³⁹ Vietnam's foreign minister agreed, declaring, "Both sides would like to have all Amerasian children in the United States. . . . the details, the procedures, will be overcome."¹⁴⁰

Upon leaving Vietnam with Minh, Mrazek vowed to pass legislation that addressed the needs of all Amerasians in Vietnam and allowed them to immigrate to the United States separately from the ODP. "It has always been my hope," Mrazek explained, "that the case of Le Van Minh represents a small ripple of hope that would grow larger . . . I feel satisfied that we have brought that day closer."¹⁴¹ In his farewell to the congressman and Minh, Thach reiterated Vietnam's support for Mrazek's plan as he exclaimed, "This time, Congressman Mrazek brings with him one Amerasian child. Next time, he will bring thousands of Amerasian children."¹⁴²

The Politics of Policy

Three days before his untimely death, Rep. Stewart McKinney, the coauthor of the Amerasian Immigration Act, introduced HR 2265, Amerasian Immigration Amendments of 1987, in the House of Representatives. The bill sought to address what McKinney viewed as the limitations of the AIA that had rendered it largely useless.[143] Still clearly bothered by the ineffectiveness of his initial legislative efforts, McKinney quoted Pearl S. Buck when he described Amerasians in Southeast Asia as "piteous, miserable, and hopeless," and called on Congress to reexamine the U.S. commitment to assist those who, "by virtue of their American parentage, deserve a chance for a better life in the United States."[144] As was the fate of many of McKinney's previous legislative proposals to address the Amerasians, the bill failed to advance out of the Judiciary Committee, and McKinney never had the chance to participate in passing Mrazek's Amerasian Homecoming Act.[145] He died on May 7, 1987, after a prolonged and private battle with AIDS.[146]

However, McKinney's decade of work on behalf of Amerasians was not in vain. Robert Mrazek continued the efforts to amend the AIA and bring Amerasians in Vietnam "home" by introducing a new and more effective law: it eliminated the AIA's requirement of an American sponsor and designated Amerasians as immigrants rather than refugees, but immigrants eligible for refugee benefits.[147] Like his predecessor, Mrazek found his efforts quickly stonewalled by Ron Mazzoli (D-KY), the chairman of the Immigration Subcommittee of the House Judiciary Committee, and Alan Simpson (R-WY), chairman of the Immigration Subcommittee of the Senate Foreign Relations Committee.[148] Five years after they supported the AIA, both Mazzoli and Simpson had little interest in taking on the Reagan administration on this issue again. No longer obsessed with paternity and blood, the administration remained staunchly opposed to separating the Amerasian issue from other points of contention with Vietnam. Singling out Amerasians, administration officials argued, undercut U.S. negotiating power by removing a powerful issue from the negotiating table and thus diminishing the ability of the United States to accomplish bigger goals.[149]

But that was not Mrazek's concern. He knew he had a very small window of opportunity in which to make change. By 1987 the average Amerasian was already seventeen-years-old, illiterate, with very little education and few job skills.[150] Mrazek understood that such challenges already made assimilation into American society difficult and that age only compounded the situation. The older Amerasians became, the less sympathetic their plight was to the American people, who would likely be more moved by the fate of abused and begging children than homeless and unemployed adults.[151] He recognized that while the MIA/POW and ODP issues were important, legislation could take years, and Amerasians simply did not have that kind of time.

Hence, in spite of the staunch political resistance to his efforts, Mrazek authored what became the Amerasian Homecoming Act. He aimed for a bill that would both address the needs of Amerasians and be acceptable to the Reagan administration. Unlike the AIA, which had depended on evidentiary proof of paternity through documents and thus proved useful to only a limited number of Amerasians, Mrazek's bill assumed that such documents did not exist. Under the AHA the only evidence Amerasians needed to prove American paternity was "their face and skin color."[152] Even with the best intentions to meet the needs of all Amerasians in Vietnam, such evidentiary requirements would force U.S. officials to categorize Amerasian applicants based on personal assumptions of what an American "looked like." However, given the absence of documented paternity, few other options existed.

According to the bill, American personnel would interview each Amerasian individually to identify evidence of American paternity. If no documentation existed, the interviews would rely on physical characteristics. Specifically, dark skin tones or "Caucasian eyes" could count as proof of paternity. Reiterating some of the arguments surrounding the AIA regarding children fathered by non-American personnel in Vietnam, Mrazek also argued that due to the large American presence during the war, it was a logical assumption that a non-Vietnamese father was American. The children Mrazek claimed were "a product of our being there," and they deserved an American response.[153]

Possibly informed by the challenges and failures experienced with the AIA and with issues that Minh now faced in his resettlement, Mrazek also had the bill loosen the immigration restrictions to allow Amerasians to bring their immediate family members with them to the United States.[154] Additionally, he designated Amerasians as immigrants but provided them with refugee benefits, which included a mandatory six-month stay in the Philippines Refugee Processing Center for cultural and language training. To alleviate concerns about immigrants, refugees, and open borders, Mrazek also ensured that qualifying Amerasians continued to count under the annual refugee ceiling for the ODP.[155]

Mrazek also seriously considered granting Amerasians birthright U.S. citizenship in the bill. However, he knew that any attempt to award blanket citizenship would ensure the bill's failure in Congress. Even as U.S. policymakers and the Reagan administration continued to deliberately use inclusionary rhetoric to describe Amerasians as the children of U.S. citizens, and current policies, including the AIA and ODP, "clearly recognized that Amerasians have a legitimate claim to live in the United States," there was little interest in going that far.[156] Excluding citizenship from the bill was "a pragmatic decision" to ensure it would pass.[157] Consequently, like all preceding Amerasian legislation, the AHA perpetuated the contradictory and uneven application of U.S. law. Claiming Amerasians as American children while failing to legitimate them through U.S. citizenship reflected the inability of lawmakers to reconcile the Amerasian mixture of race and nationality and continued to shield the nation from any formal responsibility of national paternity.

Still, citizenship would have effectively resolved the Amerasian problem by opening new immigration channels and promising Amerasians the rights and protections of the U.S. Constitution. It possibly would have also given the Reagan administration more incentive to reestablish diplomatic relations with Vietnam, to protect its American citizens. But the Amerasians remained a foreign policy problem that the Reagan administration had little interest in actually solving. It continued to insist that the discrimination Amerasians faced in Vietnam was part of Vietnam's anti-American agenda and more evidence that Vietnam was America's enemy. In refusing to negotiate with Vietnam on the Amerasian issue or separate them from the other topics of concern, the Reagan administration maintained its hard line against communism, never giving an inch, even for American children.

By 1987 President Reagan homed in on Vietnam's continued occupation of Cambodia for his anticommunist stance in Southeast Asia. In a June 1987 letter, Secretary of Defense Frank Carlucci reminded the president that normalizing relations with Vietnam must depend upon an acceptable Cambodian settlement that included the withdrawal of Vietnamese troops.[158] Consequently, the administration rejected the pressure from many members of Congress to resolve some of the smaller issues between the two countries—including the MIA/POWs and the Amerasians—as grounds for reconciliation. It cited its commitment to a free and independent Cambodia and the Cambodian noncommunist resistance. Finding common ground with Vietnam, the administration claimed, "would be viewed as a signal of weakening American resolve to stay the course" in Cambodia and could have an adverse effect on those "smaller" issues of humanitarian concern.[159]

Accordingly, the administration had no interest in diplomatic relations with Vietnam or in making the Amerasian issue soluble. Key policymakers Simpson and Mazzoli also had no interest in taking on their party over such an issue. These kinds of choices imply that Amerasians constituted nothing more than political pawns in a game of Cold War politics during the Reagan era. Mrazek understood these political layers, and thus incorporated an alternative approach to passing his bill.

On August 6, 1987, Mrazek introduced the Amerasian Homecoming Act to the House, an act to provide for the admission of Vietnamese Amerasians as immigrants to the United States for a two-year period. Arizona Republican senator John McCain introduced the sister bill to the Senate. Convinced that the AHA fulfilled the immediate needs of Amerasians and that it could pass Congress, Mrazek and his cosponsor Thomas Ridge (R-PA) submitted it to Mazzoli's Judiciary Committee. There it languished for weeks before Mazzoli told Mrazek that the bill would receive no hearings.[160] In its rejection of the bill the Judiciary Committee reasserted its commitment to the plight of Amerasians but claimed that the potential for abuse outweighed the humanitarian concern of the legislation. The committee also pointed to the ODP and the AIA and currently existing programs able to deal with the Amerasian issue.[161]

Predicting such an outcome, Mrazek had a backup plan. Thanks to a political stalemate between Congress and Reagan over ideological differences, Congress was unable to agree on a federal budget and planned to pass a continuing resolution at the end of the year to keep the government running. After gaining the necessary political support from his subcommittee and the appropriations committee, Mrazek inserted his Amerasian bill into the continuing resolution.[162] When it appeared in the House as part of the appropriations bill, Mrazek faced harsh criticism from a furious Mazzoli, who assailed a bill created by a single member of the House that never had hearings and diverged from the policy standards for U.S. relations with Vietnam.[163] However, Mazzoli could not remove the provision without rejecting the entire continuing resolution. The House approved it and sent it to the Senate, where Mrazek had a critical ally in Senator McCain, a Vietnam War veteran and former prisoner of war. McCain was remarkably sensitive to Amerasians, and he held great influence in the Senate regarding all things Vietnam. It was McCain who introduced the initial bill. With his support, and that of committee chair David Obey (D-WI), whom Mrazek credits for his savvy yet tough negotiation skills, the Homecoming Act successfully passed through the Senate and landed on Reagan's desk in December 1987 as part of a 1,194-page omnibus bill.[164] Unable to remove the Homecoming Act from the legislation, Reagan had no choice but to sign it into law.

Hope

The students at HHS were proud of their efforts. Not only had they succeeded in bringing Le Van Minh to the United States, their actions had become the catalyst for bilateral cooperation between two Cold War foes. They had, in essence, bridged the gap that existed between the United States and Vietnam for over a decade. Although there was some frustration upon Minh's arrival that the media and politicians had overlooked their contribution and hard work, the students appreciated the chance to make what they believed was a real difference.[165]

Even after they moved on from the year-long Minh campaign, the students sometimes thought about Minh from their dormitories and classrooms at Penn State (Zach and Forte) and Stanford (Sandler). For a few months, Audrey Tiernan and Gloria Blauvelt kept the students informed of Minh and the progress Mrazek made with the AHA. They were proud of their role in Minh's life and in the Homecoming Act, but for some there was guilt after hearing reports of the challenges Minh faced. Now adults with families of their own, Forte, Sandler, and Scalia all admit that there was little contact with Minh ever again. "This whole thing has made me reflect on how easily it seems we let it go," Sandler explained. "It seems really unfair to have taken someone's life and considered it a student government project . . . we should have been better about following up or ensuring that he was doing well."[166]

The fact that Minh did not attend HHS or live in the Huntington community contributed to the students' disconnect. Only months after his arrival in the United States, Minh effectively disappeared from the halls of the school and the Huntington community. In June, HHS junior Brian Dooreck promised Minh that he would not "just say welcome and forget about him," and committed to leading a school committee to monitor Minh's progress in America.[167] It is unclear if the committee ever transpired. However, by the time Tara Scalia graduated from HHS in 1988, Minh existed only in a photograph scattered among many others under the aptly titled "Homecoming" section of the HHS yearbook. In 2000 Marlo Sandler, living only minutes from Minh's last known address in San Jose, California, told *Newsday* that on her honeymoon trip to Vietnam she saw numerous homeless Amerasians and "thought about Minh the entire time."[168]

Within a year of his arrival in America, the poster child for the Homecoming Act had melted into the shadows of American society.

Neither the students at HHS, U.S. policymakers, nor the Reagan administration made any serious attempts to find Minh's father or grant Minh citizenship. Unable to pass the citizenship test, he never legally became American and continued to live the life of a refugee struggling with the challenges posed by limited language, education, and job skills.[169] It is possible that over time Minh recognized the irony of being rescued from his homeland because his American father abandoned him, only to be abandoned again by those who "saved" him. Still, thirteen years later, long after the cameras, reporters, and fame had disappeared, Minh remained adamant that he was better off in America than in Vietnam. In America, Minh exclaimed, "you have hope."[170] As Robert Mrazek witnessed the obstacles that Minh continued to face in his assimilation into America, he too hoped that the Homecoming Act, even without citizenship, would benefit Amerasians in Vietnam by allowing them to immigrate to the United States.

| Chapter Seven

"Like a Home without a Roof"

The Amerasian Homecoming Act went into effect on March 21, 1988, as a bilateral agreement between the United States and Vietnam. It provided a two-year window in which all Amerasians born in Vietnam between January 1, 1962, and January 1, 1976, and their immediate relatives could immigrate to the United States.[1] The estimated numbers of Amerasians still living in Vietnam varied in the tens of thousands. As a result, the AHA avoided imposing numerical limitations, accepting all Amerasians from Vietnam who wanted to immigrate to the United States. Approvals, however, counted under the refugee admissions ceiling of the Orderly Departure Program, and the Migration and Refugee Assistance fund financed the program.[2] The AHA used the preexisting structure of the ODP to commence immigration procedures. It replaced the UN officials responsible for interviewing and approving applicants with U.S. State Department employees who now directly decided which applicants had American fathers and could immigrate to the United States.[3] Those approved for immigration received immigrant status and refugee benefits of six months of language and culture training, as well as medical care and settlement assistance through the Philippines Refugee Processing Center (PRPC) and the Amerasian Resettlement Program (ARP).[4]

Both interventions sought to help ease the transition into American society and begin the process of assimilation.[5]

Amerasians who qualified for the AHA ranged in age from ten to twenty-six years old and by 1988 had spent critical years growing up in Vietnam. Some had families of their own.[6] By the time they applied for the AHA the majority of Amerasians had lived long enough to recognize their physical differences in Vietnam's relatively homogenous society and to internalize their marginalized status as *bui doi* or *con lai*. For many, poverty, poor education, and their association with the war compounded their ostracism. Poverty proved to be the biggest barrier to education for most Amerasians, and their Vietnamese peers generally assumed them to be both poor and uneducated. On average, white Amerasians were thirteen times and Black Amerasians thirty-nine times more likely than other Vietnamese to immigrate with low levels of education.[7] In 1989 the California Department of Social Services declared that the most important concern for Amerasians is the "self-identity crisis"—the result of having spent a lifetime ostracized, taunted, and ridiculed because of their appearance.[8]

The AHA transformed the Amerasians' "American faces" from symbols of shame to a source of pride, as the more American an Amerasian looked, the quicker their approval for the AHA and their immigration to America. Five years after the contentious debate in Congress regarding the AIA over evidentiary proof and American blood, and whether their "American faces" made them American, the AHA ensured just that. In contrast to the AIA, the AHA accepted applicants without evidentiary proof on the sole basis of their looks. According to an official of the American consulate in Vietnam, the AHA interview started and ended with "the most superficial of evaluations: a look at the applicant's face. Anyone thought to look like an American is immediately approved, regardless of whether he or she has any supporting evidence."[9] However, by relying on Amerasians' looks as proof of paternity, the AHA elevated the role of race and assumptions of bloodlines. Interviewers reverted to longstanding racial stereotypes to cast Asians and Americans into two distinct and opposing racial categories to determine nationality. Thus the AHA perpetuated the assumptions of mixed race otherness and Asian foreignness that had always complicated Amerasian existence and branded them with the stigma of illegitimacy. In this way the AHA brought the Amerasian experience in America full circle.

The Process

The application process for the AHA was a bilateral affair initiated by the Vietnamese government, which was responsible for informing Amerasians and their family members about the program. Amerasian applicants submitted petitions for an interview with U.S. officials through local Vietnamese authorities, who then approved or rejected each request, forwarding the list of approved petitions to the ODP office in Bangkok, Thailand. ODP employees rechecked the list before creating applicant files and scheduling interviews. Approved applicants and their families then traveled to Ho Chi Minh City, where teams of U.S. officials conducted the interviews. Applicants who passed the interview received a medical examination before departing for the PRPC. Applicants who failed returned home.[10]

Some U.S. officials, including Rep. Mrazek, worried that the process excluded Amerasians who lived outside of the normal channels of communication in Vietnam or who lacked access to information about the program because of poverty or illiteracy.[11] In addition, many Amerasians claimed that local Vietnamese officials actually deterred them from applying to the AHA or required them to pay bribes to submit the initial petition.[12] A 1992 review of the program by the General Accounting Office (GAO) found that in many of the rural and mountainous regions only 50 percent of Amerasians left Vietnam through the AHA. According to the report, "not every Amerasian has been informed of the program and that even of those who are aware of it, not all have been able to move into the processing stream."[13]

The fate of the tens of thousands of Amerasians who did apply rested largely in the hands of the American interviewer. As anticipated by Mrazek, most Amerasians lacked the necessary documentation to prove American paternity by blood and had only their physical appearance—skin color, eye shape, and hair—as evidence. Although the only plausible solution absent evidentiary proof, the reliance on physical appearance in the AHA unintentionally made race hypervisible and gave cover to invidious racial stereotypes. It forced American interviewers to rely on such stereotypes to determine what an American and a non-American Asian looked like. Interviewers charged with determining whether an applicant looked American or Asian relied on subjective notions of whiteness and blackness to determine paternity and thus nationality. Interviewers imposed racialized assumptions of what the presumed American father looked like by inspecting the features of Amerasians in search of "American blood."[14] In justifying the denial of an applicant, one American interviewer explained, "The child's physical appearance does not support Caucasian parentage."[15]

Often, the racial mixture of the Amerasian challenged the limits of the interviewer's understanding of whiteness and blackness as racial rationale for approving an applicant. Amerasians with Asian American, Latino, and Native American fathers—nonwhite and non-Black—proved difficult to identify. In considering the paternity of an Amerasian applicant who claimed to have a Hawaiian father, one American official admitted the difficulty in defining an "American look." In such cases, he explained, and for this applicant, his "future hangs on whether an olive-skinned kid with black hair and eyes is going to pass for being half-Hawaiian."[16]

There appears to have been little formal protocol regarding how an interviewer should determine paternity in such cases.[17] U.S. State Department employees like Alice Krupnick sometimes found it impossible to fit the Amerasian mixture cleanly into an American racial category and often sought advice from colleagues. During the interview of one boy whose paternity confounded her, Krupnick marched the child into the offices of each of her colleagues seeking advice. One responded by exclaiming, "I can't put my finger on it, but there's something different about his face," while another determined, "That kid is pure Vietnamese through and through. He's just weird looking!"[18]

The racial profiling of Amerasians to produce categories of nationality—American and Asian—once again exposed America's long and complicated relationship with mixed-race populations in general and the nation's history of exclusionary policies against people of Asian descent in particular. The reliance on racially familiar attributes as evidence of paternity presented an inverted application of blood quantum law. As we saw, blood quantum was once used as a tool of exclusion, relegating mixed race persons in America to the racial category of their nonwhite parent. In the case of the AHA however, interviewers identified the "color" of Amerasians' blood as a condition of inclusion: to determine if they were American. Thus instead of relegating Amerasians to the racial category of their nonwhite parent to deem them un-American, under the AHA, a determination of mixed blood effectively elevated Vietnamese to the status of their white or Black American fathers, deeming them racially acceptable American children approved for immigration. Amerasians who looked least like Asians and most like white or Black Americans were, for the purposes of the AHA, Americans.[19]

The reliance on looks as evidence of race and therefore, nationality, forced interviewers to juxtapose familiar American features and foreign Asian ones within a binary of racial difference that in some cases limited the inclusionary intentions of the AHA. For those Amerasians whose physical appearance was less racially distinctive or whose fathers were non-Black or nonwhite Americans, the reliance on race proved exclusionary.[20] Without clear physical evidence of biological filiation with a white or Black American father, interviewers often denied valid Amerasian applicants.[21] In each instance, interviewers relied on preconceived, subjective notions of what an American and what a non-American looked like to make their decision. This was a seemingly impossible task considering the demographic composition of the American populace and one that forced interviewers to revert to outdated colonialist interpretations of "us" Americans and "them" Asians.[22] Hence, AHA interviewers viewed the Amerasian mixture as either a racial solution or a racial problem.[23]

From Dust to Gold

Initially, however, interviewers largely ignored the racial rationale. Inspired by the excitement and goodwill surrounding the AHA, during the first two years of the program the approval rate was a perfect 100 percent.[24] American interviewers like Krupnick worked to fulfill Mrazek's vision for all Amerasians and their family members who wanted to leave Vietnam to come to the United States. Initially most interviewers seemed to agree with Krupnick that their purpose was to right the wrong committed by the U.S. government and accept a national paternal responsibility for Amerasians.[25] However, the generous approval rates brought unintended side effects that eventually soured interviewers and affected their decisions on future cases.[26]

The inclusionary language of the AHA and the corresponding media coverage of the "thousands of children fathered by Americans" and "left behind" in Vietnam, reinforced the message that Amerasians were American children.[27] U.S. media outlets described the United States as righting the wrongs of war through the AHA and linked the Amerasians' racial hybridity—American paternity—and U.S. responsibility. While promoting the narrative of the hardships and discrimination suffered by Amerasians in Vietnam, journalists often emphasized the attractiveness of the Amerasians' "American" attributes, which they implied made them more beautiful than their Vietnamese counterparts. Photographs of Amerasians with distinctive Caucasian and Black features holding pictures of their American soldier fathers accompanied such stories. A discourse of racial hybridity and the racialization of Amerasians by media outlets convinced many Americans that Amerasians were in fact American children and reminded them of their paternal responsibility.[28]

Those same discussions also persuaded Amerasians in Vietnam that they were Americans. The inclusionary language surrounding the AHA and the legislation's recognition of Amerasians' American paternity introduced a new sense of pride and value to those once condemned as the "children of dust." According to one Amerasian woman, after hearing about the AHA, "I became more familiar with America when I learned that my father was American. I thought it was a noble land and my fatherland." Another Amerasian attested that the AHA "gave me hope for a better future."[29]

The perception that the United States had finally accepted

Amerasians as American made them attractive to other Vietnamese, who now viewed them as a ticket to America. Amerasians became popular targets for pretend friends, guardians, and family members. Lacking the financial resources to travel to Ho Chi Minh City for the required interview or to pay the bribes demanded by Vietnamese officials, or simply scared to make the journey to America alone, many Amerasians accepted the offers of fake families and arranged marriages.[30] Twenty-year-old Amerasian Trinh revealed that before the AHA, many Vietnamese treated Amerasians "like dogs in the street," but after the AHA "'we began living like rich people. People can pay as much as two thousand dollars, to buy an Amerasian.'"[31] Tyler Chau Pritchard, an Amerasian who emigrated in 1991, explained the shift: "suddenly everyone in Vietnam loved us. It was like we were walking on clouds. We were their meal ticket, and people offered a lot of money to Amerasians willing to claim them as mothers and grandparents and siblings."[32]

Corruption abounded as Amerasians often had to bribe Vietnamese officials responsible for processing their paperwork and approving them for interviews. According to one Vietnamese girl, "we paid ten thousand dong per name to register and three hundred thousand dong to get a passport for the family. They 'lost' our names, and we had to pay more bribes. Then we had to pay more money to the translator at the interview site, the fat woman dripping with gold."[33] Although the average annual per capita income in Vietnam during the period was only $230, a 1992 evaluation found that the cost for Amerasians to apply for the AHA ranged from $50 to $5,000, with an average cost of $350.[34] Furthermore, because the typical American interviewer had only one year of language training before interviewing applicants, they often relied on translators supplied by the Vietnamese government to communicate.[35] For hopeful candidates this often meant yet another bribe to ensure that translators communicated their stories correctly. Those Amerasians unable to afford such favors often found their interviews sabotaged by vindictive translators.[36]

The ruse of fake families who promised to care for and love their children in exchange for a ticket to America also confused Amerasians seeking acceptance and belonging. All too often, Amerasians found themselves abandoned once they departed Vietnam, after the relationship with their bogus families deteriorated.[37] Twenty-four-year old Amerasian Phuong emphasized: "When we were in Vietnam, being interviewed, they [fake family] were very nice to me, sure. But now that we are here [PRPC], they don't need me anymore. They treat me like dirt . . . they insult me, berate me, the daughters even have attacked me. They loved the Amerasian when they need to leave Vietnam but now they despise us."[38]

Such treatment, however, did not allay the fears of many Amerasians that their fake families might be discovered. Fraud revealed during the interview process automatically disqualified Amerasians from participating in or ever reapplying to the AHA.[39] If unveiled in the PRPC, Amerasians risked permanent residency in the PRPC camp, where they were marked as criminals subject to incarceration in the camp jail.[40] Any deception uncovered once in the United States made Amerasians ineligible for refugee status and benefits. The discovery of fake families also disqualified the accompanying Amerasians from ever bringing their real families to the United States, thus disincentivizing Amerasians from reporting such deception.[41] One person highlighted the consequences for an Amerasian who reported his fake mother to the authorities: "Minh will become a secondary migrant cut loose from refugee center benefits, housing allowances, schooling, and welfare. He will become a criminal liable to expulsion from the United States, and he will be disqualified from sponsoring for immigration any of his real family members. His fake mother will get the apartment, food stamps, cash assistance, Medicare, ESL, and sympathy for having raised a 'no good' Amerasian."[42]

Early on, the issue of sham families complicated the humanitarianism behind the AHA. As the program progressed, the interview of the applicant and accompanying family proved critical in exposing fraud. Interviewers subjected Amerasians and their family members to a series of simple questions, sometimes separating family members to test for accuracy. If the stories corresponded, interviewers like Krupnick looked for subjective signs of family affiliation—physical resemblances and genuine affection. Even in cases where an interviewer suspected fraud, according to Krupnick, applicants were often reluctant to reveal the crime, likely fearing it would hinder their own chances of approval.[43]

The Interviewers

With so much subjectivity embedded in the approval process, the backgrounds and perceptions of the AHA interviewers proved critical. According to a 1990 U.S. government review of the first two years of the AHA, the training and experience of American interviewers included knowledge of refugee processing procedures, an understanding of the conditions in Vietnam and Southeast Asia, and an average of over eighteen years of service with the U.S. Immigration and Naturalization Service.[44] In reality, however, interviewers ranged in training and experience from Foreign Service officers under the U.S. State Department who worked and lived in Vietnam with Vietnamese spouses, to those with backgrounds in U.S. Border Patrol with no previous foreign experience.[45] The overlap of interviewers from different U.S. agencies introduced different and often competing ideologies about immigration, refugees, and borders. State Department employees interpreted their position as an extension of U.S. foreign policy and the nation's Cold War commitment to saving Southeast Asian refugees. They tended to assume that everyone who desired to leave Vietnam was a legitimate refugee in fear of persecution. In contrast, INS officers, under the guidance of a U.S. Justice Department committed to protecting the nation's borders from the burden of economic migrants and immigrant invasions, took a more cynical approach. They were more concerned with U.S. national security than foreign policy and sought to prevent fake refugees from entering the United States and to ensure that only those applicants who clearly fulfilled a strictly interpreted standard of "refugee" be admitted.[46]

Additionally, while most interviewers received a year of Vietnamese language training, U.S. officials admitted that it was not enough to enable them to discern the different accents, dialects, and customs of the Vietnamese people they were responsible for interviewing. Limited language skills thus forced interviewers to depend primarily on interpreters supplied by the Vietnamese government to interview applicants.[47] Interviewers also understood the dangers inherent in their inability to communicate directly to applicants and knew that interpreters could manipulate the outcome in exchange for a fee.[48] U.S. officials in fact blamed the inconsistent AHA approval rates on the reliance on Vietnamese interpreters. Unable to alleviate the situation, interviewers tended to place greater emphasis on the part of the interview they could control, emphasizing how the applicants looked more than what they said.[49]

During the first months of the AHA, twenty-seven-year-old Krupnick, fresh from her year of intensive Vietnamese language training, joined other American interviewers who embraced Mrazek's vision to approve any Amerasians who wanted to come to the United States.[50] Members of her interview team included Bill, a former USAID employee in Vietnam, and Bob, a Vietnam veteran. Both men had Vietnamese wives and Amerasian children and, thus, a personal investment in the AHA. According to Krupnick, Bill and Bob expressed genuine concern for the Amerasian applicants and those Amerasians living on the streets who daily thrust scraps of paper at them asking for help finding their fathers and pleading to be taken to America.[51] Other members of the interview team were less concerned. Former INS officers who lacked personal connections to Vietnam and who did not know the language tended to believe that most AHA applicants were motivated by economic opportunity.[52] Krupnick described them as "xenophobic good ole boys, replete with cowboy boots and suitcases full of American snack food." Unlike Bill and Bob, these interviewers ignored Amerasians who called to them on the streets, brushed away their outstretched hands, and disregarded the scraps of paper pressed upon them. Still, during the first two years of the AHA even these interviewers approached their task optimistically and took the humanitarian responsibility for Amerasians seriously, approving every applicant.[53]

Even with a 100 percent approval rate, concerns quickly emerged that policymakers had underestimated the number of qualified Amerasians and that Vietnamese officials had failed to contact those Amerasians living outside of Vietnam's major cities.[54] By 1989 resettlement and humanitarian organizations reported that many Amerasians still remained in Vietnam. In response, policymakers extended the program indefinitely.[55] At the same time, international frustration with the continuing boat exodus out of Vietnam and the almost four hundred thousand refuge-seekers held in camps in numerous first-asylum countries resulted in important changes to U.S. and international policy that took a more deliberately restrictive approach to determining who was a refugee.[56]

In 1988 the United States sought to distinguish bona fide refugees from economic migrants or opportunists leaving Vietnam. Once presumed to be refugees fleeing persecution, ODP applicants now had to show evidence of a credible fear of persecution to gain approval.[57] One year later, over seventy countries concerned about the continuation of clandestine departures from Vietnam, and seeking to share the burden and cost of the asylum and resettlement of refugees, adopted the Comprehensive Plan of Action (CPA) at the International Conference on Indo-Chinese Refugees. The CPA instituted a more orderly and legal means of departure while implementing a more restrictive screening process, which separated economic migrants who would be repatriated to their countries of origin from actual refugees who were resettled elsewhere.[58] Even though the CPA was not directed at Amerasians specifically, the emphasis in identifying "real" refugees necessarily infused a skepticism into the ODP that affected how U.S. interviewers interpreted Amerasian applicants to the AHA. In 1989 the approval rate for the AHA dropped precipitously to 36 percent.[59]

By the time Congress renewed the AHA in 1990, the initial optimism of most interview teams had dissipated, along with the remaining support and sympathy of the American public overwhelmed with "compassion fatigue" regarding Vietnam. After over ten years of dealing with the issue of Southeast Asian migration, one refugee official speculated, some Americans "are asking how much longer the American responsibility to the Indochinese is to last."[60] Resettlement organizations voiced their alarm at the recent decline in federal funding for refugee resettlement specifically for those from Southeast Asia and warned that such disinvestment could result in antirefugee sentiment within local communities that felt "unfairly burdened by new arrivals."[61]

Interviewers became more intolerant of the growing amounts of fraud and corruption in the AHA and took an increasingly conservative approach to approving applicants, especially in questionable cases. As one interviewer put it, "I assume fraud in every case I see."[62] After two years, many experienced frustration with the burden of such a subjective decision-making process and felt job burnout. For some, their intolerance exposed a lingering anger and hurt from the Vietnam War. For others, it revealed an underlying and problematic bias against Amerasians, whom they perceived as the foreign offspring of Asian prostitutes rather than the children of U.S. soldiers. Even idealistic interviewers like Krupnick admitted that after two years, "little by little I stop being quite as naïve, quite as curious, quite as engaged. I stop being quite as compassionate, quite as unbiased. I am tired. Tired of the caseload . . . ; tired of the fraud; tired of the policy changes."[63]

By the time the AHA entered its second phase, in 1991, the approval rate under the program had drastically declined to 80 percent, followed by an abysmal 20 percent in 1992.[64] The shifting numbers also reflected the inconsistent judgments among interviewers regarding what an Amerasian looked like. While one interviewer accepted 65 percent of their cases, another approved only 35 percent.[65] Understandably, many interviewers, worried about approving fake Amerasians, began to question the racial characteristics they once depended upon to determine whether an applicant was an Amerasian, narrowing the once reliable physical characteristics of whiteness and blackness that had justified claims of American paternity. Even Krupnick, who once employed liberal interpretations of an "American face" to determine acceptance, now diligently tried to fit the faces of Amerasian applicants into a more conventional version of what an American "looked like."[66] "Distinguishing features that could be mimicked by non-Amerasian Vietnamese" were particularly suspect, including skin color and hair texture; these were no longer taken for clear indicators of American paternity, complicating traditional notions of race.⁶⁷ Interviewers who wondered if applicants had lightened or darkened their skin, dyed their hair color, manufactured afros, or surgically widened their eyes were left to consider more obscure markers to determine an applicant's Americanness.⁶⁸ As one exasperated interviewer exclaimed, "usually we rely on freckles for proof."⁶⁹

Consequently, how interviewers understood the Amerasian issue more broadly became paramount to the approval process. Unfortunately for Amerasians, and reflected in the plummeting acceptance rates, an overwhelming sense of cynicism about claims of paternity and the exclusion and abuse Amerasians claimed they faced in Vietnam replaced the optimism that defined the first two years of the program. Even interviewers with Vietnamese spouses or Amerasian children began to view the applicants with more suspicion. For example, the ODP colleagues of American interviewer Robert McMahan surprisingly described him, the father of two Amerasian children, as "heartless" in his dealings with Amerasian applicants. McMahan later admitted that despite his own children, as an interviewer "I used to avoid contact with Amerasians. . . . I thought their mothers were a bunch of whores.'"⁷⁰

Many INS employees during the period expressed an anti-immigrant and sometimes racist sentiment, voicing concerns that the AHA was contributing to an "immigrant invasion" of America. One female interviewer aptly nicknamed *Nyetnik* by AHA applicants for her "boorish manners" felt very strongly that the AHA was a mistake. She emphasized the social and economic toll of immigration on America and pointed to Cuban leader Fidel Castro's decision to send Cuban "criminals" to the United States as part of the Mariel Boatlift a few years earlier. According to *Nyetnik* the AHA would have similar results as Vietnam "scrapes up its social riffraff, its schizophrenics, and criminals, and sends them to America. We're watering down our gene pool with Amerasian mental cases. We're flooding the social welfare system with fake families."⁷¹

This period of the AHA also revealed a startling willingness by interviewers to revel in racial stereotypes that may have influenced their subjective judgments. The belief that Amerasian children had predilections for criminal and negative behavior was particularly common, as interviewers often described them as "part of an unruly subset of society, 'willful,' 'stubborn,' 'unfocused,' 'they have no discipline.'"[72] Even Bill McCabe, the father of an Amerasian child and the director of the Pearl S. Buck Foundation in the Philippines, acceded to the racial stereotype of the "sneaky" Asian as he described his own children as having "manipulative, complex, divided personalities. They can look me right in the eye and lie."[73]

As pressure mounted regarding the fraud and corruption infesting the AHA, interviewers increasingly collaborated on their cases, often consulting with each other over the physical appearance of an applicant. The general rule among interviewers was that it took three no's to deny an applicant and one yes for acceptance.[74] In discussing the appearance of one applicant with a colleague, Krupnick describes how "together we discuss the boy's characteristics in front of him and the family being interviewed. 'The eyes look round and seem to be a shade of brown.'"[75] The *Seattle Times* reported on the physical assessment and denial of Amerasian applicant Hung, whose American father Carl had flown to Bangkok to be reunited with his son. "During Hung's exit interview, he was taken out into the sunlight and studied by members of the interview team. It was at this time that the 'anthropological experts' from the Orderly Departure Program, U.S. Department of State, decided that Hung did not have any Caucasian features. This meant that Hung was unacceptable for departure from Vietnam and subsequent reunification with his father in the United States."[76]

The process itself proved humiliating for the applicants; however, even as interviewers proved increasingly wary of fraud and cynical of Amerasians generally, without documentation their physical features remained their only chance for approval.

PRPC

Once accepted for the AHA, Amerasians and their families departed Vietnam for the Philippines Refugee Processing Center on the Bataan peninsula. There they joined other Vietnamese refugees in one of the ten "neighborhoods" that housed approximately seventeen hundred refugees for six months of language and culture training before resettlement in the United States.[77] The PRPC opened in 1980 to house Southeast Asian refugees immigrating to first-asylum countries. By 1989, its purpose was to prepare all Southeast Asian refugees for life in American society through assimilation that would Americanize them and equip them "to be self-reliant."[78]

Initially, American social service and resettlement organizations, including the Indochina Resource Action Center, Lutheran Immigration and Refugee Services (LIRS), and the International Catholic Migration Commission (ICMC), supported the mandatory six-month stay. They viewed the PRPC as a "good taxpayer investment" that helped Amerasians efficiently assimilate into a "productive role in American society."[79] The U.S. State Department implemented a three-prong approach to basic literacy and cultural skills that emphasized English as a second language, cultural orientation, and work orientation. Classes taught life skills, the specific and practical tasks needed to survive in America, including how to balance a checkbook, fill out a job application, apply for welfare, light a gas stove, and flush a toilet.[80]

To alleviate concerns that the refugees might become economic burdens on American taxpayers through unemployment or welfare dependency, the PRPC made economic self-sufficiency the mission of its assimilation program. Curriculum instilled in refugees the idea that good immigrants and good Americans worked hard and paid their own bills. Classes and staff members discouraged welfare dependency by constantly reminding camp residents that "most Americans think that people who stay on welfare are lazy," and that "'upward mobility is very possible for people who work hard."[81]

After six months of training to be an American, the refugees knew that while they would start at the bottom of the economic and social ladder in America they must accept their subservient position and minimum-wage job. Only through hard work and perseverance would they eventually prosper.[82] Upon leaving the PRPC, residents received a so-called statement of understanding that reiterated the objectives of the training program: "Shortly you will be arriving in the United States as a refugee. You will be sponsored and assisted by one of the Voluntary Resettlement Agencies. The goal of sponsorship is to bring you to economic self-sufficiency as quickly as possible usually through employment. The purpose is to help yourself."[83]

By 1989 reports of the dangerous and crowded conditions in the PRPC led to increasing public criticism. In his 1989 book *Alien Winds*, English professor James Tollefson, who spent sixteen months in refugee camps in Southeast Asia, including a stint with the ICMC's teacher education unit at the PRPC, criticized the training program. According to Tollefson, the PRPC's focus on economic independence—self-sufficiency and the myth of upward mobility—failed to promote civic or political responsibility among the refugees and did not prepare them to become contributing members of American society or future American citizens. By failing to teach refugees civic responsibility or prepare them to participate politically as fully functioning American citizens, Tollefson claimed, PRPC residents only learned how to participate in the U.S. economy as workers and consumers.[84] They graduated the camp understanding only that a willingness to learn, the ability to follow orders, and dependability were the keys to success in America.

English language curriculum reinforced such messaging by teaching the language of subservience, according to Tollefson. PRPC residents "are taught how to ask for permission, but not how to give orders; how to apologize, but not how to disagree; how to comply, but not how to complain."[85] They are introduced only to low-income jobs in factories and on assembly lines and "periodically, representatives of McDonald's and Mister Donut set up simulated fast food counters to teach them how to work behind a cash register."[86] The PRPC, Tollefson alleged, only equipped refugees to work minimum-wage jobs, ensuring they did not have the skills or tools to compete with working-class or middle-class Americans or have access to upward mobility or American citizenship. He compared the PRPC assimilation process with the early twentieth-century Americanization movement, which sought to rapidly assimilate certain kinds of immigrants by replacing their traditional cultures and behaviors with "proper" American ones.[87] Ironically, the movement had advocated for the exclusion of Asian immigrants, who supporters argued did not intend to become Americans and were too different, distant, and foreign to ever assimilate.[88]

During the AHA, politicians including Republican senator Alan Simpson and Colorado's Democratic governor Richard Lamm used the same racialized restrictionist immigration discourse to fuel fears of the growing threat they believed immigrants posed to America and to promote assimilation as a way to exclude the most undesirable from crossing American borders.[89] According to Simpson, assimilation was "fundamental to American public values and institutions," and those who do not adapt may "create in America some of the same social, political and economic problems which existed in the country which they have chosen to depart." Lamm agreed. The United States "can accept additional immigrants, but we must be sure they become American."[90]

Tollefson's analysis of the PRPC was widely criticized by former refugee resettlement workers and scholars: they accused him of skewing the data for his own agenda and condemned his comparison between the PRPC and the Americanization movement. Although his critiques did not focus specifically on Amerasians, who composed 30 to 40 percent of the population in the PRPC camp by 1989, many other evaluations of the PRPC did.[91] A 1988 review prepared for AHA cosponsor Thomas Ridge and specific to the Amerasian experience contradicted Tollefson's claims. Specifically, it reported that the education provided at the PRPC on democracy, capitalism, leadership, and citizenship did benefit Amerasians. According to the report, the PRPC made the Amerasians' "assimilation into a productive role in American society" quicker and easier.[92]

Even with the language and education training, however, camp life proved difficult for many Amerasians. Upon entering the PRPC their favored status as "children of gold" quickly disappeared, as their American ties no longer protected them from abuse or marginalization. Amerasians experienced mistreatment from their Vietnamese peers, and from their fake families that no longer needed to maintain the façade of kinship, now that they had their ticket to America. Such rejection compounded feelings of abandonment and exclusion experienced back home, and many joined gangs, committed crimes, or became victims of crime. Female Amerasians, often desired for their mixed-race beauty, feared the threat of rape and unwanted pregnancies.[93] Additionally, many faced confusion over their identity. Deemed the children of Americans by the AHA and admitted to the United States as immigrants, the requirement that they enter the PRPC as refugees proved confusing.[94] Consequently, many Amerasians experienced an identity divergence and the distress associated with continuous rejection.[95]

PRPC camp and resettlement workers further complicated their camp experience. Shocked by Amerasians' "Western looks," many workers initially exhibited particular compassion toward Amerasians, until they realized they behaved like Vietnamese. As one camp worker put it, Amerasians were confusing, with "Vietnamese mannerisms in American bodies."[96] Furthermore, once in the camp, no special curriculum, treatment, or acknowledgment of Amerasians as the children of American fathers existed. They faced the same experience as all other camp refugees and any discussions of paternity occurred only in the private offices of camp counselors. In fact, Amerasians composed the primary clients of the counseling units at the PRPC, as increasing numbers of Amerasian "problem cases" demanded additional resettlement resources to address the potential for hostility, violence, and depression among the newcomers.[97] Accounts of suicide and deep-rooted depression among Amerasians were common. According to Fred Bemak, a mental health expert enlisted by the National Institute for Mental Health to determine why 14 percent of Amerasians resettled in the United States attempted suicide, "we'd never seen anything like this with any refugee group."[98]

Still, counselors and other PRPC and resettlement workers often failed to associate the psychosocial and adjustment struggles of Amerasians with fatherlessness, isolation, or rejection and blamed it instead on the treatment Amerasians had faced in Vietnam. To better assist them, the Amerasian Resettlement Program concluded that the fundamental issue was the mixture of blood: "the issue of Amerasian self-identity is perhaps at the core of their problems, having both Vietnamese and American blood."[99] PRPC authorities also pointed to the poverty, discrimination, and persecution Amerasians faced in Vietnam as making them more inclined than other refugee populations to join gangs, abuse drugs, and engage in sexually dangerous behaviors.[100] In 1990, the Indochinese Community Center in Washington DC identified newly arriving Amerasians from Vietnam as the highest risk group for AIDS. Ultimately, PRPC authorities and resettlement workers assumed all Amerasians to be the victims of trauma, abuse, and psychic wounds that resulted in mental health disorders, developmental delays, inadequate socialization, low self-esteem, problematic sexual behavior, violence, and confused personal identity.[101] As a result, Amerasians were repeatedly profiled as "maladjusted young adults" with "special needs" who "posed challenges" for camp staff.[102]

Concerned about contradictions in the treatment of Amerasians and the reports of violence, abuse, and mental health issues in the camp, the Vietnam Veterans of America undertook its own investigation in 1989. The critical question for the VVA centered on whether or not Amerasians, as children of American fathers, should have to transition through the PRPC. According to the VVA, the problem with having Amerasians at the PRPC was they were not refugees. Vietnam did not accept that label and the AHA designated them as immigrants. To the VVA, the United States had a national responsibility to Amerasians "that outweighs the standing commitment that America has toward the world's refugees. The Amerasians are truly our own."[103]

For these American children, the VVA argued, the PRPC did more harm than good. It unnecessarily forced Amerasians to "postpone their long overdue arrival in the U.S.," requiring them to live in "atrocious conditions, where there is insufficient food and water, where they are crowded into billets constructed with asbestos, with people unrelated or known to them, and where their daily lives are regulated by coercion and fears." The biggest tragedy, it asserted, was that Amerasians who processed through the camp and immigrated to the United States retained the same disadvantaged status they held in Vietnam. The VVA also incorporated Tollefson's critique into their assessment, arguing that the PRPC failed to prepare Amerasians for the opportunities in America and instead reinforced their position of powerlessness by preparing them to be subjects rather than citizens and resettling them in America's urban ghettos. Thus rather than transforming Amerasians into Americans as the PRPC proposed to do, the experience degraded and reduced them from American children to refugees.[104]

Such assertions by the most politically powerful Vietnam veterans organization in the nation proved compelling. The VVA's recognition of the Amerasians' American paternity and the resulting national responsibility exposed the problematic contradiction in U.S. policy regarding the official status of Amerasians. As Amerasians departed the PRPC for their new lives in America, the concerns expressed by Tollefson and the VVA were painfully borne out.

American Dust

By 1991 the issues of fraud and corruption and problems within the PRPC undermined the good intentions that Mrazek and his supporters had for the AHA. The reality of resettlement fell far short of the inclusionary rhetoric of kinship and belonging promised by the legislation.[105] A 1989 study by the Office of Refugee Resettlement found that only 32 percent of Amerasians entering the United States had any information about their American fathers and only 2 percent of attempts to locate fathers were successful. As with the AIA, neither the government nor the military offered any help for Amerasians looking for their fathers. The majority of success stories were therefore the result of the efforts of private and nonprofit organizations, and humanitarians like Father Alfred Carroll, who continued to assist Amerasians in finding their fathers.[106] In 1992 the *Chronicle of Higher Education* reported that ten years after the passage of the AIA, Father Carroll "remained indignant" about the abandonment of Amerasians by their American fathers and the federal government. "If fathers do not fulfill their obligations," Carroll explained, "then it's the government's obligation to do it. Our government has not done that, so some individuals have picked up on it."[107]

Even without paternal acknowledgment or kinship ties, however, many Amerasians mistakenly assumed they would find the acceptance in American society that eluded them in Vietnam because they were American children.[108] While many Americans initially mistook Amerasians for native-born Americans because of how they looked, once their language difficulties or cultural differences surfaced, Amerasians encountered marginalization and exclusion reminiscent of what they had experienced in Vietnam. In 1988 the California Department of Social Services warned Americans against assumptions of racial familiarity.[109] Officials explained the importance of remembering, "the appearance of the Amerasians will fool many people into believing that they are native Americans which can cause conflict and confusion."[110]

The U.S. State Department concurred. A 1989 State Department report stated Amerasians "are not 'our' kids and they aren't 'coming home'—they are Vietnamese young adults coming to a new and unfamiliar land for which their American genes offer no special preparation."[111] Employee Kyle Horst further explained, "Just because Amerasians have blond hair or afros, we expect them to act like Americans. But it's a myth that these are 'our' kids. They are Vietnamese. We're not bringing them home. We're taking them to a foreign country."[112] Amerasians also felt the conflict and the divide, "When I was in Vietnam," one Amerasian described, "I felt more American because of how I looked. But when I came here, I felt more Vietnamese. My language, the food I eat, the way I think the way I do—it's Vietnamese."[113]

Black Amerasians especially faced difficulty in overcoming the assumptions by Americans that skin color equated to a shared racial kinship with African Americans. Missing was the common heritage, culture, and history. Some Black Amerasians sought to create that bond by educating themselves on African American culture and history. Likewise certain American resettlement services made genuine efforts to familiarize Black Amerasians with "their" Black heritage through the incorporation of Black history into the curriculum.[114] In some cases American workers educated Black Amerasians on hair care and personal grooming in hopes of easing the transition into their impending racial identity. The efforts had limited success.[115] In Phoenix, Arizona, for example, many Black Amerasians joined Black street gangs in their efforts to find racial acceptance.[116] Others, like Black Amerasian Kien, admitted that once in America, he tried to become African American by imitating Black people, "I talk how they talk, I'm a good imitator."[117] Largely however, such attempts to fit into American racial categories failed.

Within Vietnamese-American communities where Amerasians could find cultural familiarity, they often also encountered the same prejudice that they had faced in Vietnam. Their physical appearance and paternal illegitimacy continued to prevent them from blending in, and the community continued to perceive them as the poor, uneducated children of prostitutes. The rejection heightened Amerasians' sense of alienation in America.[118] A 1993 survey by the General Accounting Office found that 95 percent of Amerasians who immigrated to the United States under the AHA experienced discrimination from the Vietnamese-American community as opposed to 20 percent from American communities.[119]

As in Vietnam, Black Amerasians faced harsher treatment in America. The same survey found that 100 percent of Black Amerasians experienced discrimination from the Vietnamese community, which continued to associate Black skin tones and African Americans with racial stereotypes of crime and homelessness.[120] In the words of one Black Amerasian, "I heard in Vietnam that black people [in America] were slaves, I didn't want to be a slave."[121] Although Black Amerasian Lee Dong admitted that being around Black people in America made him feel like he had a father, he also believed that full-blooded Vietnamese did not like him because he was Black, explaining, "They look at me like I'm ugly."[122]

Ultimately, the AHA complicated the issue of race and acceptance in America for Amerasians. American interviewers used racial criteria to determine which Amerasian applicants "looked American" enough to be formally designated children of American fathers. However, the racial transformation of Amerasians into Americans proved only skin deep. Still foreigners to the cultural norms of Americans, once in the United States Amerasians found themselves again marginalized. While race was evidence of paternity and in most cases determined whether an Amerasian remained one of the "children of dust" or became one of the "children of gold," the AHA ensured that by the time they entered the United States, Amerasians remained foreigners and refugees.

Compassion Fatigue

By the end of the Reagan era, much of the national interest in the Amerasians dissipated as Americans tired of debates over immigrants and refugees and no longer felt compelled to save anyone from Vietnam.[123] The fall of the Berlin Wall in 1989 signaled the end of the Cold War and any further responsibility to rescue refugees from communism. Two years later a convincing U.S. military victory in the Gulf War relieved Americans of their Vietnam baggage. As President George H. W. Bush exclaimed, the United States had finally "kicked the Vietnam syndrome."[124] At the same time, the demoralization of AHA interviewers and their increasing intolerance for the Amerasian situation spread to the United States, where resettlement services lacked resources to deal with fake families and abandoned Amerasians. In 1995, Joseph Love, a volunteer at St. Anselm's Cross-Cultural Community Center in Garden Grove, California, one of the Amerasian resettlement sites, estimated that thirty thousand fake Amerasians and fraudulent families lived in the United States, resulting in a general disenchantment with the process.[125]

Rep. Mrazek also became concerned about the program. Discouraged by the AHA's apparent faults, Mrazek began to wonder about its merits. In addition to the media coverage and criticism, Mrazek received annual reports about the program that also detailed the proliferation of fraud, corruption, and fake families. Numerous reports of Amerasians struggling to assimilate and getting into trouble worried Mrazek, who recognized the challenges of integrating an older, illiterate, and foreign population into American society.[126] However, more troubling for Mrazek were the reports that only 2 percent of Amerasians actually found their fathers once in the United States. There was, Mrazek claims, "a lack of responsibility" in that number, from men who, he guessed, "had gone on with their lives; it was disappointing."[127]

The AHA peaked in 1992, when 18,500 Amerasians and their families entered the United States. Those numbers drastically subsided to sixteen thousand in 1993 and only thirty-five hundred in 1994.[128] Still, by 1994 the AHA had facilitated the immigration of over sixty-nine thousand Amerasians and their family members to the United States and over the next three years an additional nineteen hundred would immigrate before the program finally fizzled out.[129] In addition to the conclusion of the Cold War, compassion fatigue, and the simple reduction in numbers of Amerasians still living in Vietnam, President Bill Clinton's moves to normalize relations with Vietnam likely secured the program's demise.

There are no reliable statistics on the number of Amerasians that eventually became naturalized U.S. citizens since U.S. records count Amerasians under the annual allocation for Vietnamese nationals.[130] What is clear, however, is that some Amerasians never even attempted to obtain citizenship because they mistakenly believed that approval for the AHA had automatically conferred citizenship. Some others believed it impossible to pass the citizenship test considering their lack of education and language skills. Sometimes their citizenship status was a matter of indifference until legal issues exposed it and in some cases threatened them with deportation. In 1996 the Immigration and Naturalization Service initiated deportation procedures against Amerasian Dung Van Chau. After his conviction for two different crimes, the INS declared Chau subject to deportation to Vietnam because he lacked U.S. citizenship.[131] Chau appealed the deportation to the U.S. Court of Appeals for the Ninth Circuit on the grounds that he had immigrated to the United States in 1984 under the Amerasian Immigration Act and therefore had U.S. citizenship. The provisions of the AIA, Chau insisted, conferred citizenship by classifying its beneficiaries as children of U.S. citizens.[132] When the court demanded proof of American paternity, Chau introduced the testimony of his mother Mai Chau, who claimed that his father was an African American soldier stationed in Vietnam during the war. Even though Chau did not know his father's identity, he also testified that his father was African

American because as a child he was given the nickname "Dung Medan" or "Dung," a Black American.[133]

The court responded that despite the language of the legislation, because the AIA did not intend to grant qualifying Amerasians U.S. citizenship and because Chau was born in Vietnam, a "presumption of alienage" existed.[134] Chau, the court ruled, could not establish citizenship because he did not know the exact identity of his father.[135] In 2006 the Department of Homeland Security ruled that Chau had not proven that his father was a U.S. citizen, stating, "no evidence exists that a man who appears to be a U.S. serviceman must necessarily be one," and "service in the United States armed forces does not confer citizenship on a serviceman." Therefore, Chau was not an American citizen but an alien, and thus subject to deportation back to Vietnam.[136]

A Home without a Roof

Chau's case highlights the fundamentally exclusionary nature of U.S. Amerasian policies. Willing to take some responsibility for Amerasians in Vietnam when it served the nation's Cold War humanitarian interests, U.S. lawmakers failed to address the underlying issue of individual paternity and military responsibility. Furthermore, they proved unable to reconcile the Amerasian mixture with U.S. law. Rather, both the AIA and the AHA sent conflicting messages about the race, place, and status of Amerasians in Vietnam. The inclusionary discourse that defined Amerasians as the children of American fathers failed to equate to U.S. citizenship.

The exclusion of citizenship exposes important gaps in U.S. immigration and citizenship laws and the continued challenge in using race to determine paternity and thus nationality. Decades removed from the AHA, Amerasians continue to suffer the consequences of fatherlessness and the absence of citizenship. Amerasian political and humanitarian advocates still seek a legislative solution of national paternal responsibility. In 2003, Rep. Zoe Lofgren (D-CA), who represents San Jose, home to a large Amerasian population, proposed HR 3360, the Amerasian Naturalization Act, to confer on Amerasians from Vietnam automatic U.S. citizenship as the sons and daughters of U.S. citizens.[137] In 2007 and 2012 Lofgren introduced the Amerasian Paternity Recognition Act, which would provide automatic U.S. citizenship to Amerasians born during the Vietnam and Korean Wars.[138]

Each bill proposed to confer birthright U.S. citizenship to Amerasians who had legally entered the United States through the AHA, the AIA, or the ODP as well as to those still in Vietnam who wanted to immigrate. Lofgren introduced her bills using the familiar Amerasian narrative that highlighted the poor conditions Amerasians faced in Vietnam as a result of their American paternity. In 2003 Lofgren explained, "these individuals lived through devastation during the Vietnam War and have been mistreated by the Vietnamese government because of their mixed race." Their racial mixtures, Lofgren claimed, were undeniable evidence of U.S. paternal responsibility as was the record of previous Amerasian legislation. "There is no doubt that they are the sons and daughters of American fathers. That determination was made when the U.S. government invited these individuals to come to the United States to live." To further advance her cause, Lofgren also pointed to the urgency of closure and reconciliation, "It is time to finally close a chapter in our history that has too long denied Amerasians the opportunity to be recognized as the American citizens they are."[139] Sharing the fate of the initial attempts of her predecessor Stewart McKinney, in each case Lofgren's bills failed to make it out of committee.[140]

Consequences of War

Shortly after his rapid rise to celebrity as the poster child of the Amerasian Homecoming Act, Americans forgot Le Van Minh. His inability to assimilate quickly into American life eventually marked him as a troubled child, an all too familiar stereotype of Amerasians. Sandy Dang, who ran an outreach program for Asian youths in Washington DC, pointed to the fundamental issue: "Amerasians had 30 years of trauma, and you can't just turn that around in a short period of time or undo what happened to them in Vietnam. . . . In Vietnam, they weren't accepted as Vietnamese and in America they weren't considered Americans. . . . Of all the immigrants in the United States, the Amerasians, I think are the group that's had the hardest time finding the American Dream."[141] Minh too, found this dream elusive. At last account, the now middle-aged Minh lives in a two-bedroom home in San Jose, California (Lofgren's district), with his Vietnamese wife and two children. With little formal education, Minh makes a living distributing newspapers from the window of his car. In 2009, the Amerasian Fellowship Association, numerous members of which immigrated through the AHA, held its regional banquet in San Jose to celebrate the achievements of the Amerasian immigrant community. Minh was noticeably absent from the affair. In fact, event organizers admitted that even though Minh lived only fifteen minutes away, they had never even heard his story.[142]

Now "older and wiser," HHS alumna Marlo Sandler still wonders about Minh and the effect that the HHS efforts had on his life. Although she generally has fond memories of the events surrounding Minh and a "sense of happiness and accomplishment," she remains troubled about the aftermath and its effects on Minh. While the politicians, humanitarians, and journalists focused their attention on the larger population of Amerasians affected by the AHA, Sandler retained a more personal view. "I am impressed by [the AHA] and . . . that all these other children were given a chance to come here, but to me it is more about this one particular person." "I would be fascinated to know how Minh feels," Sandler said, and added the wish that "somehow the life that he has led, even though it maybe has not been easy, is hopefully better than what he would have had."[143]

Conclusion

The evolution of the Amerasian issue among U.S. policymakers is evidence of the ways that race, gender, and war shape understandings of what it means to be an American and to father an American. Even though the sex-based distinction embedded in U.S. immigration and citizenship law protected America and Americans from the responsibilities of caring for their foreign-born children, the guilt associated with the Vietnam War coupled with Amerasians' "American faces" demanded some accountability. U.S. leaders approved preferential immigration policies for Amerasians in the AIA and the AHA, yet failed to include birthright citizenship, which might have been a logical extension of the acknowledgment of their American paternity. The inability of U.S lawmakers to reconcile the Amerasian mixture of race and nation combined with the American legacy of exclusionary policies against mixed-race persons and people of Asian descent informed the contradictory approach.

Over time America distanced itself from the Vietnam War and increasingly viewed the aging population of Amerasians as another refugee population with refugee problems.[1] The arguments by advocates for Amerasian citizenship faded as did any chance the nation would assume paternal responsibility or accord the ultimate legal recognition of belonging. Still, the efforts of humanitarians, journalists, high school students, and congressional leaders like Patsy Mink, Stewart McKinney, Jeremiah Denton, and Robert Mrazek succeeded in bringing attention to the issue. By 1994 their efforts resulted in the resettlement of approximately seventy-five thousand Amerasians and their families in the United States.[2]

I write this at a moment in which the memory and the lessons of Vietnam have become hidden by time, technology, and politics. America's longest war is now a seemingly endless conflict in Afghanistan, Russia has alarmingly interfered in two U.S. presidential elections, and America's global role is uncertain. An increasingly transnational world has facilitated new freedom and movement, both physical and ideological, breaking down preexisting geographic borders and conceptual boundaries that have served to differentiate and categorize groups of people. In the process, policymakers continue to question membership and belonging, reconsidering and reconstituting the role of race and gender in determining who is and who is not an American.

U.S. leaders seeking to redefine the nation and its citizens in increasingly narrow ways have committed to a hypervigilant defense of national borders and racial boundaries that all too often revert to a discourse of "us" and "them." Increasingly extreme and restrictive immigration and refugee policies have targeted nonwhite and non-Western newcomers. They have denied Black and brown asylum seekers and refugees entrance into the United States, criminalized and separated families, incarcerated children in cages, and subjected thousands to deportation. Deportation has become a particularly powerful tool with devastating effects on immigrant and refugee communities, including a number of Vietnamese and Amerasians who came to the United States between 1975 and 1995 under the Amerasian legislation.

In 2017 the Trump administration reinterpreted a 2008 bilateral agreement between the United States and Vietnam that protected Vietnamese and Amerasian immigrants who came to the United States before 1995 under the ODP, AIA, or the AHA from deportation. In an effort to remove from the United States "individuals who pose a threat to national security, public safety and border security," the administration has targeted those with criminal records.[3] It removed the 2008

CONCLUSION

protections in order to deport over seven thousand Vietnamese and Amerasian refugees, the majority being "war refugees who had sided with the United States, whose loyalty was to the flag of a nation that no longer exists."[4]

Amerasians have proven to be a population particularly vulnerable to deportation. Many arrived in the United States through the AHA at young ages, alone or with fake families. Among those who struggled with issues of illegitimacy, isolation, and identity, some turned to gangs and petty crime. Decades later those choices and their criminal records, regardless of the surrounding circumstances or the harmlessness of the crime, have come back to haunt them. According to Phi Nguyen, of the Atlanta chapter of Asian Americans Advancing Justice, "some of the crimes took place in the nineties when people were initially being resettled here, growing up in poor neighborhoods and often being bullied."[5] Since deportation only applies to non-U.S. citizens, the failure of the AIA or AHA to grant Amerasians citizenship has proven concerning. Amerasians who mistakenly believed the AIA or the AHA automatically granted them citizenship or who were unable to navigate the bureaucracy of the U.S. naturalization process have become easy targets for deportation.

In December 2017, a forty-seven-year-old husband and father of three, Pham Chi Cuong, became the first Amerasian deported to Vietnam under the Trump administration. Cuong had immigrated to the United States under the AHA in 1990, and like many Amerasians he faced discrimination and abuse because of his paternity. In 2000 Cuong served eighteen months in prison for assault and battery and in 2007 he received probation for a DUI. Cuong never became a U.S. citizen, believing it unnecessary because he had immigrated under the AHA. Another Amerasian, Robert Huynh, immigrated with his mother and siblings in 1984 under the ODP. Huynh spent three years in prison in his twenties for dealing drugs. He never became a U.S. citizen, as he lacked the necessary education and language skills.[6] In 2016 Huynh, who has a son and two grandsons in Kentucky, found his American family through a DNA test. He is slated for deportation because of the crimes he committed in his twenties.[7]

In the face of the threat of deportation, the advent of DNA testing, although somewhat ironic in this case, offers Amerasians hope by confirming claims of paternity and legitimacy. In 2015 Amerasian Jimmy Miller, who immigrated to the United States in 1990 under the AHA, established Amerasians without Borders, a nonprofit organization dedicated to identifying the fathers of the hundreds of Amerasians estimated to still be living in Vietnam and helping them immigrate to the United States. In 2018 Miller reported that he had sent DNA tests to over five hundred Amerasians in Vietnam.[8] Amerasians living in the United States have used commercial DNA companies to find relatives and, if they are lucky, their fathers. For those Amerasians for whom the cost of DNA testing is prohibitive, there are a small number of nonprofit organizations that offer discounted or free testing.[9]

However, even in the cases where DNA has successfully identified an American father of an Amerasian, citizenship is not guaranteed. The U.S. Supreme Court has yet to hear any specific case regarding Amerasians, DNA, and citizenship. And numerous previous cases in which an Amerasian has proven paternity and been denied citizenship have set a discouraging precedent. In the 1998 case of *Miller v. Albright*, the Supreme Court denied Amerasian Lorelyn Miller's claim to U.S. citizenship.[10] The U.S. State Department first rejected Miller's application for citizenship on the grounds that she did not meet the requirement of majority established by the 1952 Immigration and Nationality Act.[11] At twenty-one years old, Lorelyn was simply too old to apply, and her claims of paternity were invalid. Therefore, the U.S. government determined she was not a U.S. citizen.

Lorelyn challenged the decision in front of the U.S. Supreme Court, which also ruled against her claim. According to the Court, the act of birth itself determined the biological difference between mothers and fathers for the purpose of transmitting citizenship.[12] While unwed mothers had the benefit of having given birth as evidence of biological and therefore legal filiation with their children, unwed fathers never would. Thus the court assumed an absence, outside of marriage, of biological or legal filiation between fathers and children.[13]

The ruling was one of many citizenship transmission cases brought

CONCLUSION 245

before the Supreme Court since the 1977 case of *Fiallo v. Bell* challenged the apparent sex-based discrimination embedded in U.S. citizenship law.[14] In each case, the Court maintained that "the different treatment of mothers and fathers of out-of-wedlock children was justified since the two parents are not 'similarly situated.'"[15] Critical to the argument were expectations that mothers were likely to make questionable paternity claims and an insinuation of their promiscuity— "she may not know who is the father of her child," and "two or more men may claim paternity of the same child." This was coupled with an assumption that fathers were unable to understand the consequences of their sexual acts, to count their partners, or even remember with whom they had slept.[16] According to the Court, in the "normal interval of nine months between conception and birth," the fact that the "unmarried father may not even know his child exists, and the child may not know the father's identity" justified the sex-based distinction.[17] Thus in the reasoning of the Court, fathers only came to the realization of conception, gestation, and childbirth, and mothers only aspired to tell the truth regarding paternity, through the institution of marriage. By ruling against Miller and others and upholding the sex-based distinction in U.S. citizenship law, the Court gave permission to American men and, in this case, American servicemen, to continue fathering children abroad, out of wedlock and without any fear of paternal responsibility.

Today, the sex-based discrimination in U.S. immigration and citizenship law continues to permit individual American men to father children with foreign women abroad without any concern of paternal accountability or parental responsibility. When considered in the context of the large U.S. military presence abroad, these laws, along with the unwillingness of policymakers to expose the U.S. military and U.S. servicemen to public criticism, justify the irresponsible sexual choices of American men who continue to create out-of-wedlock children.

Although fraught with numerous other issues, the Amerasian experience in Vietnam and the United States remains important and relevant. In an increasingly militarized, transracial, and transborder world, the Amerasian case forces Americans to confront the gendered legalities of U.S. citizenship and immigration laws. It requires a consideration of how those laws work in tandem with U.S. military policy and how they translate into parental and national responsibility. Furthermore, effects at the ground level of policies imposed from above are powerful and real. The Amerasian issue matters because it affected and continues to affect the lives of real people like Pham Chi Cuong, Robert Huynh, Tung Nguyen, and Le Van Minh, in critical and sometimes devastating ways. By understanding the Amerasian experience, America can begin to reckon with the defeat in the Vietnam War and recognize how it reshaped, and ought to reshape, what it means to be an American.

Notes

Introduction

1. Appy, *American Reckoning*, 227; Viet Thanh Nguyen, *Nothing Ever Dies*, 23.

2. Minh was born in September 1971 in Cam Ranh, the site of a U.S. naval base. Minh's American father, "Joe," was a corporal in the U.S. Army and spoke Vietnamese, and Le Thi Ba was a cook in the mess hall. According to Le Thi Ba, she dated Joe for over a year and he was present at Minh's birth. They lost contact after the Vietcong invaded the area and she fled to Saigon with Minh. Michael Luo, "A Beggar No More," *Newsday*, July 9, 2000; Edna Negron, "Le Van Minh's Americanization," *Newsday*, November 16, 1987.

3. Irene Virag, "Life and Times of Le Van Minh: One Boy's Journey from the Dusty Streets of Ho Chi Minh City," *Newsday*, June 22, 1987.

4. Enloe, *Maneuvers*, 29. Enloe argues that militarized women often perform their own maneuvers—or strategies to benefit from the presence of a masculinized military. See also Turner, "Shadowboxing with the Censors," 101–20.

5. See Stoler, *Carnal Knowledge*; Stoler, *Haunted by Empire*.

6. There was never an accurate accounting of the number of Amerasians in Vietnam during or after the war. U.S. government officials and humanitarian organizations varied greatly in their reports depending on the location and resources utilized. The most accurate accounts have resulted from a combination of orphanages in South Vietnam, venereal disease clinics that treated the mothers of Amerasians, and chaplains. In 1972 Don Luce of the Indochina Mobile Education Project estimated 100,000–300,000 Amerasians living in Vietnam while the U.S. government estimated 400. In March 1985 estimates hovered around 20,000. By the passage of the AHA in 1987, the range of 30,000–50,000 became the most consistent accounting reported to Congress. *Vietnam Children's Care Agency: Hearings before the Committee on Foreign Relations*, SB 2497, 92nd Cong., 2nd sess., April 5, 1972, 82; "Introduction of the Amerasian Relief Act," Cong. Rec. H1369 (March 21, 1985); *Vietnamese Amerasian Resettlement:*

Education, Employment, and Family Outcomes in the United States, U.S. General Accounting Office (hereafter GAO), March 1994, 2. For more information on accounting methods, see Shade Jr., "A Progress Report on Caring for the Amerasian," 1978, PSBI, folder Amerasians 1978–84, box Vietnam.

7. There is much disagreement about the label that best refers to Amerasians. While *bui doi* is a general term that refers to street children in Vietnam, a category that did include many Amerasians after the war, *my lai* and *con lai* refer specifically to Amerasians themselves. For a discussion of the term *bui doi*, see Doan, "Bringing the Aliens Home," 76.

8. For more on the politics of representation and the power of pictures, see Turner, "Shadowboxing with the Censors," 101–20; Chong, *Girl in the Picture*; Gray, *Cultural Moves*; Pegler-Gordon, *In Sight of America*.

9. The author commends the budding scholarship in the field of disability history and recognizes Minh's physical disability as a potential area for further historical analysis. For more on disability history, see Kudlick, "Disability History."

10. A number of scholars have used the terms "American face" and "American blood" in discussing the Amerasians, including Bass, *Vietnamerica*, and Doan "Bringing the Aliens Home."

11. Briggs, "Mother, Child, Race, Nation," 179–200; Briggs, *Somebody's Children*, 131.

12. Both Laura Briggs and Christina Klein discuss the power of this picture for child-saving in America. Briggs, *Somebody's Children*, 134–35; Klein, *Cold War Orientalism*, 176–77.

13. For more discussion on the power of Emmett Till's picture, see Tyson, *Blood of Emmett Till*.

14. For further discussion on the iconography of child victims of napalm bombs during the war, see Chong, *Girl in the Picture*; Franklin, *Vietnam and Other American Fantasies*.

15. There is an extensive scholarship on the gendered framework of the Cold War and the Vietnam War. Notably, Dean, *Imperial Brotherhood*; Stur, *Beyond Combat*; Rutenberg, *Rough Draft*; Muehlenbeck, *Gender, Sexuality and the Cold War*.

16. See, for example, Carpenter, "Gender, Ethnicity, and Children's Human Rights"; Enloe, *Maneuvers*; Moon, *Sex among Allies*; Zeiger, *Entangling Alliances*; and Plummer, *Window on Freedom*.

17. Estimates of the number of mestizos never exceeded eighteen thousand. Molnar, *American Mestizos*, 4.

18. In 1953 an official report by Japan's Division of Health and Welfare Statistics stated there were 3,490 mixed-blood children in Japan, while humanitarian Miki Sawada, founder of the Elizabeth Saunders Home, believed there were

200,000 Amerasians and Takada Masami, chief of the Children's Bureau of the Welfare Ministry, estimated 150,000. Koshiro, *Trans-Pacific Racisms*, 164.

19. The South Korean government made this estimate in the immediate aftermath of the Korean War. Eleana Kim, *Adopted Territory*, 47.

20. The June 28, 1946, birth announcement of an Amerasian baby born as a result of the U.S. occupation of Japan portrayed the baby as a "rainbow across the Pacific," a symbol of love and friendship between the U.S. and Japan. Koshiro, *Trans-Pacific Racisms*, 159.

21. Furuya Yoshio had previously led the research department in the Ministry of Health and Welfare, where he conducted eugenics studies focused on maintaining the purity of the Japanese race. Koshiro, *Trans-Pacific Racisms*, 165–68.

22. Koshiro, *Trans-Pacific Racisms*, 165–67, 198–99.

23. Eleana Kim, *Adopted Territory*, 71–72.

24. Eleana Kim, *Adopted Territory*, 46–48. Kim suggests the lack of American interest in the Amerasians in Japan resulted from Japan's status as a U.S. adversary during the Second World War and the discomfort associated with American men sleeping with Japanese women. For a discussion of the efforts of the Black press to encourage African Americans to adopt Black Amerasians from Korea, see Graves, *War Born Family*.

25. According to Kim, press accounts used the term "orphan" indiscriminately to describe Korean and Amerasian children without reference to Korean relatives. Eleana Kim, *Adopted Territory*, 48–50; Stur, *Beyond Combat*, 12.

26. Eleana Kim, *Adopted Territory*, 73.

27. Eleana Kim, *Adopted Territory*, 71–75. See also Briggs, *Somebody's Children*; Dubinsky, *Babies without Borders*; Moon, *Sex among Allies*.

28. According to Kim U.S. servicemen adopted 90 percent of the Amerasians in Japan and led the initial wave of adoptions from Korea because they were able to navigate around U.S. immigration law. Eleana Kim, *Adopted Territory*, 55, 274.

29. Eleana Kim, *Adopted Territory*, 50–51. For further discussion of the paternalism of U.S. servicemen regarding adoption of Vietnamese orphans, see Stur, *Beyond Combat*, 142.

30. Foster, *Projections of Power*, 13.

31. Koshiro, *Trans-Pacific Racisms*, 186–89.

32. Klein, *Cold War Orientalism*, 159.

33. The Refugee Relief Act issued four thousand nonquota immigrant visas to eligible orphans younger than ten years old. Eleana Kim, *Adopted Territory*, 51; Koshiro, *Trans-Pacific Racisms*, 190.

34. Koshiro, *Trans-Pacific Racisms*, 184.

35. By January 1955 the American Joint Committee sent fifteen Amerasians to the United States under the Refugee Relief Act, and by 1956, 350 Japanese and Amerasian children from Japan immigrated through a variety of private bills. Koshiro, *Trans-Pacific Racisms*, 199.

36. Eleana Kim, *Adopted Territory*, 73.

37. Appy, *American Reckoning*, xiii.

38. Kerber, "Stateless as the Citizen's Other," 1.

39. "Congressional Black Caucus," MSRC, folder 19, box 30; Winslow, *Best Possible Immigrants*, 142–80.

40. Vernon E. Jordan Jr., "To Be Equal: Vietnam and the Orphans," *Call & Post*, April 26, 1975, MSRC, folder 21, box 79.

41. Kerber, "Stateless as the Citizen's Other," 31.

42. McCarran-Walter Act of 1952, PL 82–414, 82nd Cong., 2nd sess. (June 27, 1952). Section 309 states that children born out of wedlock abroad acquired the nationality of the mother and could only obtain the nationality of the father through official legitimation.

43. For further analysis, see Collins, "Illegitimate Borders."

44. Thomas, "Blood Politics," 65–66. Assumptions that people of Asian descent could not become American frames a history of exclusionary immigration policies in the United States beginning with the 1790 Naturalization Law, which reserved U.S. citizenship for "free white persons," and including the 1870 Naturalization Act, the 1882 Chinese Exclusion Act, and the 1924 Johnson-Reed Act.

45. Thomas, "Blood Politics," 53, 67.

46. Amerasian Immigration Act of 1982, PL 359, 97th Cong., 2nd sess. (Oct. 22, 1982); Amerasian Homecoming Act of 1987, PL 100–202, 100th Cong., 1st sess. (Dec. 22, 1987) refers to an "alien residing in Vietnam . . . whose father was a U.S. citizen."

47. Thomas, "Blood Politics," 55.

48. Taylor, *Orphans of War*; O'Conner, *Chaplain Looks at Vietnam*.

49. Bass, *Vietnamerica*; Yarborough, *Surviving Twice*; and DeBonis, *Children of the Enemy*.

50. McKelvey, *Dust of Life*.

51. Gage, "Amerasian Problem," and DeMonaco, "Disorderly Departure."

52. Valverde, "From Dust to Gold," 144.

53. Valverde, "From Dust to Gold," 144.

54. Lipman, "Mixed Voices, Mixed Policy."

55. Lipman, "Face Is the Road Map," 33–68. See also Fieldston, "Little Cold Warriors"; Casavantas Bradford, "'La Niña Adorada del Mundo Socialista'"; Varzally, *Children of Reunion*.

56. Varzally, *Children of Reunion*; Winslow, *Best Possible Immigrants*, 10–12, 144, 179, 217; Graves, *War Born Family*.

57. Varzally, *Children of Reunion*, 101, 115–16.

58. Bennett and Wanhalla, *Mother's Darlings of the South Pacific*, 4, 300.

59. Previous scholars, including Bass, *Vietnamerica*; McKelvey, *Dust of Life*; and Yarborough, *Surviving Twice*, have relied primarily on interviews with Amerasians for their analysis.

60. Bass, *Vietnamerica*; McKelvey, *Dust of Life*; Yarborough, *Surviving Twice*; Kien Nguyen, *Unwanted*; and Kelly, *Year in Saigon*.

61. Scholars of American history in postcolonial studies have produced a rich and growing scholarship on the intersection of racial hybridity, identity, and nation. See Stoler, *Carnal Knowledge*; Spickard, *Almost All Aliens*; Saada, *Empire's Children*; Firpo, *Uprooted*; Molnar, *American Mestizos*.

62. Ann Laura Stoler roots these tensions in the intimate, imperial, and militarized conditions that produced the Amerasians and in the coinciding racialized and exclusionary histories of mixed-race persons and people of Asian descent. Stoler, "Sexual Affronts and Racial Frontiers," 198–237.

63. Klein, *Cold War Orientalism*; Briggs, *Somebody's Children*; Fieldston, "Little Cold Warriors."

64. Newer scholarship by Dana Sachs and Allison Varzally challenge the common narrative of Operation Babylift as a child-saving endeavor. By considering Amerasians as living, functioning, breathing human beings with agency and family ties rather than simply as objects of rescue, this scholarship complicates the Amerasian experience in critical ways. Sachs, *Life We Were Given*; Varzally, *Children of Reunion*.

65. Yen Le Espiritu argues that the myth of "rescue and liberation" acted as an antidote to the U.S. defeat in Vietnam. In the absence of a liberated Vietnam, Americans embraced "free and reformed" Vietnamese refugees grateful to the United States for their freedom. Espiritu "'We Win Even When We Lose Syndrome,'" 329. See also Espiritu, *Body Counts*, and Mimi Thi Nguyen, *Gift of Freedom*.

66. Recent works have started to recenter the Amerasians, including Winslow, *Best Possible Immigrants*; Varzally, *Children of Reunion*; and Rhodes, *Vietnam War in American Childhood*.

1. Setting a Precedent

1. Fred Rosen, interview with Audrey Tiernan, "Operation: Rescue Concerned Photography Shows a New Dimension," *American Photographer*, February 1989.

2. Rosen, "Operation."

3. Rosen, "Operation."

NOTES TO PAGES 24–27

4. Robert Lee, *Orientals*, 28; Erika Lee, *At America's Gates*, 19–109. For further consideration of American disability history and how disabled and different bodies intersect with sociocultural and geopolitical ideas of race, immigration, and empire, see Longmore and Umansky, *New Disability History*; Adams, *Sideshow U.S.A.* For a discussion of the intersection of war and disability, see Gerber, *Disabled Veterans in History*.

5. Thomas, "Blood Politics," 55–56.

6. Paul Spickard terms this as the "racial moment." Spickard, "Race and Nation," 12. For further discussion of citizenship as a tool of exclusion that perpetuates hierarchies see Yoon, "Reproducing Citizens through U.S. Militarism," 8.

7. Spickard, "Race and Nation," 17–23. There are a number of excellent sociocultural and policy studies that address this topic, including Cashin, *Loving*; Hodes, *Sex, Love, Race*.

8. Nash, "Hidden History of Mestizo America," 10–27; Root, "Within, Between and Beyond Race," 6.

9. Cashin, *Loving*, 38, 48; Hening, *Status at Large*.

10. For laws regarding marriage, inheritance, citizenship, and voting for mixed race persons, see California Supreme Court, *Perez v. Sharp*, 32 Cal. 2d 711, 198 P.2d 17 (1948) and U.S. Supreme Court, *Loving v. Virginia*, 388 U.S. 1 (1967).

11. Pascoe, *What Comes Naturally*, 2–5; Hodes, *White Women Black Men*; Spickard, *Mixed Blood*. For a consideration of antimiscegenation laws respecting Asian Americans, see Koshy, *Sexual Naturalization*, 1–17.

12. Thomas, "Blood Politics," 54. For a history of miscegenation, mixed-race, and whiteness, see Painter, *History of White People*; Pascoe, "Miscegenation Law"; and Koshy, *Sexual Naturalization*.

13. Thomas, "Blood Politics," 67; Root, "Within, Between, and Beyond Race," 3; McClintock, *Imperial Leather*, 48.

14. Basson, *White Enough to Be American?*, 4. For further discussion see Jun, *Race for Citizenship*; Hodes, *White Women Black Men*; Pascoe, *What Comes Naturally*; Spickard, *Mixed Blood*; Nakashima, "Servants of Culture."

15. Pascoe, *What Comes Naturally*, 8. For further discussion of the one-drop rule as a race-making and race-preserving tool, see Funderburg *Black, White, Other*, 13; Root, "Within, Between, and Beyond Race," 6; Pascoe, "Miscegenation Law," 482–90.

16. Thomas, "Blood Politics," 67; Funderburg, *Black, White, Other*, 13.

17. Thomas, "Blood Politics," 67.

18. The source of this information can be traced to a fan letter Hitler wrote to Madison Grant after reading Grant's book. Grant showed the letter to Leon Whitney, executive secretary of the American Eugenics Society. Whitney then

wrote about it in his unpublished memoir. Steven Kuhl references the letter in *Nazi Connection*, 85.

19. Nash, "Hidden History of Mestizo America," 23; McClintock, *Imperial Leather*, 47; Edwin Black, "Hitler's Debt to America," *Guardian*, February 5, 2004, https://www.theguardian.com/uk/2004/feb/06/race.usa.

20. Bardaglio, "Shameful Matches," 114–19.

21. Peggy Pascoe explains that until the 1967 U.S. Supreme Court case of *Loving v. Virginia*, the denial of a marriage license was the most common way to prevent domestic interracial marriage. To regulate international unions, domestic marriage laws were combined with U.S. immigration law. Pascoe, *What Comes Naturally*, 9–12. Domestic relations law through the nineteenth century prevented out-of-wedlock children from patrilineal inheritance; states tended to allow children born out of wedlock to inherit from their mothers. Collins, "Illegitimate Borders," 2150. For more information on interracial marriages between whites and Japanese see Spickard, *Mixed Blood*.

22. Collins, "Illegitimate Borders," 2139–49. The 1864 case of *Guyer v. Smith* declared that the benefit of the 1802 federal statute that awarded citizenship to foreign-born children of American citizens parents did not apply to children born out of wedlock.

23. Immigration and Nationality Act of 1952, Pub. L. 82–414, 66 Stat. 163.

24. Robert Lee, *Orientals*, 10, 28.

25. Robert Lee, *Orientals*, 10, 28. For further discussion of the development in Western popular culture of the feminine East, see Kawaguchi, *Butterfly's Sisters*.

26. Said, "Selections from *Orientalism*," 134. Also see Yu, *Thinking Orientals*, 106.

27. Thomas, "Blood Politics," 65.

28. Jacobson, *Whiteness of a Different Color*.

29. A number of Federal laws were passed to exclude the Chinese from immigration and citizenship. For the effect of those laws and others specific to Japanese immigrants and Japanese Americans, see Spickard, *Mixed Blood*, 25–33.

30. Sohoni, "Unsuitable Suitors," 592, 603; Sohoni quote from *In re Camille* [1880].

31. In re Camille, 6 F. 256 [1880] and quoted in Sohoni, "Unsuitable Suitors," 604.

32. Chan, *Asian Americans*, 28–42, 54; Robert Lee, *Orientals*, 85.

33. Jung, *Coolies and Cane*, 142.

34. In 1855 California levied an immigration tax specifically targeting Chinese immigrant workers. Native Americans and African Americans were also included. Western delegates from California and Oregon understood the value of cheap Chinese labor for their states; however, most did not believe the Chinese deserved political rights, though some western delegates like Oregon Republican

Cornelius Cole and Nevada senator William Stewart argued that because they were better educated and more industrious, the Chinese would make better citizens than African Americans. Cole, *Memoirs of Cornelius Cole*, 285–87. The U.S. Congress ratified the Fifteenth Amendment in 1870. The amendment extended suffrage to African Americans but denied it to Chinese immigrants. Out of concern that the law could open suffrage to Chinese immigrants, California and Oregon did not ratify the law until 1962 and 1959 respectively. Chan, *Asian Americans*, 28–42, 54; Robert Lee, *Orientals*, 85. Asian restriction and exclusion laws were not unique to the United States but prevalent in Canada, Mexico, Cuba, and U.S. territories. Erika Lee, *Making of Asian America*, 100–108.

35. Koshy, *Sexual Naturalization*, 7. Between 1861 and the 1967 Supreme Court decision *Loving v. Virginia*, fifteen states banned marriage between whites and Asians. Sohoni, "Unsuitable Suitors," 587.

36. Since policies already existed to exclude Japanese and Chinese, and Filipinos were U.S. nationals, the ban excluded each group. LeMay and Barkan, *U.S. Immigration*, 109; Hing *Making and Remaking*, 38.

37. U.S. federal and state governments instituted approximately fifty laws aimed at restricting and subordinating Asian immigrants. While Asians were classified in the U.S. Census by nationality—e.g., Chinese and Japanese—Black and Latin Americans were classified by race. Latin Americans were categorized as white, mulatto, or racially distinct, and whites by country of birth. Native Americans were largely omitted from this process. Matthaei and Amott, "Race, Gender, Work," 61. For further discussion of exclusionary immigration policies against Asians, see *Cahe Chan Ping v. United States* (May 13, 1889) in LeMay and Barkan, *U.S. Immigration*, 64; Daniels, *Coming to America*, 278–79.

38. Thomas, "Blood Politics," 66. On the role of race in determining U.S. immigration policies, see Chan, *Asian Americans*; Jun, *Race for Citizenship*; Koshy, *Sexual Naturalization*; Erika Lee, *Making of Asian America*; Robert Lee, *Orientals*.

39. Thomas, "Blood Politics," 66; Ozawa v. U.S., 260 U.S. 178 (1922); LeMay and Barkan, *U.S. Immigration*, 138; United States v. Bhagat Singh Thind, 261 U.S. 204 (1923).

40. Ngai, *Impossible Subjects*, 237–38; Lemay and Barkan, *U.S. Immigration*, xxxv; Immigration and Nationality Act of 1952, Office of the Historian. Accessed January 7, 2014, http://history.state.gov/milestones/1945-1952/immigration-act. For debates regarding this law see *Hearings before the President's Commission on Immigration and Naturalization*, 82nd Cong., 2nd sess., October 29, 1952, 1719–1800, 1216–17.

41. LeMay and Barkan, *U.S. Immigration*, 228.

42. Quotation attributed to Mae Ngai, "This Is How Immigration Reform Happened."

NOTES TO PAGES 33–35

43. Ngai, "This is How Immigration Reform Happened"; Chin, "Civil Rights Revolution," 273; Hing, *Making and Remaking*, 40. After the passage of the 1965 Immigration Act, 75 percent of immigrants to the U.S. were from Asia, Africa, and Central or South America.

44. Thomas, "Blood Politics," 67; Wu, *Color of Success*, 149. See also Jun, *Race for Citizenship*; Chan, *Asian Americans*; Robert Lee, *Orientals*; Espiritu, *Body Counts*; Ngai, *Impossible Subjects*, 8; Erika Lee, *At America's Gates*, 77–109.

45. Jana K. Lipman examines this intersection of policy and race in "'Face Is the Road Map.'" See also Gage, "Pure Mixed Blood"; Trautfield, "America's Responsibility"; DeMonaco, "Disorderly Departure"; Yarborough, *Surviving Twice*; Valverde, "Doing the Mixed-Race Dance," 131–44. Scholars of American history, postcolonial studies, and the métis of French Indochina have produced a rich and growing scholarship on the intersection of racial hybridity, identity, and nation, including most recently Firpo, *Uprooted*.

46. By the end of the nineteenth century, the U.S. citizenry had become less white, largely the result of the end of slavery, the Fourteenth Amendment, and European immigration. Basson, *White Enough to Be American?*, 55, 4. For a strong analysis of "whiteness" during the period, see Jacobson, *Whiteness of a Different Color*.

47. For a case study on the construction of colonial categories using race, see Briggs, *Reproducing Empire*, 4–9, 62.

48. Briggs, *Reproducing Empire*, 4–9, 62. See also Kaplan, *Anarchy of Empire*, 9.

49. Erika Lee, *Making of Asian America*, 100–101; Kauanui, *Hawaiian Blood*, 94–95.

50. Erika Lee, *Making of Asian America*, 100–101; Kauanui, *Hawaiian Blood*, 19–21, 96; Basson, *White Enough to Be American?*, 24.

51. The Hawaii Organic Act did not extend U.S. citizenship to Asian laborers (mainly from China and Japan) in Hawaii. These laborers composed approximately 60 percent of the population. Kauanui, *Hawaiian Blood*, 91–96.

52. Estimates of the number of mestizos never exceeded eighteen thousand; however, Nicholas Trajano Molnar notes this to be extraordinarily high considering there were two thousand mestizos identified in 1913 and 2,820 in 1918. Molnar, *American Mestizos*, 4, 16n4.

53. Dower, *War without Mercy*, 149. "A Progress Report," PSBI, folder Amerasian 1978–1984, box Vietnam.

54. Kramer, *Blood of Government*, 1–12; Foster, *Projections of Power*, 1–13.

55. Kramer, *Blood of Government*, 158; Dower, *War without Mercy*.

56. "From this Generation to the Next," HILA, Conrad Stanton Babcock Papers 1876–1950, folder C. S. Babcock Memoirs 194–366, box 1.

57. "From this Generation to the Next," HILA.

58. Molnar, *American Mestizos*, 3–5, 14, 155–59; Kramer, *Blood of Government*, 10–16; "A Progress Report," PSBI.

59. Molnar, *American Mestizos*, 43–45, 51–68.

60. Molnar, *American Mestizos*, 26–30.

61. Molnar, *American Mestizos*, 26.

62. Molnar, *American Mestizos*, 26–49.

63. Thomas, "Blood Politics," 68.

64. Dower, *War without Mercy*, 149; Koshiro, *Trans-Pacific Racisms*, 1.

65. Koshiro, *Trans-Pacific Racisms*, 1. Koshiro argues that the United States and Japan had mutually racist sentiment against each other as both countries competed for world control. The mutual racism defined the savagery and aggression of the war in the Pacific.

66. Dower, *War without Mercy*, 78.

67. Dower, *War without Mercy*, 310.

68. Dower, *War without Mercy*, 309.

69. Robert Bennyhoff, "Reds Kept Coming Like Droves of Cattle, U.S. Officer Reports: Disconnected Assaults in Groups," *Los Angeles Times*, July 26, 1950; Peter Kalischer, "'Like Scraping Off Ants': Unit Defending Bridge Slaughters 250 Reds," *Los Angeles Times*, August 4, 1950.

70. "Soldiers Revive 'G——' as Name for Korea Reds," *Los Angeles Times*, August 6, 1950.

71. Spickard, *Almost All Aliens*, 400. Spickard argues that the racism directed toward the Vietnamese throughout the war, specifically in the terms "g——s" and "slopes," returned to the United States with the soldiers, contributing to America's continuing tendency to view all Asians in these terms. Also see Longley, *Grunts*, 62–64, and Herring, *America's Longest War*, 186–87.

72. Quoted in Longley, *Grunts*, 63; Bilton and Sim, *Four Hours in My Lai*, 365–69; Robert Lee, *Orientals*, 190; Caputo, *Rumor of War*, xx.

73. Koshiro, *Trans-Pacific Racism*, 159.

74. Stated in a lecture on the social and biological impact of racial hybridization, January 31, 1953, in Koshiro, *Trans-Pacific Racism*, 165.

75. For further examination of the exclusion of Black Amerasians in Japan, see Koshiro, "Race as International Identity?" 61–77; and Matthaei and Amott, "Race, Gender, Work."

76. Fehrenbach, "Of German Mothers and 'Negermischlingskinder,'" 164. According to Fehrenbach, by 1950 only three thousand of an estimated ninety thousand GI babies in Germany were brown babies.

77. "Ship Tan-Yank Babies to U.S.," *Chicago Defender*, April 12, 1947; "British Families Adopt Brown Babies: Illegitimate Tots Left Behind by Negro GIs Finally

Find Homes," *Ebony*, March 1949; Sylvia McNeill, "Illegitimate Children Born in Britain of English Mothers and Coloured Americans: Report of a Survey," NAACP, "Brown Babies in Europe," file 1945–49, part 2, box A642.

78. Neither did U.S. law grant the out-of-wedlock children of white American fathers citizenship. However their whiteness enabled them to be easily assimilated into British society.

79. Stoler, *Carnal Knowledge and Imperial Power*, 15, 79–81.

80. Stoler, *Carnal Knowledge and Imperial Power*, 82–83; Saada, *Empire's Children*; Firpo, *Uprooted*, 2–3.

81. Saada, *Empire's Children*, 1–2, 184–204.

82. For the long-term effects of the forced migration of Eurasian children from Vietnam to France, see Mora-Kpai, *Indochina*.

83. Thomas, "Blood Politics," 62.

84. Uchida, "Orientalization of Asian Women."

85. Uchida, "Orientalization of Asian Women." Chinese prostitutes came to America through immigration or importation; however, not all Chinese women who immigrated to the United States were prostitutes. For further reading on interracial sexual relations in the ports of Japan and China, see Koshy, *Sexual Naturalization*.

86. Höhn and Moon, "Politics of Gender," 2, 21; Moon, *Sex among Allies*, 8. For further discussion of the American military-endorsed sex industry and service economy in South Korea, see Enloe, *Maneuvers*; Shigematsu and Camacho, *Militarized Currents*; and Jin-kyung Lee, *Service Economies*. For a broader examination of the sexualized and racialized nature of U.S. militarism abroad, see Renda, *Taking Haiti*.

87. Tokyo Rose was the general name U.S. soldiers gave to the female, Japanese-accented voices that broadcast English-language programs on Japanese radio. Unbeknown to American soldiers, these women were American. For the true story behind Tokyo Rose, see Uchida, "Orientalization of Asian Women," 166, and Duus, *Tokyo Rose*.

88. Enloe, *Maneuvers*, 66. Enloe details both the warm welcome that prostitutes received on some U.S. military bases, where they entered as "local national guests," and the army colonel who banned prostitutes from his base and prohibited the hiring of Vietnamese women as personal maids.

89. Katherine Moon posits that camptowns were places of self-exile for Korean women who had already lost their social status due to divorce, rape, sex, and illegitimate pregnancies, and were a means of economic survival. Moon, *Sex among Allies*, 3. Cynthia Enloe notes that American authorities took steps to hide evidence of the Japanese imperial military's prostitution program and

accepted it with the design of serving "sex-starved" U.S. soldiers. Enloe, *Maneuvers*, 85. Sarah Kovner argues that the U.S. occupation of Japan transformed the landscape of Japan's sex industry by abolishing licensed and legal prostitution to comply with U.S. regulations and forcing sex workers underground, making them less visible and more vulnerable to abuses. Kovner, *Occupying Power*.

90. Robert Lee, *Orientals*, 162; "Marriage by G.I.'s Problem in Korea: One Soldier in 40, the Army Finds, Weds a Korean," *New York Times*, October 24, 1965. In 1965 the *New York Times* reported that 1,265 American servicemen married Korean wives and 771 had married by October 1965.

91. Pfc. William F. Sprague, "The Problem of Marriages in the European Theater of Operations," April 1944, NARA RG498, box 3915.

92. War Department directive, circular 179, June 8, 1942, declared that marriages of any military personnel stationed in foreign countries required approval of the commanding officer at least two months in advance, a letter from a civil or ecclesiastical authority that would conduct the marriage, and an interview of the bride. The circular became the "cornerstone" of ETO directives on marriage procedure for officers and enlisted personnel. Enloe, *Maneuvers*, 44; Shukert and Scibetta, *War Brides of World War II*, 20; Various Documents, NARA, File 291.1, 1949, RG331, box 643.

93. Koshiro, "Race as International Identity?," 61–77; Zeiger, *Entangling Alliances*, Goedde, *GIs and Germans*; Shukert and Scibetta, *War Brides of World War II*.

94. The act gave permission to couples who applied for and were wed within thirty days of the law's enactment—a provision that proved unreasonable and impossible for most. This exception was reintroduced in P.L. 717 from 1950 to 1952 to coincide with the marriage requests resulting from the Korean War. Zeiger, *Entangling Alliances*, 6.

95. Enloe, *Maneuvers*, 66. Susan Brownmiller discusses prostitution during the First Indochina War, claiming the French Army imported Algerian girls to travel with mobile field brothels to satisfy the sexual needs of French soldiers. The U.S. did not continue the tradition of importing sex largely because the postwar economic devastation drove many Vietnamese women to prostitution as the only viable way to make money. Brownmiller, *Against Our Will*, 93.

96. Enloe, *Maneuvers*, 65–68.

97. Robert Lee, *Orientals*, 180.

98. Zeiger, *Entangling Alliances*, 244; Spickard, *Mixed Blood*, 133.

99. Terry, *Bloods*, 88.

100. Spickard, *Mixed Blood*, 134.

101. Enloe, *Maneuvers*, 36–45.

102. Brownmiller, *Against Our Will*, 31.

103. Brownmiller, *Against Our Will*, 109. Sergeant Camil served in Vietnam from March 1966 to November 1967. Akibayashi and Takazato, "Okinawa," 269. According to Akibayashi and Takazato, during the Vietnam War three to four Vietnamese women working in the sex industry around U.S. military bases were strangled to death each year.

104. Scales, "Soft on Defense," 379.

105. *Memorandum No. 96 "Establishment of Paternity,"* Office of the Political Adviser for Germany American Consulate General, Germany, June 17, 1947, NARA, Records of United States Occupation Headquarters, WWII, OMGUS for Germany, Records of the Civil Administration Division: General Records of Public Welfare and Displaced Persons, Bavaria, 1946–50, RG260, box 37. For more information on soldier marriages and military policies see, Zeiger, *Entangling Alliances*; Shukert and Scibetta, *War Brides*.

106. Scales, "Soft on Defense," 379.

107. Bass, *Vietnamerica*, 36.

108. Spickard, *Mixed Blood*, 135; Daniel-Wrabetz, "Children Born of War," 36; Langguth, *Our Vietnam War*.

109. This argument is taken directly from Enloe, *Maneuvers*, 67.

110. For more on the gendered framework that shaped the U.S. intervention in Vietnam see Dean, *Imperial Brotherhood*; Rutenberg, *Rough Draft*; Stur, *Beyond Combat*; and Dumancic, "Hidden in Plain Sight," 1–14.

111. Bradley, "Slouching toward Bethlehem."

112. There exists a rich scholarship on American race relations and U.S. foreign policy during the period, including Borstelmann, *Cold War and the Color Line*; Dudziak, *Cold War Civil Rights*; Plummer, *Rising Wind*; and Anderson, *Eyes Off the Prize*.

113. Huynh, "American War in Vietnamese Memory," 243–57. For more on the shared approach of U.S. officials and European colonial officials, see Foster, *Projections of Power*, 7.

114. William C. Bullitt, the American ambassador to the Soviet Union and France during the 1930s, used this description in conversation with the U.S. State Department Division of Philippine and Southeast Asian Affairs in 1947 to explain his suspicions about Vietnamese communism. Bullitt's view reiterated previous reports by the American consul to Saigon, Charles S. Reed, who noted that the Vietnamese were not "particularly industrious" nor were they known for their "honesty, loyalty or veracity." Bradley, "Improbable Opportunity," 12–14.

115. Bradley, "Improbable Opportunity"; Herring, *America's Longest War*; Foster, *Projections of Power*.

116. John F. Kennedy, "America's Stake in Vietnam," Papers of John F. Kennedy, Pre-Presidential Papers, Senate files, series 12, Speeches and the Press, box 895, folder "America's Stake in Vietnam, American Friends of Vietnam, Washington DC, 1 June 1956."

117. Thomas, "Blood Politics," 53.

118. Thomas, "Blood Politics," 52.

2. Saving Cold War Children

1. Spurling, *Pearl Buck in China*, 2.

2. Spurling, *Pearl Buck in China* 2, 38.

3. Buck published her first novel, *East Wind, West Wind*, in 1930 and won the Pulitzer Prize in 1932 for *The Good Earth*. In 1938, Buck became the first woman to win the Nobel Prize for Literature.

4. Gage, "Pure Mixed Blood," 89.

5. In 1939 the majority of states had antimiscegenation laws and fourteen states banned marriages between whites and Asians. On miscegenation, race mixing, and eugenics see, Cashin, *Loving*, 97; Pascoe, "Miscegenation Law," 464–90.

6. Era Bell Thompson, "Japan's Rejected: Teenage War Babies Face Bleak Future," *Ebony*, September 1967. For more insight on Buck's ideas of hybrid superiority, see Graves, *A War Born Family*, 198–205.

7. "Statement on the Founding of the Pearl S. Buck Foundation," *Insight Asia*, Fall 1989, PSBI, folder Insight Asia, box Insight Publication; Klein, *Cold War Orientalism*, 144. See also Nakashima, "Invisible Monster"; Robert Park, "Human Migration," 881–93; and Yu, *Thinking Orientals*.

8. Graves, *A War Born Family*, 210–11.

9. The Buck Foundation later claimed the U.S. foreign policy of containment "fathered the Amerasians" by placing U.S. troops permanently in Asia. Shade, *America's Forgotten Children*, 61. For a deeper discussion of Buck's evolution on transnational and transracial adoptions, see Graves, *A War Born Family*, 187–221.

10. Tom Tiede, "U.S. Passes Buck on GI Babies," SB 2497, 92 Cong. Rec. S13857 (daily ed. September 8, 1971). In addition to the resistance of the U.S. government, there were numerous obstacles to international adoption in the laws of South Vietnam and the regulations of the Vietnamese Ministry of Social Welfare. Testimony of Dr. James R. Dumpson, *Relief and Rehabilitation of War Victims in Indochina, part 2: Orphans and Child Welfare: Hearings before the Subcommittee to Investigate Problems Connected with Refugees and Escapees*. 93rd Cong., 1st sess., May 11, 1973.

11. Spurling, *Pearl Buck in China*, 240; Briggs, *Somebody's Children*, 151. Briggs writes that paternalism marred Buck's liberalism and advocacy for transracial

and transnational adoption. She embraced the politics of anticommunism and rescue and America's paternal responsibility for the Amerasians to ensure they overcame Asian barbarism. For a deeper discussion of Welcome House and Buck's commitment to creating interracial families, see Graves, *A War Born Family*, 191–221. For more information on the role of private organizations like the Pearl S. Buck Foundation in the emergence of international adoption see Winslow, *Best Possible Immigrants*, 15–33.

12. "Paul R. Cherney, The Aftermath of Asian Conflicts . . . The Abandoned Children of Asia," October–November 1965, PSBI, folder Amerasians, 1979–84, box Vietnam.

13. "Summary for Panel on Child Welfare," American Council of Voluntary Agencies for Foreign Service, Inc. November 30, 1966, PSBI, folder Adoption Issues 1967–68, box Vietnam Refugee Information; Judy McCann, "Welcome House Considers S. Vietnamese Adoptions," *Daily Intelligencer*, April 2 1973, PSBI, folder News Articles 1975–2000, box Vietnam Operation Babylift.

14. Thompson, "Japan's Rejected," *Ebony*.

15. Shade, "A Progress Report," PSBI.

16. Shade, "A Progress Report," PSBI.

17. Shade, *America's Forgotten Children*, 36.

18. Shade, *America's Forgotten Children*, 36.

19. Briggs, *Somebody's Children*, 152; Graves, *War Born Family*, 187–91.

20. Barnett, *Empire of Humanity*, 107.

21. Barnett, *Empire of Humanity*, 111–18. Barnett makes an interesting argument for paternalism as a force for good that underscores humanitarianism. See also Winslow, *Best Possible Immigrants*, 34–48.

22. Briggs, *Somebody's Children*, 136, 151; Winslow, *Best Possible Immigrants*, 43–48.

23. Rachel Winslow notes that the 1948 Displaced Persons Act applied only to orphans from Europe and did not include orphans from Japan. Winslow, *Best Possible Immigrants*, 43. By 1950 there were an estimated ninety thousand American GI babies in Germany and five thousand in Japan (a number humanitarians believed to be much higher). Fehrenbach, "Of German Mothers and 'Negermischlingskinder,'" 164; Koshiro, *Trans-Pacific Racisms*, 164. The U.S. government passed a number of immigration policies to address GI babies, including the War Brides Act (1945), Displaced Persons Act (1948), Korean War Brides Act (1950), and numerous amendments to the Immigration and Nationality Act.

24. For further analysis of the interdependent relationship between humanitarianism, voluntarism, and national foreign policy goals in shaping international adoption efforts after the Second World War see Winslow, *Best Possible Immigrants*.

25. Briggs, "Mother, Child, Race, Nation," 179–86.

26. Klein, *Cold War Orientalism*, 147.

27. Briggs, "Mother, Child, Race, Nation," 180; Briggs, *Somebody's Children*, 150; Eleana Kim, *Adopted Territory*, 53; Winslow, *Best Possible Immigrants*, 86–87.

28. Espiritu, *Body Counts*, 8 (quote); Dubinsky, *Babies without Borders*, 12; Klein, *Cold War Orientalism*, 145–46, 156–60.

29. "Patriotic pronatalism" is Eleana Kim's term: *Adopted Territory*, 44. For a detailed analysis of the Holt Adoption Agency, see Winslow, *Best Possible Immigrants*, 70–141. Also see Briggs, "Mother, Child, Race, Nation"; Dubinsky, *Babies without Borders*, 131; Klein, *Cold War Orientalism*, 152–60.

30. Klein, *Cold War Orientalism*, 144–50; Graves, *War Born Family*, 189.

31. Klein, *Cold War Orientalism*, 16, 174–75, 189. Klein describes this dual approach as "Cold War Orientalism." For further analysis of Pearl Buck's Amerasian adoption efforts, see Winslow, *Best Possible Immigrants*, 106–7; Graves, *War Born Family*, 187–89.

32. Klein, *Cold War Orientalism*, 174.

33. Mr. and Mrs. Richard Burton to Pearl Buck, April 20, 1972, PSBI, folder Correspondence 1972, box 44.

34. Klein, *Cold War Orientalism*, 189. For further examination of hybridity, see Dubinksy, *Babies without Borders*.

35. Extension of Remarks of Hon. John R. Dellenback, "Tribute to the Holt Adoption Agency," August 24, 1967, 90 Cong. Rec.

36. Robert Trumbull, "Amerasians: 'An Entirely New Group of Human Beings,'" *New York Times*, April 30, 1967.

37. Michael Kernan, "Children with No Country: A Champion in Pearl Buck," *Washington Post*, August 7, 1971. Kori Graves argues that Buck incorporated the potential communist threat of abandoned Amerasians into her rescue narrative as part of her transnational child welfare activism for the Amerasians in South Korea. Graves, *War Born Family*, 218–19.

38. "Save the Children," flyer, ca. 1973, PMP, folder 1, box 312.

39. "Save the Children," flyer.

40. Saada, *Empire's Children*, 24–25.

41. Mary and Ed Miyakawa, to Patsy Mink, June 14, 1973, PMP, folder 5, box 312.

42. Yarborough, *Surviving Twice*, 9; Jean Yavis Jones, Education and Public Welfare Division, "Vietnamese Adoption and Childcare," July 18, 1973, and included report, "Measures Taken for Eurasian Children Affected by the War in Indochina," June 15, 1971, PMP, folder 2, box 312. For more on French nationality law, see Plender, "New French Nationality Law," and Jennings, *Imperial Heights*.

43. Gus Constantine, "Parley Focuses on GI Babies in Vietnam," *Washington Post*, July 20, 1971, PNP, folder 4, box 312.

44. Shade, *America's Forgotten Children*, 47. Numerous reports described Nixon and Buck as having a good friendship based on a mutual interest in improving U.S.-China relations.

45. Seymour M. Hersh, "Coverup," part 1, *New Yorker*, January 22, 1972. Historian Nick Turse's work reveals that such acts of violence and barbarity against Vietnamese civilians were pervasive during the Vietnam War. Turse, *Kill Anything That Moves*.

46. Historian Jerry Lembcke argues that epithets like "baby killer" and stories of antiwar protesters spitting on returning soldiers were fabricated. Lembcke, *Spitting Image*. Also, Appy, *American Reckoning*, 184–85, 237; Appy, *Working-Class War*, 298–305.

47. Don Luce, "Amer-Asian Children in Viet Nam," in Adoption and Vietnam, SB 2497, 92nd Cong., Cong. Rec. S13854.

48. Michael Kernan, "Children with No Country: A Champion in Pearl Buck," in Adoption and Vietnam, SB 2497, 92nd Cong., Cong. Rec. S13853.

49. "Department of Defense Position Regarding Children Born out of Wedlock in Foreign Countries Where US Armed Forces Are Assigned," Pentagon, June 9, 1971, PMP, folder Immigration, Vietnamese Orphans, box 312.

50. Bass, *Vietnamerica*, 34; "Department of Defense Position Regarding Children Born Out of Wedlock."

51. Tom Tiede, "U.S. Passes Buck on GI Babies," in Adoption and Vietnam, SB 2497, 92nd Cong., Cong. Rec. S13857 (daily ed. September 8, 1971).

52. Alexander M. Haig Jr. to Richard M. Nixon, July 12, 1971 (declassified January 21, 1998), RNPL, White House Special Files: Staff Member and Office Files: John Scali, 1971–72, folder Orphans-Vietnamese, box 7. LO9, 6, A, 1, 1.

53. Bass, *Vietnamerica*, 34; Adoption and Vietnam, SB 2497, S13857.

54. Tiede, "U.S. Passes Buck on GI Babies."

55. H. R. Haldeman to John Scali, April 28, 1971, RNPL, White House Special Files: Staff Member and Office Files: John Scali, 1971–72, folder Orphans-Vietnamese, box 7. LO9, 6, A, 1, 1.

56. John Scali to H. R. Haldeman, May 12, 1971, RNPL, White House Special Files: Staff Member and Office Files: John Scali, 1971–72, folder Orphans-Vietnamese, box 7. LO9, 6, A, 1, 1.

57. Jon M. Huntsman to John Scali, May 28, 1971, RNPL, folder Orphans-Vietnamese, box 7. LO9, 6, A, 1, 1.

58. Scali to Haldeman, May 12, 1971. After the Second World War, the Korea Model became a template for transnational adoption and a solution to the problem of child displacement and social dislocations caused by war. Eleana Kim, *Adopted Territory*, 4–5. See also Graves, *A War Born Family*, 105–48.

59. Paul R. Cherney, "The Aftermath of Asian Conflicts," October–November 1965, PSBI, folder Amerasians, 1979–84, box Vietnam; "Child Welfare Problems in Vietnam: A Summary," UN Asian Conference, September 1965; [quote] letter to Pearl S. Buck, December 20, 1966, PSBI, folder Adoption Issues 1967–68, box Vietnam, Refugee Information; Winslow, *Best Possible Immigrants*, 154–55.

60. Navy Chaplain John O'Connor described the effects of orphaned Vietnamese children on U.S. servicemen: O'Conner, *Chaplain Looks at Vietnam*, 53. There were 120 registered orphanages in South Vietnam by 1974 housing a total of 17,500 Amerasian and Vietnamese children. "Agencies Licensed by the Republic of Vietnam to Facilitate Inter-Country Adoptions," Holt International Survey, PSBI, folder General Info PSBF Vietnam, box Vietnam Operation Babylift.

61. Donald L. Ranard to William H. Sullivan, May 14, 1971; Charles S. Whitehouse to John Scali, n.d., RNPL, White House Special Files: Staff Member and Office Files: John Scali, 1971–72, folder Orphans-Vietnamese, box 7. LO9, 6, A, 1, 1.

62. Quoted in Longley, *Grunts*, 154.

63. "For 3,000 Korean Orphans, Dies;" April 29, 1965, RNPL, White House Special Files: Staff Member and Office Files: John Scali, 1971–72, folder Orphans-Vietnamese, box 7. LO9, 6, A, 1, 1.

64. Scali to Haldeman, May 12, 1971; Haig to Nixon, July 12, 1971; Haldeman to Scali, April 28, 1971.

65. "Another Way the United States Has Left Its Mark on Vietnam," *New York Times*, in Adoption and Vietnam, SB 2497, 92nd Cong., Cong. Rec. S13855.

66. William H. Sullivan to John Scali, June 24, 1971, RNPL, folder Orphans-Vietnamese, box 7. LO9, 6, A, 1, 1; Haldeman to Scali, April 28, 1971.

67. After the war International Social Service and World Church Service were two of nine voluntary agencies contracted by the U.S. government for refugee assistance and resettlement. Chan, *Asian Americans*, 156; Tiede, "U.S. Passes Buck on GI Babies."

68. Rep. Donald M. Fraser, "Vietnam War Babies," 93rd Cong., Cong. Rec. H45243.

69. The bill awarded special immigrant visas to individuals residing in Vietnam with one alien and one U.S. citizen parent and determined to be orphans because abandoned by either parent or both. Rep. Donald M. Fraser, "Vietnam War Babies"; press release, May 17, 1971, PMP, Congressional/Legislative Central File, folder Immigration, Vietnamese Orphans, Correspondence Congress and Federal Agencies, 1971–72, box 313.

70. Press release, May 17, 1971, PMP, box 313.

71. Letter to Patsy Mink, May 3, 1971, PMP, Congressional/Legislative Central File, folder Immigration, Vietnamese Orphans, Correspondence Congress and

Federal Agencies, 1971–72, box 313 (italics added). For more on Hawaii's history of blood, race, and immigration, see Kauanui, *Hawaiian Blood*.

72. Peter W. Rodino to Patsy T. Mink, June 2, 1972, PMP, Congressional/Legislative Central File, folder Immigration, Vietnamese Orphans, Correspondence Congress and Federal Agencies, 1971–72, box 313.

73. Sponsors of the bill stressed cooperation with the United Nations to alleviate some of the concern. Initially proposed in the House as HR 13050 with ten cosponsors, Hatfield, Hughes, and Williams presented it to the Foreign Relations Committee, chaired by William Fulbright (D-AR), on April 5, 1972, and the Senate on April 10. The bill resurfaced in the House five times between January 3, 1973, and May 31, 1973, never making it out of committee. For more on the opposition argument, see "Children Orphaned and Wounded in Vietnam War," 92nd Cong., 2nd sess., Cong. Rec. 11928–32 (April 10, 1972).

74. For a more detailed examination and accurate accounting of the human toll, see W. Robinson, *Terms of Refuge*.

75. Appy, *American Reckoning*, xi; statistics, xiv.

76. Northshield, *Sins of the Fathers*.

77. Hon. Patsy T. Mink, "The Sins of the Fathers—Vietnam's Dying Orphans," Extension of Remarks, 93rd Cong., Cong. Rec. 22170:22173 (June 28, 1973). Heather Stur describes the "gentle warrior," a kindhearted father figure and skilled fighter, as a critical figure in the battle for hearts and minds and symbolic of the contradiction in the U.S. mission in Vietnam. Stur, "Hiding behind the Humanitarian," 228.

78. John J. O'Conner, "TV: Plight of Racially Mixed Children in Vietnam," *New York Times*, June 20, 1973, https://www.nytimes.com/1973/06/20/archives/tv-plight-of-racially-mixed-children-in-vietnam-report-by.html. Also see Klein, *Cold War Orientalism*, chap. 4.

79. Dianne Coughlin, "Vietnamese Orphans: How Can We Help?" *Star-Bulletin*, September 19, 1973, PMP, folder Immigration, Vietnamese Orphans Fact-Finding Trip, 1973, box 315.

80. Internal memo, Patsy Mink, 1973; Mink to House of Representatives, March 26, 1973, PMP, folder Immigration, Vietnamese Orphans, Correspondence Congress and Federal Agencies, 1973 Feb.–June, box 313.

81. Mink to Edward O. Craft, May 4, 1971, PMP, folder Immigration, Vietnamese Orphans, Correspondence Congress and Federal Agencies, 1971–72, box 313.

82. Internal memo, Patsy Mink, 1973; Mink to House, March 26, 1973.

83. Mink, "Sins of the Fathers."

84. As a result of reopening relations, Welcome House established the Vietnamese American Children's Fund to support and adopt Amerasians in June

1973. "W.H.A.P.G to Work alongside VACF," *Welcomer*, November 1973; "Report from VACF Field Director Victor Srinivasan," *Welcomer*, November 1973; John E. Adams, "Report from Holt in Vietnam," *Welcomer*, November 1973: all in PSBI, folder *Welcomer* Nov. 1973, box Welcome House; *The Welcomer: Welcome House Adoptive Parents Group Newsletter*, Spring–Summer 1971, no. 2, PSBI, folder *Welcomer 1972*, box Welcome House.

85. *The Orphan Problem in South Vietnam*, report of Special Study Subcommittee of the Committee on the Judiciary to Review Immigration, Refugee, and Nationality Problems, Committee on the Judiciary, House of Representatives, 93rd Cong, 1st sess., Dec. 1973, PMP, folder 9, box 315; Loren Jenkins, "Vietnam's War-Torn Children," *Newsweek*, May 28, 1973, 56; Patsy Mink, "Unloved Orphans of an Unloved War," *Washington Post*, Sept. 23, 1973, PMP, folder, Immigration, Vietnamese Orphans, box 316.

86. Jenkins, "Vietnam's War-Torn Children."

87. Jenkins, "Vietnam's War-Torn Children."

88. Patsy Mink to Ward Hussey, October 24, 1973, PMP, Legislative Central File, folder Vietnamese Orphans, box 313.

89. Patsy Mink to Peter Rodino Jr., June 23, 1973, PMP, Legislative Central File, folder Immigration Vietnamese Orphans Correspondence Congress and Federal Agencies, 1973 Feb.–June, box 313.

90. "Help for Vietnam Orphans—A National Need," New England Conference on the Children of Vietnam, April 27, 1974, PMP, Legislative Central File, folder Immigration, Vietnamese Orphans, box 316.

91. "Bill Pushed to Aid War Orphans," *Milwaukee Journal*, August 19, 1973, PMP, folder Vietnamese Orphans, box 313.

92. Marshall Wright to Joshua Eilberg, August, 7, 1973, PMP, Congressional/Legislative Central File, folder Immigration, Vietnamese Orphans, Correspondence, Congress and Federal Agencies 1973, July–Oct., box 313.

93. Illegible to Patsy Mink, August 30, 1973, PMP, Legislative Central File, folder Immigration, Vietnamese Orphans, box 316.

94. *HR 3159—A Bill for the Relief of Certain Orphans in Vietnam*, departmental report, House, Committee on the Judiciary, Department of Health, Education, and Welfare, June 19, 1973, PMP, folder Immigration, Vietnamese Orphans, box 313.

95. Heather Sigworth to Patsy Mink, July 5, 1973, PMP, folder Vietnamese Orphans, box 312.

96. Sigworth to Mink, July 5, 1973.

97. On January 29, 1973, Mink revived her initial failed bill, HR 8462, and introduced HR 3159. Marshall Wright to Joshua Eilberg, August, 7, 1973, PMP,

folder Immigration, Vietnamese Orphans, Correspondence, Congress and Federal Agencies 1973, July–Oct., box 313.

98. USAID asked the Judiciary Committee to consider modifying U.S. immigration and nationality laws to allow Amerasians to obtain American citizenship. *Relief and Rehabilitation of War Victims in Indochina Part II: Orphans and Child Welfare: Hearings before the Subcommittee to Investigate Problems Connected with Refugees and Escapees*, U.S. Senate, 93rd Cong., 1st sess., May 11, 1973, 90–94.

99. The bill proposed to make eligible for citizenship any Vietnamese Amerasian born in the Republic of Vietnam before January 1, 1974, twelve years of age or younger and placed with a family through a properly accredited adoption agency. There was some discussion between Robison, Steiger, and Mink about merging their bills; however, disagreements over the specific timing of granting citizenship prevented it. The House reintroduced the bill in March 1975 as HR 4810, where it once again failed to move past the Judiciary Committee. "Adoption of Vietnamese-American Orphans and Resettlement of Refugees," 93rd Cong., 1st sess., Cong. Rec. H18167–69 (June 5, 1973).

100. In addition to Steiger, the bipartisan effort to get the same version of the bill through committee in the House included Edward Roybal (D-CA), John Zwach (R-MN), Ancher Nelsen (R-MN), Edward Winn Jr. (R-KS), and George O'Brien (R-IL). Rodino served in North Africa and Italy and chaired the House Judiciary Committee in 1973 and 1974. The record is unclear as to why these bills did not advance out of committee; however, the investigation and trial surrounding President Richard Nixon and Watergate arguably occupied much of the attention of the committee during the period. Sheila Meehan to Patsy Mink, March 4, 1974, PMP, folder Immigration, Vietnamese Orphans, box 316.

101. "Foreign Assistance Authorization Act—Amendments," 93rd Cong., 1st sess., Cong. Rec. 4632–34 (February 20, 1973).

102. "Foreign Assistance Authorization Act." Senator Kennedy proposed three amendments: the first affirmed the willingness of the U.S. to share the burden of humanitarian relief, rehabilitation, and reconstruction for the people and nations of Indochina; the second earmarked $70 million for humanitarian assistance to refugees, civilian war casualties, war orphans, and other persons disadvantaged by the war; and the third earmarked $2million for the same purposes in Cambodia. Sen. Walter Mondale, speaking of the child victims of war, "The Children of Vietnam," 93rd Cong., 1st sess., Cong. Rec. S17088–89 (May 29, 1973). The Congressional Subcommittee on Children and Youth voiced its concerns about the future of Vietnam's child war victims, their medical treatment, and the prospects for adoption and secure family lives.

103. "Foreign Assistance Authorization Act"; *Relief and Rehabilitation of War Victims: Hearings*.

104. *Relief and Rehabilitation of War Victims: Hearings*.

105. Anis "Psychosocial Adjustment of Vietnamese Americans," 45.

106. *Vietnam Children's Care Agency: Hearings before the Committee on Foreign Relations*, U.S. Senate, 92nd Cong., 2nd sess. (April 5, 1972), 46–55. The estimated number of Black Amerasians aligned with reports that Black Amerasians composed 30 percent of all Amerasians in Vietnam and with the number reported by Victor Srinivasen, a humanitarian worker who assisted Black Amerasians in Vietnam. Gloria Emerson, "Part Vietnamese, Part Black—and Orphans," *New York Times*, February 7, 1972; David Detweller, "Fatherless Children: GI Babies in Vietnam," *Parade*, in 92nd Cong., 1st sess., Cong. Rec. S13854 (Sept. 8, 1971).

107. Because of its long history with people of various ethnicities, the value of racial purity that exists in other Asian countries like Japan is less pronounced in Vietnam. However, as in other Asian countries, skin color in Vietnam revealed deeply rooted concepts of beauty. Such racial conceptions arguably preceded the imposition of racialized French colonial categories in the nineteenth century, evidenced by assumptions of superiority and inferiority of Vietnamese to Khmers and Cham and to other mountain tribes. In Vietnam dark skin is often associated with class, representing the outdoor labor common of the peasantry, while light skin represents the wealthy. The racial hierarchy that accompanied French colonization and American intervention further embedded notions of racial difference and contempt for Black skin tones. Valverde, "Doing the Mixed-Race Dance," 140; Kowner and Demel, *Race and Racism in Modern East Asia*; Russell, "Race and Reflexivity;" Wagatsuma, "Social Perception of Skin Color in Japan."

108. See Firpo, *Uprooted*, and Koshiro, *Trans-Pacific Racisms*.

109. McKelvey, *Dust of Life*, 47; DeBonis, *Children of the Enemy*; Valverde, "Doing the Mixed Race Dance," 140.

110. Valverde, "Doing the Mixed-Race Dance," 140; Kowner and Demel, *Race and Racism in Modern East Asia*; Russell, "Race and Reflexivity."

111. Daniel Southerland, "When Fathers Were American," *Christian Science Monitor*, February 2, 1973, PMP, folder Vietnamese Orphans, box 312; Wells Klein, "The Special Needs of Vietnamese Children," *Vietnam Children's Care Agency: Hearings before the Committee on Foreign Relations*, U.S. Senate, 92nd Cong., 2nd sess. (April 5, 1972), 46.

112. American authorities noted that as a result of racial discrimination many Black Eurasian girls fathered by French African troops worked as bar girls and prostitutes, bringing additional shame to their Vietnamese families. Valverde, "Doing the Mixed-Race Dance," 140.

113. Holt International reported the statistical findings for abandonment in 1972. "Report to the Board of Directors of the Holt Adoption Program, Vietnam 1972," *Vietnam Children's Care Agency: Hearings before the Committee on Foreign Relations*, U.S. Senate, 92nd Cong., 2nd sess. (April 5, 1972), 110–12; Klein, "Special Needs of Vietnamese Children."

114. "Another Way the United States Has Left Its Mark on Vietnam," *New York Times*, in Adoption and Vietnam, SB 2497, 92nd Cong., Cong. Rec. S13855 (September 8, 1971).

115. Ranard and Gilzow, "Amerasians," UCI, Van Le files, folder 1, box 1.

116. Southerland, "When Fathers Were American," PMP.

117. Anis, "Psychosocial Adjustment of Vietnamese Americans," 42–44; *New York Times*, November 16, 1992.

118. Tad Szulc "Embassy in Saigon Calls Babies of GIs a 'Serious Concern,'" in 92nd Cong., Cong. Rec. S13853 (September 8, 1971).

119. Emerson, "Part Vietnamese, Part Black—And Orphans."

120. Klein, "Special Needs of Vietnamese Children."

121. Klein, "Special Needs of Vietnamese Children."

122. "Summary of Study Mission Recommendations Currently under Review by the Agency for International Development and the Department of State," *Relief and Rehabilitation of War Victims in Indochina Part II: Orphans and Child Welfare: Hearings before the Subcommittee to Investigate Problems Connected with Refugees and Escapees*, Senate, 93rd Cong., 1st sess. (May 11, 1973), 90–94.

123. Interview with Juanita Williams, Martin Luther King Speaks, 1972, Series 19 Audio, MARBLE, folder 13, box 613.

124. Interview with Juanita Williams, MARBLE.

125. Interview with Juanita Williams, MARBLE.

126. The focus on Black Catholic families was critical to the Williams's efforts, as the Catholic Church operated 90 percent of the orphanages in South Vietnam and Buddhist orphanages did not traditionally place children for adoption. Williams insisted that adoptive parents be Catholic. Williams to Stoney Cooks, January 1, 1972, MARBLE, collection 1083, folder 22, box 209; *Vietnam Children's Care Agency: Hearings before the Committee on Foreign Relations*, U.S. Senate, 92nd Cong., 2nd sess. (April 5, 1972), 65–68.

127. Era Bell Thompson, "The Plight of Black Babies in Vietnam," *Ebony*, December 1972.

128. Thompson, "Plight of Black Babies in Vietnam."

129. According to Kyle Longley, racial inequities in draft boards, selective enrollment in the National Guard and the reserves that catered to sons of politicians, the wealthy, and professional athletes ensured that the poor, the less

educated, the less privileged, and Black men composed the majority of combat ground forces (grunts). The death rates for Black soldiers consistently exceeded the proportion of the Black population throughout the conflict. By 1975 African Americans composed 11 percent of the American population but 13.1 percent of the deaths. Longley, *Grunts*, 9–11, 30. For more information see Eldridge, *Chronicles of a Two-Front War*; Terry, *Bloods*.

130. In January 1972 SCLC hired Victor Srinivasan to head the SCLC Viet-American Children's Program in Saigon, with an annual salary of $5,000. However, letters between Srinivasan, Juanita Williams, and Stoney Cooks reveal that by June 1972 SCLC failed to file the proper paperwork with the South Vietnam government or pay Srinivasan, who was by then caring for ten Black Amerasians under the auspices of SCLC. On December 31, 1972, SCLC notified Srinivasan that the program had been discontinued. Juanita Williams to Stoney Cooks, June 21, 1972; Victor Srinivasan to Williams, July 23, 1972; Srinivasan to Cooks, August 19, 1972; Bernard S. Lee to Srinivasan, December 31, 1972; all in MARBLE, folder 22, box 209.

131. "And Now a Domestic Babylift?" *Ebony*, June 1975; "Confusion, Controversy Cloud Viet War Orphans," *Jet*, May 15, 1975.

132. In 1975, forty thousand of the one hundred thousand American children awaiting adoption in the United States were African American. Although some domestic adoption agencies pushed African American couples and single Black women to adopt Black babies, not enough were placed to keep up with the growing numbers of available Black children. The result was a greater acceptance of interracial adoptions. "And Now a Domestic Babylift?" *Ebony*; "Confusion, Controversy Cloud Viet War Orphans," *Jet*, 15; Helen H. King, "It's Easier to Adopt Today," *Ebony*, December 1970, 120–28; Kathy Begley, "Orphans: Too Little, Too Late," *Philadelphia Inquirer*, April 13, 1975, PSBI, folder Operation Babylift.

133. Bell, *Black Power Movement and American Social Work*, 136.

134. Rachel Winslow notes that many Black social workers viewed efforts to remove Black Amerasian children from their Vietnamese families through the lens of decolonization, self-determination, and resistance. As a result, they believed that Black Amerasian children should be raised by their Vietnamese mothers and families. Winslow, *Best Possible Immigrants*, 152–53.

135. Matthew J. Harvey to Mink, November 30, 1973; "Meeting on Placement and Adoption of Vietnamese Children in American Homes," *Agency for International Development (AID)*, July 25–26, 1973, PMP, folder Vietnamese Orphans, box 313.

136. Winslow, *Best Possible Immigrants*, 148–49.

137. "Introduction to IVAC," Eggleston to Randall, February 3, 1976, MSRC, folder 5: Vietnamese Adoption Committee, box 102.

138. Walter E. Fauntroy, "National Black Political Agenda," March 24, 1972, MSRC, folder 42, box 75.

139. "Conyers and Colleagues Introduce Impeachment Resolution," May 12, 1972, MSRC, folder 30, box 75.

140. Charles C. Diggs Jr. to Nixon, July 22, 1971, RNPL, John Dean subject file 1969–1973, folder Racial Problems in the Military 2/6, box 66.

141. Herring, *America's Longest War*, 336.

142. The U.S. State Department expressed concerns about the danger facing those identified with the U.S. presence in Vietnam. Sheila Meehan to Mink, "Evacuation of Vietnamese Orphans and Humanitarian Assistance," April 11, 1975, PMP, folder Immigration, Vietnamese Orphans, Staff and Communication, box 316. The Buck Foundation reported persecution of Amerasians in Vietnam by the Communists. John Shade Jr., "The Forgotten Child," Conference for the National Organizations Advisory Council, May 8, 1980, PSBI, folder Amerasian, box Vietnam.

143. Sachs, *Life We Were Given*, 12.

144. There is no corroborating evidence in the United States for this report or many of the other claims about Amerasian persecution. "Agencies Licensed," PSBI, folder 1 General, box Vietnam Operation Babylift.

145. "Agencies Licensed," PSBI. Laura Briggs and Karen Dubinsky examine how international adoption efforts contribute to notions and narratives of saving, rescue, and survival in international adoption efforts. Briggs, *Somebody's Children*, Dubinsky, *Babies without Borders*.

146. Yarborough, *Surviving Twice*, x.

147. Thomas, "Blood Politics," 56–57.

148. Tsongas proposed HR 5187 with twenty-four cosponsors, including Patsy Mink and Romano Mazzoli. "A Bill to Confer U.S. Citizenship upon Certain Orphans," 121 no. 6 Cong. Rec. H7082 (March 18, 1975).

149. Pearl S. Buck Foundation, "The Amerasians: A Human Rights Issue and U.S. Foreign Policy Question," ca. 1980, PSBI, folder Pearl.

150. Marre and Briggs, *International Adoption*, 7.

151. Sachs, *Life We Were Given*, 65.

152. Weidenfeld, *First Lady's Lady*, 112–13.

153. Sachs, *Life We Were Given*, xii.

154. Loescher and Scanlan, *Calculated Kindness*, 107.

155. Sutter, *Indochinese Refugee Dilemma*, 61.

156. Edward Royball introduced an identical bill in the House, HR 3496, in February 1975.

157. Sen. Bob Packwood, 121 no. 8 Cong. Rec., Senate, April 7, 1975, PMP, folder 3, box 312.

158. Packwood, 121 no. 8 Cong. Rec., April 7, 1975.

159. Kathy Begley, "Orphans: Too Little, Too Late," *Philadelphia Inquirer*, April 13, 1975.

160. Sachs, *Life We Were Given*, 130–31.

161. Quoted in Sachs, *Life We Were Given*, 131.

162. Marre and Briggs, *International Adoption*, 9.

163. Marre and Briggs, *International Adoption*, 9–10. Marre and Briggs credit the decline in white children in foster care to economic and social changes that caused fewer single women to put their children up for adoption and the availability of birth control and abortion.

164. Begley, "Orphans."

165. Vernon E Jordan Jr., "To Be Equal: Vietnam and the Orphans," *Call and Post*, April 26, 1975, MSRC, folder 21, box 79.

166. "Findings of Fact and Conclusions of Law and Order" in the United States District Court for the Northern District of California, *Nguyen Da Yen, Nguyen Da Vuong and Nguyen Da Tuyen v. James Schlesinger, Secretary of Defense et al.*, June 30, 1975, PSBI, folder Legal Information, box Vietnam Operation Babylift.

167. See the arguments regarding the U.S. effort to rewrite the Vietnam War narrative to transform it from a military defeat to a humanitarian victory, in Espiritu, *Body Counts*, and Appy, *American Reckoning*.

168. McKelvey, *Dust of Life*, 11.

3. Becoming Refugees

1. Carol Lundin, "Stewart B. McKinney: The Man," accessed, May 24, 2014.

2. McKinney to Sophie Stevens, May 8, 1975, SMP, Legislative Correspondence, folder Viet-Refugees, box 26; McKinney to Paul Nakian, August 3, 1973, SMP, Legislative Correspondence, folder Foreign Affairs—Vietnam, box 13.

3. McKinney to Nakian, SMP.

4. Martini, *Invisible Enemies*, 13.

5. Appy, *American Reckoning*, xi.

6. Loescher and Scanlan, *Calculated Kindness*, 110.

7. Appy, *American Reckoning*, 228; quoted in Martini, *Invisible Enemies*, 12.

8. McKinney to Adele P. Edgerton, January 25, 1973, SMP, folder Foreign Affairs—Vietnam, box 13.

9. Espiritu, "'We Win Even When We Lose Syndrome,'" 329; Heather Stur, "Hiding behind the Humanitarian Label," 228.

10. Espiritu, "'We Win Even When We Lose Syndrome,'" 329; Appy, *American Reckoning*, 227–28; Stur, "Hiding behind the Humanitarian Label," 228.

11. Keys, *Reclaiming American Virtue*, 3; Winslow, *Best Possible Immigrants*, 11.

12. Loescher and Scanlan, *Calculated Kindness*, 110–12.

13. Chan, *Vietnamese American 1.5 Generation*, 62.

14. "Message from Ambassador Graham Martin Concerning the Evacuation," April 29, 1975, GFPL, digitized from box 3 of the National Security Administration, also included in "Last Days in Vietnam: The Embassy Evacuation," *American Experience*, Public Broadcasting Service, https://www.pbslearningmedia.org/resource/amex27ldv.ush.embassy/embassy-evacuation/.

15. Sutter, *Indochinese Refugee Dilemma*, 10, 54.

16. Sutter, *Indochinese Refugee Dilemma*, 10, 167; Loescher and Scanlan, *Calculated Kindness*, 108–12; Winslow, *Best Possible Immigrants*, 179–94.

17. "Press Conference No. 12 of the President of the United States," April 3, 1975, GFPL, Operation Babylift Press Releases, digitized from box 9.

18. Robinson, *Terms of Refuge*, 22; Sutter, *Indochinese Refugee Dilemma*, 57; "Press Conference No. 12 of the President of the United States," April 3, 1975, GFPL, Operation Babylift Press Releases, digitized from box 9.

19. Loescher and Scanlan use "calculated kindness" to describe the politics that have historically shaped the American response to refugees. Loescher and Scanlan, *Calculated Kindness*, xiv.

20. Loescher and Scanlan, *Calculated Kindness*, xviii, 102.

21. For more on the history of American humanitarianism, see Barnett, *Empire of Humanity*, and for more on human rights see Anderson, *Eyes Off the Prize*.

22. Snyder, *From Selma to Moscow*, 8–17.

23. Snyder, *From Selma to Moscow*, 15–17; Loescher and Scanlan, *Calculated Kindness*, 88.

24. Keys, *Reclaiming American Virtue*, 3, 269–72.

25. Loescher and Scanlan, *Calculated Kindness*, 114.

26. David Binder, "Ford Asks Nation to Open Its Doors to the Refugees," *New York Times*, May 7, 1975; Byrd is also quoted in Schulzinger, *Time for Peace*, 5.

27. Binder, "Ford Asks Nation to Open Its Doors."

28. Bon Tempo, *Americans at the Gate*, 147.

29. Espiritu, *Body Counts*, 94–97.

30. Espiritu, *Body Counts*, 25; Mimi Thi Nguyen, *Gift of Freedom*.

31. Henry Yu argues that the transformation of Asian Americans from an "Oriental problem" in America to good refugees and a "model minority" resulted from assumptions that Asians made successful cultural adjustments in America that resulted in academic and economic success. Yu, *Thinking Orientals*, 187.

Also see Jun, *Race for Citizenship*; Chan, *Asian Americans*; Robert Lee, *Orientals*, and Espiritu, *Body Counts*, 94–97. In 1977 Bob Suzuki published his article, "Education and the Socialization of Asian Americans: A Revisionist Analysis of the 'Model Minority,'" in which he challenged the image of the successful, educated, middle-class model minority Asian by contrasting it with the damaging characterizations that had defined Asians in American for over a century. Suzuki, "Education and the Socialization of Asian Americans."

32. Wu, *Color of Success*, 2, 149; Jun, *Race for Citizenship*, 128. Jun posits that the construction of the Asian model minority occurred as a domestic racial discourse and an expression of the neoliberal principles that emerged after the civil rights movement.

33. Yu, *Thinking Orientals*, 7–8.

34. Joseph Alsop, "Matter of Fact: July 4!," *Washington Post*, July 3, 1967, quoted in Wu, *Color of Success*, 244.

35. According to Wallace Terry and James Westheider, both combat and postwar experiences were divided along racial lines. African Americans served and died in Vietnam at disproportionate rates, making up 23 percent of the fatalities in the first half of the war. African American veterans from the Vietnam War faced unemployment rate of 33 percent, three times the national average and well above the 5.7 percent facing white veterans. Terry, *Bloods*, xiv–xv, and Westheider, *African American Experience in Vietnam*, xx, 107.

36. "The Congressional Black Caucus Views on the Vietnamese Refugees," May 8, 1975, MSRC, folder 21 Vietnamese Refugees, box 79.

37. "Congressional Black Caucus Views," MSRC.

38. William O. Walker, "Down the Big Road: 200,000 South Vietnamese," *Cleveland Call & Post*, April 26, 1975, MSRC, folder 21, box 79.

39. William O. Walker, "Down the Big Road: 200,000 South Vietnamese," MSRC; "Black Caucus Asks Refugee Aid Link to Help for Needy," *New York Times*, May 9, 1975; Richard L. Lyons, "Congress Shatters Patterns in Its Reaction to Refugees," *Washington Post*, May 9, 1975.

40. Additional factors included Haiti's value as the nearest U.S. military base to Cuba in the Caribbean, its mineral resources—gold, silver, and bauxite. "U.S. Denies Human Rights to Haitian Refugees," February 3, 1976, MSRC, folder 4, box 102.

41. "U.S. Denies Human Rights to Haitian Refugees," MSRC.

42. "U.S. Denies Human Rights to Haitian Refugees," MSRC.

43. "U.S. Denies Human Rights to Haitian Refugees," MSRC; "Jailed Haitian Refugee Attempts Suicide," press release, September 26, 1975, MSRC, folder 4, box 102. Father Antoine Adrian was one of the Haitian Fathers, a group of Roman

Catholic priests exiled from Haiti in 1969. Father Adrian was an activist against the regime of Papa Doc Duvalier.

44. Lynn Dunson, "3 Black Groups Hit Vietnam Adoptions," *Washington Star*, April 19, 1975, enclosure in Evelyn Eggleston to Carol Randal, February 3, 1976, MSRC, folder 5, box 102.

45. Tom Littlewood, "Blacks Hit 'Bias' In the Babylift," *New York Post*, April 19, 1975, enclosure in Evelyn Eggleston to Carol Randal, February 3, 1976, MSRC, folder 5, box 102.

46. Evelyn Eggleston, "Bring It Down Front, The Issue: Vietnam's Babies," August 1975; Nancy Hicks, "Black Agencies Charge Injustice in Placing of Vietnam Children," *New York Times*, April 19, 1975: enclosures in Evelyn Eggleston to Carol Randal, February 3, 1976, MSRC, folder 5, box 102. For a more extensive analysis of IVAC and how race informed the adoption efforts of Amerasians in Vietnam, see Winslow, *Best Possible Immigrants*, 142–80.

47. *Report to the Congressional Black Caucus: The Interagency Vietnam Adoption Committee*, February 6, 1976; Carol Randall to Charles Rangel, February 1976: enclosures in Evelyn Eggleston to Carol Randall, February 3, 1976, MSRC, folder 5, box 102.

48. Allen, *Until the Last Man Comes Home*, 163–64.

49. Pham Van Dong quoted in Hurst, *Carter Administration and Vietnam*, 19, and Martini, *Invisible Enemies*, 19.

50. Martini, *Invisible Enemies*, 18–19.

51. Allen, *Until the Last Man Comes Home*, 165; Martini, *Invisible Enemies*, 20.

52. In 1966 Sybil Stockdale, wife of POW Jim Stockdale, organized the National League of Families to counter the communist POW propaganda and impose political pressure on U.S. leaders to bring the POWs home. President Nixon used the POW issue to his political advantage and eventually the league became one of the most powerful small political organizations in American history. Allen, *Until the Last Man Comes Home*, 24–29; Appy, *American Reckoning*, 244; also see Heath Hardage Lee, *League of Wives*.

53. Franklin, *M.I.A. or Mythmaking in America*, 11–13. For more on victimization see Appy, *American Reckoning*, and Martini, *Invisible Enemies*.

54. Schulzinger, *Time for Peace*, 7.

55. Martini, *Invisible Enemies*, 2, 79.

56. Sutter, *Indochinese Refugee Dilemma*, 82; Hurst, *Carter Administration and Vietnam*, 28.

57. Hurst, *Carter Administration and Vietnam*, 40–44; Martini, *Invisible Enemies*, 36.

58. The outflow reached fifteen hundred people a month by the spring of 1978. Chan, *Vietnamese American 1.5 Generation*, 68.

59. According to Thomas Bass, the Amerasian issue disappeared after Operation Babylift. It resurfaced with media reports of "Rosie" and her pleas. Following the passage of the ODP, Rosie sent letters of support to the U.S. government and collected the names of numerous Amerasian children and their Vietnamese mothers in an effort to get them accepted by the new program. Bass, *Vietnamerica*, 37.

60. Martini, *Invisible Enemies*, 46–49, 76.

61. *M*A*S*H*, "Yessir That's Our Baby." The portrayal of the Amerasian in the episode promoted notions of hybrid vigor discussed by Nakashima, "Invisible Monster." The insinuations about the abandoning mother reinforce Robert Lee's argument that in the postwar era Americans continued to view the Vietnamese as "g——s," a silent and secretive alien threat to the United States. Robert Lee, *Orientals*, 190–91.

62. *M*A*S*H*, "Yessir That's Our Baby."

63. *M*A*S*H*, "Yessir That's Our Baby."

64. *M*A*S*H*, "Yessir That's Our Baby."

65. "Paternity Claims by Non-Nationals," circular no. 157, Headquarters European Command, February 15, 1949; Records of the Civil Administration Division: General Records of Public Welfare and Displaced Persons, Bavaria, 1946–50; both in NARA, Records of United States Occupation Headquarters, WWII, OMGUS Germany, record group 250, box 25. "Policy Governing Certain Marital Status of Officers, Warrant Officers or Enlisted Men," War Department, June 29, 1944, NARA, Adjutant Generals Section Operations Division Mail and Records Branch Decimal File, 1945–46, file 291-1 #1, record group 33, box 433.

66. "Paternity Claims by Non-Nationals"; "Request for Procedure of Establishing Paternity of Child," April 5, 1948, NARA, Decimal File 1945–52, Marriages, Parentage, Nationality File 291.1; record group 331, box 1260.

67. Section 309 states that illegitimate children born abroad acquired the nationality of the mother and could only obtain the nationality of the father through official legitimation. McCarran-Walter Act of 1952, PL 82–414, 82nd Cong., 2nd sess. (June 27, 1952).

68. Bass, *Vietnamerica*, 37.

69. Fiallo v. Bell, 430 U.S. 787, 97 S. Ct. 1473, 52 L. Ed. 2d 50 (1977).

70. Section 309 (c) nationality and Sections 101 (b)(1)(D) and 101 (b)(2) of the 1952 Immigration and Nationality Act exclude the relationship between an illegitimate child and its natural father from the special immigration status.

71. Justice Powell delivered the opinion of the Court, joined by Justices Burger, Stewart, Blackmun, Rehnquist, and Stevens. Justice White filed the dissenting statement and Justice Marshall filed a dissenting opinion joined by Justices Brennan and White. "Fiallo v. Bell," Oyez Project at Illinois Institute of Technology, Chicago–Kent College of Law, accessed March 11, 2015, http://www.oyez.org/cases/1970-1979/1976/1976_75_6297.

72. Antognini, "From Citizenship to Custody," 414.

73. This statement also referenced the 1957 amendment that reflected the intentional choice on the matter.

74. For further discussion of plenary power see Slocum, "Canons."

75. Fiallo v. Bell, 430 U.S. 787, 97 S. Ct. 1473, 52 L. Ed. 2d 50 (1977).

76. For subsequent Supreme Court cases regarding paternity and citizenship claims of American-fathered, foreign-born children, see *Nguyen v. INS* (2000), *Flores-Villar v. United States* (2010), *Sessions, Attorney General v. Morales* (2017).

77. The author recognizes that the numerous examples throughout U.S. history in which American humanitarianism toward refugees did not prevail complicates the narrative. The 1965 INA established the first permanent statutory basis for refugee admissions to the United States specifically targeting refugees fleeing communist countries. Hing, *Making and Remaking*, 125.

78. Hing, *Making and Remaking*, 126. This number includes all of Southeast Asia: Laos, Cambodia, Thailand, and Vietnam.

79. Hing, *Making and Remaking*, 130–35.

80. Hing, *Making and Remaking*, 124–35. On April 18, 1975, President Ford established the Interagency Task Force to coordinate the resettlement of the first wave of Vietnamese refugees, the majority of whom entered the United States between 1975 and 1980 through the parole authority of the U.S. Attorney General. The 1952 INA awarded such authority to the Attorney General to "parole" into the United Sates any alien and it was used to allow over four hundred thousand refugees from Southeast Asia to enter the country.

81. Bass, *Vietnamerica*, 37.

82. Bass, *Vietnamerica*, 37.

83. Hing *Making and Remaking*, 130–35.

84. Marsha Harris to McKinney, May 8, 1975, SMP, Series Legislative Correspondence, box 25.

85. Rep. Henry A. Waxman of California speaking in support of American assistance for Indochinese refugees, on June 26, 1979, 125 *Cong. Rec.* 16774–76.

86. *The Refugee Crisis in Southeast Asia: Hearings before the Committee on the Judiciary*, 96th Cong., 1st sess., July 26, 1979, 4.

87. S. I. Hayakawa, "Indochinese Refugees," 125 part 23 Cong. Rec. (October 25, 1979), HILA, S. I. Hayakawa papers, box 124.

88. *Refugee Crisis in Southeast Asia: Hearings*, 69.

89. During the decade, 4.5 million legal immigrants, the majority from Latin America, entered the United States. Tichenor, *Dividing Lines*, 238.

90. For more information, see collection MS2070: General files 1960–90, WFP.

91. Bob Drogin, "Charlotte, NC: A Black Backlash," *Washington Post*, August 5, 1979, HILA, S. I. Hayakawa papers, box 147.

92. Drogin, "Charlotte, NC."

93. Senator Walter Huddleston of Kentucky speaking on the high cost of refugee resettlement, July 12, 1979, 125 *Cong Rec*. 18285–87 (July 12, 1979), citing William Raspberry, "Our Own 'Wretched Refuse,'" *Washington Post*, July 4, 1979.

94. Foreign Assistance and Related Agencies Appropriations, *Hearings*.

95. Bob Drogin, "Charlotte, NC," HILA, S. I. Hayakawa papers, box 147.

96. Robert Lee, *Orientals*, 190–91.

97. Sutter, *Indochinese Refugee Dilemma*, 174; Spickard, *Almost All Aliens*, 347. Spickard suggests that the "nexus between racism, colonialism, and migration" in which terms like "g——" and "slope" were used jaded the ways in which Americans interpreted the postwar immigration.

98. Robert Lee, *Orientals*, 187.

99. Hayakawa, "Indochinese Refugees."

100. Hayakawa, "Indochinese Refugees"; Mark Stevens, "US Should 'Lift Lid' on Immigration—Hayakawa," *Christian Science Monitor*, July 9, 1979, JCL, Stephen Aiello Ethnic Group Files, folder 2/79–7/79, box 34.

101. Hayakawa, "Indochinese Refugees," quoted in Thomas, "Blood Politics," 52.

102. Throughout his political career, Hayakawa supported legislation to fund education for refugee children. Hayakawa's efforts could not turn the growing sentiment for more restrictive refugee and immigration policy, including employer sanctions to protect American workers and U.S. immigration and refugee policy reform.

103. HR 3439, 96th Cong., 1st sess., April 4, 1979.

104. HR 3439 proposed to allow illegitimate Amerasians in Korea, Vietnam, Thailand, and Laos to immigrate to the United States under the first and fourth immigration preference—unmarried and married sons and daughters of U.S. citizens. The act also proposed the establishment of a board to determine U.S. paternity via various documents and required a U.S. citizen sponsor to designate the Amerasian a legal alien. Many of these provisions would resurface in the AIA.

105. Hart Cellar Act of 1965, PL 89-236, 89th Cong., 1st sess. (October 3, 1965).

106. United States-Asian Immigration Act, H. Res. 3439, 125 Cong. Rec. H7258 (April 4, 1979).

107. United States-Asian Immigration Act.

108. United States-Asian Immigration Act.

109. United States-Asian Immigration Act.

110. Bureaucratic red tape and the reluctance of U.S. military officials to approve soldier marriages to Vietnamese women complicated the process of legitimating Amerasian children through marriage. As a result many American military men lived in common-law family units that were not recognized as formal unions for the purpose of immigration or legitimation. Yarborough, *Surviving Twice*, 36; Rhodes, *Vietnam War in American Childhood*, 195. Diana Yoon argues that U.S. military officers categorically viewed Vietnamese women as acceptable sexual partners but unsuitable spouses for military personnel and thus the U.S. military established barriers to marriage that ensured the illegitimacy of many Amerasian children. Yoon, "Reproducing Citizens through U.S. Militarism," 43.

111. John Shade Jr., "Developing Programs for Amerasians in Three Countries," 1979, PBSI, folder Amerasian Program 1979–83, no box. Estimates leading up to the 1979 Orderly Departure Program varied from a few thousand to twenty-five thousand, depending on the source. The most common methods of locating and accounting for Amerasian children were through venereal disease clinics that provided care to mothers and through chaplains who counseled American fathers on their relationships with Asian women. Shade Jr., "A Progress Report," 1978, PSBI, folder Amerasian 1978–1984, box Vietnam.

112. Shade Jr., "Progress Report." Shade insisted that U.S. military policies and practices were to blame for the illegitimacy of Amerasians. For many American men, a love affair or long-term romance with a Vietnamese woman often ended with the end of the tour, a transfer, the denial of their marriage request, or death. According to Trin Yarborough, U.S. policy during the Vietnam War required military members to spend twelve to thirteen months in Vietnam. As more troops were rotated home, more Amerasian babies were left fatherless. Yarborough, *Surviving Twice*, 11.

113. David Lawton, "Mondale Pledges More Aid for Indochinese Refugees," *Washington Post*, May 6, 1978, HILA, S. I. Hayakawa papers, box 147; Mary McGrory, "Refugees from Haiti May Become the 'Right' Kind of Boat People," *Washington Star*, November 13, 1979, JCL, Civil Rights and Justice, folder Immigration and Naturalization Service, box 11.

114. *The Orderly Departure Program from Vietnam*, GAO report, Subcommittee on Immigration, Refugees, and International Law, Committee on the Judiciary, 101st Cong., 2nd sess., 1990. Chan claims these arrivals on large passenger ships

marked a critical turning point in how first-asylum countries addressed the refugee outflow. Chan, *Vietnamese American 1.5 Generation*, 78–80.

115. Chan, *Vietnamese American 1.5 Generation*, 78–80.

116. Loescher and Scanlan, *Calculated Kindness*, 135–36.

117. Kumin, "Orderly Departure from Vietnam."

118. Opening statement of Sen. Edward Kennedy, *The Refugee Crisis in Southeast Asia: Hearings before the Committee on the Judiciary*. 96th Cong., 1st sess., July 26, 1979, 7. Secretary of State Cyrus Vance estimated that the number of boat people fatalities were in the "tens and tens of thousands." The exodus, according to Vance, was largely the result of the Vietnamese government pushing out ethnic Chinese (who composed two-thirds of those leaving by boat), economic hardships in postwar Vietnam, and Vietnam's intervention in Cambodia.

119. *Orderly Departure Program from Vietnam*, GAO.

120. Kumin, "Orderly Departure from Vietnam," 111.

121. United States–Asian Immigration Act, 125 part 21 Cong. Rec. 27567–68 (October 9, 1979).

122. According to the bill, the American sponsor was financially responsible for the Amerasian for a period of five years. HR 3439, 96th Cong., 1st sess. (April 4, 1979).

123. Although Jimmy Carter was known as the "human rights President," his inaction on behalf of the Amerasians is symptomatic of the bigger geopolitical concerns during the period. By 1979 Carter faced increasing tensions with Vietnam over the failure to normalize relations, the invasion of Cambodia and U.S.-China relations, and increasing pressure regarding American MIAs, and domestically faced rising concerns over immigration and refugee admissions. The Carter administration supported the ODP as a solution to the Amerasian issue. JCL, RAC project number NLC16-118-3-42-5; 16-13-2-22-4; 16-27-1-49-1.

124. In April 1979 the House referred the bill to the House Judiciary Committee, where members discussed it. It failed to move out of committee and therefore died in October 1979.

125. House, United States-Asian Immigration Act, 96th Cong., 2nd sess., Oct. 9, 1979.

126. Shade to Carter, July 17, 1979, JCL, White House Central File, Name files, Pearl, Q–Z folder, WHCF-Pearl.

127. HR 3439 spent much of 1980 in the Subcommittee on Immigration, Refugees and International Law of the Judiciary Committee. John Shade blamed its ultimate failure on bad timing and the 1980 presidential campaign. Shade to Carter, May 16, 1980, JCP, Pearl, Q–Z folder.

128. Chan, *Vietnamese American 1.5 Generation*, 83; Bon Tempo, *Americans at the Gate*, 178.

129. UN General Assembly, *Draft Convention Relating to the Status of Refugees*, December 14, 1950, accessed November 7, 2019, https://www.refworld.org/docid/3b00f08a27.html; Tichenor, *Dividing Lines*, 244.

130. Bill Kurtis, "The Plight of the Children Abandoned in Vietnam," *New York Times*, March 2, 1980.

131. Robb to Reagan, November 12, 1981; Brubaker to Reagan, March 29, 1982: RRPL, no. 051828, WE001, WHORM subject file.

132. The unemployment rate in America for people over sixteen years of age was 7.1 percent in 1980, 7.6 percent in 1981, 9.7 percent in 1982, and 9.6 percent in 1983 (the number of refugee arrivals in 1988 was 166,700). U.S. Department of Labor, Bureau of Labor Statistics, accessed July 6, 2014, http://data.bls.gov/timeseries/LNU04000000?years_option=all_years&periods_option=specific_periods&periods=Annual+Data; William Raspberry, "Bill Solves Some of Immigration Puzzles," *Washington Post*, May 28, 1980. See also Tichenor, *Dividing Lines*. Tichenor touches on the quandary of a U.S. public in favor of restriction and in contention with a U.S. policy of expansion.

133. The McCarran-Walter Act of 1952 is arguably America's first expansionist immigration policy and specifically benefited formerly excluded groups, including Asians. The 1965 INA was even more expansionist but maintained a numerical ceiling on immigration and recognized the new category of "refugee." Schaller and Rising, *Republican Ascendancy*, xi.

134. Lipman, "Refugee Camp in America," 70–72; Brinkley, *Reagan Diaries*, 30, 72.

135. "President Ronald Reagan's Statement on U.S. Immigration and Refugee Policy, July 30, 1981" in LeMay and Barkan, *U.S. Immigration*, 276.

4. Blood Politics

1. *HR 3405 and HR 808, Miscellaneous Immigration Reform Bills: Hearings before the Subcommittee on Immigration, Refugees, International Law*, 97th Cong., 1st sess. (November 17, 1981).

2. *HR 3405 and HR 808: Hearings*. Although the AIA included Amerasians from five Southeast Asian countries, it was a political and humanitarian response specifically to the increasing media coverage of the "American-faced" Amerasian children in Vietnam.

3. PL 359, 97th Cong., 2nd sess. (October 22, 1982).

4. Rep. Stewart McKinney, "The Warriors Children," Extension of Remarks, HR 808, 127 no. 1 Cong. Rec. H1327–28 (January 29, 1981).

5. *HR 3405 and HR 808: Hearings.*

6. Remarks of Hon. Richard L. Ottinger, 128 no. 7 Cong. Rec. H9780 (May 12, 1982) and Hon. James K. Coyne 128 no. 28 Cong. Rec. H27576 (October 1, 1982), speaking on the American responsibility for Amerasian children.

7. Erika Lee, *Making of Asian America*, 4; Wu, *Color of Success*, 1–15; Thomas, "Blood Politics," 60.

8. Ngai, *Impossible Subjects*, 229.

9. By 1981 Father Keane had arranged an estimated nine hundred adoptions of Amerasians to American families. St. Vincent's Children's Home supported seventeen Korean Amerasian students in the United States, most at Gonzaga University. The funding for the home came from private donations and from Americans for International Aid. Webb to De Losso, October 1, 1981, PSBI, folder Other Agency Info, no box.

10. *Semiannual Report to Congress*, Select Commission on Immigration and Refugee Policy, 96th Cong., 2nd sess., March 1, 1980, 55.

11. Thomas, "Blood Politics," 10.

12. Reagan sought to address the "Vietnam syndrome"—the unwillingness of U.S. leaders to use force to resist Soviet pressure or to defend foreign friends and interests. Schaller, "Reagan and the Cold War," 6.

13. Appy, *American Reckoning*, 255–56.

14. "Peace Restoring the Margin of Safety," Veterans of Foreign Wars Convention, August 18, 1980, RRPL.

15. Appy, *American Reckoning*, 259, 262.

16. Appy, *American Reckoning*, 246.

17. Appy, *American Reckoning*, 256–60.

18. Tichenor, *Dividing Lines*, 242.

19. Among the long-term costs of resettlement programs were English language and skill training. Loescher and Scanlan, *Calculated Kindness*, 198.

20. Bon Tempo, *Americans at the Gate*, 170.

21. Sureck argued that generous refugee admissions had created a permanent immigration problem: Loescher and Scanlon, *Calculated Kindness*, 197–205.

22. Kathryn Christensen, "Panel of Midwesterners Advocates Selectivity in Taking Newcomers," *Wall Street Journal*, October 14, 1980, reprinted in McClellan, *Immigrants, Refugees, and U.S. Policy*, 163. U.S. nationality law already incorporated such an approach. The preference system that replaced the quota system in 1965 emphasized family reunification, and desirable occupation, skills, or training. 1965 Immigration and Nationality Act, PL 89–236; 79 Stat. 911, 89th Cong., October 3, 1965.

NOTES TO PAGES 124–128

23. The commission was formed in 1978 at the urging of Democratic leaders Ted Kennedy and Peter Rodino.

24. Tichenor, *Dividing Lines*, 252; Ambassador Diego C. Asencio, interview by Charles Stuart Kennedy, September 11, 1986, Association for Diplomatic Studies and Training, Foreign Affairs Oral History Project.

25. In June 1980, the Senate approved a "sense of Congress" resolution that depicted the growing concerns over the overwhelming numbers of immigrants entering the United States and urging a strict limit of one hundred thousand immigrants and refugees allowed into the country from June to September of that year. "Curbs on Immigration Urged by the Senate," *Los Angeles Times*, June 19, 1980; Loescher and Scanlon, *Calculated Kindness*, 189; Tichenor, *Dividing Lines*, 249–56; Weisberg, *Ronald Reagan*, 117.

26. Loescher and Scanlan, *Calculated Kindness*, 199.

27. Christensen, in McClellan, *Immigrants*, 166.

28. Although exclusive to children whose fathers would legitimate them, Frank's bill posed a direct challenge to the U.S. policy at the heart of the Amerasian issue, section 309 of the 1952 INA. *HR 3405 and HR 808: Hearings*, 858.

29. *HR 3405 and HR 808: Hearings*, 857–934.

30. Thomas, "Blood Politics," 64.

31. Thomas, "Blood Politics," 64.

32. For further examination of how gender shaped the American experience in Vietnam and the reputations of U.S. soldiers, see Stur, *Beyond Combat*.

33. Thomas, "Blood Politics," 62; Greg Kane, interview by author, telephone, October 21, 2013.

34. Thomas, "Blood Politics," 62.

35. Thomas, "Blood Politics," 62. Evidentiary proof varied in each Asian country. Usually, the father's absence meant there was no formal evidence that the Amerasian existed.

36. Regarding HR 3405, the State Department referenced the 1977 Supreme Court decision in *Fiallo v. Bell*, which upheld the sex-based distinction between the rights of an out-of-wedlock child derived through its natural father as opposed to its natural mother. *HR 3405 and HR 808: Hearings*, 858.

37. *HR 3405 and HR 808: Hearings*, 858.

38. Varzally, *Children of Reunion*, 57; Thomas, "Blood Politics," 63.

39. Appy, *American Reckoning*, 255; Thomas, "Blood Politics," 63.

40. Thomas, "Blood Politics," 63.

41. Thomas, "Blood Politics," 64; statement of Representative Pat Schroeder, HR 3405 and HR 808, *Hearings*, 876.

42. Thomas, "Blood Politics," 64.

43. The *New York Times* published numerous photographs and stories, including a number by journalists Bill Kurtis, Gloria Emerson, and Bernard Weinraub. Weinraub traveled to Vietnam with the Vietnam Veterans of America in December 1981. There was also increasing television coverage from the major television stations, NBC, ABC, and CBS; Thomas, "Blood Politics," 64–65.

44. Statement of Rep. Pat Schroeder, *HR 3405 and HR 808: Hearings*, 876.

45. Testimony of Mr. Henry Sandri, *HR 3405 and HR 808: Hearings*, 876, 909; Thomas, "Blood Politics," 65.

46. Testimony of Mr. Henry Sandri, *HR 3405 and HR 808: Hearings*, 876–79.

47. Thomas, "Blood Politics," 65.

48. Testimony of Dr. James R. Dumpson, *Relief and Rehabilitation of War Victims in Indochina Part II: Orphans and Child Welfare: Hearings before the Subcommittee to Investigate Problems Connected with Refugees and Escapees*, 93rd Cong., 1st sess., May 11, 1973, 19.

49. *Relief and Rehabilitation: Hearings*, 19.

50. Thomas, "Blood Politics," 68.

51. Testimony of Mr. Scully, *HR 3405 and HR 808: Hearings*, 877.

52. Argument made by Cornelius Scully, director of the Office of Legislation, Regulations and Advisory Assistance in the Bureau of Consular Affairs. Scully's office oversaw the training of consular officers and visas. Testimony of Mr. Scully, *HR 3405 and HR 808: Hearings*, 881.

53. Scully confirmed the quoted statement by Chairman Romano Mazzoli regarding the efficacy of the blood test. Testimony of Mr. Scully, *HR 3405 and HR 808: Hearings*, 881.

54. Testimony of Mr. Scully, *HR 3405 and HR 808: Hearings*, 881.

55. Testimony of Mr. Scully, *HR 3405 and HR 808: Hearings*, 884–89.

56. See chapter 1 for more on the blood quantum theory.

57. Thomas, "Blood Politics," 69. Today, through scientific advancements, DNA is a reliable, although costly, test of paternity and is being used by numerous organizations dedicated to connecting Amerasians with their American fathers, including Amerasians Without Borders, established in 2015.

58. Father Alfred Carroll, interview by author, Spokane, Washington, May 24, 2013.

59. Father Carroll to Reagan, JOPA, folder Amerasian Program, box 3B.2.1; Father Alfred Carroll to Walter Fauntroy, June 28, 1982, JOPA, folder Amerasians, box 3B.2.1.

60. The author interviewed Father Carroll in 2013 at Gonzaga University's Jesuit House.

61. The program, established in May 1975, offered scholarships to aid Vietnamese refugees, and Gonzaga University pledged financial assistance for instruction in English and the opportunity of an American college education. Twenty-three Vietnamese refugees joined the GU student body in September 1975. Carroll, interview; Form Acceptance Letter to Gonzaga University, n.d., JOPA, folder Amerasian Program, box 3b.2.2.

62. "Homecoming for Sons and Daughters of Americans," Sept. 3, 1984; "A Model Program for Implementing the Forgotten Americans Act: Proposal Presented to the Sisters of the Franciscan Order of Philadelphia," March 4, 1983: JOPA, folder Amerasian Program, box 3b.2.2.

63. Carroll, interview; "Homecoming for Sons and Daughters of Americans," JOPA; "A Model Program," JOPA.

64. Fifteen college-age Amerasians arrived at Gonzaga University in 1980 on student visas, initiating Gonzaga University's Korean American Education Fund for Korean Amerasians. "Coming Home to the Land of the Their Fathers," pamphlet, Gonzaga University, n.d., private collection of Father Alfred Carroll; Carroll, interview.

65. Statement of Rev. Alfred V. Keane, SB 1698, *Hearings of the Subcommittee on Immigration and Refugee Policy*, June 21, 1982, 65, GUA, loose folder Amerasian Program, 1993–1996, box Carroll no. 1 General Amerasian.

66. "Background Information on Father Alfred V. Keane, M.M.," JOPA, Americans for International Aid, Carroll, folder B-7, box 3B.2.1.

67. Carroll, interview.

68. Pauline and John Motay to McKinney, May 12, 1975, SMP, Legislative Correspondence, N–S 1975, folder Refugees, box 25.

69. Clare Booth Luce, "Refugees and Guilt," *New York Times*, May 11, 1975, SMP, Legislative Correspondence, folder Viet Refugee.

70. Anonymous (postcard) to Carroll, October 4, 1982, JOPA, folder Plight of Amerasians, box Al. Carroll, S. J. Amerasian Program 3B.2.1.

71. Statement of Father Alfred V. Keane, *HR 3405 and HR 808: Hearings*, 900.

72. Statement of Keane, SB 1698.

73. Webb to De Losso, *Welcomer*, October 1, 1981, PSBI, folder Other Agency Info; statement of Keane, *HR 3405 and HR 808*.

74. Thomas, "Blood Politics," 56.

75. Webb to De Losso, *Welcomer*; statement of Keane, *HR 3405 and HR 808*. An example of the possible consequences from illegitimacy and the absence of citizenship occurred in Thailand. On December 31, 1972, the Thai government passed Announcement 337, revoking Thai citizenship from the Amerasians born before the date of the act and denying citizenship to future Amerasian children

for the purpose of national security. This act left Amerasian children effectively stateless. In February 1978, the Thai government overturned it, explaining that the change was due to humanitarian concerns and international agreements and that the government recognized that, in the case of the Amerasians, because the fathers were out of the country, it was the responsibility of the Thai citizen mothers to raise them as Thai citizens. James Steele, "The Amerasian Outreach Project, Final Evaluation," September 24, 1982, PSBI.

76. *Half American, Half Forgotten*, ca.1982, Gonzaga University Video, GUA.

77. Carroll, Christmas letter, December 1982; "Americans from Korea at Gonzaga University," July 26, 1982, JOPA, folder Letters from Senators, box 3B.2.

78. Statement of Keane, *SB 1698*; Amerasian Program, GUA, Loose Folder Correspondence Amerasian Stuff, 1993–96, box Carroll no. 1 General Amerasian.

79. Ziglar, *Steps to the Top*, 204.

80. Ziglar, *Steps to the Top*, 204.

81. "A Loving Couple Brings Home the Littlest Victims of War," *People*, December 23, 1974.

82. According to reports, Americans for International Aid had over one thousand airline employees who flew mercy missions to transport children from Southeast Asia, South and Central America, and India. The majority of the AIA escorts were associated with British Airways, Braniff, Cascade, Delta, Eastern, and Northwest Orient airlines. "Suzanne Williams: An Eager Escort for US-Bound Orphans," *Christian Science Monitor*, 1982. Lawrence Kilman, "Airline Employees Aid Poor Children," *Sarasota Herald-Tribune*, December 16, 1981. "Inspiring Women," June 1988. For a history and a critique of transnational and transracial adoptions see Briggs, *Somebody's Children*; Dubinsky, *Babies without Borders*.

83. The Darraghs credited their interest in the plight of Vietnam's orphans to Betty Tisdale, the chairman of the board of the An Lac orphanage in Saigon. There was much dissension and concern surrounding Tisdale's massive evacuation of children (20 percent of whom were Amerasian) during Operation Babylift after a lawsuit found that many of the children were not orphans and did not have the proper release from parents or guardians for evacuation or adoption. The lawsuit created tension between the government-approved adoption organizations. Even the Buck Foundation criticized Tisdale and the Darraghs for failing to legally evacuate the children. "More Vietnamese Orphans due in Georgia Tuesday," *Tuscaloosa News*, April 14, 1975. "Findings of Fact and Conclusions of Law and Order," U.S. District Court for the Northern District of California, Nguyen Da Yen, Nguyen Da Vuong and Nguyen Da Tueyn v. James Schlesinger, Secretary of Defense, et al., June 30, 1975; memos from M. Daniel Bailey to PSBF Board of Directors, May 23, 1975, and July 22, 1975, PSBI, folders Vietnam

Refugees—Operation Babylift, 1975–77, General Info PSBF Vietnam no. 1; Legal Information 1975, box Vietnam Operation Babylift. Also see Sachs, *Life We Were Given*, 184–211.

84. Crescent Dragonwagon, "Saving the World—One Kid at a Time," *McCalls*, n.d., SMP, subject files A, Series 7, folder Amerasians, box 132.

85. "Sad Eyes, Happy Eyes," Americans for International Aid newsletter, ca. 1982, 36–50; Nancy M. Fox to Welcome House Board of Directors, PSBI, folder America's Forgotten Children.

86. PL 97-359, 97th Cong., 96 Stat, 1716, October 22, 1982; Amerasian Children Relief Act of 1985, 131 Cong. Rec. 33: H1369 (1985); Amerasian Amendments of 1987, 133 Cong. Rec., 70: E1687.

87. Shade had a rather tumultuous career with PSBF, where he was the executive director from 1978 to 1984. Shade Jr. "Amerasian Kids: Problem for Congress," November 1981, PSBI, folder Amerasians, folder 1978–84, box Vietnam.

88. Shade Jr. "Amerasian Kids."

89. "The Amerasian Children," 126 no. 11 Cong. Rec. 14046 (June 11, 1980); Shade Jr., "A Progress Report," PSBI, folder Amerasians, box Vietnam.

90. Shade Jr., "Problem for Congress," PSBI.

91. Shade Jr., "Problem for Congress," PSBI.

92. John A. Shade Jr., "The Forgotten Child—The Amerasian in Indochina," May 8, 1980, PSBI, folder Amerasians 1978–1984, box Vietnam.

93. "Bring the Dust Children Home" *New York Times*, July 12, 1982.

94. Shade Jr., "Developing Programs for Amerasians in Three Countries," PSBI, folder Amerasian programs.

95. Anis, "Psychosocial Adjustment of Vietnamese Amerasians," 69.

96. Anis, "Psychosocial Adjustment of Vietnamese Amerasians," 70.

97. William Drozdiak, "Strangers in Their Own Land," *Time*, September 14, 1981.

98. *HR 3405 and HR 808: Hearings*, 921.

99. SB 1698, *Amerasian Immigration Act: Hearings*, 28.

100. Robert D. McFadden, "Jeremiah A. Denton Jr., 89 Dies," *New York Times*, March 28, 2014.

101. The U.S. government initiated Operation Homecoming in March 1973, successfully bringing 591 American POWs home to the United States.

102. Mary McGrory, remarks on Sen. Jeremiah Denton, 128 no. 1 Cong. Rec. S7 (January 25, 1982); Duggan, *Jeremiah Denton*, 66–67.

103. Duggan, *Jeremiah Denton*, 67.

104. Frank Morring Jr., "Denton Praises Family Emphasis of Head Start," *Birmingham Post-Herald*, March 11, 1981, JDPA, box 61.

105. By 1982 Father Keane had arranged over nine hundred adoptions in the U.S. of Amerasian children from Korea. "Amerasian Children Meeting our Responsibilities," Extension of Remarks, HR 808, 128 no. 13 Cong. Rec. (July 23, 1982).

106. Sen. Jeremiah Denton, in support of S1698, 127 no. 17 Cong. Rec. (Oct 1, 1981), JDPA, folder Floor Statements 97th Congress, box 60.

107. "National Adoption Week," 127 no. 22 Cong. Rec. 28837–38 (November 23, 1981); Duggan, *Jeremiah Denton*, 66–69.

108. The Senate amended the language of the original bill from, "A bill to amend the Immigration and Nationality Act to provide preferential treatment in the admission of certain children of United States Armed Forces Personnel," to "certain children of United States citizens." SB 1698, *Amerasian Immigration Act: Hearings*, 14; Amerasian Immigration Act of 1982, PL 359, 97th Cong., 2nd sess. (October 22, 1982).

109. SB 1698, *Amerasian Immigration Act: Hearings*, 14.

110. SB 1698, *Amerasian Immigration Act: Hearings*, 29.

111. SB 1698, *Amerasian Immigration Act: Hearings*, 26.

112. SB 1698, *Amerasian Immigration Act: Hearings*, 29.

113. SB 1698, *Amerasian Immigration Act: Hearings*, 44.

114. Mary McGrory, "The Leviathan of Government Gets Education in Compassion," *Washington Post*, June 22, 1982, GHP, folder 50, box 36.

115. "Denton's Amerasian Bill Passes Senate," September 29, 1982, JDPA, RG 600, folder 1982—Press Releases, box 83.

116. Tom Fuller, Richard Manning, Stryker McGuire, Vern E. Smith, and Ron Moreau, "What Vietnam Did to Us: Survivors of Charlie Company Relive the War and the Decade Since," *Newsweek*, December 14, 1981, 46–97.

117. Herring, *America's Longest War*, 347; Longley, *Grunts*, 175–79. For the experience of African American veterans see Terry, *Bloods*.

118. Scott, *Politics of Readjustment*, 75; Richard Sisk, "The War among the Vets," *Daily News*, May 30, 1982, JDPA, folder Statements, box 32.

119. Bobby Muller, interview by author, telephone, December 7, 2013.

120. Muller interview.

121. Muller initially founded the Vietnam Veterans Coalition (later the VVA) with Stuart Feldman, an advocacy organization for Vietnam veterans with the purpose of publicizing veterans' issues. By 1979 VVA had begun to mobilize veterans into a political force specifically around the issue of Agent Orange. Scott, *Politics of Readjustment*, 75.

122. In 1981 the Veterans Administration officially accredited the VVA as an official veterans' organization, giving it the necessary political leverage to address the concerns of Vietnam veterans.

123. Sisk, "War among the Vets."

124. Muller interview; Bernard Weinraub, "In Vietnam, Tears as the Past Is Remembered," *New York Times*, December 27, 1981; Sisk, "War among the Vets."

125. Weinraub, "In Vietnam, Tears as the Past Is Remembered."

126. Muller interview.

127. "Bring the Dust Children Home," *New York Times*, July 13, 1982.

128. Doan, "Bringing the Aliens Home," 71, 75. Doan examines the tension between what he terms the popular yet "false narratives" surrounding the Amerasians and their lived experiences.

129. Chuong and Le Van, *Amerasians from Vietnam*, 58.

130. For further discussion of the orphan trope and specifically the "suffering war orphan" as an anticommunist figure of the Cold War, see Jodi Kim, "An Orphan with Two Mothers," 860.

131. Thomas, "Blood Politics," 58.

132. Thomas, "Blood Politics," 59. Historian Edwin Martini describes the U.S. effort to reconstruct the history of the Vietnam War by recasting U.S. involvement as benevolent and moral as "historical inversion." Martini, *Invisible Enemies*, 7. Also see Stur, *Beyond Combat*, 4, 142.

133. Briggs, "Mother, Child, Race, Nation," 180–81, 185.

134. Doan, "Bringing the Aliens Home," 83. Doan argues the terms "American blood" and "American face" commonly used to describe Amerasians are meaningless considering there is no default American and that "American" is a national category, not a racial or ethnic one.

135. Greg Kane, interview by author, telephone, October 21, 2013.

136. Kane, interview.

137. Doan, "Bringing the Aliens Home," 75; Bass, *Vietnamerica*, 70–71.

138. Kane, interview.

139. Mike Wallace, "Honor Thy Children," *60 Minutes*, CBS, September 19, 1982; Schulzinger, *Time for Peace*, 188–91.

140. Wallace, "Honor Thy Children."

141. Gary Tanous to Ronald Reagan, ca. 1982, RRPL, ID no. 070522, IM161533, WHORM, subject file Amerasian Children.

142. At the time of Jeanna Mare's birth in 1967, her parents Gary and Mai Tanous were married and resided in Saigon. In 1968 the family moved to Vancouver, Canada, where the couple separated. Mai returned to Saigon with their daughter, and the couple later divorced. Bob Beck, "Quest for Daughter in Vietnam Getting Increasingly Futile," *Columbian*, n.d. RRPL, ID #070522, IM161533, WHORM, subject file Amerasian Children.

143. Beck, "Quest for Daughter," RRPL. The newspaper article provides a different spelling of "Jeanna Mare."

144. Wallace, "Honor Thy Children."

145. Quoted in Varzally, *Children of Reunion*, 83; Thomas, "Blood Politics," 58.

146. Wallace, "Honor Thy Children"; Bass, *Vietnamerica*, 37–38; Thomas, "Blood Politics," 58.

147. Thomas, "Blood Politics," 58.

148. Wallace, "Honor Thy Children," September 19, 1982.

149. 128 no. 18 Cong. Rec. S25338 (September 28, 1982). The Senate passed S1698 during this session.

150. "Forgotten Americans in Asia," Americans for International Aid newsletter, n.d., 36–50, GHP.

151. SB 1698, *Amerasian Immigration Act: Hearings.*

152. "Denton's Amerasian Bill Passes Senate," press release, September 29, 1982, JDPA, folder 1982 Press Releases, box 83; Preferential Treatment in Admission of Certain Children of US Citizens, 128 no. 20 Cong. Rec. H27269–73. HR 808 passed the House on October 1, 1982.

153. The votes in the Senate on September 28, 1982, and the House on October 1 were "voice votes." There is no record of individual votes as a result. S. 1698 (97th): An Act to Amend the Immigration and Nationality Act to Provide Preferential Treatment in the Admission of Certain Children of United States Citizens, GovTrack.us, accessed February 1, 2015, https://www.govtrack.us/congress/bills/97/s1698.

154. 128 no. 20 Cong. Rec. H27269–70 (October 1, 1982).

155. 128 no. 20 Cong. Rec. H27269–70 (October 1, 1982).

156. 128 no. 20 Cong. Rec. H27269–70 (October 1, 1982).

157. Mary McGrory, "The Leviathan of Government Gets Education in Compassion," *Washington Post*, June 22, 1982, GHP, folder 50, box 36.

158. See remarks regarding American responsibility for Amerasian children, 128 Cong. Rec. 27270–73 (October 1, 1982).

159. Relations between the United States and Vietnam were often strained during the 1980s as a result of discrepancies and miscommunication about American POWs and MIAs said to still be living as well as the remains of those killed in Vietnam and recovered by Vietnam. *American POW/MIAs in Southeast Asia: Hearings before the Subcommittee on Asian and Pacific Affairs*, 97th Cong., 2nd sess., September 30, 1982. Thomas Bass asserts that the Amerasian issue was simply an opportunistic way for Vietnam to accuse the United States of being hypocritical and untrustworthy. Bass, *Vietnamerica*, 35.

NOTES TO PAGES 151–156

160. Before 1986 the ODP functioned through an office in Bangkok, Thailand, with UN officials acting as processing liaisons in Vietnam. Under this system, bureaucratic morass, intensive document requirements and checks, and significant time delays characterized each level of Amerasian processing. When these operational inefficiencies resulted in a significant case backlog, Vietnam installed a unilateral moratorium on processing. DeMonaco, "Disorderly Departure," 644.

5. Window Dressing

1. Remarks of the President in the Signing Ceremony for Immigration and Nationality Act Amendment, October 22, 1982, JOPA, folder Gonzaga University Amerasian Program Congressional Action, box 3B.2; Ronald Reagan, Remarks on Signing a Bill Providing for the Immigration of Certain Amerasian Children, October 22, 1982.

2. Remarks of the President, JOPA.

3. Remarks of the President, JOPA.

4. Remarks of the President, JOPA.

5. Ronald Reagan to Father Alfred Keane, October 25, 1982, RRPL, WHORM, subject file Amerasian Children.

6. Ronald Reagan to Jeremiah Denton (also sent to Stewart McKinney, Carl Levin, Alan Simpson, Strom Thurmond, Hamilton Fish Jr., Romano Mazzoli, and Father Alfred Keane), October 25, 1982, RRPL, WHORM, subject file Amerasian Children.

7. Statements of Congressmen Bereuter and Gilman, 128 no. 20 Cong. Rec. H27269–70 (October 1, 1982); Thomas, "Blood Politics," 69–70.

8. The Amerasian experience in the American foster care system is a fascinating and unexplored area for future research. *Midyear Consultation on U.S. Refugee Programs for Fiscal Year 1986: Hearings before the Subcommittee on Immigration and Refugee Policy*, 99th Cong., 2nd sess., Senate, 73.

9. Vietnam's foreign minister, Nguyen Co Thach, specifically voiced the Socialist Republic of Vietnam's concerns about the AIA.

10. *Los Angeles Times*, December 19, 1982.

11. Mike Wallace, "Honor Thy Children," *60 Minutes*, CBS, September 19, 1982.

12. Application for Immigration at Refugees an [sic] American Halfbreed Children, *Amerasian Immigration Act of 1982: Hearings*, 97th Cong., 2nd sess., June 21, 1982, 60.

13. John Shade to Ronald Reagan, November 19, 1982, RRPL, WHORM, subject file Amerasian Children.

14. Jeffords, *Hard Bodies*, 7–13. Jeffords argues that in contrast to Jimmy Carter's effeminate and "weak body" administration, Reagan's masculine identity

projected a strength and "hard body" that proved attractive to American voters. Jeffords suggests the combination of a "hard body" model and the image of a "sensitive family man" were "overlapping components of the Reagan Revolution" that comprise both a strong militaristic foreign policy and domestic economy and traditionally patriarchal social values.

15. Michael Kilian, "Reagans' Close Relationship Didn't Always Include Kids," *Baltimore Sun*, June 6, 2005. Actor David Ogden Stiers noted that Reagan "preached family values, but presided over a dysfunctional family." See also Longley, "When Character Was King?," 91–93.

16. Dowland, *Family Values and the Rise of the Christian Right*, 4–10.

17. Dowland, *Family Values and the Rise of the Christian Right*, 158.

18. Jeffords, *Hard Bodies*, 8–13.

19. Dowland, *Family Values and the Rise of the Christian Right*, 177.

20. Lipman, "Mixed Voices, Mixed Policy," 62.

21. While Congress could have passed legislation to address soldier behavior, the power to change U.S. military policy rested with the Department of Defense. In this case, neither chose to act.

22. William Raspberry, "Bill Solves Some of Immigration Puzzles," *Spokesman Review*, April 13, 1982.

23. Shade to Reagan, November 19, 1982.

24. Richard Childress to William P. Clark, September 21, 1982, RRPL, WHORM, subject file Amerasian Children.

25. Testimony of James Purcell, Bureau of Refugee Programs, *Midyear Consultation on U.S. Refugee Programs for Fiscal Year 1986: Hearings*, 99th Cong., 2nd sess., Senate, 103.

26. *Los Angeles Times*, December 19, 1982.

27. Director Outreach Program INS Central Office, *Report on Public Law 97-359*, January 6, 1986, JOPA, folder Gonzaga University, Amerasian Program Congressional Action, box 3B.2. Al Carroll, S. J. Amerasian Program.

28. Raspberry, "Bill Solves Some of Immigration Puzzles."

29. Shade to Reagan, November 19, 1982.

30. Specifically, the act states: "To provide preferential treatment in the admission of certain children of United States citizens." Amerasian Immigration Act, PL 97-359, 97th Cong., Oct 22, 1982.

31. Shade to Reagan, November 19, 1982.

32. Per U.S. law Amerasians older than fourteen years of age did not qualify for adoption. "Important memo from Welcome House," *Welcomer*, 1980, PSBI, folder *Welcomer* 1970, box Welcome House.

33. Shade to Reagan, November 19, 1982.

34. Adopted Amerasians did not automatically become U.S. citizens; they had to apply for naturalized U.S. citizenship and had to wait until two years after finalizing the adoption to begin the process. "Important memo from Welcome House," *The Welcomer*, 1980, PSBI, folder Welcomer 1970, box Welcome House.

35. Shade to Reagan, November 19, 1982.

36. For a similar case regarding the métis in Vietnam see Saada, *Empire's Children*.

37. Allen, *Until the Last Man Comes Home*, 212–13; Schulman, *Seventies*.

38. Myra MacPherson, "The Militant Morality of Jeremiah Denton," *Washington Post*, December 7, 1980.

39. As quoted in Schulzinger, *Time for Peace*, 21–22.

40. As quoted in Schulzinger, *Time for Peace*, 21–22.

41. Reagan gave his "Evil Empire" speech, in which he condemned the Soviet Union as the world's nexus of evil, on March 8, 1983, in an address to the National Association of Evangelicals in Orlando, Florida.

42. The Vietnam syndrome described the apparent weakness of the nation in the post–Vietnam War era and the unwillingness of U.S. leaders to use force against communism or to defend American interests. Reagan pledged to cure the nation of its "syndrome" for political advantage. Schaller, "Reagan and the Cold War," in *Deconstructing Reagan*, 6.

43. Schulzinger, *Time for Peace*, 189–91. See also Jeffords, *Hard Bodies*, and Martini, *Invisible Enemies*.

44. Martini, *Invisible Enemies*, 42, 79. Edwin Martini describes the "war by other means" as the U.S. effort to reclassify Vietnam as the enemy and pursue openly hostile and unprecedented economic and diplomatic policies against the Vietnamese. Initiated under the Carter administration, Reagan continued the policy.

45. Schulzinger, *Time for Peace*, 189–91. For more on Reagan's struggles, see Mayer, "Reagan and Race," and Longley, "When Character was King?"

46. Lyn Nofziger to Edwin Meese, James Baker, Michael Deaver, and William Clark, July 18, 1982, RRPL, WHORM, subject file Amerasian Children.

47. Nofziger to Meese, Baker, Deaver, Clark, July 18, 1982.

48. Mayer, "Reagan and Race," 85; Schaller and Rising, *Republican Ascendency*, 84–88.

49. Schaller and Rising, *Republican Ascendency*, 84–88.

50. Schaller and Rising, *Republican Ascendency*, 88. Historian Nikhil Pal Singh argues that Reagan's presidency effected a historical shift from the War on Poverty to the War on Drugs, which reinvented and renewed coded racist appeals through the use of racial imagery—a Black underclass of "wild youths and welfare

queens"—to attack tax-supported government services for America's working poor and unemployed. Singh, *Black Is a Country*, 9–11.

51. Helen Heran Jun argues that the Reagan administration's attack on social welfare programs and publicly funded institutions was an extension of the neoliberal Americanism that emphasized personal responsibility and self-sufficiency. The Reagan administration ignored the reality that the majority of welfare recipients during the period were white women, and produced the "welfare queen" as the image of "black female reproduction as a pathological excess" sustained by welfare. Jun, *Race for Citizenship*, 126. For further discussion of the representation of the Black mother as the welfare queen see Roberts, *Killing the Black Body*; Josh Levin, "The Welfare Queen," *Slate*, December 19, 2013, http://www.slate.com/articles/news_and_politics/history/2013/12/linda_taylor_welfare_queen_ronald_reagan_made_her_a_notorious_american_villain.html.

52. Weisberg, *Ronald Reagan*, 70–71; Mayer, "Reagan and Race," 70; Schaller and Rising, *Republican Ascendancy*, 84–85.

53. Childress to Clark, September 21, 1982; "President Reagan's Visit to Thailand," November 8–9, 1983, JCL, RAC NLC 131-10-9-4-1 [declassified, June 9, 2008].

54. Individual American sponsors and private aid agencies financed the AIA, and qualifying Amerasians were admitted under existing refugee admissions allotments for the ODP (sixty-four thousand in fiscal year 1983). As a result, Amerasian admissions amounted to an insignificant cost to the country. *Annual Refugee Consultation: Hearings before the Subcommittee on Immigration and Refugee Policy*, 98th Cong., 1st sess., Senate, Sept. 26, 1983, 31–33.

55. Martini, *Invisible Enemies*, 78–79. Less than a decade after secretary general of the Vietnamese Communist Party Le Duan promised "a radio, a television, and a refrigerator" to every family, Vietnamese leaders faced the realities of a struggling postwar economy, international tensions, a costly war in Cambodia, and a hostile United States.

56. Lipman "Mixed Voices, Mixed Policy"; Martini, *Invisible Enemies*, 40–115; Schulzinger, *Time for Peace*, 21–41.

57. For analysis of U.S.-Vietnam relations and Vietnam's occupation of Cambodia, see Martini, *Invisible Enemies*, 93–115; Schulzinger, *Time for Peace*, 22–24.

58. Martini, *Invisible Enemies*, 79–80.

59. Martini, *Invisible Enemies*, 79–80, 104; Schulzinger, *Time for Peace*, 22.

60. Allen, *Until the Last Man Comes Home*, argues that America's infatuation with the MIA/POW issues and specifically captivity and recovery, was the way Americans addressed the military defeat in the Vietnam War.

61. Young, "Vietnam War in American Memory," 253.

62. Shortly after the fall of Saigon, the Congressional Committee on Missing Persons in Southeast Asia held a major investigation of the POW/MIA issue in December 1976, and concluded there were no POWs in Indochina.

63. Longley, *Grunts*, 188–89. Longley contends that the sense of betrayal felt by many Vietnam veterans after the war diminished during the Reagan era as more memorials and events commemorated their service and sacrifice, including parades—New York City, Houston, and Chicago—and memorials in Clifton, Arizona, and San Angelo, Texas.

64. Brinkley, *Reagan Diaries*, 277; Ronald Reagan, Remarks at Dedication Ceremonies for the Vietnam Veterans Memorial Statue, November 11, 1984, American Presidency Project, accessed January 1, 2014, http://www.presidency.ucsb.edu/ws/?pid=39414; Longley, *Grunts*. For more information about the Vietnam Veterans Memorial see Haas, *Carried to the Wall*.

65. Ronald Reagan, Message to the Congress Transmitting a Report on POWs and MIAs in Southeast Asia, April 30, 1985, Ronald Reagan Presidential Library, accessed January 1, 2018, https://www.reaganlibrary.gov/research/speeches/43085b.

66. Ronald Reagan, Message to the Congress, April 30, 1985.

67. Ronald Reagan, Remarks at Memorial Day Ceremonies Honoring an Unknown Serviceman of the Vietnam Conflict, May 28, 1984, Ronald Reagan Presidential Library, accessed January 1, 2015.

68. Brinkley, *Reagan Diaries*, 128.

69. Bruce Franklin makes the argument that popular culture helped these stories infiltrate the American consciousness. Franklin, *M.I.A. or Mythmaking in America*.

70. Martini, *Invisible Enemies*, 122.

71. Franklin, *M.I.A. or Mythmaking in America*, 139–40.

72. Franklin, *M.I.A. or Mythmaking in America*, 136–38.

73. Franklin, *M.I.A. or Mythmaking in America*, 139 (quote); Sidney Blumenthal, "The Mission," *New Republic*, July 6, 1992; Allen, *Until the Last Man Comes Home*, 255.

74. Sen. Jeremiah Denton, remarks, POW/MIA Recognition Day, July 9, 1982, JDPA, folder Denton, box 34/151.

75. *Americans Missing in Southeast Asia: Hearings before Subcommittee on Asian and Pacific Affairs*, 99th Cong., 1st sess., House, June 27, 1985, 19. Tighe argued that the United States should establish diplomatic relations with Vietnam in order to resolve the MIA/POW issue.

76. Allen, *Until the Last Man Comes Home*, 2.

77. Allen claims that Vietnamese officials often insisted on economic assistance in exchange for further cooperation on the issue, likely to compensate for

the billings of dollars pledged to them by President Nixon in the Paris Agreement but never paid. Allen, *Until the Last Man Comes Home*, 5.

78. Donald Dodd to Pearl S. Buck Foundation, January 18, 1986, PSBI, folder Operation Forget-Me-Not, box Vietnam, Refugee Information.

79. According to Commodore Thomas A. Brooks, assistant deputy director for collection management, Defense Intelligence Agency, of the 122 unresolved live sighting reports in 1985, almost half were of Caucasian men walking freely in Vietnam, not under guard, some with Vietnamese wives and families, assumed to be Soviet advisers, Western European diplomats or press, etc. After eliminating such reports, forty-three unresolved reports of Americans in captivity remained—seventeen from Vietnam. *Americans Missing in Southeast Asia: Hearings*, 66.

80. *Americans Missing in Southeast Asia: Hearings*, 65–67.

81. *Americans Missing in Southeast Asia: Hearings*, 65.

82. James Rosenthal, "The Myth of the Last POWs," *New Republic*, July 1, 1985.

83. James Rosenthal, "Myth of the Last POWs."

84. The Nixon administration used the cause of America POWs in Vietnam to rally public opinion in pressuring the Vietcong to obey the Geneva principles concerning the rights of POWs. Nixon also elevated the profile of the National League of Families of Americans Missing in Southeast Asia, publicizing the pain and anguish of families of American POWs through press conferences, speaking engagements, and demonstrations. President Reagan reignited this strategy with the MIA issue. Allen, *Until the Last Man Comes Home*, 215–19.

85. Allen, *Until the Last Man Comes Home*, 218–22. Many members of the league pushed Reagan for action on the MIA/POW issue, not just symbolism. Action meant actually bringing live prisoners home and achieving a full accounting. By his second term, it became more apparent to league members that the Reagan administration had little interest in cooperating with Hanoi to achieve a full accounting or acting out its promoted commitment to bringing missing Americans home.

86. Rosenthal, "Myth of the Last POWs."

87. Bass, *Vietnamerica*, 35.

88. Although the ODP remained the most effective process for the safe and orderly departure and resettlement of Southeast Asian refugees, including Amerasians, it certainly was not the most efficient. Robinson, *Terms of Refuge*, 172–73; Sutter, *Indochinese Refugee Dilemma*, 69.

89. Nan Robertson, "Amerasian War Orphans Come to U.S.," *New York Times*, April 18, 1984.

90. Colin Campbell, "24 Children of American Fathers, Happy but Tearful, Leave Vietnam," *New York Times*, Oct. 8, 1982.

91. Joseph Cerquone, "Vietnam's American Children: Refugees in a War That Won't End," *Commonweal*, April 25, 1986, 241. Cerquone and his wife would later become foster parents to an Amerasian girl, My Phuong. He wrote about his experience in the *Washington Post* in 1990. Joseph Cerquone, "A Divided Life," *Washington Post*, June 10, 1990.

92. Statement of Sanford Mevorah and Charles Printz from the New York based Human Rights International. "Three-Year Plan U.S. Will Admit 'Amerasian' Kids," *Desert Sun*, September 12, 1984.

93. Mary Ellen Finnerty Nachbur to Ronald Reagan, August 11, 1983, RRPL, WHORM, subject file Amerasian Children.

94. Prior to its passage McKinney worried about the consequences of excluding the Philippines from the AIA. He acknowledged the tremendous numbers of Amerasians in the Philippines and the concerns of the numerous servicemen who contacted him about their Amerasian children in that country. One active duty Navy sailor begged McKinney to include the islands and citizenship for the Amerasians. After the AIA passed, McKinney reiterated his concern for the Philippines, but his frustration with the law's limitations in the countries where it did apply demanded his immediate attention. Robert W. Blue Jr. to McKinney, July 30, 1982, SMP, subject files, folder Amerasian, box 131.

95. McKinney to Mazzoli, July 12, 1984, SMP, subject files A, folder Amerasians, box 131.

96. While the Justice Department and Immigration and Naturalization Service employees charged with granting refugee status and admission sought to limit the numbers of Indochinese refugees, the Department of State, more concerned with the geopolitical effects of U.S. refugee policy, assumed that everyone fleeing Southeast Asia qualified as a refugee. Bon Tempo, *Americans at the Gate*, 192; Loescher and Scanlan, *Calculated Kindness*, 200–208; Tichenor, *Dividing Lines*, 246–57; Joseph Cerquone, "Vietnam's American Children: Refugees in a War That Won't End," *Commonwealth*, April 25, 1986, 239–41, SMP, subject files, folder Amerasian, box 132; Asian-American Conference, American Council of Voluntary Agencies in Foreign Service, New York, October 4–5, 1984, 1–61.

97. Loescher and Scanlan, *Calculated Kindness*, 207.

98. After visiting Vietnam in 1983 Simpson was incensed about what he saw as abuse of the ODP. Purcell, *We're in Danger!*, 216–17; Le Xuan Khoa, "U.S. Refugee Program in Southeast Asia," April 11, 1986, UCI, folder 1, box 1.

99. According to James Purcell, in 1983 Simpson complained to Secretary Shultz about the ineffectiveness of the ODP and condemned the willingness of

the Reagan administration to declare Amerasians refugees so they could immigrate through the ODP. Purcell, *We're in Danger!*, 217–20.

100. *Midyear Consultation on U.S. Refugee Programs for Fiscal Year 1986: Hearings before the Subcommittee on Immigration and Refugee Policy*, 99th Cong., 2nd sess., Senate, 103.

101. *Midyear Consultation on U.S. Refugee Programs for Fiscal Year 1986: Hearings*, 102.

102. Purcell, *We're in Danger!*, 218.

103. Powell A. Moore to Arlen Specter, n.d., RRPL, WHORM, subject file Amerasian Children.

104. "Vietnam Official Wants Talks on Amerasians," *New York Times*, July 31, 1984.

105. This label applied to both the Amerasians of Vietnam and the political prisoners from the war still confined in Vietnam's reeducation camps. *Annual Refugee Consultation: Hearings before the Subcommittee on Immigration and Refugee Policy*, 99th Cong., 1st sess., Senate, September 17, 1985, 6; Cerquone, "Vietnam's American Children."

106. *Annual Refugee Consultation: Hearings*, Sept 17, 1985, 6.

107. Proposed by the United States on September 11, 1984, and successfully presented to Vietnamese authorities in October 1984. *Annual Refugee Consultation: Hearings*, Sept 17, 1985, 6; Asian-American Conference, October 4–5, 1984.

108. "Amerasian Children in Vietnam," U.S. Department of State, n.d., PSBI, folder Adoption Issues 1967–68, box Vietnam, Refugee Information; *Refugee Consultation: Hearings before the Subcommittee on Immigration and Refugee Policy of the Committee on the Judiciary*, 97th Cong., 2nd sess., Senate, September 29, 1982, 96; *Midyear Consultation on U.S. Refugee Programs for Fiscal Year 1986: Hearings*, 102; *Midyear Consultation on Refugee Programs for Fiscal Year 1987: Hearings before the Subcommittee on Immigration and Refugee Affairs*, Senate, 100th Cong., 1st sess., Senate, June 30, 1987, 138.

109. *Midyear Consultation on Refugee Programs for Fiscal Year 1987: Hearings*, 108; *Report on the Amerasian Issue*, Vietnam Veterans of America Foundation, August 1989, UCI, Van Le files, folder 42, box 1.

110. Lipman, "Mixed Voices, Mixed Policy," 62.

111. In FY 1985, 69,000 refugees entered the United States and in FY 1986 62,000, a decline of 8 percent. Southeast Asian refugee arrivals in FY 1985 were 49,853 and in FY 1986 were 45,391, a 9 percent drop reflecting the admissions ceiling that year of 45,500. However, the monthly flow of Southeast Asian refugees remained fairly stable throughout the decade. The annual ODP admission ceiling remained at 8,500 for FY 1985 through FY 1987. U.S. Department of Health

and Human Services, Refugee Resettlement Program report, 100th Cong., 1st sess., January 31, 1987, 7.

112. Between FY 1982 and 1986, 3,552 Amerasians total entered the United States as part of the ODP. *Midyear Consultation on U.S. Refugee Programs for FY 1986: Hearings*, 105; *Annual Refugee Consultation: Hearings*, Sept 17, 1985, 6; Asian-American Conference, October 4–5, 1984, 6-8.

113. McKinney to Mazzoli, April 16, 1985, SMP, subject files A, folder Amerasian, box 132.

114. "Amerasian Issue," October 22, 1985, SMP, subject files A, folder Amerasian, box 132.

115. "Amerasian Issue," October 22, 1985; Carroll to McKinney, October 4, 1985, SMP, subject files A, folder Amerasian, box 132.

116. Carroll to McKinney, October 4, 1985; discussion with Greg Kane by Tom Michaud, SMP, folder Amerasian, box 132.

117. Jack Dolan, "McKinney: Amerasian Immigration Too Slow," May 7, 1985, *Advocate*, SMP, subject files A, folder McKinney, box 132.

118. Dolan, "McKinney," SMP.

119. Barbara Crossette, "Hanoi Asks to End Amerasians' Issue," *New York Times*, Oct. 20, 1985.

120. *American POW/MIAs in Southeast Asia: Hearings before the Subcommittee on Asian and Pacific Affairs*, 97th Cong., 2nd sess., House, September 30, 1982.

121. Admission of Certain Children of U.S. Armed Forces Personnel, SB 1698, 128 no. 19 Cong. Rec. S25338–41 (September 28, 1982); Preferential Treatment in Admission of Certain Children of U.S. Citizens, HR 808, 128 no. 20 Cong. Rec. H27269–73 (October 1, 1982).

122. Kane, interview.

123. Amerasian Children Relief Act, HR 1684, 131 Cong. Rec. H1369 (March 21, 1985).

124. Amerasian Children Relief Act, HR 1684.

6. The Amerasian Homecoming Act

1. "Vietnam Student Seeks Aid," *Long Islander*, June 19, 1975.

2. "For Son Tran: No Return: But LI Gives Student a Home," *Long Island Press*, June 11, 1975.

3. See Longley, *Morenci Marines*.

4. Sforza, *Portrait of a Small Town III*, xvii.

5. *Urban Renewal Plan for Huntington Village*, May 19, 1959, HTCA, folder 1959–61, RG02, box 48; folder Urban Renewal CAC for a Workable Program, box 13284, 083-10; Sforza, *Portrait of A Small Town III*.

6. "Welcome Home Captain David E. Baker," *Long Islander*, April 5, 1973.

7. Longley, *Morenci Marines*, 5.

8. "Young and Old Join March, Reading List of War Dead," *Long Islander*, September 4, 1969, 1.

9. Joy Anne Wellman and Mrs. Francis Wellman, "2,000 Pounds Sent to South Vietnam," *Long Islander*, June 15, 1967; "Flag That Flew over Capitol Is Raised over Honor Roll on Village Green," *Long Islander*, November 16, 1967.

10. Initially there were forty names listed as killed in action; another died after the initial inscription of the memorial and, after the war ended, two others were listed as MIA. Anita Singer, "Huntington Women Plant Tree Memorial to Viet Dead," *Long Islander*, April 27, 1972.

11. "When the Cherry Blossoms Are in Bloom: Vietnam Memorial Trees Are Now in a Blaze of Color," *Long Islander*, May 6, 1993.

12. "Welcome Home Captain David E. Baker."

13. "Welcome Home Captain David E. Baker."

14. Espiritu, "Body Counts"; Stur, "'Hiding behind the Humanitarian Label.'"

15. Martin C. Evans, "Vietnam War Refugee Was Welcomed on LI, and the Bond Endures," *Newsday*, June 26, 2017.

16. "Sponsors Needed for Vietnamese Refugees," *Bethpage Tribune*, August 14, 1975.

17. Joye Brown, "30 Years Ago LI Family Took in Young Vietnamese Refugees," *Newsday*, November 28, 2009.

18. Keys, *Reclaiming American Virtue*.

19. Jeff Somer, "The Amerasian Dilemma," *Newsday*, November 4, 1985.

20. Gloria Blauvelt, interview by author, telephone, July 20, 2018. Tiernan's photograph of Minh initially ran in Jeff Somers, "Report from Vietnam," *Newsday*, November 4, 1985. In February 1986 additional photographs of Minh appeared in the newspaper. Mark Carfi-Bellerose Terrace, "A Language Barrier," *Newsday*, July 4, 1987.

21. Reports in *Newsday* during the period consistently described Minh as the "crippled boy," eliciting criticism from the disabled community; Blauvelt, interview, July 20, 2018.

22. Paul Marinaccio, "Students Trying to Help a Boy Half a World Away," *Newsday*, November 9, 1986.

23. Marlo Sandler, interview by author, telephone, December 11, 2015.

24. The HHS students and staff consulted with Dr. Hugo A. Keim, a New York surgeon, to diagnose Minh's medical issues. Keim agreed with previous diagnoses that Minh suffered from polio and would need a series of operations to

walk properly. Blauvelt, interview, July 20, 2018; Paul Marinaccio, "Students Get Help in Bid for Orphan," *Newsday*, January 30, 1987.

25. Sandler, interview; Sue (Forte) Gerbavsits, interview by author, Huntington NY, June 8, 2018.

26. Tara (Scalia) Quilty, interview by author, Huntington NY, 2018.

27. (Forte) Gerbavsits, interview.

28. Gloria Blauvelt, "Students Reach Out to a Needy Child," *New Horizons* (Huntington Free School District), no. 2, 1986–87.

29. Edna Negron, "At Huntington High, Minh's the Main Topic," *Newsday*, June 2, 1987.

30. Negron, "At Huntington High."

31. Blauvelt's description is of the reception students received from Vietnam veterans when speaking at the Lions Club in Northport, New York. Gloria Blauvelt, interview by author, telephone, April 18, 2019.

32. Blauvelt, interview, July 20, 2018; Irene Virag, "Lawmakers Ask Shultz to Help Amerasian," *Newsday*, March 7, 1987; Rep. Bob Mrazek, "Biography of Le Van Minh," press release, n.d. [1987].

33. Blauvelt, interview, July 20, 2018.

34. Although Blauvelt managed to secure a free medical evaluation and treatment for Minh through Dr. Hugo Keim at a Shriner's hospital, Minh was not able to take advantage. Blauvelt, interview, April 18, 2019.

35. Blauvelt started covering sports for the *Long Islander* in 1969. Blauvelt, interview, July 20, 2018.

36. "The Sea Breeze Awards," Ana Sims-Phillips, May 25, 1987, Marlo Sandler personal papers.

37. Robert Mrazek, interview by author, telephone, September 8, 2012; Marinaccio, "Students Trying to Help."

38. Sandler, interview.

39. Mrazek, interview.

40. *Report on the Amerasian Issue*, Vietnam Veterans of America Foundation, August 1989, UCI, Van Le files, folder 42, box 1.

41. "In Our Father's Land: Vietnamese Amerasians in the United States," United States Catholic Conference Migration and Refugee Services, 1985, UCI, folder 2, box 20. For further discussion see Bass, *Vietnamerica*, DeBonis, *Children of the Enemy*, and McKelvey, *Dust of Life*. In May 1987, Minh admitted his mother was alive and emotional over his departure and wanted to come to the United States with him. Paul Wedel, "I am Amerasian," UPI, May 30, 1987, Marlo Sandler personal collection.

42. According to historian Ann Laura Stoler, identifiable attributes that link national and racial identity are central to inclusionary discourses and exclusionary practices that frame the colonial dilemma of the mixed-race individual. Stoler, *Carnal Knowledge and Imperial Power*.

43. Jeff Sommer, "The Amerasian Dilemma," *Newsday*, November 4, 1985.

44. Paul Marinaccio, "Amerasian's Case Makes Headway," *Newsday*, November 30, 1986; Paul Marinaccio, "Vow of Help for Crippled Amerasian," *Newsday*, December 13, 1986.

45. Irene Virag, "Orphan Becomes a Symbol of Diplomacy," *Newsday*, March 25, 1987.

46. Irene Virag, "Le Van Minh's Friends Celebrate," *Newsday*, April 28, 1987; Irene Virag, "Goodbye . . . and Hello," *Newsday*, May 31, 1987.

47. The promotion of the "familiar" traits by *Newsday* reporters is another example of Edward Said's Orientalism, in which the eye and hair color of Le Van Minh symbolized his place in the familiar Western world of "us" and his displacement in the strange, Eastern world of "them." Said, *Orientalism*, 43–44.

48. Sandler, interview, and (Scalia) Quilty, interview.

49. Mrazek, interview.

50. Marc Kaufman, "Diplomats Agree on Outline of Plan to Release Amerasians," *Houston Chronicle*, October 12, 1986.

51. Mrazek, interview.

52. Mrazek, interview.

53. U.S. and Vietnamese officials desired to reconcile the Amerasian issue after the suspension of the ODP in January 1986. The last Amerasian approved by the ODP left Vietnam in May 1986. Robert Mrazek office, "The Amerasian Problem," press release, May 30, 1987, Marlo Sandler personal collection; Kaufman, "Diplomats Agree."

54. HHS Student Government to Nguyen Dang Quang, October 27, 1986, Marlo Sandler personal collection.

55. HHS Student Government to Nguyen Dang Quang.

56. The meeting occurred on December 12, 1986. Although diplomatic relations between the two countries did not exist in 1986, Vietnam was part of the United Nations and did have a representative office in New York City. Marinaccio, "Vow of Help for Crippled Amerasian"; Mrazek, interview.

57. Sandler, interview; (Scalia) Quilty, interview.

58. Dave Zach, "A Message from G.O.," *Dispatch*, n.d., ca. December 1986. Sue (Forte) Gerbavsits personal collection.

59. Marinaccio, "Amerasian's Case Makes Headway"; Mrazek, interview. Barbara Crossettes, "Vietnam Appears to Hinder an Emigration Accord," *New York*

NOTES TO PAGES 189-191

Times, August 22, 1987; "Orderly Departure Statistics as of October 1986," *Midyear Consultation on Refugee Programs FY 1987: Hearings before the Subcommittee on Immigration and Refugee Affairs*, 100th Cong., 1st sess., Senate, June 30, 1987. The ODP backlog of 26,379 persons to the United States included 12,422 who had previously received approval to immigrate to the United States.

60. Crossettes, "Vietnam Appears to Hinder an Emigration Accord."

61. Crossettes, "Vietnam Appears to Hinder an Emigration Accord."

62. Marinaccio, "Amerasian's Case Makes Headway"; Mrazek, interview; Crossettes, "Vietnam Appears to Hinder an Emigration Accord"; "Orderly Departure Statistics as of October 1986," *Midyear Consultation*.

63. Sandler, interview.

64. Sandler, interview.

65. Blauvelt, interview, 2018.

66. Marinaccio, "Vow of Help for Crippled Amerasian."

67. Marinaccio, "Vow of Help for Crippled Amerasian." Official reports listed three thousand Amerasians on the backlog list. Even while the program was suspended, departures from Vietnam for people already approved continued at drastically reduced levels, decreasing from an average of 704 refugee departures a month to 483 a month. Appendix 4, *Midyear Consultation on Refugee Programs FY 1987, Hearings before the Subcommittee on Immigration and Refugee Affairs*, 100th Cong., 1st sess., June 30, 1987.

68. At its peak the ODP backlog listed 3,825 refugees as "Persons Approved Yet Not Medically Cleared" and 1,912 "Approved but Will Not Yet Be Telexed to Vietnam." The former category covered those with expired medical exams, an increasing number because medical exams were impossible under the suspension. The latter category included those who had never received a medical exam and who were now also unable to complete that process. As a result, refugee departures from Vietnam to the United States declined from an average of 704 a month to 483 a month—levels comparable to early 1983. "The Orderly Departure Program: The Need for Reassessment," *Midyear Consultation on Refugee Programs FY 87: Hearings before the Subcommittee on Immigration and Refugee Affairs*, 100th Cong., 1st sess., June 30, 1987, 156.

69. Midyear Consultation on U.S. Refugee Programs for *FY 1987: Hearings before the Subcommittee on Immigration and Refugee Affairs*, 100th Cong., 1st sess., June 30, 1987, 108; *Midyear Consultation on U.S. Refugee Programs for FY 1986, Hearings before the Subcommittee on Immigration and Refugee Policy*, 99th Cong., 2nd sess., June 20, 1986, 108; *Report on the Amerasian Issue*, Vietnam Veterans of America.

70. Mrazek, interview; Virag, "Lawmakers Ask Shultz to Help Amerasian."

71. *Midyear Consultation on Refugee Programs FY 1987: Hearings*; Paul Marinaccio, "New Strategy for Helping Amerasian," *Newsday*, January 6, 1987.

72. Marinaccio, "New Strategy for Helping Amerasian," Sue (Forte) Gerbavsits personal collection.

73. Gloria Blauvelt, "HHS Students Deliver 27,808 Petition Signatures to Local Congressman on Behalf of Amerasian Boy," *Long Islander*, February 12, 1987; (Scalia) Quilty, interview.

74. Marc Kaufman, "U.S. and Vietnam Reach Accord on Amerasians," *Philadelphia Inquirer*, October 9, 1986; Kaufman, "Diplomats Agree."

75. Virag, "Lawmakers Ask Shultz to Help Amerasian."

76. Mrazek, interview.

77. Virag, "Lawmakers Ask Shultz to Help Amerasian"; Mrazek, interview.

78. Minh revealed these details in a *Newsday* interview in 2000. Michael Luo, "A Beggar No More," *Newsday*, July 9, 2000.

79. Luo, "A Beggar No More."

80. Virag, "Orphan Becomes a Symbol of Diplomacy." Rep. Thomas Ridge (R-PA), a decorated Vietnam War veteran active in negotiations over American MIA/POWs, accompanied Mrazek on a second trip to Vietnam to negotiate the specifics of the Amerasian Homecoming Act.

81. Sandler, interview.

82. (Forte) Gerbavsits, interview.

83. Irene Virag, "Le Van Minh's Friends Celebrate," *Newsday*, April 28, 1987.

84. Virag, "Le Van Minh's Friends Celebrate." Interestingly, VVA member and Westbury businessman Greg Kane was also reportedly in attendance at the HHS assembly, having "recently visited Le Van Minh in Ho Chi Minh City." "Assembly for Amerasian Boy," *Long Islander*, April 23, 1987.

85. Virag, "Le Van Minh's Friends Celebrate."

86. Virag, "Le Van Minh's Friends Celebrate."

87. Irene Virag, "Mrazek Leaves Today on a Mission of Mercy," *Newsday*, May 26, 1987.

88. Virag, "Mrazek Leaves Today." Virag wrote a series of articles from May to August 1987 about Minh's immigration experience to the United States.

89. Virag, "Goodbye . . . and Hello."

90. Virag, "Goodbye . . . and Hello."

91. Virag, "Goodbye . . . and Hello."

92. Sandler, interview.

93. Robert Mrazek personal video collection, May 1987.

94. Irene Virag, "Blackjack and 'Gimme Five': Amerasian Learning Americana from a Bangkok Hospital Bed," *Newsday*, June 1, 1987.

95. In 2000 Minh explained that he had spoken out of anger when he claimed his mother had abandoned him to the streets. In reality, Minh admitted that he ran away from home because his stepfather abused him. Luo, "A Beggar No More"; Negron, "At Huntington High."

96. Virag, "Blackjack and 'Gimme Five.'"

97. Sandler, interview.

98. Irene Virag, "Minh Coming Home Tomorrow," *Newsday*, June 3, 1987.

99. Edna Negron, "100 Students Greet Minh," *Newsday*, June 5, 1987.

100. Negron, "100 Students Greet Minh"; Joshua Botkin, "Goodnight Saigon, Good Morning America," *Dispatch HHS Newspaper*, June 21, 1987, Sue (Forte) Gerbavsits personal collection.

101. Negron, "100 Students Greet Minh."

102. Gail Ellen Daly, "Students Meet Minh," *Huntington Weekender*, June 13, 1987.

103. (Scalia) Quilty, interview, and Sandler, interview.

104. Gloria Blauvelt, letter to the editor, *Dispatch*, HHS newspaper, June 21, 1987. Sue (Forte) Gerbavsits personal collection.

105. Irene Virag, "Minh's First Day Home,'" *Newsday*, June 6, 1987.

106. Irene Virag, "Minh Faces Challenge of Private Life," *Newsday*, June 14, 1987; Sandler, interview.

107. Edna Negron, "'We Can Make a Difference,'" *Newsday*, June 22, 1987.

108. Sandler, interview.

109. Daly, "Students Meet Minh"; "*Newsday* Community Affairs: High School of the Year," *Newsday*, May 29, 1987.

110. "My Father's Not Home," (film proposal), East Bay Studios, June 23, 1987, Marlo Sandler personal collection.

111. Amerasians who grew up with consistent relationship with a mother (biological, foster, or adopted) had a much better psychological outcome than those who did not. Many of the Amerasian street-children did not have this benefit. McKelvey and Webb, "Long-Term Effects," 1013; Bemak and Chung, "Vietnamese Amerasians."

112. "Vietnamese Amerasians: Practical Implications of Current Research," Office of Refugee Resettlement; "Amerasian Families and American Fathers," Interaction Amerasian Resettlement Program: UCI, SEARAC, folder 2 Amerasians Information, box 20.

113. "In Our Fathers' Land: Vietnamese Amerasians in the United States," United States Catholic Conference, November 1985, UCI, SEARAC, folder 2, box 20.

114. "GAO Request for Completion of Survey to Evaluate Outcomes of AHA," St. Anselm's Immigrant and Refugee Community Center, March 8 1993, UCI, folder 44, box 1; "In Our Fathers' Land," United States Catholic Conference;

"Vietnamese Amerasians: Practical Implications of Current Research," Office of Refugee Resettlement; "Amerasian Families and American Fathers," UCI, box 20. According to the 1993 survey, 98 percent of Amerasians who immigrated to the United States via the Amerasian Homecoming Act were unproductive in their father searches. This number would remain consistent for Amerasians from Vietnam over the next decade and was compounded by the fact that by 1989, only 32 percent arriving in America came with information about their fathers.

115. "Vietnamese Amerasians: Practical Implications of Current Research," Office of Refugee Resettlement; "Amerasian Families and American Fathers," UCI.

116. Kane, interview.

117. Carroll, interview.

118. Bemak and Chung, "Vietnamese Amerasians," 79–88.

119. Trautfield, "America's Responsibility to the Amerasian Children."

120. Memo no. 89 to All Affiliated URM and Resettlement Programs, July 20, 1985, UCI, SEARAC, folder 2, box 20.

121. Memo no. 89 to All Affiliated URM and Resettlement Programs.

122. Irene Virag, "Life and Times of Le Van Minh," *Newsday*, June 22, 1987. According to the 1985 U.S. Catholic Conference survey, Minh's challenges were common among Amerasians who entered the United States as unaccompanied minors. Twenty-two percent of Amerasians who entered America without family members did not want to leave their families or friends in Vietnam. "In Our Fathers' Land," United States Catholic Conference.

123. Virag, "Minh Coming Home Tomorrow."

124. Virag, "Minh Faces Challenges of Private Life"; Mrazek, interview.

125. (Scalia) Quilty, interview.

126. (Forte) Gerbavsits, interview.

127. Rep. Bob Mrazek, *Report, Third District, New York*, July 1987, Sue (Forte) Gerbavsits personal collection.

128. Mrazek, interview.

129. Mrazek, interview.

130. Minh petitioned for his mother and half-siblings to come to the United States through the ODP in Thailand, as Vietnam had yet to resume ODP processing to the United States. The LIRS, his Vietnamese-speaking social worker, and the Kinneys assisted Minh with the process. Edna Negron, "Homesick, Minh Sends for Mom," *Newsday*, August 21, 1987; Mrazek, interview.

131. Edna Negron, "Le Van Minh's Americanization," *Newsday*, November 16, 1987.

132. Negron, "Le Van Minh's Americanization."

133. David Lamb, "Children of the Vietnam War," *Smithsonian*, June 2009, http://www.smithsonianmag.com/people-places/Children-of-the-Dust.html.

134. Lamb, "Children of the Vietnam War"; Chan, *Vietnamese American 1.5 Generation*.

135. Mrazek, interview; Robert Mrazek, personal video collection, May 1987.

136. Claims that government policy prevented Amerasians from attending school were common during the period, as was the denial of such accusations by the Vietnam government. However, most Amerasians describe the abuse and discrimination suffered at the hands of classmates in school as reasons that they did not attend. In either case, Amerasians were largely poorly educated and poor. Ranard and Gilzow, "The Amerasians"; McKelvey, *Dust of Life*, 8–15.

137. Mrazek, interview.

138. Robert McKelvey posits that the lack of interest among the American public toward immigrants and refugees by the 1990s greatly contributed to the large decline in acceptance rates under the Homecoming Act. He labeled the phenomenon "compassion fatigue" to describe the public reaction to immigration reform during the decade. McKelvey, *Dust of Life*, 120; Bernard Gwertzman, "The Debt to the Indochinese Is Becoming a Fiscal Drain," *New York Times*, March 3, 1985.

139. Mrazek, interview.

140. Peter Eng, "Vietnam Sends Amerasian Teenager to United States," *Associated Press*, May 30, 1987.

141. Irene Virag, "Mrazek Pushes for More," *Newsday*, May 31, 1987.

142. Virag, "Mrazek Pushes for More."

143. The bill included eliminating the birth cut-off date, extending the legislation to incorporate Amerasians born in the Philippines, Japan, and Taiwan, reducing the period of required sponsorship, and permitting mothers to accompany minor children. It also called for sponsorship by civic and church organizations and reduced the amount of time required for sponsorship from five to two years. Extension of Remarks, 133, pt. 70 Cong. Rec. H E1687 (May 4, 1987).

144. Extension of Remarks, 133, pt. 70 Cong. Rec. H E1687 (May 4, 1987).

145. Legislative Calendar, Committee on the Judiciary, House, 134, no. 24 Cong. Rec. (Oct. 22, 1988).

146. Clifford D. May, "McKinney Dies of Illness Ties to AIDS," *New York Times*, May 8, 1987; "1987: Rep. Stewart B. McKinney Dies," *Stamford (CT) Advocate*, May 6, 2012, http://stamfordadvocate.com/local/article/1987-Rep-Stewart-B-McKinney-dies-3538540.php.

147. Virag, "Mrazek Pushes for More."

148. It is likely that Stewart McKinney's failing health contributed to the lack of communication between him and Mrazek. Mrazek claims he had no

knowledge of any previous Amerasian legislation and created the AHA from scratch. However, numerous humanitarians and politicians, including McKinney, previously discussed many of the components that ended up in the Homecoming Act. Mrazek, interview.

149. Mrazek, interview.

150. According to a 1993 survey of the AHA, 40 percent of Amerasians immigrating between 1991 and 1992 were illiterate in Vietnamese, 95 percent had low education levels, 90 percent few or no job skill, and 80 percent few or no English skills, more than double the percentage of other Vietnamese refugees. "Amerasian Survey," UCI, Saint Anselm's Cross-Cultural Community Center Records, folder 44, box 1.

151. Nicholas Goldberg, "Vietnam to Release Amerasians," *Newsday*, January 20, 1988.

152. *Midyear Consultation on Refugee Programs FY 1987: Hearings*, S136. This is in contrast to the AIA. While the AIA allowed officials to consider physical appearance in determining the paternity of an Amerasian, they preferred documentation to looks. In October 1982, the U.S. director of the ODP, Donald I. Colin, initiated a "short priority list" of groups that American officials deemed priority for the ODP. On that list, Colin identified "documented Amerasian children," effectively limiting access to the ODP to those Amerasians with documented evidentiary proof of paternity. Amerasian Immigration Act, PL 97-359, 97th Cong., 2nd sess. (Oct. 22, 1982); Mrazek, interview.

153. Mrazek, interview.

154. "Amerasian Families and American Fathers: Considerations for Responses to Tracing Requests," InterAction Amerasian Resettlement Program, UCI, SEARAC, folder 2 Amerasian Information, report 1985-87, box 20.

155. Although the AHA designated the Amerasians immigrants, the funding for the program came from the Migration and Refugee Assistance fund. "Refugee Admissions for Fiscal Year 1990," *Hearings before the Subcommittee on Immigration, Refugees and International Law*, 101st Cong., 1st sess., September 12-13, 1989, 159; Foreign Operations, Export Financing, and Related Programs Appropriations Bill, 1989, House Committee on Appropriations, 100th Cong., 2nd sess., May 19, 1988, 85.

156. *Amerasian Resettlement Planning Committee Report*, March 14-15, 1988, and April 18-19, 1988, UCI, Van Le Files, folder 1 Amerasian Resettlement Reports, box 1.

157. Mrazek, interview.

158. Frank C. Carlucci to Ronald Reagan, June 15, 1987, RRPL, ID no. 480701, CO172, WHORM: Amerasian Children.

NOTES TO PAGES 209-213

159. J. Edward Fox to Dante B. Faschell, n.d., RRPL, ID no. 575191, CO172, WHORM: Amerasian Children.

160. 133, no. 16 Cong. Rec. 22797, 22917, 22923 (August 6, 1987); Mrazek, interview; John R. Bolton to Peter W. Rodino, November 10, 1987, ID no. 58021, CO172; J. Edward Fox to Peter W. Rodino Jr., October 13, 1987, RRPL ID no. 555040, CO172: WHORM, Amerasian Children.

161. Bolton to Rodino, November 10, 1987.

162. Mrazek's use of the appropriations committee for the AHA challenged the limits of the congressional committee system. While the appropriations committee decided the allocation of funds, the authorizing committee—the House Foreign Affairs Committee in this case—created policy. According to Mrazek, because he did not have the cooperation of the authorization committee on the AHA, he took it upon himself to create policy, writing the bill and adding it to the continuing resolution.

163. There was intense debate in the House surrounding the continuing resolution and specific criticism of the opportunity it provided to automatically pass bills without debate or discussion in the House or Senate. To read the specific debates see 153 Cong, Rec. H10911.

164. On August 6, 1987, McCain introduced S1601 in the Senate, the counterpart to Mrazek's HR 3171, the Amerasian Homecoming Act. This bill failed to move past committee.

165. Daly, "Students Meet Minh."

166. Sandler, interview.

167. Negron, "100 Students Greet Minh."

168. Luo, "A Beggar No More."

169. Luo, "A Beggar No More."

170. Luo, "A Beggar No More."

7. "Like a Home without a Roof"

1. The AHA specified immediate family members as "the spouse, child, or mother, or [one who] has acted as the next of kin" (with specified limitations). PL 202-100, Amerasian Homecoming Act, HR 3568, 100th Cong., 1st sess.

2. In both cases, there were safeguards put in place in case the number of applicants exceeded the ceiling or costs exceeded what was earmarked for the program. *President's Refugee Admissions Proposal FY 1988: Hearings before the Committee on the Judiciary*, 100th Cong., 1st sess., September 23, 1987, 107; Foreign Operations, Export Financing, and Related Programs Appropriations Bill, 1989; House, Appropriations Committee, 100th Cong., 2nd sess., May 19, 1988, 85.

3. American officials conducted personal interviews in Ho Chi Minh City, rather than relying on UN interviewers. After the initial interview, approved applicants traveled to Bangkok, Thailand, where U.S. officials made a final decision. Applicants were subject to a final identity check at the airport prior to boarding a plane to the Philippines Refugee Processing Center.

4. PL 202-100, Amerasian Homecoming Act, HR 3568, 100th Cong., 1st sess.; Mabry, "We're Bringing Them Home," 22–26.

5. The resettlement program emerged from a cooperative agreement with the American Council for Voluntary International Action, composed of 116 national voluntary resettlement organizations and the Office of Refugee Resettlement for the purpose of supporting local community efforts to "enhance the services provided to Amerasians and their families." Upon arrival at the PRPC, files for each Amerasian were sent to the Refugee Data Center in the United States, which placed them with one of the approved resettlement agencies. Upon their departure from the PRPC, the resettlement agency assisted with placing the Amerasian and family members either with near relatives already in the United States or in one of the fifty-five cluster sites approved by the Department of Health and Human Services, Program Evaluation and Methodology Division, *Initial Observation and Findings of Amerasian Homecoming Act*, GAO, report to Hon. Robert J. Mrazek and Hon. Thomas J. Ridge, November 16, 1992; *Vietnamese Amerasian Resettlement: Education, Employment, and Family Outcomes in the United States* report to congressional requesters, GAO, March 1994.

6. According to the 1994 GAO report, 88 percent of Amerasians who entered the United States through the AHA did so with families, usually parents and siblings. Four percent immigrated with spouses. Only 12 percent came to America alone. *Vietnamese Amerasian Resettlement*, GAO, 32–34.

7. A 1985 study found most Amerasians arrived at the PRPC with an average of six years of education. Ranard and Gilzow, "Amerasians." By 1994, a U.S. GAO study determined that the dysfunctional family structure and poor educational backgrounds that Amerasians brought with them to the United States impeded their progress. *Vietnamese Amerasian Resettlement*, GAO, 3; Valverde, "Doing the Mixed Race Dance," in *Sum of Our Parts*, 132–35.

8. *Amerasians' Special Needs Report*, Department of Social Services, California Health and Welfare Agency, August 1989, UCI, Saint Anselm's Cross-Cultural Community Center Records, folder 8, box 1 Amerasian Records.

9. *Wall Street Journal*, February 28, 2002; Thomas, "Blood Politics," 71.

10. *Initial Observation and Findings*, GAO.

11. *Initial Observation and Findings*, GAO.

12. *Initial Observation and Findings*, GAO. Also see McKelvey, *Dust of Life*, and Bass, *Vietnamerica*.
13. *Initial Observation and Findings*, GAO.
14. Mabry, "We're Bringing Them Home," 33.
15. Colin Powell to President Ronald Reagan, April 19, 1988, RRPL, ID no. 541476SS, IM 541476, WHORM; Thomas, "Blood Politics," 71.
16. Bass, *Vietnamerica*, 6; Lipman, "Face Is the Road Map," 58.
17. Lipman, "Face Is the Road Map," 58–60.
18. Krupnick, "Benefit of the Doubt," 88.
19. Yoon, "Reproducing Citizens through U.S. Militarism," 89.
20. Thomas, "Blood Politics," 71.
21. *Initial Observation and Findings*, GAO; Krupnick, "Benefit of the Doubt."
22. Said, *Orientalism*; Yu, *Thinking Orientals*, 7.
23. Henry Yu argues that America's infatuation with Asians as both a racial "problem" and a racial "solution" (referring to the model minority stereotype that emerged in the second half of the twentieth century) is rooted in an inability to reconcile the two. Yu, *Thinking Orientals*, 7, 190.
24. *Orderly Departure Program from Vietnam*, GAO, 1.
25. Krupnick, "Benefit of the Doubt," 46–58; Yoon, "Reproducing Citizens through U.S. Militarism," 86.
26. Anis, "Psychosocial Adjustment of Vietnamese Amerasians," 53.
27. "Amerasian Children Owed U.S. Aid," *Sun-Sentinel* (Fort Lauderdale FL), January 24, 1988, 4G.
28. Lipman, "Face Is the Roadmap," 54–55.
29. Amerasian online survey by author, April 1, 2011.
30. *Initial Observation and Findings*, GAO. According to Bass, the motivations for many included guilt, money, family obligations, blackmail, and fear of crossing the ocean alone. Bass, *Vietnamerica*, 125.
31. Bass, *Vietnamerica*, 129.
32. Lamb, "Children of the Vietnam War."
33. Bass, *Vietnamerica*, 128.
34. *Initial Observation and Findings*, GAO.
35. *Initial Observation and Findings*, GAO; Krupnick, "Benefit of the Doubt," 48.
36. In the 1992 review of the AHA, U.S. officials reported that some Amerasians complained that Vietnamese interpreters manipulated the interview outcome. If paid a proper bribe, interpreters coached applicants on how to answer the interview questions and translated their responses favorably. As rejection rates increased with the program by 1990, valid

Amerasians reportedly paid for such services to increase their chances of acceptance. *Initial Observation and Findings*, GAO, 8; Mabry, "We're Bringing Them Home," 34.

37. Debonis, *Children of the Enemy*, 12. Bemak and Chung, "Vietnamese Amerasians" and Bass, *Vietnamerica* further expose that fake families, termed "buyers" by Bemak and Chung, often abandoned the Amerasians at the PRPC and in America, leaving them to fend for themselves.

38. DeBonis, *Children of the Enemy*, 12.

39. *Vietnamese Amerasian Resettlement*, GAO, 3.

40. "Administrative hold," the delaying or canceling of departure for the United States, was the ultimate sanction in the PRPC for those who violated camp rules, failed to complete the work requirements, were suspected of criminal behavior, or who had certain medical conditions, including pregnancy and mental illness. Additionally, the Philippine military units that provided camp security at the PRPC operated the "monkey house," jails in which they could hold refugees without charges or hearings indefinitely. This, too, was used to punish those refugees accused or suspected of crimes, political subversion, or breaking camp rules. Tollefson, *Alien Winds*, 130–33.

41. *Initial Observation and Findings*, GAO.

42. Bass, *Vietnamerica*, 126.

43. Krupnick, "Benefit of the Doubt," 52. During her time as an interviewer, Krupnick claims that only once in four years did an Amerasian confess that the family accompanying him to the interview was fake.

44. *Orderly Departure Program from Vietnam*, GAO.

45. Yoon, "Reproducing Citizens through U.S. Militarism," 86.

46. Sutter, *Indochinese Refugee Dilemma*, 172–77.

47. *Initial Observation and Findings*, GAO, 7.

48. *Initial Observation and Findings*, GAO, 8.

49. *Initial Observation and Findings*, GAO. Vietnamese officials reported that the rejection rates of ODP interviewers varied from 60 to 90 percent.

50. Krupnik, "Benefit of the Doubt," 46.

51. Krupnik, "Benefit of the Doubt," 47.

52. Krupnik, "Benefit of the Doubt," 47; Sutter, *Indochinese*, 172–75.

53. Krupnik, "Benefit of the Doubt," 47.

54. Valverde, "From Dust to Gold," 151–53.

55. Reporting organizations included the Lutheran Immigration and Refugee Services and the Indochina Resource Action Center. In 1990, the U.S. government extended the program. In 1991, in an effort to encourage Amerasians to apply, the Vietnamese government announced that the program would stop in

NOTES TO PAGES 223–226 313

January 1992. The announcement resulted in confusion for many Amerasians, who thought they had missed the deadline and were unaware, even though the U.S. government listed the duration of the program as "open-ended," that they could still apply. *Initial Observation and Findings*, GAO, 5. *Consultation on Refugee Admissions for Fiscal Year 1990: Hearings before the Committee on the Judiciary, Subcommittee on Immigration and Refugee Affairs*, 101st Cong., 1st sess., September 15, 1989, 199–202.

56. Chan, *Vietnamese American*, 86.
57. *Orderly Departure Program from Vietnam*, GAO.
58. Chan, *Vietnamese American 1.5 Generation*, 86–87; Robinson, *Terms of Refuge*, 187–98.
59. *Orderly Departure Program from Vietnam*, GAO.
60. Sutter, *Indochinese Refugee Dilemma*, 213.
61. *Consultation on Refugee Admissions for Fiscal Year 1990: Hearings*, 14.
62. Bass, *Vietnamerica*, 55.
63. Krupnik, "Benefit of the Doubt," 57.
64. *Initial Observation and Findings*, GAO, 7.
65. Mabry, "We're Bringing Them Home," 34–35.
66. For further discussion on racial categorization during the ODP interviews see Yoon, "Reproducing Citizens through U.S. Militarism," 89; DeMonaco, "Disorderly Departure," and Mabry, "We're Bringing Them Home," 33.
67. *Initial Observation and Findings*, GAO, 7.
68. There are many cases of Vietnamese attempting to pass as Amerasians by manipulating their looks. For more information see Bass, *Vietnamerica*; Yarborough, *Surviving Twice*; McKelvey, *Dust of Life*; DeBonis, *Children of the Enemy*.
69. Lipman, "Face Is the Roadmap," 58.
70. Bass, *Vietnamerica*, 26.
71. Bass, *Vietnamerica*, 54. The word *nyetnik* means "naysayer" in Russian. Bass reports that this particular interviewer reminded the Amerasians of the boorish manner of the Russians they had encountered.
72. Bass, *Vietnamerica*, 27.
73. Bass, *Vietnamerica*, 27. Robert Lee posits that Asians in America have historically been cast as economic, social, and sexual threats. Racial stereotypes portrayed Asians as alien threats to the American nation and family. Thus, the "sneaky" Asian reinforced fears that Asians in America in the post–Vietnam War era continued to threaten American unity and remained the "enemy." They became scapegoats for America's economic decline and the psychic trauma of the war. Lee, *Orientals*, 8–9, 190.
74. *Wall Street Journal*, February 28, 2002.

75. Krupnick, "Benefit of the Doubt," 50.

76. "Why Hasn't U.S. Let Amerasian Immigrate," *Seattle Times*, December 21, 1988.

77. Even as "immigrants" the Amerasians remained under the auspices of annual refugee allotments for the ODP and refugee resettlement provisions. Mabry, "We're Bringing Them Home," 40.

78. The PRPC opened in 1980, initially housing Southeast Asian refugees immigrating to various first-asylum countries. By 1989, the PRPC was used almost exclusively by the United States. Yoon, "Reproducing Citizens through U.S. Militarism," 106–12. Tollefson, *Alien Winds*, xvii.

79. The ICMC developed and administered the curriculum taught to residents at the PRPC and received support from the Refugee Service Center of the Center for Applied Linguistics contracted by the Department of State. By the time the PRPC closed in 1994, many resettlement organizations had low opinions about the camp. *Implementing the Amerasian Homecoming Act: A Close Look at the Philippine Refugee Processing Center*, report prepared for Rep. Tom Ridge, Oct. 12, 1989, UCI, Van Le Files, folder 1, box 1 Amerasian Resettlement Reports, 1989–93; Mabry, "We're Bringing Them Home," 12, 42.

80. Tollefson, *Alien Winds*, 53, 63, 69; Keith B. Richburg, "Philippines Camp Helps Prepare Asian Refugees for Life in U.S.," *Washington Post*, March 26, 1988.

81. Tollefson, *Alien Winds*, 57; Yoon, "Reproducing Citizens through U.S. Militarism," 114.

82. Some scholars compared the PRPC curriculum to the Americanization programs of the early twentieth century. Tollefson, *Alien Winds*, 58. For more information see Benton-Cohen, *Inventing the Immigration Problem*.

83. Mabry, "We're Bringing Them Home," 49.

84. Tollefson, *Alien Winds*. 57.

85. Yoon, "Reproducing Citizens through U.S. Militarism," 116; Tollefson, *Alien Winds*, 75.

86. Richburg, "Philippines Camp."

87. The Americanization movement emerged from the 1911 Dillingham Commission report, which recommended restrictive immigration policies to ensure only assimilable immigrants—those whose traditional cultures and races were familiar to Americans—became American. Tollefson, *Alien Winds*, 45–58. See also Benton-Cohen, *Inventing the Immigration Problem*; Gerstle, *American Crucible*.

88. In *Thinking Orientals*, Henry Yu argues that even after attempts to assimilate appropriately, the geographic distance and cultural difference of Asians framed them as "permanent outsiders" in America.

89. The threat of the "unassimilable" immigrant was the focus of much nativist discourse and immigration policy during the nineteenth and early twentieth centuries. Jacobson, *Whiteness of a Different Color*. For further discussion see Daniels, *Coming to America*; Hoxie, *A Final Promise*.

90. Hing, *Making and Remaking*, 7–8.

91. Tollefson, *Alien Winds*. Critics claimed that Tollefson failed to account for the changes and improvements made at the PRPC since his departure in 1986. In a review of *Alien Winds*, Donald A. Ranard and Douglas F. Gilzow stated, "We find half-truths, inaccuracies, misleading examples, and simplistic generalizations." Still, Tollefson's work remains one of the only primary source accounts written about the PRPC and as such makes an important contribution. Ranard and Gilzow, "Comments on James W. Tollefson's 'Alien Winds'"; Felsman, "Alien Winds: The Reeducation," 272–74.

92. *Implementing the Amerasian Homecoming Act*, report prepared for Rep. Tom Ridge.

93. Valverde, "From Dust to Gold," 155.

94. Yoon, "Reproducing Citizens through U.S. Militarism," 106.

95. Bemak and Chung, "Vietnamese Amerasians."

96. Mabry, "We're Bringing Them Home," 232–35.

97. Yoon, "Reproducing Citizens through U.S. Militarism," 120–21. It was common for American resettlement organizations to collect mental health data on the Amerasian residents at the PRPC in efforts to better serve them once they arrived in the United States. Mabry, "We're Bringing Them Home," 43–46.

98. Prof. Bemak established this percentage in a 1991–92 study. Lamb, "Children of the Vietnam War."

99. Mabry, "We're Bringing Them Home," 242.

100. Some Amerasians in the PRPC did join gangs, engage in crime, face arrest, and exhibit mental health challenges, all acts that sometimes delayed or suspended their departure to the United States. DeBonis, *Children of the Enemy*, 6; Bemak and Chung, "Vietnamese Amerasians."

101. Yoon, "Reproducing Citizens through U.S. Militarism," 120. Reports determined that this group was most likely to experience poverty, most likely to participate in unsafe sex, and most unlikely to receive medical care or education because of the language barrier. Amerasian women were sexually active earlier than other Vietnamese women and reports showed that high rates of teen pregnancy coupled with low self-esteem led many to prostitution and drugs. Amerasian men were also identified as most likely to visit prostitutes and to practice unsafe sex. *Amerasians and AIDS: The Need for Intensive, Targeted Prevention Efforts*, September 1990, UCI, SEARAC, attachment B, folder 26, box 20.

102. Yoon, "Reproducing Citizens through U.S. Militarism," 120.

103. *Report on the Amerasian Issue*, Vietnam Veterans of America Foundation, August 1989, UCI, Van Le files, folder 42, box 1.

104. *Report on the Amerasian Issue*, Vietnam Veterans of America.

105. *Amerasians' Special Needs Report*, Department. of Social Services, California Health and Welfare Agency; Bemak and Chung, "Vietnamese Amerasians," 79–88; Levi, "Legacies of War," 421.

106. Studies found that the number of Amerasians who wanted to reunite with their American fathers ranged from 25 to 54 percent and that only a small percentage of those actually searched for their father. Bemak and Chung, "Vietnamese Amerasians"; *Vietnamese Amerasians: Practical Implications*, UCI, folder 2, box 20; "Request for Completion of Survey to Evaluate Outcomes of AHA," St. Anselm's Immigrant and Refugee Community Center, March 8, 1993, UCI, Saint Anselm's Cross-Cultural Community Records, folder 44, box 1.

107. Peter Monaghan, "Gonzaga U. Helps Amerasian Children of GIs Make a New Start in the United States," *Chronicle of Higher Education*, December 9, 1992, A29, Amerasian Stuff, 1993–96, Amerasian Program GUA, folder Correspondence, box General Amerasian.

108. *Amerasians' Special Needs Report*, Department of Social Services, California Health and Welfare Agency.

109. By 1988, 46 percent of all refugees arriving in the United States settled in California, including more than five thousand Amerasians. State Coordinators Meeting October 1988, Working Group, UCI, SEARAC, folder 1, box 1.

110. *Amerasians' Special Needs Report*, Department of Social Services, California Health and Welfare Agency.

111. Ranard and Gilzow, "Amerasians," 6.

112. Bass, *Vietnamerica*, 27.

113. Ranard and Gilzow, "Amerasians," 6.

114. *New York Times*, November 16, 1992.

115. Mabry, "We're Bringing Them Home," 246.

116. *Amerasians*, Gandini Multifilm.

117. *Amerasians*, Gandini Multifilm.

118. Robin Levi posits that the rejection faced by Amerasians from the Vietnamese-American community was less severe than that which they faced in Vietnam but still compounded feelings of alienation and abandonment. Levi, "Legacies of War," 421–22; Valverde, "Doing the Mixed Race Dance," 134–37.

119. "Request for Completion of Survey," St. Anselm's Immigrant and Refugee Center.

120. "Request for Completion of Survey," St. Anselm's Immigrant and Refugee Center; David Gonzales, "For Afro-Amerasians, Tangled Emotions," *New York Times*, November 16, 1992.

121. Gonzales, "For Afro-Amerasians, Tangled Emotions." For more on Black Amerasians' racial assimilation and identity, see Williams and Thornton, "Social Construction of Ethnicity."

122. *Amerasians*, Gandini Multifilm.

123. McKelvey, *Dust of Life*, 120. McKelvey attributes the large decline in acceptance rates for the AHA to declining public interest in immigrants and refugees by the 1990s.

124. Schaller and Rising, *Republican Ascendency*, 110–15.

125. Huyen Friedlander, "Bui Doi: From Children of Dust to Children of Gold," *VietNow*, October 31, 1995.

126. The GAO reported that 80 percent of Amerasians from Vietnam were functionally illiterate in English, compared to 45 percent of other Vietnamese refugees; 40 percent were illiterate in Vietnamese, 95 percent had low education level, and 90 percent had few or no job skills. "Request for completion of survey," St. Anselm's Immigrant and Refugee Center.

127. Mrazek, interview.

128. In 1997 only 809 Amerasians and accompanying family members immigrated to the United States under the AHA. *Annual Report, Refugees, FY 1997*, Office of Policy and Planning, Department of Justice, Immigration and Naturalization Service, July 1999, 101st Cong., 2nd sess., 4, 9.

129. *Annual Report, Refugees, FY 1997*, Office of Policy and Planning, 4, 9; *Yearbook of Immigration Statistics, FY 1986–2004*, Department of Homeland Security, http://www.dhs.gov/yearbook-immigration-statistics-2004-0. Although the AHA continued to exist, the funding associated with the program disappeared.

130. Official naturalization statistics for FY 1991–2003 lists only region and country of birth. *Yearbook of Immigration Statistics, FY 1991–2003*, Department of Homeland Security, www.dhs.gov/yearbook-immigration-statistics-2003-1.

131. The Bureau of Immigration Appeals found that the INS had proved its case, and ordered Dung Van Chau deported as an alien convicted of two crimes of moral turpitude. Immigration and Nationality Act ("INA") § 241(a)(2)(A)(ii), 8 U.S.C. § 1251(a)(2)(A)(ii) (1994), https://caselaw.findlaw.com/us-9th-circuit/1054646.html.

132. Chau v. INS, 247 F.3d 1026,1027 (9th Cir. 2001).

133. Chau v. Dept. of Homeland Security, 424 F Supp. 2d 1159, 1160 (D. Ariz. 2006), https://casetext.com/case/chau-v-us-dept-of-homeland-sec.

134. Chau v. Dept. of Homeland Security.

135. The Ninth Circuit Court transferred the case back to the U.S. District Court in Arizona. Chau v. INS.

136. Chau v. Dept. of Homeland Security. In the 2006 case, Chau admitted that he had not immigrated under the AIA but as an Amerasian refugee under the ODP because of the AIA requirement that the mothers of Amerasians release them for immigration. In order to bring his family with him, Chau testified, he had to use the ODP. This revelation placed the burden of his case on proof of paternity and legitimation.

137. In 2005 Lofgren announced the same bill, now HR 2684, still titled the Amerasian Naturalization Act.

138. The 2007 proposal was designated HR 4007; in 2012 it became HR 5156. The Amerasian Paternity Recognition Act, April 27, 2012, Zoe Lofgren, HR 5156, 112th Cong., 2nd sess.

139. "Lofgren Introduces Citizenship Bill for Children Born in Vietnam to American Servicemen and Vietnam" press release, Oct. 22, 2003.

140. In 2012 HR 5156 failed to advance past the Judiciary Committee on Immigration and Border Security.

141. Lamb, "Children of the Vietnam War."

142. Lamb, "Children of the Vietnam War."

143. Marlo Sandler Interview.

Conclusion

1. *Vietnamese Amerasian Resettlement: Education, Employment, and Family Outcomes in the United States*, GAO, March 1994.

2. *Vietnamese Amerasian Resettlement*, GAO, 1; *Yearbook of Immigration Statistics, FY 1986–2004*, Department of Homeland Security.

3. Simon Denyer, "Thousands of Vietnamese, Including Children of U.S. Troops, Could Be Deported under New Policy," *Washington Post*, August 31, 2018.

4. Michael Tatarski, "Why Is the U.S. Deporting Protected Vietnamese Immigrants?" *Diplomat*, June 5, 2018, https://thediplomat.com/2018/06/why-is-the-us-deporting-protected-vietnamese-immigrants/; Shannon Dooling, "40 Years after the Vietnam War, Some Refugees Face Deportation under Trump," National Public Radio, https://www.npr.org/2019/03/04/699177071/40-years-after-the-vietnam-war-some-refugees-face-deportation-under-trump.

5. Denyer, "Thousands of Vietnamese."

6. Denyer, "Thousands of Vietnamese."

7. Denyer, "Thousands of Vietnamese."

8. Humanitarian organizations estimate around four hundred Amerasians are still in Vietnam. However, Miller's claim to have tested five hundred call that

NOTES TO PAGES 244–245

number into question. It is likely most estimates do not account for the Amerasians still living in rural areas. Jackie Montalvo, "Son of U.S. Soldier Left Behind in Vietnam Helps Other 'Amerasians' Reunite with Families" *NBC News*, June 15, 2018, https://www.nbcnews.com/news/asian-america/son-u-s-soldier-left-behind-vietnam-helps-other-amerasians-n882946.

9. Tony Tran, "People Always Ask 'What Are You?' A DNA Kit Gave Me the Unexpected Answer," *Huffington Post*, May 8, 2018, https://www.huffpost.com/entry/people-always-ask-what-are-you-i-finally-learned-the-unexpected-truth-via-a-dna-kit_n_5af07e06e4b041fd2d2936d3.

10. Miller was born out of wedlock in the Philippines to a Filipina mother, Luz Penero, and an American father, Charlie Miller, who legitimated his daughter before Lorelyn applied for citizenship.

11. The Immigration and Nationality Act of 1952, PL 414, 66 Stat. 163 (enacted June 27, 1952). According to the law, legitimation of paternity for children born abroad out of wedlock to American fathers had to occur before the child's eighteenth birthday.

12. Antognini, "From Citizenship to Custody," 432; The question for the Court was whether 9 U.S.C. Section 1409—establishing upon birth the U.S. citizenship of illegitimate, foreign-born children whose mothers are citizens but failing to do the same if only their fathers are U.S. citizens—violated the Fifth Amendment's equal protection guarantees. The Court ruled that it did not. "Miller v. Albright," Oyez Project at Illinois Institute of Technology, Chicago–Kent College of Law, accessed March 10, 2015, http://www.oyez.org/cases/1990-1999/1997/1997_96_1060.

13. Since fathers can't confirm their paternity through childbirth, U.S. law allows unwed fathers to confer birthright citizenship by legitimating their child and claiming paternity if four requirements are satisfied: (1) there exists a blood relationship, (2) the father was a citizen at the time of birth, (3) the father provides a written agreement to provide financial support until the age of majority (eighteen), (4) until the age of eighteen, the person is (a) legitimized under the law of his or her residence or domicile and the father (b) gives written acknowledgment of paternity under oath and (c) paternity is established by competent court.

14. Additional Supreme Court cases include *Fiallo v. Bell* (1977), *Nguyen v. INS* (2000), and *Flores-Villar v. United States* (2010).

15. "Miller v. Albright, Secretary of State."

16. Fiallo v. Bell, 430 U.S. 787, 97 S. Ct. 1473, 52 L. Ed. 2d 50 (1977).

17. The Supreme Court's decision was 6–3, Justices Rehnquist, Stevens, O'Connor, Scalia, Kennedy, and Thomas ruling for Albright, and Justices Souter, Ginsburg, and Breyer against. "Miller v. Albright," Oyez Project.

Bibliography

Archives/Manuscript Materials

CBS	CBS News Archive.
GFPL	Gerald R. Ford Presidential Library, Grand Rapids MI.
GHP	Gary Hart Papers, University of Colorado Boulder Libraries.
GUA	Gonzaga University Archives, Spokane WA.
HHSA	Huntington Historical Society Archive, Huntington NY.
HHSM	Huntington High School Heritage Museum, Huntington NY.
HILA	Hoover Institution Library and Archives, Stanford University.
HTCA	Huntington Town Clerk's Archives, Huntington NY.
JCL	Jimmy Carter Library, Atlanta GA.
JDPA	Jeremiah Denton Personal Papers, Auburn University Archives.
JOPA	Jesuit Oregon Province Archives, Spokane WA (subsequently moved to the Jesuit Archives and Research Center, St. Louis MO).
MARBLE	Manuscript, Archives, and Rare Book Library, Emory University.
MSRC	Moorland-Spingarn Research Center, Howard University, Manuscript Division.
NAACP	NAACP Papers, Library of Congress, Washington DC.
NACP	National Archives at College Park, College Park MD.
NARA	National Archives, Washington DC.
PMP	Patsy Mink Papers, Manuscript Division, Library of Congress, Washington DC.
PSBI	Archives of the Pearl S. Buck House, Pearl S. Buck International, Perkasie PA.
RNPL	Richard Nixon Presidential Library, Yorba Linda CA.
RRPL	Ronald Reagan Presidential Library, Simi Valley CA.
SMP	Stewart B. McKinney Papers. Archives and Special Collections at the Thomas J. Dodd Center, University of Connecticut Libraries.
SWHA	Social Welfare History Archives, University of Minnesota.

UCI	Southeast Asian Archive, Special Collections and Archives, University of California–Irvine Libraries.
WFP	Walter E. Fauntroy Papers, Special Collections Research Center, George Washington University.

Published Works

Adams, Rachel. *Sideshow U.S.A.: Freaks and the American Cultural Imagination*. Chicago: University of Chicago Press, 2001.

Ahern, Joseph M. "Out of Sight, Out of Mind: United States Immigration Law and Policy as Applied to Filipino-Amerasians." *Pacific Rim Law and Policy*, 1992.

Akibayashi, Kozue, and Suzuyo Takazato. "Okinawa: Women's Struggle for Demilitarization." In *Bases of Empire: The Global Struggle against U.S. Military Posts*, edited by Catherine Lutz and Cynthia Enloe, 243–69. New York: New York University Press, 2009.

Allen, Michael J. *Until the Last Man Comes Home: POWs, MIAs, and the Unending Vietnam War*. Chapel Hill: University of North Carolina Press, 2009.

Amerasian. Produced and directed by Gandini Multifilm. New York: Cinema Guild, 1998. Videocassette, 55 min.

Anderson, Carol. *Eyes Off the Prize: The United Nations and the African American Struggle for Human Rights, 1944–1955*. Cambridge, UK: Cambridge University Press, 2003.

Anis, Joyce. "Psychosocial Adjustment of Vietnamese Amerasians." PhD diss., University of Minnesota, 2006.

Antognini, Albertina. "From Citizenship to Custody: Unwed Fathers Abroad and at Home." *Harvard Journal of Law & Gender* 36 (August 6, 2013): 405–68.

Appy, Christian. *American Reckoning: The Vietnam War and Our National Identity*. New York: Penguin Books, 2016.

———. *Working-Class War: American Combat Soldiers & Vietnam*. Chapel Hill: University of North Carolina Press, 1993.

Bardaglio, Peter W. "'Shameful Matches': The Regulation of Interracial Sex and Marriage in the South before 1900." In *Sex Love Race: Crossing Boundaries in American History*, edited by Martha Hodes, 112–38. New York: New York University Press, 1999.

Barnett, Michael. *Empire of Humanity: A History of Humanitarianism*. Ithaca NY: Cornell University Press, 2011.

Bass, Thomas A. *Vietnamerica: The War Comes Home*. New York: Soho Press, 1996.

Basson, Laura. *White Enough to be American?: Race Mixing, Indigenous People, and the Boundaries of State and Nation*. Chapel Hill: University of North Carolina Press, 2008.

Baviera, Aileen S. P. "Implications of the U.S.-Philippine Enhanced Defense Cooperation Agreement." *Asia Pacific Bulletin* 262 (May 9, 2014). EastWestCenter/APB, http://www.eastwestcenter.org/sites/default/files/private/apb262.pdf.

Bell, Joyce. *The Black Power Movement and American Social Work*. New York: Columbia University Press, 2014.

Bemak, Fred, and Rita Chi-Ying Chung. "Vietnamese Amerasians: Psychosocial Adjustment and Psychotherapy." *Journal of Multicultural Counseling and Development* 25 (January 1997): 79–88.

Bennett, Judith A., and Angela Wanhalla, eds. *Mother's Darlings of the South Pacific: The Children of Indigenous Women and U.S. Servicemen, World War II*. Honolulu: University of Hawaii Press, 2017.

Benton-Cohen, Katherine. *Inventing the Immigration Problem: The Dillingham Commission and its Legacy*. Cambridge MA: Harvard University Press, 2018.

Biddiscombe, Perry. "Dangerous Liaisons: The Anti-Fraternization Movement in the U.S. Occupation Zones of Germany and Austria, 1945–1948." *Journal of Social History* 34, no. 3 (Spring 2001): 611–47.

Bilton, Michael, and Kevin Sim. *Four Hours in My Lai: A War Crime and Its Aftermath*. London: Viking, 1992.

Bon Tempo, Carl J. *Americans at the Gate: The United States and Refugees during the Cold War*. Princeton NJ: Princeton University Press, 2008.

Borstelmann, Thomas. *The Cold War and the Color Line*. Cambridge MA: Harvard University Press, 2001.

Bradley, Mark. "An Improbable Opportunity: America and the Democratic Republic of Vietnam's 1947 Initiative." In *The Vietnam War: Vietnamese and American Perspectives*, edited by Jayne Werner and Luu Doan Huynh, 3–23. New York: M. E. Sharpe, 1993.

———. "Slouching toward Bethlehem: Culture, Diplomacy, and the Origins of the Cold War in Vietnam." In *Cold War Constructions: The Political Culture of United States Imperialism, 1945–1966*, edited by Christian G. Appy, 11–34. Amherst: University of Massachusetts Press, 2000.

Briggs, Laura. "Mother, Child, Race, Nation: The Visual Iconography of Rescue and the Politics of Transnational and Transracial Adoption." *Gender and History* 15, no. 2 (August 2003): 170–200.

———. *Reproducing Empire: Race, Sex, Science, and U.S. Imperialism in Puerto Rico*. Berkeley: University of California Press, 2002.

———. *Somebody's Children: The Politics of Transracial and Transnational Adoption*. Durham NC: Duke University Press, 2012.

Brinkley, Douglas, ed. *The Reagan Diaries*. New York: HarperCollins, 2007.

Brownmiller, Susan. *Against Our Will: Men, Women and Rape*. 1975. Reprint, New York: Ballantine Books, 1993.

Brubaker, Rogers. *Citizenship and Nationhood in France and Germany*. Cambridge MA: Harvard University Press, 1992.

———. "Migration, Membership, Modern Nation-State: Internal and External Dimension of the Politics of Belonging." *Journal of Interdisciplinary History* 41, no. 1 (Summer 2010).

Burkhardt, William R. "Institutional Barriers, Marginality, and Adaptation among the American-Japanese Mixed Bloods in Japan." *Journal of Asian Studies* 42, no. 3 (May 1983): 519–44.

Campt, Tina. *Other Germans: Black Germans and the Politics of Race, Gender, and Memory in the Third Reich*. Ann Arbor: University of Michigan Press, 2004.

Caputo, Philip. *A Rumor of War*. New York: Holt, 1996.

Carpenter, Charli. "Gender, Ethnicity, and Children's Human Rights." In *Born of War: Protecting Children of Sexual Violence Survivors in Conflict Zones*, edited by Charli Carpenter, 1–20. Bloomfield CT: Kumarian Press, 2007.

Casavantas Bradford, Anita. "'La Niña Adorada del Mundo Socialista': The Politics of Childhood and U.S.-Cuba-U.S.S.R. Relations, 1959–1962." *Diplomatic History* 40, no. 2 (April 2016): 296–326.

Cashin, Sheryll. *Loving: Interracial Intimacy in America and the Threat to White Supremacy*. Boston: Beach Press, 2017.

Chan, Sucheng. *Asian Americans: An Interpretive History*. Boston: Twayne Publishers, 1991.

———, ed. *Remapping Asian American History*. Walnut Creek CA: AltaMira Press, 2003.

———, ed. *The Vietnamese American 1.5 Generation: Stories of War, Revolution, Flight, and New Beginnings*. Philadelphia: Temple University Press, 2006.

Chin, Gabriel. "The Civil Rights Revolution Comes to Immigration Law: A New Look at the Immigration and Nationality Act of 1965," *North Carolina Law Review* 75 (1996): 273–347.

Chong, Denise. *The Girl in the Picture: The Story of Kim Phuc and the Vietnam War*. New York: Penguin, 2001.

Choy, Catherine. *Global Families: A History of Asian International Adoption in America*. New York: New York University Press, 2013.

Chrisman, Laura, and Patrick Williams, eds. *Colonial Discourse and Post-Colonial Theory: A Reader*. New York: Columbia University Press, 1994.

Chuong, Chung Hoang, and Le Van. *The Amerasians from Vietnam: A California Study*. Folsom CA: Southeast Asia Community Resource Center, 1994.

Cole, Cornelius. *Memoirs of Cornelius Cole, Ex-Senator of the United States from California*. New York: McLoughlin Brothers, 1908.

Collins, Kristin A. "Illegitimate Borders: *Jus Sanguinis* Citizenship and the Legal Construction of Family, Race, and Nation." *Yale Law Journal* 123, no. 2134 (2014): 2134–235.

———. "A Short History of Sex and Citizenship." *Boston University Law Review* 91, no. 11–61 (July 2011): 1485–515.

———. "When Fathers' Rights Are Mothers' Duties: The Failure of Equal Protection in Miller v. Albright." *Yale Law Journal* 109, no. 7 (May, 2000): 1669–708.

Cooper, Frederick, and Ann Laura Stoler, eds. *Tensions of Empire: Colonial Cultures in a Bourgeois World*. Berkeley: University of California Press, 1997.

Daniels, Roger. *Coming to America: A History of Immigration and Ethnicity in American Life*. New York: Harper Perennial, 2002.

Daniel-Wrabetz, Joana. "Children Born of War Rape in Bosnia-Herzegovina and the Convention on the Rights of the Child." In *Born of War: Protecting Children of Sexual Violence Survivors in Conflict Zones*, edited by Charli Carpenter, 21–39. Bloomfield CT: Kumarian Press, 2007.

Dean, Robert. *Imperial Brotherhood: Gender and the Making of Cold War Foreign Policy*. Amherst: University of Massachusetts Press, 2003.

DeBonis, Steven. *Children of the Enemy: Oral Histories of Vietnamese Amerasians and Their Mothers*. Jefferson NC: McFarland, 1995.

Demmer, Amanda C. *After Saigon's Fall: Refugees and U.S.-Vietnamese Relations 1975–2000*. Cambridge, UK: Cambridge University Press, 2021.

———. "The Last Chapter of the Vietnam War: Normalization, Nongovernmental Actors, and the Politics of Human Rights, 1975–1995." PhD diss., University of New Hampshire, 2017.

DeMonaco, Mary Kim. "Disorderly Departure: An Analysis of the United States Policy toward Amerasian Immigration." *Brooklyn Journal of International Law* 15, no. 6 (1989): 641–709.

Doan, Trúc. "Bringing the Aliens Home: The Influence of False Narratives on Judicial Decision Making in the Amerasian Context." *Asian American Law Journal* 24, no. 3 (2017): 69–96.

Dowd, Nancy. "Fathers and the Supreme Court: Founding Fathers and Nurturing Fathers." *Emory Law Journal* 54, no. 3 (2005): 1271–333.

Dower, John. *War without Mercy: Race and Power in the Pacific War*. New York: Pantheon Books, 1986.

Dowland, Seth. *Family Values and the Rise of the Christian Right*. Philadelphia: University of Pennsylvania Press, 2015.

Dubinsky, Karen. *Babies without Borders: Adoption and Migration across the Americas*. New York: New York University Press, 2010.

Dudziak, Mary. *Cold War Civil Rights: Race and the Image of American Democracy*. Princeton NJ: Princeton University Press, 2000.

Duggan, Joseph P. *Jeremiah Denton: A Political Portrait*. Mobile AL: Traditional Press, 1986.

Dumancic, Marko. "Hidden in Plain Sight: The Histories of Gender and Sexuality during the Cold War." In *Gender, Sexuality, and the Cold War*, edited by Philip E. Muehlenbeck, 1–12. Nashville TN: Vanderbilt University Press, 2017.

Duus, Masayo. *Tokyo Rose: Orphan of the Pacific*. New York: Kodansha America, 1979.

Eldridge, Lawrence. *Chronicles of a Two-Front War: Civil Rights and Vietnam in the African American Press*. Columbia: University of Missouri Press, 2012.

Enloe, Cynthia. *Bananas, Beaches and Bases: Making Feminist Sense of International Politics*. Berkeley: University of California Press, 1990.

———. *Maneuvers: The International Politics of Militarizing Women's Lives*. Berkeley: University of California Press, 2000.

Espiritu, Yen Le. *Body Counts: The Vietnam War and Militarized Refugees*. Berkeley: University of California Press, 2014.

———. "The 'We Win Even When We Lose' Syndrome: U.S. Press Coverage of the Twenty-Fifth Anniversary of the 'Fall of Saigon.'" *American Quarterly* 58, no. 2 (June 2006): 329–52.

Fehrenbach, Heide. "Of German Mothers and 'Negermischlingskinder': Race, Sex and the Postwar Nation." In *The Miracle Years: A Cultural History of West Germany*, edited by Hanna Schissler, 164–85. Princeton NJ: Princeton University Press, 2001.

———. *Race after Hitler: Black Occupation Children in Postwar Germany and America*. Princeton NJ: Princeton University Press, 2005.

Felsman, Kirk J. "Alien Winds: The Reeducation of America's Indochinese Refugees." *Journal of Refugee Studies* 3 no. 3 (1990): 272–74.

Fieldston, Sara. "Little Cold Warriors: Child Sponsorship and International Affairs." *Diplomatic History* 38, no. 2 (April 2014): 240–50.

Firpo, Christina Elizabeth. *The Uprooted: Race, Children, and Imperialism in French Indochina, 1890–1980*. Honolulu: University of Hawaii Press, 2016.

Foster, Anne L. *Projections of Power: The United States and Europe in Colonial Southeast Asia, 1919–1941*. Durham NC: Duke University Press, 2010.

Franco, Vincent, and Gail Dolgin, dirs. *Daughter from Danang*. Watertown MA: Interfaze Educational Productions, 2003. DVD, 83 min.

Franklin, Bruce. *M.I.A. or Mythmaking in America: How and Why Belief in Live POWs Has Possessed a Nation*. New Brunswick NJ: Rutgers University Press, 1992.

———. *Vietnam and Other American Fantasies*. Amherst: University of Massachusetts Press, 2001.
Funderburg, Lise. *Black, White, Other: Biracial Americans Talk about Race and Identity*. New York: William Morrow, 1994.
Gage, Sue-Je Lee. "The Amerasian Problem: Blood, Duty, and Race." *International Relations* 21, no. 1 (2007): 86–102.
———. "Pure Mixed Blood: The Multiple Identities of Amerasians in South Korea." PhD diss., Indiana University, 2007.
Gallicchio, Marc. *The African American Encounter with Japan and China: Black Internationalism in Asia, 1895–1945*. Chapel Hill: University of North Carolina Press, 2000.
Gerber, David A. *Disabled Veterans in History*. Rev. ed. Ann Arbor: University of Michigan Press, 2012.
Gerstle, Gary. *American Crucible: Race and Nation in the Twentieth Century*. Princeton NJ: Princeton University Press, 2001.
Goedde, Petra. *GIs and Germans: Culture, Gender and Foreign Relations, 1945–1949*. New Haven CT: Yale University Press, 2003.
Graves, Kori A. *A War Born Family: African American Adoption in the Wake of the Korean War*. New York: New York University Press, 2020.
Gray, Herman S. *Cultural Moves: African Americans and the Politics of Representation*. Berkeley: University of California Press, 2005.
Haas, Kristin. *Carried to the Wall: American Memory and the Vietnam Veterans Memorial*. Berkeley: University of California Press, 1998.
Hening, William Waller. *Status at Large: Being a Collection of all the Laws of Virginia from the First Session of the Legislature in the Year 1619*. Charlottesville: University of Virginia Press, 1988.
Herring, George C. *America's Longest War: The United States and Vietnam, 1950–1975*. New York: McGraw-Hill, 1979.
Higham, John. *Strangers in the Land: Patterns of American Nativism, 1860–1925*. New Brunswick NJ: Rutgers University Press, 2002.
Hing, Bill Ong. *Defining America through Immigration Policy*. Philadelphia: Temple University, 2004.
———. *Deporting Our Souls: Values, Morality, and Immigration Policy*. Cambridge, UK: Cambridge University Press, 2006.
———. *Making and Remaking Asian America through Immigration Policy, 1850–1990*. Stanford CA: Stanford University Press, 1993.
———. *White Women Black Men: Illicit Sex in the 19th-Century South*. New Haven CT: Yale University Press, 1999.

Höhn, Maria. *GIs and Fräuleins: The German-American Encounter in 1950s West Germany*. Chapel Hill: University of North Carolina Press, 2002.

Höhn, Maria, and Seungsook Moon. "The Politics of Gender, Sexuality, Race, and Class in the U.S. Military Empire." In *Over There: Living with the U.S. Military Empire from World War Two to the Present*, edited by Maria Höhn and Seungsook Moon, 1–36. Durham NC: Duke University Press, 2010.

Hoxie, Frederick E. *A Final Promise: The Campaign to Assimilate the Indians, 1880–1920*. Lincoln: University of Nebraska Press, 2001.

Hurst, Steven. *The Carter Administration and Vietnam*. New York: St. Martin's Press, 1996.

Huynh, Luu Doan. "The American War in Vietnamese Memory." In *The Vietnam War: Vietnamese and American Perspectives*, edited by Jayne Werner and Luu Doan Huynh, 243–47. New York: M. E. Sharpe, 1993.

Jacobson, Matthew Frye. *Whiteness of a Different Color: European Immigrants and the Alchemy of Race*. Cambridge MA: Harvard University Press, 1999.

Jeffords, Susan. *Hard Bodies: Hollywood Masculinity in the Reagan Era*. New Brunswick NJ: Rutgers University Press, 1993.

Jennings, Eric T. *Imperial Heights: Dalat and the Making and Undoing of French Indochina*. Berkeley: University of California Press, 2011.

Johnson, James D. *Combat Chaplain: A Thirty-Year Vietnam Battle*. Denton: University of North Texas Press, 2001.

Jun, Helen Heran. *Race for Citizenship: Black Orientalism and Asian Uplift from Pre-Emancipation to Neoliberal America*. New York: New York University Press, 2011.

Jung, Moon-Ho. *Coolies and Cane: Race, Labor, and Sugar in the Age of Emancipation*. Baltimore MD: Johns Hopkins University Press, 2008.

Kaplan, Amy. *The Anarchy of Empire in the Making of U.S. Culture*. Cambridge MA: Harvard University Press, 2002.

Kauanui. Kehaulani, J. *Hawaiian Blood: Colonialism and the Politics of Sovereignty and Indigeneity*. Durham NC: Duke University Press, 2008.

Kawaguchi, Yoko. *Butterfly's Sisters: The Geisha in Western Culture*. New Haven CT: Yale University Press, 2010.

Kelly, Katie. *A Year in Saigon: How I Gave Up My Glitzy Job in Television to Have the Time of My Life Teaching Amerasian Kids in Vietnam*. New York: Simon and Schuster, 1992.

Kennedy, John F. *A Nation of Immigrants*. 1964. Reprint, New York: Harper Perennial, 2008.

Kerber, Linda. "The Stateless as the Citizen's Other: A View from the United States." *American Historical Review* 112, no. 1 (February 2007): 1–34.

Keys, Barbara J. *Reclaiming American Virtue: The Human Rights Revolution of the 1970s*. Cambridge MA: Harvard University Press, 2014.
Kim, Eleana. *Adopted Territory: Transnational Korean Adoptees and the Politics of Belonging*. Durham NC: Duke University Press, 2010.
Kim, Jodi. *Ends of Empire: Asian American Critique and the Cold War*. Minneapolis: University of Minnesota Press, 2010.
———. "An Orphan with Two Mothers: Transnational and Transracial Adoption, the Cold War, and Contemporary Asian American Cultural Politics." *American Quarterly* 61, no. 4 (December 2009): 855–80.
Kim, Nadia Y. *Imperial Citizens: Koreans and Race from Seoul to L.A*. Stanford CA: Stanford University Press, 2008.
Klein, Christina. *Cold War Orientalism: Asia in the Middlebrow Imagination, 1945–1961*. Berkeley: University of California Press, 2003.
Koshiro, Yukiko. "Race as International Identity? 'Miscegenation' in the U.S. Occupation of Japan and Beyond." *Amerikastudien/American Studies* 48, no. 1 (2003): 61–77.
———. *Trans-Pacific Racisms and the U.S. Occupation of Japan*. New York: Columbia University Press, 1999.
Koshy, Susan. *Sexual Naturalization: Asian Americans and Miscegenation*. Stanford CA: Stanford University Press, 2004.
Kovner, Sarah. *Occupying Power: Sex Workers and Servicemen in Postwar Japan*. Stanford CA: Stanford University Press, 2013.
Kowner, Rotem, and Walter Demel, eds. *Race and Racism in Modern East Asia*. Boston: Brill, 2012.
Kramer, Paul. *The Blood of Government: Race, Empire, the United States, and the Philippines*. Chapel Hill: University of North Carolina Press, 2006.
Kroes, Rob. *Them and Us: Questions of Citizenship in a Globalizing World*. Urbana: University of Illinois Press, 2000.
Krupnick, Alison. "The Benefit of the Doubt." *Harvard Review* 28 (2005): 46–58.
Kudlick, Catherine J. "Disability History: Why We Need Another 'Other.'" *American Historical Review* 108, no. 3 (June 2003): 763–93.
Kuhl, Steven. *The Nazi Connection: Eugenics, American Racism, and German National Socialism*. Oxford, UK: Oxford University Press, 2002.
Kumin, Judith. "Orderly Departure from Vietnam: Cold War Anomaly or Humanitarian Innovation?" *Refugee Survey Quarterly* 27, no. 1 (2008).
Kuo, Karen. *East Is West and West Is East: Gender, Culture, and Interwar Encounters between Asia and America*. Philadelphia: Temple University Press, 2013.
Lamb, David. "Children of the Vietnam War: Born Overseas to Vietnamese Mothers and U.S. Servicemen, Amerasians Brought Hard-Won Resilience to Their

Lives in America." *Smithsonian*, June 2009. http://www.smithsonianmag.com/people-places/Children-of-the-Dust.html.

Langguth, A. J. *Our Vietnam War: The War, 1954–1975*. New York: Simon and Schuster, 2002.

Lee, Erika. *At America's Gates: Chinese Immigration during the Exclusion Era 1882–1943*. Chapel Hill: University of North Carolina Press, 2003.

———. *The Making of Asian America: A History*. New York: Simon and Schuster, 2015.

Lee, Heath Hardage. *The League of Wives: The Untold Story of the Women Who Took On the U.S. Government to Bring Their Husbands Home*. New York: St. Martin's Press, 2019.

Lee, Jin-kyung. *Service Economies: Militarism, Sex Work, and Migrant Labor in South Korea*. Minneapolis: University of Minnesota Press, 2010.

Lee, Robert. *Orientals: Asian Americans in Popular Culture*. Philadelphia: Temple University Press, 1999.

LeMay, Michael, and Elliott Robert Barkan, eds. *U.S. Immigration and Naturalization Laws and Issues*. Westport CT: Greenwood, 1999.

Lembcke, Jerry. *The Spitting Image: Myth, Memory, and the Legacy of Vietnam*. New York: New York University Press, 1998.

Levi, Robin S. "Legacies of War: The United States Obligation toward Amerasians." In *Mixed Race America and the Law: A Reader*, edited by Kevin R. Johnson, 413–23. New York: New York University Press, 2003.

Lim, Maria Teresa M. "Removal Provisions of the Philippine–United States Military Bases Agreement: Can the United States Take It All." *Loyola of Los Angeles Law Review* 20 (1987).

Lipman, Jana K. "'The Face Is the Road Map': Vietnamese Amerasians in U.S. Political and Popular Culture, 1980–1988." *Journal of Asian American Studies* (February 2011): 33–68.

———. "Mixed Voices, Mixed Policy: Vietnamese Amerasians in Vietnam and the United States." Master's thesis, Brown University, 1997.

———. "A Refugee Camp in America: Fort Chaffee and Vietnamese and Cuban Refugees, 1975–1982." *Journal of American Ethnic History* 33, no. 2 (Winter 2014): 57–87.

Loescher, Gil, and John A. Scanlan. *Calculated Kindness: Refugees and America's Half Open Door 1945–Present*. New York: MacMillan, 1986.

Longley, Kyle. *Grunts: The American Combat Soldier in Vietnam*. New York: M. E. Sharpe, 2008.

———. *The Morenci Marines: A Tale of Small Town America and Vietnam*. Lawrence: University Press of Kansas, 2013.

———. "When Character was King? Ronald Reagan and the Issues of Ethics and Morality." In Kyle Longley, Jeremy D. Mayer, Michael Schaller, and John W. Sloan, *Deconstructing Reagan: Conservative Mythology and America's Fortieth President*, 90–119. Armonk NY: M. E. Sharpe, 2007.

Longmore, Paul K., and Lauri Umansky, eds. *The New Disability History: American Perspectives*. New York: New York University Press, 2001.

Lundin, Carol. "Stewart B. McKinney: The Man." William and Mary School of Education, accessed May 24, 2014. http://education.wm.edu/centers/hope/resources/documents/bios.pdf.

Mabry, Philip James. "We're Bringing Them Home: Resettling Vietnamese Amerasians in the United States." PhD diss., University of Pittsburgh, 1996.

Marre, Diana, and Laura Briggs, eds. *International Adoption: Global Inequalities and the Circulation of Children*. New York: New York University Press, 2009.

Martindale, Carolyn. *The White Press and Black America*. New York: Praeger, 1986.

Martini, Edwin A. *Invisible Enemies: The American War on Vietnam 1975–2000*. Amherst: University of Massachusetts Press, 2007.

*M*A*S*H*. "Yessir That's Our Baby." Season 8, episode 15. Directed by Alan Alda. Aired December 31, 1979, on CBS. 20th Century Fox TV.

Matthaei, Julie, and Teresa Amott. "Race, Gender, Work: The History of Asian and Asian American women." *Race Class* 31, no. 61 (1990): 61–80.

Mayer, Jeremy D. "Reagan and Race: Prophet of Color Blindness, Baiter of the Backlash." In Kyle Longley, Jeremy D. Mayer, Michael Schaller, and John W. Sloan, *Deconstructing Reagan: Conservative Mythology and America's Fortieth President*, 70–89. Armonk NY: M. E. Sharpe, 2007.

Mazon, Patricia, and Reinhild Steingrover, eds. *Not So Plain as Black and White: Afro-German Culture and History, 1890–2000*. Rochester NY: University of Rochester Press, 2005.

McClellan, Grant S., ed. *Immigrants, Refugees, and U.S. Policy*. New York: H. Wilson, 1981.

McClintock, Anne. *Imperial Leather: Race, Gender, and Sexuality in the Colonial Contest*. New York: Routledge, 1995.

McKelvey, Robert S. *The Dust of Life: America's Children Abandoned in Vietnam*. Seattle: University of Washington Press, 1999.

McKelvey, Robert S., and John A. Webb. "Long-Term Effects of Maternal Loss on Vietnamese Amerasians." *Journal of the American Academy of Child Adolescence* 32, no. 5, (September 1993).

McLeod, Mark W. *The Vietnamese Response to French Intervention, 1862–1874*. New York: Praeger Press, 1991.

Molnar, Nicholas Trajano. *American Mestizos, the Philippines, and the Malleability of Race, 1898–1961*. Columbia: University of Missouri Press, 2017.

Moon, Katherine H. S. *Sex among Allies: Military Prostitution in U.S.-Korea Relations*. New York: Columbia University Press, 1997.

Mora-Kpai, Idrissou, dir., *Indochina: Traces of a Mother*. New York: Third World Newsreel. Documentary. DVD, 2002.

Muehlenbeck, Philip E., ed. *Gender, Sexuality and the Cold War: A Global Perspective*. Nashville TN: Vanderbilt University Press, 2017.

Nakashima, Cynthia L. "An Invisible Monster: The Creation and Denial of Mixed Race People in America." In *Racially Mixed People in America*, edited by Maria Root, 162–78. London: Sage, 1992.

———. "Servants of Culture: The Symbolic Role of Mixed-Race Asians in American Discourse." In *The Sum of Our Parts: Mixed-Heritage Asian Americans*, edited by Teresa Williams-León and Cynthia L. Nakashima, 42–47. Philadelphia: Temple University Press, 2001.

Nash, Gary B. "The Hidden History of Mestizo America." In *Sex Love Race: Crossing Boundaries in American History*, edited by Martha Hodes, 10–32. New York: New York University Press, 1999.

Ngai, Mae M. *Impossible Subjects: Illegal Aliens and the Making of Modern America*. Princeton NJ: Princeton University Press, 2004.

———. "This Is How Immigration Reform Happened 50 Years Ago: It Can Happen Again." *Nation*. October 2, 2015. https://www.thenation.com/article/this-is-how-immigration-reform-happened-50-years-ago-it-can-happen-again/.

Nguyen, Kien. *The Unwanted: A Memoir of Childhood*. Back Bay Books, 2002.

Nguyen, Mimi Thi. *The Gift of Freedom: War, Debt, and Other Refugee Passages*. Durham NC: Duke University Press, 2012.

Nguyen, Viet Thanh. *Nothing Ever Dies: Vietnam and the Memory of War*. Cambridge MA: Harvard University Press, 2016.

Northshield, Robert. *The Sins of the Fathers*. National Broadcasting Company. Telecast, June 19, 1973.

O'Conner, John. *A Chaplain Looks at Vietnam*. Cleveland OH: World Publishing, 1968.

Oh, Arissa. "A New Kind of Missionary Work: Christians, Christian Americanists, and the Adoption of Korean GI Babies, 1955–1961." *Women's Studies Quarterly* 33, no. 3/4 (Fall–Winter 2005): 161–88.

Painter, Nell Irvin. *The History of White People*. New York: W. W. Norton, 2011.

Park, Bongsoo. "Intimate Encounters: Racial Frontiers: Stateless GI Babies in South Korea and the United States, 1953–1965." PhD diss., University of Minnesota, 2010.

Park, Robert E. "Human Migration and the Marginal Man." *American Journal of Sociology* 33, no. 6 (May 1928): 881–93.
Pascoe, Peggy. "Miscegenation Law, Court Cases, and Ideologies of 'Race' in Twentieth-Century America." In *Sex, Love, Race: Crossing Boundaries in North American History*, edited by Martha Hodes, 464–90. New York: New York University Press, 1999.
———. *What Comes Naturally: Miscegenation Law and the Making of Race in America*. Oxford, UK: Oxford University Press, 2010.
Pegler-Gordon, Anna. *In Sight of America: Photography and the Development of U.S. Immigration Policy*. Berkeley: University of California Press, 2009.
Pivar, David J. "The Military, Prostitution, and Colonial Peoples: India and the Philippines, 1885–1917." *Journal of Sex Research* 17, no. 3 (August 1981): 256–69.
Plender, Richard. "The New French Nationality Law." *International and Comparative Law Quarterly* 23, no. 4 (October 1974): 709–47.
Plummer, Brenda Gayle. *Rising Wind: Black Americans and U.S. Foreign Affairs, 1935–1960*. Chapel Hill: University of North Carolina Press, 1996.
———, ed. *Window on Freedom: Race, Civil Rights, and Foreign Affairs, 1945–1988*. Chapel Hill: University of North Carolina Press, 2003.
Purcell, James N. Jr. *We're in Danger! Who Will Help Us?: Refugees and Migrants: A Test of Civilization*. Bloomington IN: Archway Publishing, 2019.
Quigley, Thomas E. *American Catholics and Vietnam*. Grand Rapids MI: William B. Eerdmans Publishing, 1968.
Ranard, Donald A., and Douglas F. Gilzow. "The Amerasians." *American Perspectives on Refugee Resettlement*, Washington DC Refugee Service Center newsletter, no. 4, June 1989.
———. "Comments on James W. Tollefson's 'Alien Winds: The Reeducation of America's Indochinese Refugees' and Elsa Auerbach's Review: Two Readers React." *Teachers of English to Speakers of Other Languages* 24, no. 3 (Autumn 1990): 529–41. http://www.jstor.org/stable/3587246.
Renda, Mary A. *Taking Haiti: Military Occupation and the Culture of U.S. Imperialism*. Chapel Hill: University of North Carolina Press, 2001.
Rhodes, Joel P. *The Vietnam War in American Childhood*. Athens: University of Georgia Press, 2019.
Roberts, Dorothy. *Killing the Black Body: Race, Reproduction, and the Meaning of Liberty*. New York: Pantheon Books, 1997.
Robinson, W. Courtland. *Terms of Refuge: The Indochinese Exodus and the International Response*. London: Zed Books, 1998.
Romano, Renee C. *Race Mixing: Black-White Marriage in Postwar America*. Cambridge MA: Harvard University Press, 2003.

Root, Maria. "Within, Between, and Beyond Race." In *Racially Mixed People in America*, edited by Maria Root, 3–11. London: Sage, 1992.

Rotberg, Robert I. *The Mixing of Peoples: Problems of Identity and Ethnicity*. Stamford CT: Greylock Publishers, 1978.

Russell, John. "Race and Reflexivity: The Black Other in Contemporary Japanese Mass Culture." *Cultural Anthropology* 6, no. 1 (February 1991): 3–25.

Rutenberg, Amy. *Rough Draft: Cold War Military Manpower Policy and the Origins of Vietnam-Era Draft Resistance*. Ithaca NY: Cornell University Press, 2019.

Saada, Emmanuelle *Empire's Children: Race, Filiation, and Citizenship in the French Colonies*. Translated by Arthur Goldhammer. Chicago: University of Chicago Press, 2012.

Sachs, Dana. *The Life We Were Given: Operation Babylift, International Adoption, and the Children of War in Vietnam*. Boston: Beacon Press, 2010.

Said, Edward. "Selections from *Orientalism*." In Patrick Williams and Laura Chrisman, *Colonial Discourse and Post-Colonial Theory: A Reader*, 132–49. New York: Columbia University Press, 1994.

Scales, Ann. "Soft on Defense: The Failure to Confront Militarism." *Berkeley Journal of Gender, Law and Justice* (2005): 369–93.

Schaller, Michael. "Reagan and the Cold War." In Kyle Longley, Jeremy D. Mayer, Michael Schaller, and John W. Sloan, *Deconstructing Reagan: Conservative Mythology and America's Fortieth President*, 3–40. Armonk NY: M. E. Sharpe, 2007.

Schaller, Michael, and George Rising. *The Republican Ascendancy: American Politics, 1968–2001*. Wheeling IL: Harlan Davidson, 2002.

Schulman, Bruce. *The Seventies: The Great Shift in American Culture, Society, and Politics*. 2001. Reprint, Cambridge MA: De Capo Press, 2002.

Schulzinger, Robert. *A Time for Peace: The Legacy of the Vietnam War*. Oxford, UK: Oxford University Press, 2006.

Schwenkel, Christina. *The American War in Contemporary Vietnam: Transnational Remembrance and Representation*. Bloomington: Indiana University Press, 2009.

Scott, Wilbur J. *The Politics of Readjustment: Vietnam Veterans since the War*. New York: Aldine De Gruyter, 1993.

Sforza, Alfred V. *Portrait of A Small Town III: Huntington Station "A New Perspective": A Critical Review of a Vanished Community, A Narrative That Must Be Told*. Huntington NY: Alfred V. Sforza, 2006.

Shade, John. *America's Forgotten Children: The Amerasians*. Perkasie PA: Pearl S. Buck Foundation, 1980.

Shalom, Stephen R. "Securing the U.S.-Philippine Military Bases Agreement of 1947." *Bulletin of Concerned Asian Scholars* 22, no. 4 (October–December 1990).

Shigematsu, Setsu, and Keith L. Camacho, eds. *Militarized Currents: Toward a Decolonized Future in Asia and the Pacific*. Minneapolis: University of Minnesota Press, 2010.

Shukert, Elfrieda Berthiaume, and Barbara Smith Scibetta. *War Brides of World War II*. Novato CA: Presidio Press, 1988.

Singh, Nikhil Pal. *Black Is a Country: Race and the Unfinished Struggle for Democracy*. Cambridge MA: Harvard University Press, 2004.

Slocum, Brian G. "Canons, the Plenary Power Doctrine and Immigration Law." *Florida State University Law Review* 34: 363–411.

Snyder, Sarah B. *From Selma to Moscow: How Human Rights Activists Transformed U.S. Foreign Policy*. New York: Columbia University Press, 2018.

Sohoni, Deenesh. "Unsuitable Suitors: Anti-Miscegenation Laws, Naturalization Laws, and the Construction of Asian Identities." *Law and Society Review* 41, no. 3 (September 2007): 587–618.

Spickard, Paul. *Almost All Aliens: Immigration, Race, and Colonialism in American History and Identity*. New York: Routledge, 2007.

———. *Mixed Blood: Intermarriage and Ethnic Identity in Twentieth Century America*. Madison: University of Wisconsin Press, 1989.

———. "Race and Nation, Identity and Power: Thinking Comparatively about Ethnic Systems" In *Race and Nation: Ethnic Systems in the Modern World*, edited by Paul Spickard, 1–29. New York: Routledge, 2005.

Spurling, Hilary. *Pearl Buck in China: Journey to the Good Earth*. New York: Simon and Schuster, 2010.

Stoler, Ann Laura. *Carnal Knowledge and Imperial Power: Race and the Intimate in Colonial Rule*. Berkeley: University of California Press, 2002.

———, ed. *Haunted by Empire: Geographies of Intimacy in North American History*. Durham NC: Duke University Press, 2006.

——— "Sexual Affronts and Racial Frontiers." In *Tensions of Empire: Colonial Cultures in a Bourgeois World*, edited by Frederick Cooper and Ann Laura Stoler. Berkeley: University of California Press, 1997, 198–237.

Stur, Heather. *Beyond Combat: Women and Gender in the Vietnam War Era*. Cambridge, UK: Cambridge University Press, 2011.

———. "'Hiding behind the Humanitarian Label': Refugees, Repatriates, and the Rebuilding of America's Benevolent Image after the Vietnam War." *Diplomatic History* 39, no. 2 (April 2015): 223–44.

Sturdevant, Sandra, and Brenda Stoltzfus. *Let the Good Times Roll: Prostitution and the U.S. Military in Asia*. New York: New Press, 1993.

Sutter, Valerie O'Connor. *The Indochinese Refugee Dilemma*. Baton Rouge: Louisiana State University Press, 1990.

Suzuki, Bob H. "Education and the Socialization of Asian Americans: A Revisionist Analysis of the 'Model Minority' Thesis." *Amerasian* 4:2 (1977): 23–51.

Taylor, Rosemary, in collaboration with Wende Grant. *Orphans of War: Work with the Abandoned Children of Vietnam 1967–1975*. London: Collins, 1988.

Terry, Wallace. *Bloods: An Oral History of the Vietnam War by Black Veterans*. New York: Random House, 1984.

Thomas, Sabrina. "Blood Politics: Reproducing the Children of 'Others' in the 1982 Amerasian Immigration Act." *Journal of American–East Asian Relations* 26, no. 1 (February 13, 2019): 51–84.

Tichenor, Daniel J. *Dividing Lines: The Politics of Immigration Control in America*. Princeton NJ: Princeton University Press, 2002.

Tollefson, James. *Alien Winds: The Reeducation of America's Indochinese Refugees*. New York: Praeger, 1989.

Trautfield, M. T. "America's Responsibility to the Amerasian Children: Too Little, Too Late." *Brooklyn Journal of International Law* 10, no. 1 (1984): 54–82.

Turner, Karen. "Shadowboxing with the Censors: A Vietnamese Woman Directs the War Story." In *Cinema, Law, and the State in Asia*, edited by Corey K. Creekmur and Mark Sidel, 101–22. New York: Palgrave Macmillan, 2007.

Turse, Nick. *Kill Anything That Moves: The Real American War in Vietnam*. New York: Picador, 2013.

Tyson, Timothy. *The Blood of Emmett Till*. New York: Simon and Schuster, 2017.

Uchida, Aki. "The Orientalization of Asian Women in America." *Women's Studies International Forum* 21 (1998): 161–74.

United Nations High Commissioner for Refugees. *Out of the Shadows: Ending Statelessness in the Americas*. Statement of Anne C. Richard. The Newsseum. Washington DC, November 18, 2014.

U.S. Navy. *Chaplains with Marines in Vietnam, 1962–1971*. By Cdr. Herbert L. Bergsma, CHC. Bureau of Navy Personnel news kit, January 7, 1970. History and Museums Division Headquarters, U.S. Marine Corps, Washington DC: Library of Congress Volumes in the Marine Corps Vietnam series, 1970.

———. Memorandum, "Narrative Report for August 1968," from Lt. Nathan O. Loesch, Chief of Chaplains, U.S. Navy Reserves, Chaplain River Assault Flotilla One (Alpha Group), to Commander in Chief, U.S. Pacific Fleet. September 7, 1968.

U. S. President. Address before a Joint Session of the Congress Reporting on the United States Foreign Policy. Gerald Ford, April 10, 1975. *Public Papers of the Presidents of the United States*. Washington DC: Office of the Federal Register, National Archives and Records Service, 1974–77. John T. Woolley and Gerhard Peters, *The American Presidency Project* [online]. Santa Barbara CA.

———. Statement Announcing Humanitarian Assistance for Refugees in the Republic of Vietnam. Gerald Ford, March 29, 1975. *Public Papers of the Presidents of the United States.* Washington DC: Office of the Federal Register, National Archives and Records Service, 1974–77. John T. Woolley and Gerhard Peters, *The American Presidency Project* [online]. Santa Barbara CA.

———. Statement following Evacuation of United States Personnel from the Republic of Vietnam. Gerald Ford, April 29, 1975. *Public Papers of the Presidents of the United States.* Washington DC: Office of the Federal Register, National Archives and Records Service, 1974–77. John T. Woolley and Gerhard Peters, *The American Presidency Project* [online]. Santa Barbara CA.

———. Statement on the Crash of a C-5A Cargo Plane on a Mercy Flight from Saigon, Republic of Vietnam. Gerald Ford, April 4, 1975. *Public Papers of the Presidents of the United States.* Washington DC: Office of the Federal Register, National Archives and Records Service, 1974–77. John T. Woolley and Gerhard Peters, *The American Presidency Project* [online], Santa Barbara CA.

———. Statement on the Release of an American Prisoner in Lao. Gerald Ford, September 18, 1974. *Public Papers of the Presidents of the United States.* Washington DC: Office of the Federal Register, National Archives and Records Service, 1974–77. John T. Woolley and Gerhard Peters, *The American Presidency Project* [online], Santa Barbara CA.

———. Statement on Signing the Foreign Assistance and Related Programs Appropriations Act, 1975. Gerald Ford, March 27, 1975. *Public Papers of the Presidents of the United States.* Washington DC: Office of the Federal Register, National Archives and Records Service, 1974–77. John T. Woolley and Gerhard Peters, *The American Presidency Project* [online]. Santa Barbara CA.

U.S. State Department. *East Asia and the Pacific: The Roads Behind and Ahead.* Gaston J. Sigur, Assist. Sec. for East Asian and Pacific Affairs. Address before the Philadelphia World Affairs Council, June 6 1988. Bureau of Public Affairs, Office of Public Communication, Editorial Division.

———. *Fact Sheet: U.S. Expands Orderly Departure for the Vietnamese Refugees.* Dispatch, April 1, 1991.

———. Memo to Ambassador Graham Martin from Henry Kissinger Providing an Update on Arrangements to Evacuate U.S. Citizens from South Vietnam, April 19, 1975. Declassified October 4, 1994. Declassified Documents Reference System, Farmington Hills MI: Gale, 2010. Gerald R. Ford Presidential Library.

———. *Report of the Indochinese Refugee Panel: Midyear Consultation on U.S. Refugee Programs for Fiscal Year 1986: Hearing before the Subcommittee on*

Immigration and Refugee Policy. April 17, 1986. Senate, 99th Cong., 2nd sess., June 20, 1986, 61–67.

———. "Sensitive Exclusively Eyes Only via Martin Channels Saigon." Memo from Graham Martin to Henry Kissinger, April 18, 1975. Declassified February 3, 1995. Declassified Documents Reference System, Farmington Hills MI: Gale, 2010. Digitized from GFPL, NSA box 3, files Backchannel Messages.

U.S. Department of Defense. *Final Interagency Report of the Reagan Administration on the POW/MIA Issue in Southeast Asia.* January 19, 1989.

Valverde, Kieu-Linh Caroline. "Doing the Mixed-Race Dance: Negotiating Social Spaces within the Multiracial Vietnamese American Class Typology." In *The Sum of Our Parts: Mixed-Heritage Asian Americans,* edited by Teresa Williams-León and Cynthia L. Nakashima, 131–43. Philadelphia: Temple University Press, 2001.

———. "From Dust to Gold: The Vietnamese Amerasian Experience." In *Racially Mixed People in America,* edited by Maria P. P. Root, 144–61. Newbury Park CA: Sage, 1992.

Varzally, Allison. *Children of Reunion: Vietnamese Adoptions and the Politics of Family Migrations.* Chapel Hill: University of North Carolina Press, 2017.

Wagatsuma, Hiroshi. "The Social Perception of Skin Color in Japan." In *Color and Race,* edited by John Hope Franklin, 407–43. Boston: Houghton Mifflin, 1968.

Watanna, Onoto. *"A Half Caste" and Other Writings.* Urbana: University of Illinois Press, 2003.

Weidenfeld, Sheila. *First Lady's Lady: With the Fords at the White House.* New York: G. P. Putnam's Sons, 1979.

Weisberg, Jacob. *Ronald Reagan.* New York: Henry Holt, 2016.

Westheider, James. *The African American Experience in Vietnam: Brothers in Arms.* Lanham MD: Rowman and Littlefield, 2008.

———. *Fighting on Two Fronts: African Americans and the Vietnam War.* New York: New York University Press, 1999.

Williams, Teresa Kay, and Michael C. Thornton. "Social Construction of Ethnicity versus Personal Experience: The Case of Afro-Amerasians." *Journal of Comparative Family Studies* 29, no. 2 (Summer 1998): 225–67.

Winslow, Rachel Rains. *The Best Possible Immigrants: International Adoption and the American Family.* Philadelphia: University of Pennsylvania Press, 2017.

Wu, Ellen D. *The Color of Success: Asian Americans and the Origins of the Model Minority.* Princeton NJ: Princeton University Press, 2014.

Yarborough, Trin. *Surviving Twice: Amerasian Children of the Vietnam War.* Washington DC: Potomac Books, 2005.

Yoon, Diana. "Reproducing Citizens through U.S. Militarism: Amerasians and Descent Based Membership." PhD diss., New York University, 2010.

Young, Marilyn B. "The Vietnam War in American Memory." In *The Vietnam War: Vietnamese and American Perspectives*, edited by Jane S. Werner and Luu Doan Huynh, 248–57. New York: M. E. Sharpe, 1993.

Yu, Henry. *Thinking Orientals: Migration, Contact, and Exoticism in Modern America*. Oxford, UK: Oxford University Press, 2002.

Zeiger, Susan. *Entangling Alliances: Foreign War Brides and American Soldiers in the Twentieth Century*. New York: New York University Press, 2010.

Ziglar, Zig. *Steps to the Top*. Gretna LA: Pelican Publishing, 1985.

Index

adoption: of Black Amerasians, 70, 75, 76, 77, 83; Cold War and, 8–9, 11; and conservatism, 140; "Korea model" of, 59; national paternal responsibility and, 55–56, 62, 65; and racial discrimination, 97–98; racial distinctions and, 11; Second World War and, 50–53, 133; and U.S. citizenship, 79–80, 136; Vietnam and, 51, 63, 66–67, 69. *See also* Operation Babylift

Amerasian Homecoming Act (AHA), 12, 23, 180, 312n36; application process, 215–17; and concerns of fraud, 222–26; immigration numbers, 236; passage of, 210, 212; public support for, 224; and Robert Mrazek, 204, 209–10. *See also* Huntington High School; Minh, Le Van; Mrazek, Robert J.

Amerasian Immigration Act (AIA), 12–13, 119, 153; amendments to, 206–8; criticism of, 158–59, 169; debates over, 126–30, 140–41; and family separation, 155–57, 208; limitations, 154–59, 168–74; MIA issues and, 164; national paternity and, 119–21, 132, 136, 138; Reagan administration and, 160–63, 166–68. *See also* McKinney, Stewart

Amerasian Resettlement Program, 213–14, 230

Amerasians, 2–8, 185, 189, 237; African American attitudes toward, 82–83; categorization of, 109, 112, 115, 147, 168–69; and compassion fatigue, 235–36; and debates around paternity, 68, 121; and Department of Defense policy, 102–3; deportation of, 243–44; dual exclusion of, 50; after *Fiallo v. Bell*, 104, 245; historiography of, 13–17; and identity, 10–11, 120; and Korea model, 59; Korean, 132; after Korean War, 9; media coverage of, 116, 147–49, 184; and national belonging, 91; and nineteenth-century imperialism, 34–35; ODP program, 112–14, 173; origins of term, 50; paternity and, 126–31; in popular culture, 101–2, 199; during postwar refugee crisis, 111–12; during POW/MIA debates, 100, 165; pride, 217–18, 233; self-narrativization of, 146. *See also* Black Amerasians; national paternal responsibility; paternity

Americans for International Aid, 133, 135–36, 139

Anderson, John, 69

Asian American studies, 13

Asian exclusion, 30–34

Asiatic Barred Zone Act (1917), 31

assimilation, 13, 100, 108, 125; difficulties of, 201–3, 207; Philippines Refugee Processing Center and, 227–29

Ba, Le Thi, 1–2

Ban Me Thout, 79, 99

Biden, Joseph, 93

Black Amerasians: and aftermath of Operation Babylift, 97; in Japan, 7, 39, 233; race and, 10, 13, 68, 200; and racial kinship with African Americans, 73–77; in Vietnam, 71–78, 234

Blauvelt, Gloria, 181–83; and campaign for Le Van Minh, 189–92, 194, 198–99; after Minh's arrival, 211

blood quantum, 2, 68, 217; in Amerasian legislation, 217; definition and history of, 26–27, 32, 36; and Vietnamese ideas on race and blood, 71

Brenden, Marta, 192

Buck, Pearl S., 5, 8, 18; Amerasian activism, 49–52, 55; background, 49–50. *See also* Pearl S. Buck Foundation

bui doi, 3, 142, 201, 214, 248n7

Byrd, Robert, 93

Cambodia, 100, 105; Vietnamese occupation of, 162, 205, 209
Carroll, Alfred, 121, 132–36, 149, 173, 201
Carter, Jimmy, 99–100, 111–15
Chinese Exclusion Act (1882), 31
Church World Service, 61, 71, 76
citizenship: after AHA, 237, 241–42; AHA and, 236; AIA and, 142, 158–59; after amendments to AIA, 208–9; anti-Blackness and, 38–40; arguments against, 113; birthright, 24–25, 103, 120, 201, 238; and civilization discourse, 36; contradictory language of, and AIA and ODP, 201; and exclusion, 30–31, 237; history of race and, 26–30, 121; legislative efforts to extend, 64–67, 80, 84; national quotas, 31–32; ODP program, 112; paternity and, 27–28, 103–4; racial qualifications, 30–31; during refugee crisis, 109; sex-based distinction, 245. *See also* blood quantum; national paternal responsibility; sex-based distinction
Cold War, 123–25, 175, 209; child saving and, 6, 8–10, 53; concerns over mixed-race offspring during, 54, 174; conclusion of, 235–36; and humanitarianism, 13, 53, 89, 111, 116, 158; and legacies of Vietnam War, 145; and racism toward Asians, 38, 108; Reagan and, 156–60, 162–64, 166, 169; refugees and, 91–93, 122–24, 221, 235
Communism: adoption and containment of, 8, 54, 80; Amerasians as victims of, 89, 145–46, 161; American racism and, 43–44; authoritarian allies against, 96; loss of China to, 38; refugees from, 53, 91–93, 123–25, 128. *See also* Cold War
Comprehensive Plan of Action, 223
Congressional Black Caucus, 77–78; responses to adoption of Amerasians, 97; responses to refugee crises, 94–96
con lai, 3, 214, 248n7
Conyers, John, Jr., 77, 96

Dan, Quang Phan, 81
Darragh, Jodie, 135–36, 139, 153, 173
Dellenback, John R., 54–55
Dellums, Ronald, 95
Democratic Republic of Vietnam, 98
Denton, Jeremiah, 136, 139–42, 149, 159, 165
Department of Defense (DoD), 57–59, 102, 114

Department of Health Education and Welfare, 67, 76, 83, 113
Diggs, Charles, Jr., 78
Dong, Pham Van, 66, 98–99
Duvalier, Papa "Doc," 96

East Wind, West Wind (Buck), 50, 260n3
Ebony Magazine, 75, 82
Emerson, Gloria, 73
eugenics, 27, 131

Falwell, Jerry, 156
Fauntroy, Walter, 132
Fiallo v. Bell, 102–4, 245
First Indochina War, 40, 46, 55, 71, 258n95
Ford, Betty, 81–82
Ford, Gerald, 80, 90–91; advocating for refugees, 93–95; MIA issues, 98–99
Foreign Assistance Authorization Act, 70
(Forte) Gerbavsits, Sue, 181–82, 187, 194, 198, 203, 211
Fourteenth Amendment (1868), 26, 30
France, 40, 55, 102, 138
Frank, Barney, 125–31
Fraser, Donald, 62, 92

Geary Act (1892), 31
Gentleman's Agreement, 31
gentle warriors, 64, 88
Gerbavsits, Sue (Forte). *See* (Forte) Gerbavsits, Sue
Giang, Dung Vo, 188
GI babies, 6, 9, 15, 136
Grant, Madison, 27, 252n18
Guyer v. Smith, 27–28, 45, 253n22

Haldeman, H. R., 58, 60
Hatfield, Mark, 63
Hayakawa, Samuel Ichiye (S. I.), 105–6, 108–9
Holt Adoption Agency, 50, 53, 76
"Honor Thy Children" (*60 Minutes* episode), 147–49
Hughes, Harold, 59, 63
humanitarianism: and Amerasian Immigration Act, 158, 162, 191; Cold War and, 53, 55, 63, 116; and Le Van Minh, 183, 185–87, 196; mixed-race children and, 52–53, 59; Nixon and, 56; refugee crises and, 89–93, 105–7, 112; Vietnamese Amerasians and, 61–63, 83–84, 90–91, 171

human rights, 92, 96, 100, 111; citizenship and, 136. *See also* humanitarianism
Huntington High School: legacy of, 211; Le Van Minh and, 181–83, 187–88, 191–92; media coverage of, 199; Son Tran and, 177–80; victory of, 194

illegitimacy, 3, 125, 185, 215; Black Amerasians and, 73; citizenship and, 47, 51–52, 103, 137; consequences of, 138, 234, 243; imperialism and, 7–8; in Vietnam, 10, 58–59, 65–68; U.S. evacuation and, 45
Immigration and Naturalization Act of 1952, 103
Immigration and Naturalization Act of 1965, 104
Immigration and Naturalization Services, 96, 108–9, 123; role in Amerasian Homecoming Act, 222–26
imperialism, 33; and paternity, 6–7; prostitution and, 41–42; and regulation of wartime sex, 45
In re Camille, 30
Interagency Vietnamese Adoption Committee (IVAC), 76, 97
International Social Services, 50, 59, 61, 73
Isidore, William, 96

Japan, 7–9, 41; attitudes toward Amerasians in, 39, 51, 55, 62; and Second World War, 37–39, 42
Jordan, Barbara, 96
jus sanguine citizenship, 25

Kane, Greg, 127, 146, 173, 200, 201
Keane, Alfred, 121, 127, 129, 132, 133–40, 149
Kennedy, Edward "Ted," 56, 69–70, 82, 112
Kim Phúc, Phan Thi, 6
Kinney family, 202–3
Kissinger, Henry, 88, 98
Klein, Wells, 73–75
Kurtis, Bill, 115

Le Thi Ba. *See* Ba, Le Thi
Le Van Minh. *See* Minh, Le Van
Lofgren, Zoe, 237–39
Long, Clarence D., 107
Lutheran Immigration and Refugee Services (LIRS), 192, 201–2, 227

marielitos, 116, 226
Martin, Graham, 45, 81, 90–91

Mazzoli, Ronald, 149, 169–70, 206, 209–10
McCain, John, 209–10
McKelvey, Robert, 71, 84, 199–200; background, 87–89; early legislative efforts, 109–14
McKinney, Stewart, 5, 307–8n148; and AIA, 119–21, 139, 150; amending AIA, 169–75, 206
mestizos, 35–37, 39, 40, 45, 136, 255n52. *See also* mixed-race people
métis, 40, 55, 71. *See also* mixed-race people
Michener, James, 54
Minh, Le Van, 3, 23, 144–45, 202; arrival in the United States, 202–4; and campaign to bring to U.S., 181–83, 187–88; difficulties assimilating, 238–39; immigration of, 195–97; media coverage of, 198–99; national negotiations over, 191–94; portrayals of, 185–86. *See also* Huntington High School
Mink, Patsy Takemoto, 5, 45, 56; biography, 65; and citizenship for Amerasians, 67; early legislative efforts, 62, 65–66, 68, 69; and Operation Babylift, 78, 80
miscegenation, 7, 26–27, 50; nineteenth-century fears of, 33–34; wartime regulation of, 42–44; white-Asian, 31
mixed-race people, 3, 17; Americans' racial attitudes toward, 24–25; blood quantum and, 32; citizenship and, 33, 51–52, 136; exclusion of, 35, 113–14, 130; French approaches to, 55–56; history of, 25–29; Japanese racial attitudes toward, 39
model minority, 33, 96, 108, 273n31
Mondale, Walter, 106, 111
Mrazek, Robert J., 5, 307–8n148; Huntington High School and, 183–84, 187–89, 192–93; relationship with Le Van Minh, 195, 202; restarting ODP, 204–6
Muller, Bobby, 142–43
My Lai massacre, 3, 56–57, 101

National Association of Black Social Workers, 76
National League of Families of American Prisoners and Missing in Southeast Asia (NLF), 99, 165, 167
national paternal responsibility, 3, 5, 9; arguments in favor of, 65, 83–84, 89; Nixon administration and, 61–62; steps toward, 154, 218, 237–38
Naturalization Law (1790), 29

Newsday: coverage of Le Van Minh, 179–87, 189, 203, 211. *See also* Tiernan, Audrey

Nixon, Richard: attitude toward Amerasians, 56–60. *See also* Nixon administration

Nixon administration: and Amerasians and South Vietnam, 61–62, 69; lack of interest in Amerasians, 56–58, 67; and racism in the military, 77–78. *See also* Nixon, Richard

normalization, 100, 154, 208–11; Reagan administration and, 162, 163, 205–7; reconciliation trips and, 143–44

Northshield, Robert, 64

Obey, David, 210
O'Neil, Tip, 95
Operation Babylift, 80–83, 90, 97, 135, 251n64
Orderly Departure Program (ODP), 111–14, 168–72; after Amerasian Homecoming Act, 213, 223; Le Van Minh family and, 203; reform of, 188; suspension of, 181
orientalism, 28–29; and gender, 41–42, 46
orphans, 135; abandonment of Amerasian, 79–80; Black Amerasian, 72, 76; depictions of, 55, 80, 168; Filipino-American, 36; French colonial, 40; Operation Babylift, 82–83; in contrast to refugees, 11; South Korean, 7–8; in Vietnam, 62, 64–72, 135
othering, 29, 48, 109, 130, 214–15
Ozawa v. the United States, 32

Packwood, Bob, 81
Page Act (1875), 31–32, 41
paternalism, 8, 37, 88
paternity, 3, 12; AHA and, 207–8; AIA and, 121, 127–29; citizenship and, 27–28, 84; civilizing, 36; discrimination and, 112–12, 243; evaluating individual claims of, 57, 68–69, 110, 216; historiography of, 13–14; Le Van Minh and, 185, 194; media coverage of, 5–6, 79; military and, 45, 102–3; paternalism and, 8; political debates surrounding, 89, 109, 112, 120, 129; reform and, 114, 141, 168; Supreme Court and, 102–3, 133–34. *See also* national paternal responsibility
patriotic pronatalism, 53
Pearl S. Buck Foundation, 66, 110, 114; accounts after Communist victory, 79–80; advocacy for AIA, 138–39; proposal for Amerasian processing center, 185
Philippines, 6–7, 35. *See also* Philippines Refugee Processing Center

Philippines Refugee Processing Center, 213–14; Amerasian Immigration Act and, 208, 227–32; corruption, 232–33

Prisoners of War (POW) / Missing in Action (MIA), 63, 98–100; Reagan administration and, 162–68, 205, 207

Quang, Nguyen Dang, 188
Quilty, Tara (Scalia). *See* (Scalia) Quilty, Tara

Raspberry, William, 107
Reagan, Ronald, 99, 115, 119, 159. *See also* Reagan administration
Reagan administration: Amerasians in foreign policy of, 207–9; anticommunist agenda, 163; approach to AIA and ODP, 171–72; attitude toward Amerasians, 174; debates over AIA, 124–25, 140, 153–54, 160; family separation policy, 155; on immigration, 124; and media criticism over AIA, 142; and POW issues, 164–67; racialization of Amerasians, 130–31; on reunification of families, 128; revising legacy of Vietnam, 122–23
Reagan Doctrine, 160–61
reeducation camp prisoners, 162, 171
Refugee Act of 1980, 115–17, 123, 170, 174
Refugee Relief Act (1953), 8, 249n33
refugees, 19; African American concerns over, 93–95; and anti-immigration sentiment, 123, 133–34; and categorizing Amerasians, 88–92, 173; and continued international crises, 223; fleeing Communism, 91–94; Haitian, 96, 105, 115; opposition to resettlement of, 107–8, 223–24; and racial dimensions of policy after Vietnam, 96–98, 106–7; in Second World War, 106; after Vietnam War, 99–100, 104–5. *See also* Orderly Departure Program
Robison, Howard, 69, 81, 83
Rodino, Peter, 62–63, 69

Said, Edward, 29
Salvatore, Jim, 181
Sandler, Marlo: and campaign for Le Van Minh, 181–82, 184, 186, 197, 203; reflections on Le Van Minh, 211, 239
Save the Children, 50, 55
Scali, John, 59–60
(Scalia) Quilty, Tara, 181–82, 186–87, 202, 211
Schroeder, Pat, 125–26, 128–31

Select Commission on Immigration and Refugee Policy, 116, 123–25
sex-based distinction, 20; and exclusion of Amerasians, 39; and *Fiallo v. Bell*, 103–5; gender and, 41; legal foundation of, 28, 34, 39, 45–46; reform efforts, 113, 120–21, 125–26
Shade, John, 129, 136–38, 149, 157–59
Shultz, George, 170–71, 193
Simpson, Alan, 141, 170, 206, 209, 229
The Sins of the Fathers (NBC special), 63–65
Snepp, Frank, 81
Southern Christian Leadership Conference, 74–75
South Korea, 7, 59–60, 121, 134; Amerasian immigration from, 158
South Vietnam: adoption from, 51, 60–61, 66–67, 71–72; defeat of, 78–79; fate of former American allies in, 90; racial attitudes in, 71–73; women and sex-work in, 43
statelessness, 11, 54–55, 67, 121
Steiger, William, 69, 81, 83
Sumner, Charles, 31

Thach, Nguyen Co, 174, 205
Thieu, Nguyen Van, 60, 81
Thompson, Era Bell, 76
Thurmond, Strom, 105–6
Tiernan, Audrey: photograph of Le Van Minh, 16, 17, 23–24, 181–83, 185, 187, 189, 192, 193, 195, 196, 199, 211

Truman, Harry, 32, 46, 53
Trump administration, 242–44
Tsongas, Paul, 80, 83

"unassimilable," categorization as, 12, 33–34, 48, 94
United Nations High Commissioner on Refugees (UNHCR), 111–12, 157, 188
United States v. Bhagat Singh Thind, 32
U.S. Agency for International Development (USAID), 69, 76
U.S. Immigration and Nationality Act (1952), 28, 109, 113
U.S. Supreme Court, 32, 102

Vance, Cyrus, 111
Vietnam Children's Care Agency, 63
Vietnamization, 60
Vietnam Veterans of America (VVA), 127, 142–43, 173
Virag, Irene, 186, 194–97

Wallace, Mike, 146–49, 155, 184
War Brides Act, 43, 261n23
Waxman, Henry, 105
Welcome House, 50, 54, 260–61n11, 265n84
Williams, Harrison, 63
Williams, Juanita, 74–75

Zach, David, 181, 187–89, 198–99, 203, 211

In the Borderlands and Transcultural Studies series

Indigenous Sacraments: Christian Rituals and Local Responses at the Fringes of Spanish America, 1529–1800
by Oriol Ambrogio Gali

The Storied Landscape of Iroquoia: History, Conquest, and Memory in the Native Northeast
by Chad Anderson

Country of the Cursed and the Driven: Slavery and the Texas Borderlands
by Paul Barba

How the West Was Drawn: Mapping, Indians, and the Construction of the Tran-Mississippi West
by David Bernstein

Chiricahua and Janos: Communities of Violence in the Southwestern Borderlands, 1680–1880
by Lance R. Blyth

The Borderland of Fear: Vincennes, Prophetstown, and the Invasion of the Miami Homeland
by Patrick Bottiger

Captives: How Stolen People Changed the World
by Catherine M. Cameron

The Allure of Blackness among Mixed Race Americans, 1862–1916
by Ingrid Dineen-Wimberly

Intermarriage from Central Europe to Central Asia: Mixed Families in the Age of Extremes
edited and introduced by Adrienne Edgar and Benjamin Frommer

Words Like Birds: Sakha Language Discourses and Practices in the City
by Jenanne Ferguson

Transnational Crossroads: Remapping the Americas and the Pacific
edited by Camilla Fojas and Rudy P. Guevarra Jr.

Conquering Sickness: Race, Health, and Colonization in the Texas Borderlands
by Mark Allan Goldberg

Creek Internationalism in an Age of Revolution, 1763–1818
by James L. Hill

The Forgotten Diaspora: Mesoamerican Migrations and the Making of the U.S.-Mexico Borderlands
by Travis Jeffres

Globalizing Borderlands Studies in Europe and North America
edited and with an introduction by John W. I. Lee and Michael North

Of Corn and Catholicism: A History of Religion and Power in Pueblo Indian Patron Saint Feast Days
by Andrea Maria McComb Sanchez

Illicit Love: Interracial Sex and Marriage in the United States and Australia
by Ann McGrath

Shades of Gray: Writing the New American Multiracialism
by Molly Littlewood McKibbin

The Limits of Liberty: Mobility and the Making of the Eastern U.S.-Mexico Border
by James David Nichols

In Praise of the Ancestors: Names, Identity, and Memory in Africa and the Americas
by Susan Elizabeth Ramírez

Between Black and Brown: Blaxicans and Multiraciality in Comparative Historical Perspective
by Rebecca Romo, G. Reginald Daniel, and J Sterphone

Native Diasporas: Indigenous Identities and Settler Colonialism in the Americas
edited by Gregory D. Smithers and Brooke N. Newman

Shape Shifters: Journeys across Terrains of Race and Identity
edited by Lily Anne Y. Welty Tamai, Ingrid Dineen-Wimberly, and Paul Spickard

Scars of War: The Politics of Paternity and Responsibility for the Amerasians of Vietnam
by Sabrina Thomas

The Southern Exodus to Mexico: Migration across the Borderlands after the American Civil War
by Todd W. Wahlstrom

To order or obtain more information on these or other University of Nebraska Press titles, visit nebraskapress.unl.edu.

www.ingramcontent.com/pod-product-compliance
Lightning Source LLC
Chambersburg PA
CBHW052242180925
32849CB00002B/27